THE PRESIDENCY OF THE EUROPEAN COUNCIL OF MINISTERS

The Presidency of the European Council of Ministers

IMPACTS AND IMPLICATIONS FOR
NATIONAL GOVERNMENTS

Edited by Colm O Nuallain
Institute of Public Administration, Dublin

in collaboration with
JEAN-MARC HOSCHEIT,
European Institute of Public Administration, Maastricht

Preface by
NEILS ERSBOLL' Secretary-General,
The Council of the European Communities, Brussels.

PUBLISHED IN ASSOCIATION WITH THE
EUROPEAN INSTITUTE OF PUBLIC ADMINISTRATION

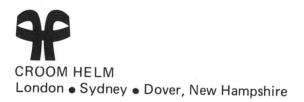

CROOM HELM
London ● Sydney ● Dover, New Hampshire

© 1985 European Institute of Public Administration
Croom Helm Ltd, Provident House,
Burrell Row, Beckenham, Kent BR3 1AT

Croom Helm Australia Pty Ltd, First Floor,
139 King Street, Sydney, NSW 2001, Australia

British Library Cataloguing in Publication Data

The Presidency of the European Council of
    ministers: impacts and implications for
    national governments
    1. Council of Ministers
    I. Nuallain, Colm O.   II. Hoscheit, Jean-Marc
    341.24'22   JN30

    ISBN 0-7099-0946-2

Croom Helm, 51 Washington Street,
Dover, New Hampshire 03820, USA

Printed and bound in Great Britain by
Biddles Ltd, Guildford and King's Lynn

TABLE OF CONTENTS

Table of Contents

LIST OF FIGURES AND TABLES

PREFACE
Mr Niels Ersbøll, Secretary-General,
The Council of the European Communities, Brussels

The role of the Presidency of the Council has been growing steadily over the years of the existence of the Community, in a way that would probably not have been possible to foresee when the founding Treaties were drawn up.

There are several reasons for this. It is partly because the Council's legislative activity has extended to areas outside and beyond the virtually 'automatic' timetables laid down in the Treaties; decisions can no longer be all semi-automatic, they must be the fruit of long and arduous inter-government negotiation. Added to this is the fact that the legislative body has now ten viewpoints to reconcile, rather than six. Another partial explanation is surely the emergence over the last decade of the European Council, a body which has grown up outside the Treaties to provide the Presidency with an unstructured forum in which considerable influence can be exercised.

The role of the Presidency has then greatly increased and the challenge facing each Member State, as its turn comes round, is immense, namely, to plan, direct and inspire a programme of work in a multitude of fields in the smoothest and best coordinated manner; to search for the compromise that makes decision possible; to represent the Community, and negotiate on its behalf, **vis-à-vis** the Community's associated partners and the countries seeking accession; to represent the Council **vis-à-vis** the European Parliament in situations, becoming more and more frequent, where real and skilful negotiation is called for, as well as **vis-à-vis** public opinion and the press.

There is very little codification of the powers that the Presidency can assume to help it in these tasks. Historians would get little help from a mere study of the Council's 'Rules of Procedure'. Experience shows us that each Presidency has different concepts of the amount of authority that it can assume, but for a determined Presidency, with a clear vision of what it wishes to obtain, the armoury is considerable. It can virtually decide the timing of meetings, the length of time to be given to each topic, the way in which each topic is treated and (perhaps most important) whether or when a vote should be taken.

Preface

Parallel with decisions on how best to use the machinery of the Council, each Presidency is faced with a daunting task of internal organisation. It has to find a means to ensure, within itself, effective central authority covering all the multitude of areas under discussion in its six-months period of office. It must be clear about its own priorities at all levels and this calls for an effort of both horizontal and vertical coordination that is highly demanding on the national civil service concerned.

The differences of the Member States are reflected in their Presidencies. Political clout, or the personality of one or other minister concerned, or his or her domestic prestige, may easily have an effect on the success in achieving elusive decisions. Differences in the interest that the Member State has in specific matters under consideration, or in the development of the Community in general, may well colour its own definition of what a successful Presidency should be.

It is also true that the present system of periods of six months is not ideal. Hardly has a Presidency begun to master the intricacies of the function than it must hand it over to its successor. Successful efforts to bring complicated and politically difficult matters to the point of agreement often require more than six months of hard work. There is no guarantee that the next Presidency can or will carry on from where the last one stopped. It is however not realistic to contemplate any major change in this basic system in the foreseeable future. The idea of lengthening the period of each Presidency has never won sufficient support, and the idea of shortening it has never been seriously considered. Therefore the search for improvements will most likely have to continue within the present framework. Some improvements will have to come from within each of the Member States themselves, such as better internal coordination (the nomination of ministers with European responsibilities has been mooted), others would entail certain adjustments to present arrangements.

What such adjustments could be will undoubtedly constitute a fertile area for the deliberations of the new Spaak Committee, decided on at Fontainebleau. The 'Three Wise Men' in their report of 1979, without advocating a full-blown 'troika' system for the Presidency of the Council, did tentatively suggest a certain elasticity at the level of working groups, whereby a Member State could continue in the chair if this were beneficial to a particular dossier, and this could well be one of the possibilities resurrected within the new Spaak Committee. Another possibility might be an adaptation of the role of the Council Secretariat. Another approach might be to define better ways in which the present **ad hoc** methods of Presidency planning at six-month intervals could be replaced by an agreed, more coherent and longer term programme.

The present study seems to me to be singularly useful to all those who want and need to understand the functioning of the Council. I also hope that ministers and civil servants preparing for the Presidency of their country will read it and reflect upon it.

INTRODUCTION
Mr Colm O Nuallain, Dublin

The accession of countries to the European Communities has added a new and important dimension to the responsibilities of their public services. It has affected many facets of the work of ministries and departments - in particular those dealing directly with Community matters. In the process, the responsibilities and work of many national civil servants have been significantly altered and extended. Their workstyles and even their lifestyles have also been radically changed.

The impact of these changes on national administrations has not, as yet, received evaluative attention commensurate with their significance. A number of studies have appeared on Community adaptation made by the British, Danish, Dutch, French and German bureaucracies (Wallace (1) and (2), Christensen (3), Lindberg and Scheingold (4), Gebert and Pepy (5).) The OECD organised a colloquium which was held in Alcala de Henares in 1982 to review experience of existing Member States. The countries involved in the first enlargement - Denmark, Ireland and the United Kingdom - presented their experience to the prospective Member States - Greece, Portugal and Spain. Other Member States were also represented and contributed from their experience (O Nuallain (6)). The OECD was interested not only in the possibility of a transfer of information, experience and insights, but also in the problems and possibilities of management improvement in this context. Nevertheless, commentators have noted a dearth of basic information in this field in rather sharp contrast to the substantial commitment of public resources and the increasing influence of Community policies in the countries involved.

There is, therefore, a need - increasing as the Community evolves and expands - to record, examine, compare and draw conclusions from the practice and experience of the various Member States in adapting to and coping with the challenges and responsibilities of Community membership. While much of the practice undoubtedly derives from a unique combination of socio-political, cultural and other factors and is **sui generis,** certain organisational and procedural expedients and practices almost certainly are not similarly culture bound. Comparative insights would also be likely to lead to useful adjustment or adaptation of existing organisational or, perhaps in some instances, political behaviour. The need to compare practices and experiences is further emphasised by the political and public preoccupation in virtually all Member States with the need to contain the growth in public sector size and expenditure, and with public service reform. Public service involvement in European affairs is now so extensive in all Member States that it must be a significant factor in any review of the public service. It would thus serve a number of Community and national interests to study the impact of Community membership and European affairs on national administrations.

A comprehensive study of this nature would be a formidable and protracted undertaking. There is, however, a particular feature of the responsibilities of Community membership which affects every Member State in turn and in which the impact of the European dimension is greatly increased. This is the revolving responsibility of the Presidency of the Council of Ministers. The Presidency throws into sharper focus the adaptation that has to be made by the national administration not only to the Presidency itself but to Community membership generally. It is, therefore, a discrete, useful and more manageable context in which to attempt - at least in the first instance - to review the impact of European affairs on national administrations. It is also the responsibility of Community membership that bears most heavily on new Member States. It is very much in their interest to learn about the implications of the Presidency for their national administration. For these reasons the European Institute of Public Administration (EIPA) decided to undertake a research project focusing on the Presidency.

The project had considerable merits in its own right. It was, so far as was known, one of the first projects of its kind to focus on the Presidency (7). It had considerable relevance as a form of case study in European co-operation. It also had relevance as a significant contribution in the field of comparative public administration. The EIPA therefore saw it as a piece of applied research which should be of interest and value to politicians and administrators - both national and international - and to academics in a number of disciplines, but especially in European Studies and Public Administration. Because of its own role at the European level, the EIPA also hoped that the project might provide relevant material for its own programmes and, to the extent to which it elicited interest at the European and national levels, might stimulate further study and research.

Turning to the subject matter of the project itself, we may note that, in the early years of the European Communities, the Presidency did not cause any special difficulties for a country because the policy-making process was still relatively limited and there was a smaller number of Member States. The Treaty commitments were very much to the fore and the Commission was playing a very active role. However, as time passed the role of the Council became more important and, hence, that of the Presidency. The Presidency has become, for all Member States, an increasing burden as a consequence of the increase in membership of the EC; in the scope of its activities; and in the extent and complexity of the EC policy-making processes. The development of European Political Co-operation has also added to the burden and assumed importance for the Presidency. Yet there has been a paucity of comparative information on the administrative arrangements and procedures which have been adopted by the various national bureaucracies to cope with the Presidency. The relatively little information available would suggest that these arrangements and procedures were to some extent developed on an ad-hoc and pragmatic basis. In consequence the research study was designed:

1) to document basic information on the organisational and administrative arrangements and procedures which were adopted by the various national bureaucracies in preparing for and managing the Presidency; (it was proposed to encompass such matters as
   - inter-ministerial coordination and communication
   - means of resolving possible conflicts
   - the preparations within ministries
   - the role of the Permanent Representation and relations with the European Community institutions
   - training for staff involved in or affected by the Presidency
   - the Presidency and European Political Co-operation
   - national expectations and objectives);

2) to determine the views and perceptions of key national officials directly involved in the work associated with the Presidency and, in particular, their suggestions for adaptation and change; (key national officials were seen as including:
   - staff assigned to the Permanent Representation
   - staff who participate in management committees, working groups etc. as national delegates or representatives
   - staff who have to chair or preside over such committees or groups
   - staff, especially those in the major economic ministries, who brief ministers and other national representatives);

3) to outline the major issues and problems in the adaptation of the various bureaucracies towards the EEC Presidency;

4) to describe the problems encountered by the Commission of the EC in relation to the term of the Presidency and in relation to national bureaucracies and their administrative traditions;

5) to describe the role of the Secretariat of the Council in the management of the Presidency;

6) finally, given the intended practical and applied nature of the research, to give possible suggestions for a better and more effective preparation and implementation of the numerous tasks of the Presidency (8).

The project was intended to cover each of the nine Member States over the period 1973-83. Each of them had, by the end of that period, discharged the Presidency role on at least two occasions and might therefore be presumed to have had the opportunity of reviewing their experience and adjusting to it. Because of Greece's accession and its interest it was agreed that it should, so far as practicable, be brought within the ambit of the project.

The project was carried out by researchers in each of the countries obtaining information from key informants by interview in a relatively structured manner. Information was also obtained in the Secretariats of both the Council and the Commission. One researcher reviewed the tasks and evolution of the Presidency to-date and synthesised some of the more significant findings from the national papers in a comparative perspective.

The research team received excellent co-operation from Ministries of Foreign Affairs, major economic ministries, Permanent Represent-ations, Secretariats of the Council and Commission and all others whom they approached. This was very important for the success of the project. It also reinforced the impression of those responsible for the research that projects of this nature can help to build bridges between practitioners and academics to their mutual advantage.

First drafts of national reports were reviewed in a workshop by the team of researchers. An effort was made to harmonise the structure and content of reports to facilitate comparative study. This was not fully realised but, given the wide international involvement and national divergences of practice and approach, a reasonable degree of conformity was secured. Further information for the final draft reports was obtained during the workshop. These latter reports were, in turn, reviewed in the light of discussions and information obtained during a colloquium organised by the European Institute of Public Administration and held in November 1983 at the Erenstein Castle (The Netherlands). The participants in the colloquium were given copies of the final drafts of the national reports which were regarded and used as background documents. Discussion at the colloquium was focused on salient aspects of the research theme with the assistance of a number of prominent people with special knowledge and experience. In addition, presentations were made reviewing the role of the Presidency in the Treaties and as it has evolved and developed: comparing national philosophies in relation to the European Communities and the Presidency; and formulating some general conclusions as they appeared to emerge from the project at that stage. The colloquium was, in fact, itself regarded as providing a further and most important input to the study in its crucial concluding stage. The proceedings of this colloquium have been published separately in the series of the EIPA Working Papers (no. 84/1).

Among the general conclusions reached in discussion at the EIPA colloquium was the judgement that, in the Community framework, the Presidency has reached a plateau for a number of reasons:

1) the reform of the Presidency is linked to the reform of the institutions;
2) governments are stretched in handling the Presidency in terms both of human resources and ideas;
3) the economic environment is not conclusive to speedy consensus on reform.

To savour and understand the underlying reasons for this and other conclusions and to ascertain the extent to which the objectives of the study were realized, readers are encouraged to continue reading. Before doing so, however, I would ask their indulgence to allow me to discharge the pleasant task of thanking the people who with their help have made

Introduction

this research project possible. In the first place this applies to Dr S. Schepers, Director General of the EIPA who was the real initiator of this research. From among the staff of the EIPA, whose commitment was evident from the first to the last day, I would like to mention Mr J-M. Hoscheit whose help in terms both of content and organisation has been very valuable at the different stages of the research and whose assistance in the editing of the publication was extremely useful. The same recognition applies to Ms M. O'Leary who was at that time lecturer at the EIPA, and whose efficient action helped to overcome many problems.

Finally and last but certainly not least, I have to thank the many people both at national and European level who were willing to listen and answer the enquiring and detailed questions of our researchers. Without their contributions and those of the participants in the Erenstein Castle colloquium, among whom I would like to mention the main speakers - Dr H. Wallace, Mr J-L. Dewost, Mr J-P. Costes and Dr K.P. Klaiber, this book would not have seen the light of day.

REFERENCES

(1) H. Wallace, National Governments and the European Community (P.E.P., London, 1973).

(2) H. Wallace, The Impact of the European Communities on National Policy-Making, in M. Hodges (ed.) European Integration, Penguin, London, 1972.

(3) J.G. Christensen, Adapting Public Administration for Participation in Supra-national Bodies, Institute of Political Science, University of Aarhus, Denmark, July 1981.

(4) L.N. Lindberg, and S.A. Scheingold, Europe's Would-be Polity, Prentice Hall, New York, 1970.

(5) P. Gebert and D. Pepy. Eds., Les décisions dans les Communautés européennes, Presses Universitaires de Bruxelles, Bruxelles, 1969.

(6) C. O Nuallain, Membership of the European Communities: Adaptation Implications for Prospective Member States. Paper presented at an international meeting on Adapting Public Administration for Participation in Supra-national Bodies, Alcala de Henares, July, 1981, (OECD).

(7) For an earlier study, see: G. Edwards and H. Wallace, The Council of Ministers of the European Communities and the President-in-Office, Federal Trust, London, 1977.

(8) Research Guidelines: The Impact of the Presidency of the European Community on National Administrations, European Institute of Public Administration, Maastricht, 1982 (mimeo).

LIST OF CONTRIBUTORS

Michel vanden Abeele

Directeur de l'Institut d'Etudes Européennes, Université Libre de Bruxelles, Bruxelles.

Jørgen Grønnegaard Christensen

Professor at the Institute of Political Science, University of Aarhus, Aarhus.

Geoffrey Edwards

Research Associate at the David Davies Memorial Institute for International Studies, London.

Niels Ersbøll

Secretary General of the General Secretariat of the Council of the EC.

Jean-Marc Hoscheit

Chargé de cours en administration européenne et comparée à l'Institut Européen d'Administration Publique, Maastricht, et Chargé de cours à l'Institut de Formation Administrative, Luxembourg.

Max Jansen

Lecturer at the Europa Instituut, University of Amsterdam, Amsterdam.

Marian O'Leary

Former Lecturer at the European Institute of Public Administration, Maastricht and now Administrator at the Commission of the European Communities, Luxembourg.

List of Contributors

Philipe Moreau Defarges

Chargé de Mission auprès du Directeur de l'I.F.R.I. et Professeur à l'Institut d'Etudes Politiques, Paris.

Colm O Nuallain

Director of the Institute of Public Administration, Dublin, and Vice-President of the Scientific Council of the European Institute of Public Administration, Maastricht.

Antonio Papisca

Professeur à la Faculté des Sciences Politiques, Université de Padova, Padova.

Elfriede Regelsberger

Research Associate at the Institut für Europäische Politik, Bonn.

Panos Tsakaloyannis

Former Lecturer in Politics at the University of Athens, now Senior Lecturer at the European Institute of Public Administration, Maastricht.

Helen Wallace

Lecturer in Public Administration at the Civil Service College, London, and Visiting Professor at the College of Europe, Brugge.

Wolfgang Wessels

Director of the Institut für Europäische Politik, Bonn, and Visiting Professor at the European Institute of Public Administration, Maastricht.

LIST OF ABBREVIATIONS

A
ACP   African, Caribean and Pacific countries associated with the EEC.

ASEAN   Association of South-East Asian Nations.

C
CAP	Common Agricultural Policy.
CECA	Communauté Européenne du Charbon et de l'Acier.
CEE	Communauté Economique Européenne.
CEI	Commission Economique Interministérielle.
CIEC	Commission Internationale de l'Etat Civil.
CIPE	Comité Interministeriel pour la Programmation Economique.
CMCES	Comité Ministériel de Coordination Economique et Sociale.
CMPE	Comité Ministériel de la Politique Extérieure.
CMREE	Comité Ministériel des Relations Economiques Extérieures.
CoCo	Coordination Commission.
Coreper	Comité des représentants permanents.
COREU	Correspondance Européenne (direct communication system among foreign ministries).
CPE	Coopération Politique Européenne.
CPRS	Central Policy Review Staff.
CSCE	Conference on Security and Co-operation in Europe.

D
DATAR	Délégation à l'Aménagement du Territoire et Action Régionale.
DCE	Departmental Committee on Europe.
DGAE	Direction Générale des Affaires Economiques.
DGAP	Direction Générale des Affaires Politiques.

E
EAGGF	European Agricultural Guidance and Guarantee Fund.
EC	European Community.

List of Abbreviations

ECD	European Community Department.
ECOFIN	Council of Economic and Finance Ministers.
ECU	European Currency Unit.
EEC	European Economic Community.
EFTA	European Free Trade Association.
EMS	European Monetary System.
EP	European Parliament.
EPC	European Political Co-operation.
EQ(O)	European Questions (Official).
EQ(S)	European Questions (Strategic).
ERDF	European Regional Development Fund.
F	
FEDER	Fonds Européen de Développement Régional.
G	
GATT	General Agreement on Tariffs and Trade.
GD	Grand-Duché (de Luxembourg).
GEPE	Groupe d'Etudes Politiques Européennes.
I	
ISEA	Commission for International Social and Economic Affairs.
K	
KYSYM	Greek Government Committee.
M	
MAE	Ministère des Affaires Etrangères.
MAFF	Ministry of Agriculture, Fisheries and Food.
MEP	Member of the European Parliament.
MFO	Multinational Force and Observers.
MP	Member of Parliament.
N	
NATO	North Atlantic Treaty Organisation (OTAN).
O	
OD Committee	Overseas and Defence Committee.
OD(E)	Overseas and Defence (Europe).
OECD	Organisation for Economic Co-operation and Development (OCDE).
ONU	Organisation des Nations Unies (UNO).
P	
P 11	Service des Organisations européennes.
R	
REZ	Council for European Affairs (Raad voor Europese Zaken).

List of Abbreviations

S

SCA	Special Committee on Agriculture.
SER	Social and Economic Council (Sociaal Economische Raad).
SGCI	Secrétariat Général du Comité Interministeriel.
STABEX	Stabilisation des Recettes d'Exportation.

T

TEPSA	Trans-European Policy Studies Association.

U

UEBL	Union Economique Belgo-Luxembourgeoise.
UEO	Union de l'Europe Occidentale (WEU).
UK	United Kingdom.
UN	United Nations (ONU).
UNCTAD	United Nations Conference on Trade and Development.
URSS	Union des Républiques Socialistes Soviétiques (USSR).
USA	United States of America (EU).
USSR	Union of Socialist Soviet Republics (URSS).

V

VAT	Value Added Tax.

Chapter 1

THE PRESIDENCY OF THE COUNCIL OF MINISTERS OF THE
EUROPEAN COMMUNITY: TASKS AND EVOLUTION
Dr Helen Wallace, London

INTRODUCTION

The European Community (EC) has no clear focal point within its various
institutions. Though both the Council of Ministers and the Commission
have Presidents, the buck stops with neither. No single political office-
holder can lay claim to pre-eminent authority or influence. There is
little scope for the systematic exercise of political leadership in the
form with which we are familiar from the experience of the national
state. Indeed the very term 'presidency' is a source of distorted images
whether we think of the strong role of a French or American President
or of the constitutionally limited but significantly dignified role of an
Italian or German President. In analysing the Presidency of the Council
of Ministers of the EC we must banish all such analogies, and instead
recall that the first task of the Presidency is as chairman and that the
deliberate diffusion of political authority militates against the
emergence of any concentration of influence, let alone power. The
Council Presidency has proved a useful barometer of shifts in the
institutional balance within the EC, but it has not been their instigator.

The drafters of the basic Treaties establishing the three European
Communities were both ambitious and innovative. In their search for a
new form of collective government they introduced a constitutional
framework that had no direct parallels or precedents elsewhere, tinged
though it was by federal and confederal analogies. On the one hand their
ambitions stretched to the long-term goal of establishing a new kind of
super-state or supranational authority. Yet caution and realism dictated
that this had to be tempered by a gradualist process of building
consensus and consent, through which nation states could develop
sufficient mutual trust to permit co-operation to become tighter, new
institutional dynamics to emerge and a common legal system to be set in
place. The result was a curious blending and blurring of legislative and
executive functions within the Council of Ministers and what became the
Commission.

If the more ambitious plans were to be realised the Commission
would develop into the central executive subject to guidance from a kind
of 'Council of Elders'. But over the short to medium term it had to be
accepted that the Community experiment was conditional, that it would

1

require periodic and positive affirmation from the representatives of the participating states. The founders of the European Community sought to combine the possible with the desirable: the Commission was endowed with the potential to emerge as the driving force of integration; but the Council of Ministers was to be the essential medium through which policies were to be negotiated and legislation endorsed, until such a time as, in a sense, a more orthodox division of powers could be achieved. In this event the basic design also changed between the Treaty of Paris and the Treaties of Rome as the participating governments pulled back from supranationalism. The outcome of the Luxembourg crisis in 1966 reinforced this trend.

Thus the Council of Ministers emerged as a curious hybrid and interim institution, a halfway house between established national political systems and the fragile Community embryo. Simultaneously it was to exercise a collective Community function and to be the sounding board of the Member States. Its members were to combine the roles of negotiators and legislators, highly abnormal in terms of conventional democratic practice. Collegiately and individually, the representatives of governments were charged with pinning down the proposals of the Commission and translating them into acceptable and tolerable commitments. Yet the blueprint could not be realised unless they were actively to conspire to hand over much of their own political authority or at least to share it generously, or without some catalyst to translate diverse national viewpoints into a consensus and collective action.

All of these contradictions are embodied in the office of the Council Presidency. Every six months the Presidency rotates among the Member States, giving each in turn the opportunity to experience in acute form the nature-defying task of simultaneously pushing and hauling. From the most senior ministers down to junior officials national representatives find themselves caught between the instinct for self-protection and the need to take a broader and more collective view of the overall Community interest. To perform adequately in such circumstances demands considerable political and administrative agility, all the more so when action by the Council has direct legal, economic and political consequences.

In retrospect it is astonishing that at the outset very little thought was apparently given to clarifying the functions and operations of the Council Presidency or indeed the Council more generally. Its contemporary features, like those of the Council as a whole, are the result of practice not of prescription. The Presidency of the 1980s, as an institution, represents a combination of reactions to events, the follower not the creator of fashion and convention. What is clear, is that the strong version of the Community idea, as embodied in the Treaty of Paris establishing the European Coal and Steel Community, anticipated only a modest and formal role for the Council Presidency. Two key principles were entrenched: first that the Presidency would be exercised by the Member States (rather than by a collective representative, as in NATO, the Secretary General) and second that each Member State would occupy the office in turn on a basis of parity, irrespective of size, political weight or any other distinction. The lack of political attributes however was evidenced by the prescription that the Presidency rotated every three months giving no government the chance to dominate the show before the next took over. The Rome Treaties, in explicitly locating more authority within the Council of Ministers, maintained the same basic principles of rotation and parity, but extended the term of office to six months. This permitted more time for business to be organised by the incumbent and opened the door for the Presidency to emerge as an important wielder of influence and as a vehicle through which a collective Council view could be achieved and expressed.

During the 1950s and for much of the 1960s basically it did not seem to make more than a marginal difference of style and occasionally personality which government occupied the chair. The agenda of Council sessions was more or less pre-ordained by Treaty commitments. The Commissioners chose to be activist and were able to be extremely influential, not just in proposing policies, but also in mediating and building packages. In a period of rapid growth and comparatively ready consensus on economic issues, relatively few dossiers raised major political storms, even though the views of governments differed. Had de Gaulle's design, embodied in the Fouchet Plan, for an explicitly inter-governmental Community, taken off, the story might have been different. But largely the role of the Presidency was literally to chair meetings and to fulfil various procedural tasks, in association with the tiny General Secretariat of the Council. During this period there was, however, one harbinger of developments to come. In the wake of the 1965 Luxembourg crisis it is fairly clear that the Italian Presidency played an important role of conciliation. The Commission was, of course, a party to the dispute and not well placed to act as honest broker, but in any case it is questionable whether even then the Commission had the political authority to knock heads together on a so highly political issue as defining the boundary between national sovereignty and political integration. In retrospect the events of 1965/66 marked a turning point which altered the institutional balance and specifically activated the previously dormant potential of the Presidency.

Gradually, then, towards the end of the 1960s and apace during the 1970s the Presidency came to occupy a more pivotal role. This resulted from the combination of several different factors: a more explicit discussion within the Council over how most appropriately to manage business; the rapid proliferation of Councils at ministerial level and of working groups; the vesting in the Community Council of the problems of inter-ministerial coordination in national capitals; changes in the political and economic environment of the EC; and the burgeoning of Community action on the broader international stage, notably, but not solely, through European Political Co-operation. Equally important was the gradual decrease in the power and effectiveness of the Commission as a purposive and independent political executive. Whatever the reasons for this, the result was to create a vacuum in terms of agenda setting, consensus building and collective representation into which the Council Presidency has stepped. The consequence has been to ascribe to the Presidency burdens, functions and opportunities for leverage which were not explicitly part of the initial institutional design. Yet this has not produced a clear and agreed view of the role of the Presidency. It is virtually impossible to find appropriate analogies from national political

3

practice, but the original notion was probably a hybrid between the formal role of head of state (signing legislation, sometimes representing the collectivity and occasionally assisting political concertation) and the modest guiding role of the president of a legislature. As we move into the contemporary period some commentators and the occasional incumbent have been tempted to look to the Presidency to play the role of proxy Prime Minister, at least in the modest way the office is exercised in a country like the Netherlands as primus inter pares.

THE FORMAL ROLE OF THE PRESIDENCY

By the time of the merger of the EC institutions in 1967, following the amending Treaty of 1965, the Council of Ministers had begun to acquire a complexity and variety barely foreseen in the 1950s. One of the results was an explicit attention to the procedures of the Council, notably reflected in the formalisation of Coreper (the Committee of Permanent Representatives), the legal establishment of the Council Secretariat and the clarification of the procedure governing Council business. The framework for this was the establishment of 'Rules of Procedure' for the Council, as required by Article 5 of the Merger Treaty, though curiously they were not formally and publicly adopted by the Council until 24 July 1979 (1). These allocated several distinct functions to the Presidency as follows:

a)   planning the calendar and convening of meetings;

b)   formulating provisional agendas of the Council (but to include any items requested in due time by any Member State or the Commission);

c)   signing the minutes of meetings drawn up by the General Secretariat of the Council;

d)   signing acts adopted by the Council, with the Secretary General;

e)   ensuring that acts are properly published;

f)   chairing Coreper and other working groups;

g)   acting as the collective point of contact for third parties.

In effect these Rules of Procedure entrenched what had long been practice. They laid down the formal, managerial and representative functions of the Presidency, but qualified them with numerous references to the scope for 'any member of the Council' or the Commission to challenge the chair and to the need for the Council to act collectively. No substantive power was delegated to the Presidency.

This very limited definition of Presidency functions was perhaps all that was necessary in a procedural document. Governments did not need to formalise the more political roles of the Presidency and in any case

4

there where then, and remain today, significant differences of view over how extensively or specifically the role of the Presidency should be defined. The role of the General Secretariat of the Council was specified in Council discussion in autumn 1980 **(2)**.

THE PROLIFERATION OF COUNCIL BUSINESS

Steadily over the years and occasionally with phrenetic intensity, the work of the Council has increased. This is reflected in the frequency of ministerial sessions, the number of committees and working groups (Coreper at least twice a week and upwards of 150 working groups) and the length of agendas. This has had a two-fold effect. In the first place it means that any government approaching its term in the Presidency has to contemplate providing chairmen for a vast range and volume of meetings, from Prime Minister (in the French case - President) down to relatively junior officials. Thus the Presidency has become more onerous and more demanding of specific preparation; if only to ensure that the appropriate people are in the appropriate rooms with documents, interpretation, secretariat and advisers. Secondly, however, the work of managing the Council has become not just the handling of individual meetings but attempting to coordinate the whole, (or perhaps to offset the practices which militate against coordination). Thirdly the increased number of informal Councils means that meetings take place at which the Commission by definition cannot play as clear a role as might be implied by the Treaties since the agenda does not consist of formal proposals.

Amidst this institutional labyrinth there has been a temptation to clutch at any available vehicle for expediting business and for steering complex dossiers through the Council. While this phenomenon has not yielded a consensus on explicitly upgrading the role of the Council Presidency, **faute de mieux** it has in practice fallen to the Presidency with the Council Secretariat to ensure that necessary business is transacted, that timetables are, as far as possible, respected and that priorities and linkages are established.

Significantly periodic proposals for improving the performance of the Council, as an institution, have tended to include suggestions for building on the role of the Presidency. Proposals in this vein have been embraced in the largely unpopular Belgian suggestion of lengthening the period in office to a whole year, the Tindemans Report on European Union and the Report of the Three Wise Men, as well as several less official recommendations. A package of reforms was steered through the Council under the 1974 German Presidency designed to improve the coherence and cohesion of Council activities. These formalised the responsibilities of the Council Presidency for coordination within the Council and improved liaison with the Commission **(3)**.

In its conclusions to the meeting of 1-2 December 1980, the European Council (under a Luxembourg Presidency) commenting on the Report of the Three Wise Men reaffirmed the spirit of the 1974 Reforms and adumbrated the importance of the Presidency.

Within the Council of Ministers:

> The prime role of the Presidency, assisted at all levels by the General Secretariat, involves in particular organizing work, preparing Council agendas, monitoring progress in discussions within working groups and coordinating the work done with a view to ensuring the consistency of Council decisions (4).

This made explicit the substantial role of the Council Secretariat and exhorted the Presidency to respond to the problems of 'compartmentalisation' within the Council. Significantly the statement recognised that this depended in large measure on better coordination within Member States. Lest anyone be in any doubt, the document reaffirmed the need for Coreper to act as an effective two-way valve between Ministers and working groups to expedite business, to meet deadlines and to clarify issues of principle, with the Presidency guiding, monitoring and nudging.

It should be noted that increasingly the view within the Council has been that institutional tinkering while useful cannot substitute for, nor of itself create substantive agreement on policy.

THE MIRROR OF NATIONAL PRACTICE

Increasingly, discussion of the functioning of the Council as a whole, and of the Presidency in particular, has come to include an awareness that these reflect the way in which individual governments handle Community business. Indeeed this is the reason for this study being extended to include an appraisal of national policy processes for formulating instructions for Council sessions, Coreper and working groups. The detailed implications for governments will be evaluated later in the volume, but it is equally important to recognise just how much national practice has determined the working methods of the Council.

Community business now penetrates to the furthest reaches of individual governments and national administrations. All governments are torn between the pull of functionalist logic, namely to let the ministers and officials who understand a dossier deal with it, and the requirement to ensure that they have a collective sense of priorities and of the linkages between different dossiers. Inevitably there are tensions and demarcation lines within governments as different groups, ministries and levels are brought into play by the creeping advance of the Community agenda.

The Council of Ministers stands witness to this on a Community-wide basis. The proliferation of Councils and working groups in specialised areas is the understandable result of the experts claiming a role in Community-level negotiation and legislation. The attempts to assert the role of Coreper, the General Council of Foreign Ministers and of the European Council stand testimony to the efforts of ministers and officials at the centre of national governments to look at issues in the round and to ensure that left and right hand operate in a synchronised fashion. Both centripetal and centrifugal tendencies work simultaneously. Broadly speaking, studies of national decision-making suggest that in practice it is extremely difficult, if not impossible, for central coordination units in national capitals to have an adequate overview of the development of Community policies except on a clutch of highly sensitive and central dossiers. If this is so, then it is simply unrealistic to expect the Council of Ministers as a whole to act in a consistent and coherent manner across the board, but equally it is a delusion to expect the Presidency to be able to substitute for lacunae and competition in national capitals. Where one can expect the Presidency to make a mark is either by competently managing the specialised areas or by a sensitive and sensible approach to critical and controversial dossiers.

Nor are the differences of view within national capitals simply a reflection of bureaucratic rivalry for its own sake, though elements of this do impinge. Just as important differences of view are the legitimate expression of different constituencies - the farmers, the traders, the keepers of the public purse and so on, as articulated by separate government departments and ministers, real interests and real conflicts of interest are at stake. In this sense the EC Council mirrors not only the formal differences in the attributions of ministerial competence, but the pluralist character of West European politics and administration with all its tensions and contradictions.

THE CHANGING ECONOMIC AND POLITICAL ENVIRONMENT

Economically as the EC was enlarged in the 1970s it found itself simultaneously, beset with two new phenomena. On the one hand the Treaties were beginning to run out of steam in the sense of having led to the achievement of many, if not most, of their precisely expressed goals, leaving the more vaguely defined areas of co-operation to be given substance. On the other hand the EC, like the international economy as a whole, became gripped by recession, by the evaporation of a ready consensus on economic doctrine and by claims for a reorientation of policies to accommodate both new economic factors and new Member States in successive enlargements. Even the most adroitly constructed institutions would have been under strain in such circumstances and the Council of Ministers, in common it must be said with most participating governments, rapidly began to show the signs of both policy confusion and fissiparous tendencies. The last decade has not been one in which it has been easy to achieve good government. It was unrealistic to expect the Council of Ministers to succeed while individual governments were struggling, or to expect the Presidency to discover a golden key with which to unlock the door to a new consensus.

Moreover by the mid-1970s it was evident that neither could the Commission, however inventive, produce solutions to which the Council would with relief assent. The Commission has itself become internally more divided, issues have become more politicised and problems of how to distribute the burdens and benefits of integration have become more intense. The Commission has acquired more of its own vested interests with the passage of time. As the 'eleventh Member State' it is less well placed to behave impartially. With the Commission less able and perhaps less willing to act as the package-broker, something of a vacuum has been created. The increased role of the Presidency thus in part represents an adaptive response from within the Council. But the task of the Presidency, in helping to push forward a consensus, has not become easier. The nature of the issues and dossiers makes it increasingly hard for any government in the Presidency, except perhaps Luxembourg, to adopt a detached approach. It is difficult to avoid partisanship when major interests are at stake, but the need for political leadership, or at least a political steer, has become more acute. The result broadly has been an appreciation that particular Presidencies may serve to edge discussion closer towards agreement, tempered by a recognition that no government is immune from countervailing domestic pressures.

INTERNATIONAL RESPONSIBILITIES: THE GROWTH OF EUROPEAN POLITICAL CO-OPERATION

European Political Co-operation (EPC) was established initially only because it was to be located outside the conventional Community framework. In the absence of agreement on any new secretariat and without at first any role for the Commission, it fell to the Presidency to fulfil the role of manager and secretariat for the new venture. The Luxembourg Report of 27 October 1970 adopted the rotating Presidency from the EC and charged it with convening and hosting meetings and with providing the secretariat and 'material organisation' (i.e. funding) for those meetings. In addition the Presidency would once a year report to the European Parliament. The Copenhagen Report of 23 July 1973 took this further by establishing a direct communication system (COREU) among Foreign Ministries to be coordinated by the Presidency and more elaborate links between the Presidency and the embassies of partners (5). A formalised link was introduced via the Presidency to Coreper and the Council of Ministers to handle linkages between the Community and EPC. Subsequently, the Gymnich meeting of June 1974 agreed that the Presidency should speak for the then Nine in any dialogue covering EPC ground with friendly governments (6).

The Presidency's functions in relation to EPC are in some respects quite different from those within the Community. EPC has few instruments for action other than by consultation, declaration and spokesmanship. There are no policies to manage or legislation to negotiate and implement. The participants are almost all ministers and officials from Foreign Ministries and thus escape many of the problems of coordination and of dealing with technical dossiers which beset their colleagues dealing with Community business. Thus the prime task of the Presidency is to maintain the now intense dialogue on foreign policy issues. The absence however of any organisations with the functions of either the Commission or the Council Secretariat means that it falls to the Presidency, not only to constitute the infrastructure of EPC, but to promote (in so far as any individual government so wishes) the development of EPC both generally and on particular issues. There are no institutional scapegoats to blame for failures to make progress, but neither is there an 'acquis communautaire' on which to rest if discussion

8

is stalled.

Discussions have taken place over the years about the desirability and feasibility of strengthening or extending the infrastructure of EPC. Two factors have conjoined to focus this discussion on the Presidency. First, doubts and controversies persist over the merits of establishing an independent political secretariat. Second, a fair amount of mutual and self-congratulation among Foreign Ministries has served to foster the argument that reliance on the Presidency is justified unless EPC were to take a quantum leap forward. Yet the Soviet invasion of Afghanistan cruelly exposed the inadequacy and discontinuities engendered by reliance on the six-monthly rotation. Eventually in the London Report of October 1981 several reforms were hammered out (7).

This report reflected the common concern of participants in EPC to gear the management of EPC to a more rapid and effective role in responding to international crises and in developing a common approach. The Presidency was thus exhorted to make more systematic arrangements to ensure continuity, forward looking studies and operational support. In particular, a 'flying secretariat' was established, whereby the incumbent Presidency would be assisted by a seconded official from each of the preceding and succeeding Presidencies. This institutionalised the 'troika' principle of co-operation and some division of tasks between successive Presidencies. This has the dual advantage of intermeshing a little more the Foreign Offices of the Ten at working level and of alleviating the problems of some smaller Member States in handling representation and coordination in posts abroad. Thus, for example, routinely the Luxembourg Presidency relies on Dutch collaboration particularly in overseas posts, and the Greeks and French worked closely together on some issues in 1983. First experiences of the flying secretariat suggest that it has made a valuable, if modest, contribution to the functioning of EPC.

The document also itemised the responsibilities of the Presidency for representation abroad, handling informal 'Gymnich' meetings, maintaining a dialogue with the European Parliament and coordinating EPC discussions with the Community business, especially important in cases such as the Falklands crisis where the instruments for sanctions depended on the Treaty of Rome. The Presidency, however, has few sticks or carrots with which to beat or lure partner governments in order to expedite discussions, and equally, as was evident in the Athens meeting of September 1983, the Presidency can resist on some issues even the combined weight of the other nine partners.

These arrangements have marked a significant evolution in the functions of the Presidency or at least an increasing acceptance of the case that the EPC mechanisms need some reinforcement, if more effective results are to be achieved. The consensus that the time is not (yet) ripe for an independent secretariat reflects in part the cautions of member governments about new institutions, whether because formalised structures would not be appropriate or through resistance to institutions outside the strict Community framework. The strengthening of the Presidency-based infrastructure, however, also reflects a high degree of satisfaction and mutual congratulation at the successful performance of the Presidency as an institution in its own right. More recently, the

Solemn Declaration on European Union of 1983 (through a much modified form of the original Genscher-Colombo proposals) has committed the member governments to strengthen 'the Presidency's powers of initiative, of coordination and of representation in relations with third countries ... and ... the operational support for successive Presidencies, corresponding to the increasing tasks which they have to perform...' (8).

THE SEVERAL ROLES OF THE COUNCIL PRESIDENCY

An earlier study of the Presidency identified five distinct functions: as manager of Community business; as a source of political initiatives; as package broker in negotiations; as a focus of liaison with other Community institutions; and as a representative of the Community in external relations (9). In all of these functions the Presidency exercises responsibilities, but without either formal powers or political leverage of a systematic character.

A. The Management of the Council

The formal role of the Presidency, identified earlier, is indisputably the main priority of the office. A Presidency cannot be judged successful unless the basic technical tasks of management have been carried out with thoroughness and care, through the conduct of the chair in a businesslike manner, by keeping the machine turning smoothly and purposefully. Credit for such success can generally however be measured only in terms of the approval of ministers and officials from the other Member States or the other Community institutions. A government holding the Presidency can expect to win few laurels from the wider public at home or abroad in return for the effort it puts into running the Council efficiently, unless by great procedural skill it can also create a general sense of purpose in the Community. On the other hand, lack of attention to detail or inadequate preparation can cause blockage and resentment which reflect badly on both the Presidency and the Council as a whole.

In practice the time-table is worked out in conjunction with the other member goverments, with some opportunity for the Presidency, either unilaterally or in response to requests from the other governments or the Commission, to fit in extra meetings or to delay convening sessions. In any event, a backlog of work tends to accumulate towards the end of each presidential period that provides a rush of ministerial meetings in June and December, and an unevenness in the distribution of work between the first half-year and the second which is significantly eroded by the summer holidays.

The Presidency is also responsible for convening all the committees and working groups of officials which prepare Council sessions, except for those few that have special procedures for electing their own chairman which, like the Monetary Committee are joint Commission-Council organs. Some like Coreper and the Special Committee on Agriculture (SCA) have an automatic calendar of meetings, others meet rather more erratically. Sheer numbers mean that there are great constraints on time-tabling, partly due to the demands for rooms and interpreting facilities and because a limited number of Ministers and key officials cannot physically manage to cover more than a certain number of meetings.

It is certainly the case that the Presidency stands to win or lose credit depending on its ability and willingness to cope with these organisational duties. Nor is it simply a question of administration: ministerial sessions are more or less productive depending on whether the negotiations at official level have been completed in time and with adequate thoroughness. Coreper, in particular, has a vital and pivotal role which the Presidency neglects at its peril. A government cannot achieve its targets unless it has succeeded in moving the dossiers up and down the Council hierarchy and used Coreper to pull the various layers of negotiations together within the available time. The national Permanent Representations play a crucial part in supporting and to a large extent embodying the Presidency. A distinction must be drawn between those Councils, committees and working groups which meet frequently and those which provide the forum for occasional and specialised areas of work. In the former case individuals in the chair are likely to have considerable accumulated experience of the EC and of each other, while in the latter group are to be found participants and thus frequently chairmen who may have difficulty in fulfilling the presidential role effectively.

Would-be reformers have attempted to identify a more explicit role for the Presidency as a coordinator of Council negotiations. The reforms of 1973/74 sought to attribute to the Presidency, especially through its Foreign Minister, a more active responsibility for coordination. The La Marlia procedure, agreed in October 1975, required the Council to call for monthly reports summarising progress in the various sectors of the Community 'with particular reference to the questions examined by the specialist councils' (10). Its purpose was not simply to improve coordination in a technical sense but to open the way for more constructive debate on the issues on which Technical Councils had reached deadlock. But it deteriorated into a catalogue of dossiers under discussion. It thus failed to provide the focus originally intended and became redundant.

On the whole, coordination within the Council has been perceived as an intractable Community problem, but the agenda of negotiation has increasingly come to require a more coherent Council-wide approach. The debate over restructuring in 1981 and the follow-up to the Stuttgart Mandate of 1983 have depended **inter alia** on how far the Council could mesh together different strands of a complex bundle of issues. While the Presidency cannot substitute for political agreement it can help to provide the conditions which might foster consensus. This eluded the British Presidency in 1981 and proved more than the Greeks could accomplish in 1983 though in both cases this may reflect the depth of controversy rather than the performance and resources of the chair.

There is no question that the volume of work associated with EPC has become immense. The Presidency takes direct responsibility during its term of office for convening around 60 to 80 meetings including up to four ministerial sessions, monthly meetings of political directors and regular sessions of political correspondents (their deputies) and an ever-increasing number of working groups on specific issues. Most of these meetings take place in the capital of the Presidency and are serviced by the political and geographic departments that in most administrations cover EPC business. One of their advantages, by comparison with colleagues dealing with EC business, is that on the whole they are not weighed down by involvement in complex and time-consuming inter-ministerial coordination in advance of EPC meetings. The rapid extension of the consultative network of EPC has also brought within the machinery, diplomats in embassies in Community capitals, in third countries and in delegations to other international organisations, especially the United Nations. The Foreign Ministry of the Presidency is, in addition, responsible for regular communications with the other nine through the COREU network that links the Foreign Ministries of the Ten. Under the Gymnich formula agreed in 1974 the Presidency liaises with the United States government on topics under discussion among the Nine, now Ten, and there is constant pressure for extending the privileged dialogue to other countries. Moreover, since agreement on the London Report of 1981, the formal and informal responsibilities of the Presidency have been both clarified and modestly expanded (as outlined earlier).

In practice this growth of activity has had the result that for Foreign Ministries and diplomats in posts outside the EC the Presidency often is seen as, in large measure, a matter of running political co-operation. During the six months of office, and indeed in the run-up to it, this may consume more time, resources and indeed enthusiasm than regular Community business. Much, however, depends on the extent to which particular Foreign Ministries are engaged in the management of Community business as distinct from EPC. Obviously in all cases the Permanent Representations with substantial diplomatic staffs play a vital part in the preparation for and management of the Presidency.

It is perhaps a reflection of the current state of the EC that, in practice, most member governments would argue that the very task of keeping the Council ship afloat is their predominant concern during the Presidency. It is non-controversial in the sense that both the Dutch and the French, with their very different views about Community institutions, can agree that the work of the Council must be procedurally facilitated as far as possible. It is a sufficiently taxing role to occupy and preoccupy ministers and officials. The additional responsibility for Foreign Ministries of managing political co-operation generates what most see as a more than adequate workload.

Interestingly, the Council Secretariat, while preserving its collective loyalty to the Council as a whole, has, in effect, become largely a Presidency Secretariat in a much more explicit sense than was previously the case. Perhaps it always was, in that the Secretariat from the outset provided the infrastructure for the organisation of meetings as well as contributing the considerable weight of its legal advice on emerging legislation. But during the 1970s this became more focused and more explicit. The appointment of a Secretary-General, Niels Ersbøll, with political weight and aspirations has helped to foster this trend. It however also reflects the growing responsibilities of the Presidency and the contribution which can be made by a detached secretariat, without a substantive interest of its own, to identifying the scope and procedural requirements for moving business forward, as the secretariats which serve either the Head of Government or ministers collectively often do at the national level.

Yet here also practice varies considerably among governments, as the national case-studies demonstrate. Some work hand in glove with the Council Secretariat whether by preference or because of the scarce resources of staff in their national administrations. Others co-operate closely, as is virtually unavoidable, on procedural arrangements, but put less weight on taking the advice of the Secretariat on how to manage dossiers. Also individual officials of the Secretariat may be more or less committed to or effective in supporting the Presidency. Much depends in practice on personal relationships and the qualities of particular individuals. Often in very specialised areas chairmen with limited experience of the EC will not look to the Council Secretariat for help, sometimes with deleterious consequences. There has been some discussion of the appointment to the Secretariat of a collective spokesman for the Council as distinct from the current more limited operation of briefing the press on Council sessions, but this does not currently have significant support.

B. The Promotion of Political Initiatives

Observers of the Community increasingly suggested in the 1970s that the enhanced importance of the Council Presidency had endowed it with some scope for generating political initiatives. This expectation was most evident in press commentaries and in the national reactions of domestic publics to their respective politicians appearing to 'take over' the running of the Community for six months. At the beginning of his term of office the Foreign Minister of the government in the chair is faced with a barrage of questions about his intentions; at the end he is called to account for his achievements and those of his colleagues and officials. Outside observers look for both the promotion of specific national objectives and spectacular breakthroughs on new Community policies.

Four arguments can be put forward to justify such an ambitious view of the Presidency. First, the increasing weight of the Council **vis-à-vis** the Commission has incorporated some of the power of initiative that formally resides with the Commission. Second, the managerial role of the Presidency is assumed to confer a positive influence on the outcome of Council negotiations. Third, the glamour of European Councils increases the threshold of public expectation projected on to the host country. Fourth, efforts to impose a distinctive national style on the Presidency imply the search for nationally cherished objectives. The weight of these arguments suggests that governments should define specific targets to be sought during their term of office, and that their success or failure should be shared according to how many of these targets have been achieved. The practice is now well-established that each incoming Presidency presents a 'State of the Community' message to the European Parliament and outlines a programme of action to other governments at the start of the first General Council session, and subsequently to the waiting press corps.

Such an image of the Presidency was always grossly simplistic. The constraints of each government are considerable and six months is a very brief period in which to demonstrate dramatic progress. Quite often a chairman may be able to cut through a deadlock in Council negotiations, but the final agreement may still require further refinement that enables a subsequent Presidency to claim the credit for the actual decision. Similarly a Presidency may be able to announce the eventual agreement on a thorny problem even though it had little to do with promoting the crucial agreement. A government is however also dependent on the political and economic climate of its period in office, and thus the victim of both its domestic position and the situation within the Community as a whole. A government may take over the Presidency full of ambitious plans, only to have them undermined by other preoccupations, an unexpected crisis, a sudden distraction or a stubborn lack of co-operation from other governments. The difficult climate of Community negotiations in recent years has tended to diminish expectations that such initiatives are likely to be very successful. In any case the realities of Brussels negotiation are that almost as much depends on the infrastructure of committees of officials labouring their way through thick and awkward dossiers as on the higher profile debates among ministers.

In practice therefore a more modest type of target-setting, by emphasising particular items of current business, is more common. It has become quite usual for incoming Presidencies to stress a number of key issues among those already under negotiation and to outline a new formula for achieving agreement on them. They can then try to push the discussion further or more quickly. This is a less glamorous approach to initiatives, but one which, in principle, allows a government to demonstrate that its period in the chair has produced tangible gains in terms of Community policies. Even this more modest goal is however fraught with difficulties. In the first place, the ability to promote particular issues effectively depends on how skilful a Presidency is in a managerial sense. Secondly, it is not easy to plan in advance those issues that are likely to be amenable to active promotion. Both the Commission and the Council Secretariat offer guidance to the Presidency in the papers they submit at the beginning of each new term of office. Individual governments may also sketch out a list of priorities beforehand, although the practice varies significantly. There is little agreement amongst those involved on how much prior planning is either desirable or possible. Some governments prefer to adopt a wait-and-see approach and then seize upon likely topics just as they take on the Presidency. Others devote considerable efforts in the few months that precede their entry into the chair to pinpointing those areas of negotiation that appear ready for special attention during their term of office.

Procedural innovation is **per contra** an area which offers the Presidency some scope for initiatives. The record tends to show that this has been more productive in EPC than in the more cumbersome procedures of the Council. Thus, for example, the West German government in April 1974 convened the private meeting of Foreign Ministers at Schloss Gymnich to introduce more informal consultations into political co-operation, and the British government pressed for what became the London Report of 1981.

Lastly and most controversially, the Presidency provides scope for emphasising special national interests. It is tempting to infer that such initiatives are particularly attractive to governments attempting to make the most of their term of office. Indeed it is the aspect of the Presidency that in principle seems to offer the greatest gains in domestic political terms, especially to those who are less interested in the Community as a whole and more concerned to see demonstrable national rewards from Community membership. It is however a double-edged weapon, since biased chairmanship is likely to provoke the active resentment of other governments. However attractive national politicians and officials may find it to use every Community resource possible to promote their favoured causes, too explicit an emphasis on narrow national interests is countered by ready charges of partiality. Indeed the more experienced of those involved in the Community argue consistently that the Presidency is more likely to be costly in terms of national interest, since the pressures on the contrary demand proof of Community-mindedness. Governments can thus be handicapped in fostering national causes, and if they cling during the six months' span to so blinkered an approach their Presidency as a whole is likely to be discredited. Here we must however recognise that we are discussing a domain where perceptions are crucial. What a government in the chair may regard as a fair and sensible approach may appear to partners to be strikingly partisan.

C. The Presidency as a Package-Broker

It is commonly a function of the chair in any committee to use its position to promote agreement on the issues under discussion. The Presidency of the Council of Ministers thus automatically carries some responsibility for developing a consensus and for identifying possible compromises. In the early years of the Community the assumption was that the Commission would actively mediate among the differing interests of member governments. The fail-safe mechanism envisaged by the Treaties was the progressive introduction of majority voting to impose agreement if arbitration by the Commission was unsuccessful. However these two methods of reaching a consensus have proved in the first case insufficient and in the second unacceptable. The Commission continues to try to mediate, particularly at ministerial level, sometimes effectively but often fruitlessly. As a consequence, there has been some shift of attention to the Presidency of the Council as an alternative architect of compromise. A more active assertion of the powers of the chair, it is argued, can pressure governments to be conciliatory. Given that a large proportion of dossiers are actually settled at the level of officials (before being ratified formally by ministers), the search for compromise by the Presidency can be important in working groups and senior committees such as Coreper. The fact that a large number of chairmen are officials from the relevant Permanent Representation helps to orient them towards a collective approach and to detach them from their national spokesmen.

The burden on governments is still further increased if this additional role of mediation is to be performed with any success. Moreover it requires an explicit separation for the government occupying the chair between the Community-oriented role required of a mediator and the regular role of members and officials in acting as the spokesmen of their governments' narrower interests. This has both practical and political repercussions. In particular, chairmen need to be familiar with the detailed postures of each government and thus to spend a considerable amount of time identifying the reasoning behind publicly enunciated positions. This may require either spending time in advance of meetings gathering intelligence from the members of Permanent Representations, from the Commission and from the Council Secretariat or direct consultations in the capital of other governments to clear the ground for the final stage of negotiations. Preparing the ground in this way is especially onerous as an additional claim on the time of ministers, though perhaps less of a problem for the officials chairing committees, since the majority of these are normally full-time specialists on Community or Community-related matters. The Council Secretariat as a matter of practice includes in its brief for the Presidency a section on the position of Member States. Increasingly, ministers and officials define it as part of their job during the Presidency to set aside time for bilateral visits to their counterparts. This has been most common among Agriculture Ministers, but has become more prevalent latterly in other sectors too. It is important to recognise that the cumbersome constitutional conventions of the formal Council hierarchy often impede 'imaginative solutions'. While bilateral contacts and active Presidencies cannot guarantee breakthroughs, they may sometimes serve to open up alternative options and packages. It also falls to officials to advise their ministers on the scope for constructive bilateralism.

Yet here again the capacity to deliver as an effective package-broker is closely tied to the procedural dexterity of the Presidency. Obvious skills of timing and diplomacy in the chair facilitate mediation. Only if time is saved on unproductive discussion is it possible for the chair to focus attention on issues amenable to resolution. Close co-operation at all levels with the responsible Commissioners and their officials is crucial. It is also the normal practice, for example, for Council officials to prepare notes of guidance for the Presidency indicating the lines of possible compromise. During the run up to the Stuttgart European Council of June 1983, for example, the German Presidency worked extremely closely with the Council Secretariat. Whatever the limitations on achievement, the concept of 'the Presidency compromise' now seems to be built into Council negotiations.

There is however also a sensitive political dimension to this package-broking role. A government in the chair, which happens also to have a strong vested interest in the outcome of any given issue, is obviously ill-placed to assume the mantle of a neutral arbitrator. By contrast, a Presidency which is freed of commitment to a particular outcome, because its government is little affected by a proposal, can more easily stand back and argue the Community interest and promote,

16

without incurring suspicion, a compromise position. It has always been easier, for example, for the Luxembourgers to put themselves forward as mediators than for the French or British. Of the larger Member States only the Italians have regularly and productively assumed the mantle of conciliation, to particularly good effect in 1965 and 1980. Occasionally chairmen seize on the fact that they are under pressure to identify with the Community interest in order to carry their own governments along with decisions on which they might otherwise have expressed reservations. Thus chairmen of committees who are drawn from the Permanent Representations often welcome their term of office as an opportunity to induce in their home-based colleagues a more co-operative attitude to Community negotiations.

D. Liaison with other Community Institutions

The initial definition of the Presidency's role included a formal responsibility for communications between the Council of Ministers and other Community institutions. One key relationship is that between the Council Presidency and the Commission over the forthcoming business of the Council and Coreper. The Commission, through its General Secretariat, has adopted the practice of preparing six-monthly reports for each new Council Presidency on the state of play of the various policy proposals under discussion. Often the chairmen of technical councils and Council Committees establish close links with their counterparts among the Commissioners and in the Directorates-General of the Commission in order to improve consultation on important areas of negotiations, though much depends on the goodwill and conscientiousness of the particular individuals involved.

Staff in the Commission generally argue that a Council Presidency is more likely to be effective if the incumbent government establishes close and regular contacts with Commissioners and the services and thus themselves often seek contacts with the Presidency. As a matter of common practice, the incoming President of the Foreign Affairs Council will meet the Commissioners to exchange views on the negotiating programme of the next six months. The President of Coreper regularly meets the President of the Commission and the Secretary-General of the Council, and there are less frequent but important meetings with all Permanent Representatives. This round of informal but systematic contacts has become increasingly important in preparing sessions of Coreper, and since Presidents of Coreper are normally experienced members of this 'club' they serve to interweave the roles of the Presidency, the Council Secretariat and the Commission. Yet national practices and preferences for activating the dialogue between Council Presidency and Commission vary so much that it is difficult to reach hard and fast conclusions about what actually happens let alone about what makes for a mutually reinforcing complementarity of roles.

The Council Presidency has also become increasingly important in acting as the channel for liaison between the Council and the directly elected European Parliament for both Community business and issues raised in political co-operation. The sheer increase in the volume of Council work has generated a parallel increase in contacts with the

Parliament. As pressure from the Parliament for greater attention has strengthened, so the demands on the Presidency to make regular reports and to answer questions have grown. This has required a heavy commitment of time by ministers of the government in the chair especially by the Foreign Minister. It has now become an established practice for the Foreign Minister to present a 'State of the Community' message to the Parliament at the beginning of each six-monthly term which sets out a programme or delineates the priorities envisaged as important. In addition, European parliamentarians expect ministers from the Presidency to be available regularly after each Council session to report on negotiations and to respond to fairly thorough questioning. Foreign Ministers also inform the Political Committee in camera of what has been agreed in political co-operation meetings. In some areas, such as agriculture, it is common for ministers to attend a session of the relevant Committee of the Parliament. These appearances before the Parliament have acquired considerable importance and are neglected by the Presidency only at the cost of heavy criticism from parliamentarians, though some ministers bear the reproaches more readily than others. At the level of officials too member governments have expanded their coverage of discussion and debate within the European Parliament, especially during the Presidency.

There are, however, major problems for the government of the Presidency in fitting this substantial commitment into a heavily crowded time-table. Foreign Ministers find it difficult to be present in the Parliament regularly and many delegate this job to junior ministers, though this can provoke resentment. An interesting innovation was the decision by the European Council in June 1981 that the President of the European Council should report in person to the Parliament. This was agreed under an enthusiastic Dutch Presidency after the electoral defeat of Mr Giscard d'Estaing who would not have countenanced it. The London Report and the 'Solemn Declaration on European Union' of 1983 confirmed this.

In addition, the evolving role of the Parliament on budgetary matters has generated both a political requirement and procedures for managing inter-institutional relationships. The budgetary 'trilogue' compels the Presidents of the Council, Commission and Parliament to seek consensus and concertation on certain budgetary disputes (11). This, combined with the procedures for conciliation on financial legislation, is gradually compelling, at least in formal terms, more regular and structured exchanges between the Council, Parliament and Commission Presidencies. Here, as in all contacts with the Parliament, the overt responsibility falls on ministers from the current Presidency and practices vary according to the political preferences of both governments as such and of individual ministers. Yet it also adds significantly to the workload of national officials in preparing the ground for ministers. The Council Secretariat plays an important part in coordinating replies to parliamentary questions and in briefing the Presidency before and during sessions of the Parliament.

A further development has been the practice by the President of the Parliament of making prior contacts with each government about its next Presidency and of holding informal meetings during the term of office with the Council and Commission Presidents, a development which perhaps contains the germ of a collective and inter-institutional approach to political leadership within the EC.

E. The Presidency as Spokesman
Acting as a collective spokesman both for the EC and for the Ten in a variety of international contexts has become one of the chief tasks of the Council Presidency. As the external relations of the Community have expanded, so different formulae have been agreed for representing common positions, which have come to impose more and more of this responsibility on the Presidency. Since the establishment of political co-operation, the representational role of the Presidency has taken a quantum leap forward now that the Ten have become actively involved in foreign policy collaboration in various new areas and problems that hitherto were the sole responsibility of individual Member States.

Underlying this development has run a persistent argument over competences and who has the right to speak for the EC and its members on what occasion. The Commission has been able to retain primacy only on those areas of policy where the authority of the Treaties or subsequent decisions are absolutely clear. For areas of shared or contested competence a compromise procedure was agreed - the so-called Rome Formula. This allowed the Commission to present and defend the agreed Community position, but entitled the Council Presidency to supplement this on behalf of governments. The role of the Presidency thus emerged as what has come to be known as the 'bicephalous' Presidency or dual spokesmanship. As a consequence, the Council Presidency has found itself more and more heavily involved in representational work, not least because the number of such grey areas of international negotiations has increased rather rapidly. Another difficult area has been representing the EC at western economic summits where the EC is spoken for either by a regular member or by an occasional member, depending on who occupies the Council Presidency, with Commission contributions since 1977 on areas within Community competence (12). Interestingly there have been pressures for European-hosted summits to be held during the EC Presidential terms of France, Germany, Italy, or the UK, thus obviating the need to expand temporarily the membership of the deliberately restricted club. In a few instances, where some of the Member States have been caught up with an issue (such as the Siberian gas pipeline), the Presidency has acted as a point of contact with the rest of the EC.

The evolution of political co-operation has given the Council a far more precise responsibility for acting as the spokesman of the Ten. Both the London Report of 1981 and the Solemn Declaration on European Union of 1983 have highlighted the importance of a scope for developing this role. There are several different dimensions to this: acting as spokesman in some international fora like the UN and the CIEC; discussions with other governments either in their capitals or in the capital of the Presidency; the occasional input of a Community dimension to bilateral talks between another government and the government that happens to hold the Presidency; and the specific liaison arrangements made to keep the US Government regularly informed of developments in political co-operation. The representation of the Ten through the Presidency in these issues, is uncontentious in so far as they exclude matters of Community competence, but it may cause sensitive problems on other grounds. Moreover, foreign policy resources in administrative terms make it easier for some Community governments than for others to act as spokesmen of the Ten in all the countries and international fora which are relevant at any given moment. In addition, the Presidency is only able to represent the Ten in a substantive sense where a common position has been agreed already. Thus in some instances the Presidency may be able only to state what the Member States have agreed without any scope for further discussion, in contrast, for example, to cases where the Presidency is empowered to pursue discussions (or in the inter-institutional context negotiations) on behalf of the Council collectively.

SOME PRELIMINARY CONCLUSIONS

The shape of the Presidency's role and functions has not changed dramatically in recent years, but some elements have been thrown into sharper relief. EPC has become more established and more important, at least in the sense of its agenda of awkward issues. Perhaps also the rift exposed between the Americans and the West Europeans on issues such as the Siberian pipeline is indicative of pressures towards a still more consolidated and collective approach by the Ten on foreign policy issues. Security issues have floated back into the Community arena, though not at this stage in a very tangible form. Yet there are tensions within EPC and a wide spectrum of views on some issues. Managerial effectiveness and sensitive agenda setting may help, but they are not a substitute for compatible interests or a consensus on action.
The Federal Trust study concluded in 1977:

> It is, however, open to question how much longer the rather **ad hoc** arrangements for the Presidency can survive or whether it can take on still further duties without it either placing an intolerable load on each Member Government in turn or causing a progressive deterioration in the workings of the Council of Ministers.
> (Edwards and Wallace)

As I have argued in this paper, the Presidency has not acquired further duties, though some, such as liaison with the Parliament, may have become more onerous and others more a matter of routine. Governments do not, by and large, argue that the load is intolerable, though there is significantly no enthusiasm for extending the term of office beyond six months. Perhaps, on the contrary, there is now a sense of **déjà vu**: all governments with the exception of the Greek have been round the course at least twice since the Presidency's role was clearly extended. As this 'routinisation' has crept in there has perhaps been a downgrading of expectations by each government of both itself and its partners. Poor conduct of meetings is received with irritation, smooth management is welcomed as helpful. Little investment is made in dreaming up ambitious blueprints for reforming the operations of the Council. Governments look for differences of style and emphasis from successive presidencies and expect individual personalities to have an impact on specific areas of work. But they do not expect profound differences of approach because the Council machine will tick over more or less.

Over the last few years the EC has been through a very difficult period, reflected in hard and sometimes abortive negotiations in the Council, though it would be quite erroneous to ascribe this to malfunction of the Presidency. Yet policy interests and institutional resources do interact. Perhaps the most striking development has been an increased sense of frustration with what is perceived as the conventional Council straightjacket where the search for consensus can so easily be condemned to move at the pace of the slowest or most eccentric government on any given issue. There is also a striking mismatch between the highly segmented structures of the Council and the package of inter-connected policy choices over restructuring, CAP reform, budget financing and enlargement. The Presidency, as such, has made little apparent contribution in general terms to resolving this dichotomy. The temptation to look for other ways of pushing dossiers forward is strong in some quarters. On the margins of Council meetings and in direct contacts through capitals informal negotiations have become increasingly important as an adjunct to or substitute for the formal Brussels forum. Sometimes these involve the Presidency, but by no means always, though an alert Presidency may be well placed to build bridges between formal and informal negotiations. Whatever label one chooses from the several now on offer, some version of 'variable geometry' seems set fair to gain greater currency, perhaps rather by gradual changes in practice than by explicit agreement. Notions of some countries or groups of countries having a privileged role in certain areas or of only some governments participating in some decisions begin to look like more than a veiled hint.

This kind of development puts the Presidency in an interesting but exposed position. Everything about the Presidency symbolises the effort to achieve two objectives: first, a rough parity amongst the Member States, even though everyone knows that actual degrees of influence and interests are less evenly spread; and second, an attempt to balance national and Community perspectives. Maintenance of parity is contested and contestable on a number of grounds. Community and national perspectives are difficult to identify and seem particularly fluid. In the past the Council has often laboriously, and almost always late, adapted itself to changing pressures. On its own a redefinition of the role of the Presidency probably does not offer much scope for further adaptation. But on past performance it is a useful barometer of a changeable institutional climate (13).

21

REFERENCES

(1)   Official Journal of the EC, no. L 269/1, 25 October 1979.
(2)   Official Journal of the EC, no. L261, 4 October 1980.
(3)   Bulletin of the EC, 2-1974, pp. 103-4. See also the Joint Declaration by the President of the Council and the President of the Commission of 2 April 1974, Bulletin of the EC 3-1974, pp. 9f.
(4)   Conclusions of the European Council (meeting 9 1-2 December 1980) on the Report on European Institutions, Council of the EC, Brussels, 1981.
(5)   Bulletin of the EC, 9-1973, pp. 14-21.
(6)   Bulletin of the EC, 6-1974, pp. 123-125.
(7)   Entitled 'Report on European Political Co-operation' the London Report was published in Europe Documents no. 1174 of 17 October 1981.
(8)   Europe Documents no. 1263 of 22 June 1983.
(9)   Geoffrey Edwards and Helen Wallace, The Council of Ministers of the European Community and the President in-Office, Federal Trust, London, 1977, also published in German by Europa Union Verlag, 1978.
(10) Bulletin of the EC, 11-1975, p. 85.
(11) Official Journal of the EC C194/1982/1., 30 June 1982.
(12) See: G. Bonvicini and W. Wessels 'The European Community and the Seven' in: C. Merlini (ed.) Economic Summits and Western Decision-Making, Croom Helm, London, 1984.
(13) For a discussion of the possible future development of the Presidency, chapter 12 p. 261 ff.

Chapter 2

LA PRÉSIDENCE DU CONSEIL DES MINISTRES DES COMMUNAUTÉS EUROPÉENNES: RAPPORT NATIONAL SUR LA BELGIQUE
M. Michel vanden Abeele, Bruxelles (1)

INTRODUCTION

Comme le signale Henri Simonet, l'idée européenne en Belgique fait l'objet d'une bienveillance générale. Elle est entrée dans le domaine des idées reçues, c'est-à-dire celles dont on ne discute pas. Mais cette bienveillance se double parfois d'un peu d'indifférence (2). Certes, les grands dossiers politique et économique européens qui ont une influence sur la Belgique font l'objet de débats parlementaires et de commentaires dans les media. Mais l'idée même de la participation à la Communauté n'est pas en jeu; il n'y a pas d'opposition exprimée à celle-ci, quelque soit la tendance politique. Les déclarations gouvernementales successives témoignent d'ailleurs de cette adhésion à l'édification européenne. A l'occasion de l'installation du gouvernement Tindemans-Hurez en juin 1977, référence est d'ailleurs faite expressément à l'impulsion que pourrait donner la Belgique à 'l'accentuation de la dimension européenne de sa politique extérieure durant la période où la Belgique présidera le Conseil des Ministres de la Communauté européenne' (3).

Il est communément admis en effet que l'appartenance de la Belgique au Marché Commun lui procure des avantages certains. L'économie profite de la libéralisation des échanges et de l'accès à un marché étendu. L'agriculture belge a largement tiré parti des dispositions de la politique agricole commune. Le pouvoir d'influence extérieure, fondé sur des politiques communes et sur la solidarité, a permis au pays de mieux s'insérer dans les relations économiques internationales et d'améliorer la sécurité de ses approvisionnements.

Le pouvoir de négociation et le rôle politique limité d'un petit pays se trouve amplifié par son appartenance à une Communauté dont l'existence en tant que partenaire commercial est désormais reconnue et surtout au moment où prend naissance une réelle coopération politique européenne.

Mais si la Belgique bénéficie de son appartenance à la Communauté, elle en connaît également les conséquences. C'est ainsi que les disciplines communes sont parfois ressenties comme des freins à la mise en oeuvre de politiques plus autonomes. Dans un passé récent, on peut relever un certain nombre de conflits entre des intérêts politiques nationaux et les dispositions européennes. C'est le cas, par exemple, du

23

respect des règles européennes en matière d'aide à finalité régionale, de la recommandation de la Commission en matière d'indexation des prix et salaires qui fut un des éléments d'une crise gouvernementale, ou encore des tensions entre les régions dans la mise en oeuvre des mesures de restructuration de la sidérurgie sur base des dispositions prises par la Communauté.

Dès lors, si l'appartenance à la Communauté n'est pas un objet de discussion, les modalités des relations entre la Belgique et ses régions d'une part, et la Communauté européenne et les autres pays membres d'autre part, font l'objet de multiples discussions, tant du point de vue politique qu'au niveau administratif.

Trois particularités méritent, en outre, d'être soulignées dans une approche globale des relations entre la Belgique et la Communauté européenne.

La première est l'émergence du phénomène régional qui caractérise la vie politique, mais également la structure administrative de la Belgique. Les relations entre la Belgique et la Communauté sont désormais influencées par les diversités régionales qui s'organisent progressivement. Certes, les systèmes d'information et de coordination qui existent continueront à fonctionner, mais il apparaît indispensable de réfléchir aux modes d'association des régions dans le processus décisionnel. D'ores et déjà, certaines matières régionalisées ou même des dossiers d'intérêt national sont sujets à des discussions tant au sein des Exécutifs régionaux qu'au niveau des responsabilités régionales des ministres appartenant au gouvernement.

Dans la Belgique nouvelle qui s'organise, les équilibres politiques et administratifs ne sont pas encore établis. L'exercice des responsabilités régionales au regard des problèmes internationaux et européens devrait faire l'objet d'un examen approfondi. Il est prématuré de prévoir comment vont s'établir les équilibres; ce n'est d'ailleurs pas l'objet de la présente communication, mais il est évident que la régionalisation introduit une nouvelle dimension dans les relations extérieures de la Belgique.

La deuxième particularité du système belge réside dans le haut degré de 'politisation' des rapports avec la Communauté. Ceci tient essentiellement au fait que le système de gouvernement en Belgique est caractérisé par le développement d'une structure politique très importante en nombre, influente auprès des responsables ministériels: il s'agit du système des cabinets. Chaque ministre dispose en effet d'un et parfois de plusieurs cabinets lorsqu'il exerce diverses fonctions ministérielles. Ces cabinets sont composés de collaborateurs en nombre croissant, en dépit de la volonté souvent exprimée d'en limiter le nombre (4).

Ce système d'organisation et son évolution marquent fortement le style administratif adopté en Belgique. Dans de nombreux cas, les dossiers échappent totalement à l'administration traditionnelle pour être traités uniquement au niveau des cabinets ministériels. Bien que ce ne soit pas fréquemment le cas en ce qui concerne les matières européennes, pareille évolution du système rend plus compliqué le suivi de certains dossiers, en particulier lorsqu'il y a un changement dans les responsabilités ministérielles. Par contre, le maintien des dossiers au niveau politique permet à ceux-ci d'évoluer en fonction des événements, caractérisant une grande adaptation de la politique belge à la recherche des compromis.

Ceci conduit à la troisième caractéristique. Il s'agit du rôle particulier que jouent bien souvent les responsables et les représentants belges dans les enceintes européennes, à savoir une fonction indéniable d'arbitre ou de conciliateur. Caractérisés, selon le mot de Paul-Henri Spaak, par leur 'impartialité active', les Belges ont voulu jouer un rôle moteur pour faire progresser les choses dans le domaine européen. Ceci se rencontre tant au niveau politique où nombreux sont les hommes politiques qui ont acquis une dimension internationale grâce à leur action européenne (5), qu'au niveau administratif où, selon une règle non écrite, les fonctionnaires belges ont bien souvent cherché à faire avancer les dossiers en privilégiant les intérêts européens plutôt qu'en s'attachant simplement à défendre des positions purement nationales (6). Ceci prédispose les Belges à jouer un rôle actif, en particulier au cours des périodes où la Belgique assume les responsabilités de la présidence du Conseil des Communautés (7).

ROLE ET INTERVENTION DU GOUVERNEMENT ET DU PARLEMENT

Caractérisé par l'existence de gouvernements de coalition, le Conseil des Ministres en Belgique est l'autorité décisionnelle suprême du pouvoir exécutif. C'est au niveau du Conseil des Ministres que se prennent les grandes décisions politiques, que s'élaborent les compromis, que s'établit le projet de Budget. C'est le Conseil des Ministres, présidé par le Premier ministre, qui adopte les projets d'arrêtés royaux et les projets de lois, qui fixe la position du gouvernement face au Parlement, et qui définit également la politique étrangère.

Toutefois, la pratique s'est développée d'organiser des comités ou des Conseils de Ministres restreints qui prennent des décisions dans des matières particulières.

Comités ministériels

La composition, les compétences et l'organisation de ces comités varient suivant les gouvernements; celui-ci fixe lors de sa création les dispositions qui régissent le fonctionnement de ces comités, mais parfois la pratique diffère des décisions; certains comités peuvent prendre plus d'importance; d'autres ne sont quasi jamais réunis.

Sont actuellement compétents en matière européenne, le Comité ministériel de coordination économique et sociale (CMCES), le Comité ministériel de la politique extérieure (CMPE) et le Comité ministériel des relations économiques extérieures (CMREE).

a) Le CMCES:

Il s'agit de l'ancien Comité ministériel économique qui avait été créé en 1938 pour émettre des avis à l'intention du Conseil des Ministres; il fut réformé en 1947, en ce sens qu'il devenait alors plus indépendant du Conseil des Ministres. De même, il a vu sa compétence étendue au domaine social en 1961 et il a été réorganisé à plusieurs reprises (8).

Tout en veillant à l'indispensable coordination, ce Comité se prononce sur les aspects économiques, financiers et sociaux de la politique gouvernementale; il établit les programmes des investissements publics, en fixe le calendrier et en règle l'exécution.

b) Le CMPE:

Ce Comité se prononce sur les aspects économiques, financiers et sociaux de la politique gouvernementale dans toutes les questions où l'aspect de politique extérieure est prédominant (9).

A noter que la composition de ces deux premiers comités est fixée par le Premier ministre qui en désigne le président, et que les membres du gouvernement qui ne font pas partie d'un comité sont invités à y participer pour l'examen des affaires les concernant particulièrement.

c) Le CMREE:

Ce Comité a été créé par le dernier gouvernement parce qu'il y avait 'urgence dans les circonstances actuelles de procéder à la création d'un comité ministériel chargé d'élaborer une politique économique extérieure coordonnée et efficace au sein du gouvernement' (10).

Ce Comité est présidé par le ministre des Relations extérieures (11).

d) Le Conseil des Ministres

Le Conseil des Ministres, enfin, reste l'organe de coordination gouvernementale qui peut être saisi par le ministre compétent ou sur rapport d'un conseil ministériel restreint lorsqu'il s'agit d'un problème de grande importance ou qui conditionne l'existence du gouvernement.

Dans tous ces comités, le ministre des Relations extérieures, responsable de la politique étrangère, joue un rôle important. Il est assisté par son administration et par son cabinet pour qui les affaires européennes constituent une tâche prioritaire.

Secrétaire d'Etat

Dans certains cas, la structure gouvernementale comprend également un secrétaire d'Etat.

Ainsi, le gouvernement mis en place juste avant la période de la présidence de 1982 a créé un secrétariat d'Etat aux Affaires européennes.

Si la présidence belge précédente (en 1977) ne connaissait pas ces structures comprenant un secrétariat d'Etat, cette institution n'était cependant pas inconnue, puisqu'il y avait déjà eu dix ans auparavant un secrétaire d'Etat adjoint au ministre des Affaires étrangères qui s'occupait entre autres choses, des affaires européennes (M. Fayat). Ce secrétariat d'Etat a existé au cours du gouvernement Eyskens-Cools II (janvier 1972 - novembre 1972). De même la Belgique a connu un ministre des Affaires européennes (M. Van Elslande) pendant le gouvernement Vanden Boeynants - De Clercq (mars 1966 - février 1968).

Ces deux premières expériences n'ont pas été très concluantes; elles ont introduit une certaine dichotomie dans la gestion des affaires européennes.

Dans le cas du gouvernement Martens de 1982, le fait que le secrétaire d'Etat aux Affaires européennes (M. De Keersmaeker) soit de la même famille politique que le ministre Leo Tindemans et qu'il dispose en outre des compétences les plus larges sur les problèmes agricoles ne crée pas cette fois les mêmes problèmes que par le passé.

La création du secrétariat d'Etat aux Affaires européennes, outre les raisons d'équilibre dans la répartition des portefeuilles, est due au fait que l'on a estimé que l'ensemble des problèmes agricoles était si étroitement lié à la politique européenne qu'il valait la peine d'en charger spécifiquement un secrétaire d'Etat. De plus, la création du secrétariat d'Etat permet de décharger le ministre des Relations extérieures dans l'exécution de certaines tâches, tant dans le cadre de la Communauté européenne que dans celui des relations extérieures (par ex. relations avec le Conseil de l'Europe).

Cette formule est également intéressante lorsque le ministre assume la présidence, le secrétaire d'Etat pouvant assurer la fonction de représentant des intérêts du gouvernement belge.

En période normale, le secrétaire d'Etat peut aisément remplacer le ministre des Relations extérieures. Compte tenu de la législation belge, le secrétaire d'Etat reste subordonné au ministre. C'est le Roi (par arrêté royal) qui détermine les attributions et les limites dans lesquelles le secrétaire d'Etat peut prendre seul une décision.

Rôle du Parlement et des groupes de pression

Le Parlement intervient dans les questions européennes générales lors du vote du Budget et notamment en ce qui concerne le budget des Affaires étrangères et le budget de l'Agriculture. De même, par de nombreuses questions parlementaires, le Parlement intervient dans le débat et peut orienter les options politiques défendues par le gouvernement. Il apparaît toutefois que le débat parlementaire est souvent coloré de préoccupations à caractère régional ou culturel et que le Parlement ne trouve pas dans la structure politique et administrative belge actuelle, une réponse à des préoccupations d'influence des régions sur les décisions européennes.

Le ministre des Relations extérieures est, semble-t-il, sensible à cette évolution et a pris le soin d'informer au préalable le Parlement et en particulier la Commission des affaires étrangères sur les positions qu'il entendait défendre à l'occasion des grands débats européens et en particulier préalablement à la présidence. Plusieurs déclarations officielles du gouvernement témoignent d'ailleurs de cette volonté d'informer le Parlement sur l'évolution des problèmes européens.

Mais le Parlement prend surtout conscience de la dimension européenne des politiques à l'occasion de grands débats sur des problèmes nationaux ou régionaux. Il en est ainsi, par exemple, des discussions sur la politique monétaire ou sur la sidérurgie, sur la restructuration industrielle ou sur la recherche. C'est à l'occasion de ces discussions que le gouvernement et le Parlement élaborent des schémas de référence où l'Europe prend sa place. Il n'y a guère eu de débat sur des sujets européens au sens strict, hormis la discussion de la loi relative aux élections du Parlement européen (12).

En dehors du Parlement, multiples sont les canaux d'information et de consultation qui, organisés ou non sous forme de groupes de pression, peuvent influencer le gouvernement et l'administration sur les matières européennes. Quels que soient les sujets ou les départements concernés, les intérêts des groupes économiques et sociaux ont de multiples occasions de s'exprimer en Belgique, que ce soit par:

- l'envoi de lettres ou de notes d'organisations diverses faisant valoir les desiderata des uns, les aspects économiques et sociaux auxquels tiennent particulièrement les autres, les intérêts nationaux, régionaux ou locaux;
- un certain nombre de visites effectuées dans les différents ministères par les représentants de ces groupes d'intérêts.

Ces contacts se font, soit au niveau politique (ministres et cabinets), soit au niveau de l'administration. Lorsque les revendications ne sont pas trop divergentes de la ligne suivie par le département concerné, elles sont généralement acceptées et s'introduisent aisément dans la philosophie défendue par la délégation belge. Cette perméabilité des influences ne signifie pas cependant que seront défendus indifféremment, sans analyse, tous les intérêts de tous les groupes de pression. L'administration et le système politique belge sont rompus à la technique des compromis et une longue tradition influence les choix dans une optique généralement pro-européenne. Les intérêts nationaux sont toujours examinés dans cette perspective européenne.

LA COORDINATION INTERMINISTERIELLE

Un nombre important de départements ministériels et de services sont concernés par les questions européennes, en fonction de divers sujets désormais affectés par la dimension européenne. Toutefois, deux départements, celui des Affaires étrangères et celui des Affaires économiques occupent dans ces matières une place privilégiée. Dans une certaine mesure, le département de l'Agriculture et celui des Finances sont largement impliqués dans le processus de décision européen qui les concerne. Dans chaque cas, distinction doit être faite entre le niveau de responsabilité politique et le niveau administratif. Ainsi, dans le domaine des relations extérieures il existe au niveau politique:

- le ministre des Relations extérieures;
- le chef du cabinet du ministre des Relations extérieures (le cabinet comprend 11 personnes, et en particulier la cellule européenne qui compte 4 membres, dont l'un chargé des relations avec le Parlement, un autre assurant la liaison avec le secrétaire d'Etat aux Affaires européennes);
- le secrétaire d'Etat aux Affaires européennes (qui n'a pas de cabinet pour cette matière).

Au niveau administratif, outre le secrétaire général du département qui joue un rôle de coordination de l'information, sont essentiellement impliqués dans les affaires européennes:

- la direction générale de la politique;
- le service des organisations européennes (P 11) qui en dépend et qui compte trois personnes de rang 1, c'est-à-dire de niveau universitaire;
- une direction d'administration et de coordination des affaires européennes (couramment appelée service Europe) qui comprend neuf personnes.

A titre occasionnel, d'autres fonctionnaires du département qui dépendent de la direction des relations extérieures bilatérales, de la direction des relations économiques internationales ou de la direction de la politique économique ou financière extérieure sont également concernés par les questions européennes.

Au département des Affaires économiques, ce sont essentiellement les fonctionnaires qui représentent le département dans la Commission économique interministérielle et leurs services qui s'occupent des matières européennes.

Les autres ministères n'ont pas de cellule européenne propre; toutefois, certains services, en particulier au département de l'Agriculture et à celui des Finances, sont organisés en fonction du rôle important qui est le leur dans les négociations qui leur sont spécifiques. Certains ministres veillent également à ce que leur cabinet comprenne un spécialiste des affaires européennes.

Il en est ainsi pour le Premier ministre qui dispose dans ses services d'un conseiller pour les relations diplomatiques et pour les questions européennes, dont le rôle est important compte tenu des responsabilités du chef de gouvernement dans le cadre des réunions du Conseil européen.

Le Premier ministre ne dispose toutefois pas d'infrastructure spécifique pour assurer la présidence du Conseil européen. Cette infrastructure dépend du département des Affaires étrangères.

D'une manière pratique, la liaison entre le département des Affaires étrangères et les services du Premier ministre est assurée par le conseiller du Premier ministre pour les questions extérieures. C'est lui qui transmet au cabinet des Affaires étrangères les priorités souhaitées par le Premier ministre. C'est également lui qui a établi, en liaison avec les Affaires étrangères et le Secrétariat général du Conseil, les procédures de préparation du Conseil européen (contacts avec la Commission, contacts préalables avec les autres chefs de gouvernement ou chefs d'Etat). Son rôle est particulièrement important lorsque la Belgique exerce la présidence du Conseil. Au cours de la présidence exercée par la Belgique en 1977, le Premier ministre s'est adjoint deux conseillers en plus de son conseiller diplomatique.

Au cours de la présidence de 1982, le Premier ministre s'est adjoint un seul conseiller en plus de son conseiller chargé des questions des relations extérieures.

Contrairement à d'autres présidences du Conseil européen, le Premier ministre belge ne semble pas avoir voulu profiter en 1982 de la présidence du Conseil européen pour prendre des initiatives particulières. Le Premier ministre a toutefois joué un rôle important dans la recherche de consensus sur les questions débattues au moment de la présidence de la Belgique, notamment les épineuses questions budgétaires.

Les structures de coordination
La coordination des problèmes européens est subrepticement passée du département des Affaires économiques au département des Affaires étrangères. Cela s'explique non seulement par la personnalité des responsables chargés des affaires européennes dans ces départements, mais aussi par le fait que les affaires européennes couvrent maintenant nombre de secteurs différents qui nécessitent une véritable coordination de nature politique, qui dépasse parfois la dimension économique.

Cette évolution n'est pas concrétisée dans les textes. Il convient également de remarquer que la coordination entre les départements et au niveau politique existe à de multiples niveaux.

On distingue actuellement la réunion de coordination du lundi matin au ministère des Relations extérieures et le rôle de la Commission économique interministérielle (CEI).

a) La réunion de coordination du lundi matin au ministère des Relations extérieures
Il s'agit d'une réunion qui est présidée par un haut fonctionnaire de ce ministère et à laquelle participent un représentant de chacun des départements économiques et financiers ou du cabinet concerné, le représentant permanent et/ou son adjoint et les représentants de tous les départements dont la présence est jugée nécessaire (c'est-à-dire les personnes désignées par leur ministre pour suivre les activités européennes).

Cette réunion revêt une importance pratique parce qu'elle joue en fait le rôle d'instance centrale. D'aucuns l'appellent d'ailleurs la 'coordination générale'; il y a parfois 30 à 35 personnes qui y assistent.

b) La Commission économique interministérielle (CEI)
Créée de longue date (en août 1938), la CEI est une commission administrative, présidée par le secrétaire général du ministère des Affaires économiques, composée de hauts fonctionnaires représentant divers ministères. Elle doit en principe assumer un rôle de coordination en matière économique, préparer les décisions du Conseil des Ministres et en particulier du C.M.C.E.S. (Comité ministériel de coordination économique et sociale) et peut se voir confier des tâches d'exécution des dispositions légales et réglementaires relatives au commerce et aux relations extérieures (13).

Le rôle de la CEI a varié dans le temps. La CEI n'assume que rarement désormais le rôle de préparation des décisions du C.M.C.E.S., préparation qui est dévolue à l'heure actuelle à des contacts entre les cabinets les plus intéressés. Toutefois, la CEI, ayant réformé son organisation interne en 1965, conserve des attributions spécifiques dans le domaine de la coordination à l'égard des affaires européennes. La CEI dispose d'un comité permanent et de 12 sous-commissions qui couvrent des sujets techniques, notamment:

-   le groupe des questions CECA qui a mission d'examiner les questions posées par l'application du Traité CECA;
-   le groupe des questions CEE/problèmes divers;
-   le groupe des questions CEE/problèmes agricoles;
-   le groupe des questions CEE/problèmes douaniers;
-   le groupe 'Licences des produits agricoles et alimentaires'.

Fonctionnement des mécanismes de coordination

La pratique établit que toute communication et que toute information de nature européenne, par exemple les communications de la Commission, sont transmises par la Représentation permanente au ministère des Affaires étrangères qui en assume la distribution aux départements ministériels intéressés.

Au niveau du ministère des Affaires étrangères, c'est le 'service des organisations européennes' (P11) qui est chargé de cette fonction de dispatching.

Remarquons également que la Représentation permanente veille aussi dans la plupart des cas à informer directement le département ministériel compétent, notamment par le fait que la Représentation permanente est composée de représentants des départements ministériels les plus intéressés aux questions européennes.

Cette circulation de l'information se fait d'une manière pragmatique. Il n'y a pas d'organigramme précis en matière de responsabilité européenne et il appartient au chef du service d'intégration des politiques européennes du département des Affaires étrangères de veiller à ce que l'information soit transmise aux services compétents. Lorsqu'il y a doute ou conflit de compétences, les questions sont généralement tranchées sans difficultés par le groupe CEE/problèmes divers de la CEI.

Au sein du département des Affaires étrangères, le service des organisations européennes est en contact étroit avec la direction d'administration et de coordination des affaires européennes (plus communément appelée 'service Europe') qui elle, est chargée de la préparation des positions que défendra la Belgique, notamment dans le domaine économique. C'est le 'service Europe' qui assume notamment la coordination qui s'organise au sein de la CEI, en liaison avec le département des Affaires économiques.

Evolution des compétences

En dépit des apparences, il n'y a pas de contradiction entre les deux niveaux de coordination assurée d'une part par la réunion du lundi et assumée par le service des organisations européennes (P11), et la coordination assumée au niveau administratif par la CEI, dont s'occupe plus particulièrement le 'service Europe'.

La CEI ayant une existence légale, ses travaux ont une valeur administrative certaine, concrétisée par l'existence de notes et de comptes rendus officiels de réunions interministérielles. Ces notes permettent à la Représentation permanente d'établir une position officielle de la Belgique. D'autre part, la coordination du lundi permet d'établir une position politique qui peut encore évoluer en fonction des discussions au Conseil et de l'évolution nécessaire vers un compromis.

Il faut remarquer que la présence des institutions européennes à Bruxelles facilite grandement les liaisons avec la Représentation permanente qui est très aisément associée aux travaux de préparation, notamment au cours de la réunion de coordination du lundi.

Au niveau de la procédure, la CEI est saisie d'une tâche d'analyse et de coordination par l'évocation de problèmes au cours de la réunion du lundi ou encore à l'initiative d'un département ministériel qui souhaite évoquer une question dans le cadre d'une nécessaire coordination des positions. Des procédures simples d'évocation des problèmes sont établies à cet effet.

La réunion de coordination du lundi a pour objet de faire un tour de table sur l'ensemble des problèmes évoqués soit au Coreper, soit en préparation d'un prochain Conseil. Cette réunion n'a pas pour but d'aller au fond des questions soulevées, celles-ci devant faire l'objet, si c'est nécessaire, d'une coordination ultérieure plus poussée. Les accords intervenus au sein de la CEI et des groupes spécialisés de la CEI sont par ailleurs évoqués au cours des réunions de coordination du lundi, au fur et à mesure de l'évocation des problèmes en question.

Ainsi on voit apparaître au niveau de la coordination hebdomadaire les problèmes les plus politiques, tandis que les problèmes techniques sont réglés au sein de la CEI. Certaines orientations politiques sont débattues, par exemple sur des sujets tel que le financement futur de la Communauté, dans la réunion de coordination hebdomadaire, tandis que l'approfondissement de cette question ou l'établissement de positions sur le droit des sociétés, la politique industrielle ou les problèmes informatiques sont précisés au sein de réunions spécifiques de la CEI ou de groupes spécialisés.

L'enchevêtrement des mécanismes de coordination rend difficile le jugement sur la prédominance d'un département ministériel par rapport à un autre. Il est certain qu'une impulsion est donnée par le département des Affaires étrangères, notamment par le fait que ce sont ses représentants qui président la réunion hebdomadaire, mais il n'en reste pas moins vrai que la CEI, dont le secrétariat est assuré par les Affaires économiques, conserve un rôle important du point de vue administratif. Elle offre en effet aux administrations concernées une structure souple rendant possible une coordination rapide et efficace et permettant aux départements 'techniques' de faire valoir leur point de vue.

Quels sont les moyens utilisés pour résoudre les conflits éventuels?

Si les problèmes ne peuvent pas être résolus au niveau des instances administratives (CEI et coordination hebdomadaire), ils seront traités au niveau ministériel, soit au niveau du C.M.C.E.S, lorsqu'il s'agit d'un problème typiquement économique (par exemple la sidérurgie), soit au niveau du comité de politique extérieure, s'il s'agit d'un problème relevant plus particulièrement des relations internationales.

Il n'y a toutefois pas de rigidité dans le traitement des questions.

Ainsi, si certains problèmes ne sont pas réglés au niveau de la CEI, l'évocation de ces problèmes dans la réunion hebdomadaire à laquelle participent des représentants des cabinets ministériels, peut parfois régler la question. De même, lorsqu'une question importante nécessite l'approbation politique des ministres, elle peut indifféremment être traitée au C.M.C.E.S., au Comité ministériel de politique extérieure ou au sein du Conseil des Ministres lui-même.

LA PREPARATION DES POSITIONS AU SEIN DES MINISTERES

Contrairement à d'autres Etats où il n'y quasiment pas d'intermédiaires entre le ministre et son administration, l'habitude s'est développée en Belgique d'utiliser les cabinets ministériels. Dans la formation de ces derniers, les ministres veillent généralement à s'entourer aussi bien de gens de leur propre famille politique, qui assurent notamment le contact avec le parti et avec les intérêts locaux et régionaux, que de gens provenant de l'administration, lesquels assurent généralement le lien avec cette dernière (14).

Le cas du ministère des Relations extérieures est exemplaire à cet égard. Bien que politique, le cabinet est surtout composé de fonctionnaires issus du département, ce qui facilite une interaction permanente entre le ministre et son administration. Il existe une osmose quasi permanente entre le cabinet et l'administration. Le cabinet est là pour demander à l'administration de creuser les idées du ministre et pour porter au ministre les idées de l'administration. Cette dernière a une grande influence dans la prise de décision. Il convient d'ajouter cependant que la personnalité même du ministre reste essentielle; il est tenu compte de ce facteur lors de la répartition des portefeuilles. Son action est renforcée par le poids qu'occupe le ministre au sein du monde politique et de son propre parti.

Le fonctionnement du département des Affaires étrangères, bien que hiérarchisé, n'est guère bureaucratique. Des contacts peuvent être pris de façon informelle, à l'occasion de rencontres fortuites ou par l'office de communications verbales. Des contacts peuvent être pris également de façon formelle par le biais de convocations à des réunions.

De la même manière se développent les contacts entre les spécialistes du département avec les fonctionnaires détachés auprès de la Représentation.

Comme les dossiers européens concernent la plupart du temps différents départements ministériels, la liaison entre ces derniers est facilitée par le caractère informel qui est généralement adopté par l'administration belge dans le traitement des questions européennes. Le fait que les affaires européennes sont traitées depuis longtemps par des personnes compétentes, relativement peu nombreuses, qui se connaissent personnellement et vivent au jour le jour l'actualité européenne, rend très fluide la communication, facilite les compromis, explique l'aisance avec laquelle l'administration belge peut supporter le surcroît de travail qu'exige la période où la Belgique assume la présidence.

Les procédures de prise de décision: le traitement d'un dossier
Il convient de distinguer:

- d'une part, le domaine couvert par les traités européens qui met en action différents départements, et où le travail consiste essentiellement en une coordination des positions, en ce sens que la majorité des problèmes discutés au niveau de la Communauté européenne ne sont pas de la compétence exclusive des Affaires étrangères;
- d'autre part, la coopération politique qui elle, concerne essentiellement le ministère des Relations extérieures.

a) En ce qui concerne les domaines couverts par les Traités
Au fur et à mesure que les problèmes se présentent au niveau du Conseil et du Coreper, le service qui est chargé de l'intégration européenne au sein du département des Affaires étrangères prend les initiatives nécessaires pour organiser les réunions de coordination et pour dresser les notes qui serviront au représentant permanent et/ou au ministre.

Un temps fort de cette coordination est la réunion du lundi. Tous les lundis matin a lieu au ministère des Affaires étrangères, une réunion de coordination organisée sous l'autorité du directeur général de la politique, et parfois, présidée par lui. Cette réunion, à laquelle participent aussi bien des membres des cabinets que des personnes déléguées par différents départements intéressés aux affaires européennes, a pour objet de parcourir tous les problèmes qui viennent en discussion au cours de la semaine, particulièrement au niveau du Comité des représentants permanents ou au niveau des prochaines réunions des Conseils des Ministres de la Communauté.

La réunion touche généralement une dizaine de points au minimum, lesquels intéressent plusieurs départements.

Si au cours de la discussion, on en vient à constater qu'il y a des problèmes plus précis ou plus techniques qui se posent et qui ne concernent qu'un ou deux départements, l'affaire est renvoyée à des réunions de coordination ad hoc qui sont organisées en cours de semaine, soit à la Commission économique interministérielle, soit à un sous-groupe qui s'organise en conséquence.

b) En ce qui concerne la coopération politique
En ce qui concerne la coopération politique, c'est le service P11, relevant de l'autorité du directeur général de la politique, qui assure la responsabilité de la coopération politique.

Les dossiers sont d'abord établis au niveau de la direction générale de la politique. Ensuite il peut y avoir une coordination au sein du département des Affaires étrangères avec les autres directions et avec les représentants des services intéressés. Après avoir consulté les membres du cabinet les plus intéressés, la direction générale de la politique fait parvenir au ministre son avis. Le ministre est ainsi appelé à approuver la ligne défendue au niveau de l'administration et il peut ainsi suivre les conseils qui lui sont donnés en la matière.

Il existe également une réunion mensuelle organisée le vendredi précédant la réunion du Conseil des Ministres des Affaires étrangères. Sur base de ce qui a été dit la veille au niveau du Coreper, un ordre du jour 'commenté' à l'intention du ministre est dressé au cours de cette réunion. Cette note consiste en une énumération des points pour chacun desquels sont exposés:

-   le problème en cause;
-   l'état dans lequel se présente l'affaire;
-   les idées le concernant émises par les uns et les autres;
-   la position belge qui pourrait être suivie en la matière.

C'est sur base de cet ordre du jour 'commenté' qu'est préparé, par le département et le cabinet, le dossier du ministre.

La plupart du temps, cette première réunion, placée sous la responsabilité de la direction générale de la politique, est suivie d'une réunion qui se tient parfois le dimanche sous la présidence du ministre lui-même. Participent à cette réunion, outre le représentant permanent et le directeur général de la politique, les membres les plus intéressés des services et du cabinet chargés des questions qui seront discutées lors du Conseil.

Des procédures analogues de préparation sont mises en place dans les autres départements à l'occasion des réunions des Conseils des Ministres spécialisés (Agriculture, Economie et Finances, Transport). Les représentants de ces ministères coordonnent leur position à l'occasion des réunions du lundi au département des Relations extérieures. Dans le cas des réunions du Conseil Eco-Fin, des contacts étroits sont également établis avec la Banque nationale, en particulier lorsque sont évoquées des questions monétaires qui ont fait l'objet d'une préparation au sein du Comité monétaire de la CEE où la Belgique est représentée par des agents de la Banque nationale.

Sur un certain nombre de matières et selon le style de travail des ministres concernés, l'influence du cabinet est plus forte que sur d'autres. Lorsque c'est le cas, les réunions de coordination permettent de dégager des orientations politiques qui ne font plus l'objet de discussions au niveau de l'administration, celle-ci complétant les orientations par des arguments d'ordre technique.

Il est toutefois évident qu'il est impossible de prévoir toutes les situations qui peuvent survenir lors de la négociation en Conseil. Le ministre dispose en fin de compte d'une large marge de manoeuvre; il reste l'acteur principal et dispose d'ailleurs de l'expérience et des réactions de nature politique que susciteront ses prises de position lors des discussions au Conseil.

ROLE DE LA REPRESENTATION PERMANENTE ET RELATIONS AVEC LES INSTITUTIONS EUROPEENNES

Composition - Département d'origine
La Représentation permanente comprend 25 membres dont le représentant permanent (M. l'ambassadeur Noterdaeme) et le représentant

permanent adjoint (M. Marc Lepoivre).

La Représentation permanente comprend, par origine, 14 diplomates ou assimilés et 11 personnes en provenance d'autres départements spécialisés:

- 14 qui sont donc originaires ou rattachés au département des Relations extérieures;
- 2 qui sont originaires ou rattachés au département des Affaires économiques;
- 4 qui sont originaires ou rattachés au département des Finances;
- 1 qui est originaire de la Banque nationale;
- 2 qui sont originaires du département de l'Agriculture;
- 1 qui est originaire du département des Communications;
- 1 qui est originaire du département de l'Emploi et du Travail.

En ce qui concerne les grades et les catégories, la situation est extrêmement variable: certains diplomates sont à leur première affectation tandis que les représentants des autres départements ne sont presque jamais des gens qui sont en début de carrière; il s'agit de conseillers, de premiers conseillers, d'inspecteurs ou d'inspecteurs généraux.

La mobilité est également différente. Les diplomates, dans certains cas, ne restent que pour une période limitée, analogue à celle de postes diplomatiques normaux. D'autres diplomates sont quasi des représentants permanents de carrière! Les représentants d'autres départements sont généralement nommés de longue date. A la Représentation permanente, il n'y a guère de mobilité.

En ce qui concerne l'organisation interne, il y a une division en fonction des formations spécifiques des membres de la Représentation permanente, découlant de leur appartenance à leur département d'origine. Le représentant permanent et le représentant permanent adjoint exercent des fonctions générales, tandis que les autres membres exercent, dans la plupart des cas, des fonctions spécifiques et sectorielles.

La Représentation permanente comprend également un membre chargé du dispatching (membre du groupe ANTICI).

Il faut noter le rôle essentiel que jouent dans la coordination des questions européennes, tant le membre du groupe ANTICI de la Représentation permanente, que le correspondant 'Europe' au département des Affaires étrangères. Le choix adéquat de ces deux personnes et leur collaboration sont essentiels pour le bon fonctionnement de la coordination de la politique européenne de la Belgique.

Relations entre la Représentation permanente et l'administration

Etant sur place à Bruxelles, les contacts avec les administrations sont extrêmement aisés. Les membres de la Représentation permanente participent non seulement aux réunions de coordination du lundi (soit le représentant permanent, soit son adjoint assisté de certains membres), mais également aux réunions de la CEI sur les sujets spécifiques.

Certaines réunions de la CEI se déroulent d'ailleurs dans les locaux de la Représentation permanente.

La Représentation permanente a également certains contacts directs avec des départements ministériels lorsqu'il s'agit de préparer un Conseil ou lorsqu'une question spécifique est posée à la Belgique. Dans la plupart des cas cependant, la Représentation permanente veille à passer par le service de coordination du département des Affaires étrangères.

La Représentation permanente participe très activement à la préparation des Conseils des Ministres sectoriels, elle vise également à informer le département des Affaires étrangères des résultats, tant de la préparation de ce Conseil que de la réunion même de ce Conseil.

La Représentation permanente dispose d'une marge d'appréciation qui lui permet de jouer bien souvent un rôle de compromis dans les affaires européennes. Toutefois, lorsqu'il y a eu au préalable des réunions interministérielles de coordination ou lorsque la position a été clairement définie, soit au sein de la réunion de coordination hebdomadaire, soit par une décision ministérielle, la Représentation permanente se trouve dans une position beaucoup plus forte pour défendre un point de vue national, d'autant plus qu'elle se sent soutenue par le ministre concerné. Ceci est particulièrement vrai pour des cas où les intérêts de la Belgique ont été précisés et déterminés d'une manière constante dans le temps.

La Représentation permanente entretient des contacts étroits avec les institutions européennes. Ainsi au cours de la dernière présidence, la Représentation permanente s'est fortement appuyée sur le Secrétariat général du Conseil. La Représentation permanente a des contacts suivis également avec les fonctionnaires de la Commission, en particulier avec certains fonctionnaires de nationalité belge et avec le cabinet du commissaire belge. Ces contacts sont des contacts de nature informelle; ils s'insèrent également dans une relation triangulaire entre des fonctionnaires nationaux, des fonctionnaires de la Commission de la Communauté européenne et la Représentation permanente.

Un problème particulier: l'association des régions aux négociations européennes

La Représentation permanente éprouve les mêmes difficultés que le département des Relations extérieures lorsqu'il s'agit de prendre en considération la dimension 'régionale' des questions européennes. La tâche de la Représentation permanente est à cet égard compliquée par la structure politique complexe du gouvernement de la Belgique et des Exécutifs régionaux.

La participation des Communautés culturelles et linguistiques et des régions à l'élaboration de la mise en oeuvre des politiques européennes n'est pas organisée de manière satisfaisante.

Rares sont jusqu'à présent, au stade de l'élaboration des prises de position belge dans le cadre des différents Conseils de la Communauté européenne, les cas où les régions sont associées à la décision. Ceci en dépit des compétences qui leur sont d'ores et déjà clairement dévolues, par exemple dans le domaine de l'environnement ou dans les domaines de la politique industrielle, pour les secteurs qui ne sont pas des secteurs nationaux.

Il existe toutefois au département des Affaires étrangères une volonté de trouver d'une manière pragmatique, une solution aux problèmes de l'association des régions à la détermination des positions belges dans le cadre de la politique européenne. Les responsables de la cellule européenne ont été instruits d'associer plus étroitement les régions aux prises de décision en matière européenne, mais il n'y a pas à l'heure actuelle de mécanisme formel de consultation qui ait été mis en place. Une des raisons évoquées est le manque de structures administratives correspondantes, tant au niveau des Exécutifs régionaux qu'au niveau des Communautés culturelles ou linguistiques.

Le problème se complique encore lorsque des décisions européennes qui touchent des matières qui sont formellement dévolues aux Communautés culturelles sont prises. Ainsi, à l'occasion de la réunion des ministres de la Culture, réunis à Naples à l'initiative du ministre Colombo, on a vu la Belgique être représentée par deux ministres compétents, chacun pour les matières culturelles de sa communauté linguistique (M. Moureaux, pour la Communauté francophone et M. Poma, pour la Communauté flamande).

La question n'est guère difficile lorsqu'il s'agit d'une réunion informelle des ministres, comme ce fut le cas pour les ministres de la Culture, mais le problème reste entier s'il s'agit d'un Conseil des Ministres de la Communauté où des décisions sont prises et où les représentants des deux régions pourraient avoir des positions différentes. Il semble qu'il serait utile à cet égard de préciser le champ de compétences des régions et des Communautés linguistiques en matière de relations diplomatiques, car la loi du 8 août 1980 sur la réforme institutionnelle ne règle pas l'ensemble du problème.

LA PRESIDENCE DU CONSEIL ET LA COOPERATION POLITIQUE

Avant la présidence

La préparation de la présidence, que la Belgique a assumée de janvier à juillet 1982, a commencé au moins six mois à l'avance avec la mise en place d'un groupe appelé 'comité de préparation de la présidence belge'. Ce groupe fut à la base de l'organisation d'un certain nombre de réunions spécifiques qui se déroulèrent au département des Relations extérieures et qui regroupaient tous les départements concernés par la future présidence.

Ces réunions avaient pour but, d'une part, de mettre en place des automatismes, d'autre part, d'élaborer le programme de la présidence.

S'il ne s'agissait pas de préparer systématiquement les administrations à la prise en charge de la présidence, du fait qu'elles étaient déjà rodées par plusieurs présidences antérieures, il s'agissait de les informer et de leur rappeler un certain nombre de principes, c'est-à-dire une sorte de déontologie, et des règles pratiques à suivre pour qu'une présidence soit fructueuse. Ces principes furent approuvés lors d'une réunion en novembre 1981 et transcrits dans une note intitulée 'Quelques principes généraux et lignes de conduites pour la présidence belge en 1982 au Conseil des Communautés européennes' (15). Cette note fut envoyée ensuite à tous les départements intéressés.

En ce qui concerne le programme de la présidence, il a été établi au cours de réunions successives où chaque département a pu apporter sa contribution. Un programme d'action, sous forme de document global, fut approuvé en décembre 1981; ce programme inclut certaines précisions qui ne se retrouvent pas dans le discours-programme que le président du Conseil présenta devant le Parlement européen en janvier 1982. Le programme de la présidence a également été établi en liaison avec le Secrétariat général du Conseil et avec la Commission des Communautés européennes.

Il faut également ajouter une première tentative d'associer les milieux académiques à l'élaboration du programme lors de la présidence de 1982. L'impact de cette première expérience s'est révélé quelque peu réduit, compte tenu du fait que le rapport préparé par le Groupe d'Etudes Politiques Européennes (GEPE - section belge de TEPSA), à la demande du ministre Charles-Ferdinand Nothomb en septembre 1981, fut remis à son successeur Leo Tindemans en cours de présidence, en février 1982 **(16)**.

Pendant la présidence

D'une manière générale, l'organisation des services est restée identique à celle qui existe en temps normal.

Il faut noter toutefois que la direction générale de la politique du département des Affaires étrangères s'est vue augmentée d'une quatrième division, chargée plus particulièrement de l'organisation matérielle des réunions ministérielles, notamment celles qui se tiennent au Palais d'Egmont.

Cette division a été dirigée par un fonctionnaire (chef de service), assisté de quelques spécialistes. Cette nouvelle division était indispensable, compte tenu des difficultés soulevées par l'organisation de réunions ministérielles et du Conseil européen au Palais d'Egmont (sécurité, accueil, problèmes des communications). Cette division fut créée spécialement pour la période de la présidence et dissoute au 1er juillet 1982.

Toujours au sein du département, la division 'Europe' s'est vue adjoindre un fonctionnaire ainsi que des supports logistiques, notamment au point de vue dactylographique.

En ce qui concerne les procédures, on a mis en place une instance de liaison entre le cabinet et l'administration pour faire le point sur les tâches spécifiques de la présidence. Cette instance de liaison se réunissait en fait tous les quinze jours.

Si la présidence belge n'a pas impliqué une augmentation importante du cadre administratif, il faut souligner l'augmentation importante des charges et des responsabilités tant au niveau politique qu'au niveau administratif pendant la période de présidence.

Le chef du cabinet du ministre des Relations extérieures qui, auparavant, ne s'occupait des questions européennes qu'épisodiquement, s'est vu attribuer la responsabilité, au sein du cabinet, du dossier européen. Le cabinet s'est vu également adjoindre un spécialiste de la

Représentation permanente, en vue de soutenir l'action du cabinet pendant la présidence.

De plus, compte tenu du changement de gouvernement qui était intervenu quelques semaines avant janvier 1982, la mise en place du nouveau ministre des Relations extérieures a permis d'organiser, au sein du cabinet, une équipe beaucoup plus axée sur les affaires européennes que la précédente. Cette évolution a permis que se constitue au niveau politique, une équipe spécialement compétente en matière européenne:

- un ministre, considéré par ses partenaires comme un spécialiste des affaires européennes;
- un chef de cabinet expert en la matière auquel a été adjoint un membre du cabinet provenant de la Représentation permanente.

Pour le cabinet tout entier, les affaires européennes et la présidence ont été considérées d'ailleurs comme la priorité principale de leur action.

Procédure de la présidence

La préparation du Conseil des Affaires étrangères a vu s'accentuer le rôle de coordination du département des Affaires étrangères, en particulier au cours des réunions de coordination du vendredi et surtout du dimanche soir. La réunion du dimanche soir regroupait, outre les spécialistes du département des Affaires étrangères, des représentants du Secrétariat général du Conseil et l'équipe de la Représentation permanente.

Le Secrétariat général du Conseil fournit non seulement un appui logistique à la présidence; il permet d'établir pour la présidence les éventuelles solutions d'arbitrage.

La dualité des intérêts (ceux de la présidence et ceux de la Belgique) oblige le ministre, son cabinet, la Représentation permanente et l'administration belge à un surcroît d'activités pour établir d'une part, quelle sera la position que défendra le représentant de la Belgique et d'autre part, quels pourraient être les compromis possibles à établir au niveau de la présidence. Ceci explique que la période de la présidence est un moment de grande effervescence, tant au niveau du cabinet, de la Représentation permanente que de l'administration. Cette double fonction mobilise les esprits et demande un surcroît de travail important.

La préparation du Conseil européen implique en plus la nécessité d'assurer une information complète au Premier ministre et à son cabinet pour qui les affaires européennes ne constituent pas toujours une priorité.

Cette préparation de la présidence au niveau du Premier ministre a cependant été grandement facilitée dans le cas de la Belgique, par le fait qu'il existe une bonne liaison entre les Affaires étrangères et les services du Premier ministre, et par le fait que le chef du cabinet du Premier ministre (M. Jacques van Ypersele) connaissait de longue date les questions européennes, étant notamment un ancien président du Comité monétaire.

Tout comme pour le département des Affaires étrangères, les

autres départements ont dû pendant la présidence, remplir une double fonction:

- représenter les intérêts belges dans les négociations européennes;
- présider les réunions et rechercher des compromis indispensables.

Au niveau de la préparation des différents Conseils, chaque département a suivi les procédures usuelles des préparations des dossiers européens, mais a veillé à assumer également le rôle qu'implique la présidence.

Ainsi au département de l'Agriculture, les réunions préparatoires aux réunions européennes, impliquant notamment la préparation du dossier du ministre, étaient simplement allongées par rapport aux réunions normales en vue de préparer non seulement la position belge, mais de rechercher également quel pouvait être le rôle de la présidence.

Au département des Affaires économiques, une préparation spécifique a parfois été demandée au service d'études du département, en ce qui concerne les solutions à imaginer pour la présidence des Conseils.

Un autre exemple de cette participation des départements est la difficile recherche d'un compromis en matière budgétaire (problème de la contribution britannique), où les travaux préparatoires ont été réalisés tant au sein de la Représentation permanente belge qu'au sein des départements ministériels intéressés, cela afin de tenter d'appréhender le problème dans sa globalité, et non pas seulement en défendant le point de vue de la Belgique.

Tant l'administration que la Représentation permanente ont fait face à un surcroît de tâches, spécialement au niveau de la préparation des réunions ministérielles, mais surtout au niveau de la préparation du Conseil européen. Remarquons également que la préparation du Sommet économique de Versailles en 1982 a nécessité un accroissement des activités européennes au sein du cabinet du Premier ministre, par le fait que la Belgique représentait, conjointement avec le président de la Commission, les intérêts de la Communauté et des petits pays membres de la Communauté non présents à Versailles. Ceci a obligé le chef de cabinet du Premier ministre à jouer son rôle de 'sherpa' et à participer à de nombreuses réunions préparatoires au Sommet économique de Versailles.

Présidence et coopération politique

Une autre tâche spécifique de la présidence qui requiert énormément de temps et d'efforts consiste dans des voyages que le président du Conseil est obligé de faire. L'intensité de ces voyages était particulièrement importante, compte tenu de la volonté exprimée par le ministre des Relations extérieures de jouer un rôle dans le domaine de la coopération politique (Moyen-Orient) et de la nécessité de préparer le Sommet économique de Versailles.

La présidence belge a été confrontée à un nombre important de crises internationales (Pologne, Malouines, Liban).

La présidence a eu recours au système de 'crisis management' qui avait été établi suite à la réunion de Londres; ce système a fonctionné correctement.

Plus particulièrement, l'équipe d'assistance à la présidence, prévue en exécution des dispositions du rapport de Londres, a bien fonctionné dans le cadre de la coopération politique, et s'est insérée harmonieusement dans le fonctionnement des institutions communautaires. En Belgique, le service chargé de l'intégration européenne, qui fait partie de la direction générale de la politique, est compétent en la matière. Une division de la direction générale de la politique s'occupe du secrétariat de la coopération politique européenne. Il faut remarquer que dans cette matière, le Secrétariat général du Conseil n'est pas compétent et que les tâches de coordination et de secrétariat reposent entièrement sur la présidence.

Cependant, dans le cadre du système de la 'troïka' imaginé à Londres en 1981, la division de la direction générale de la politique fut renforcée par l'arrivée d'un diplomate britannique et d'un diplomate danois. Ces personnes furent intégrées dans le service de la coopération politique pour assister le président dans l'exercice de certaines démarches et remplir certaines tâches de secrétariat. La coopération politique, au point de vue administratif, comprenait donc quatre personnes à l'époque de la présidence belge: 2 fonctionnaires belges, 1 fonctionnaire britannique et 1 danois. Cette équipe a été renforcée par du personnel d'exécution, mobilisé au sein du département des Affaires étrangères.

Notons également que certains postes diplomatiques ont été renforcés dans le but d'améliorer la coordination européenne sur certains dossiers. C'est ainsi que la présidence belge a renforcé sa délégation à New-York pour assurer une meilleure coordination des Dix dans le cadre des Nations Unies.

Présidence et relations extérieures

La présidence belge a veillé à assurer la représentation de la Communauté vis-à-vis de l'extérieur.

Dans le domaine de la coopération politique, on a en particulier renforcé certains liens d'informations existant antérieurement, entre autres les contacts avec la Norvège. Mais l'effort le plus conséquent a été de représenter la Communauté dans les négociations entamées avec les principaux pays suivants:

- les Etats-Unis
  En liaison avec la Commission, la présidence belge a assuré le suivi des consultations à tous les niveaux, avec les Etat-Unis. La présidence belge (Premier ministre, ministre des Relations extérieures) mandatée par le Conseil a effectué une visite aux Etats-Unis du 16 au 21 février.
- le Japon
  En exécution des orientations du Conseil, la présidence belge a visité le Japon dans la perspective d'une ouverture croissante du marché intérieur japonais aux exportations communautaires.

La Présidence des CE: Rapport national sur la Belgique

- Pays A.C.P.
  La présidence a fait accepter un compromis relatif aux ressources du STABEX.
- Pays du Bassin méditerranéen
  Outre les efforts pour l'aboutissement des négociations relatives aux Protocoles financiers méditerranéens (hormis Israël), la présidence a effectué une mission d'évaluation en Turquie sur les perspectives d'évolution démocratique de ce pays.
- Pays asiatiques
  Participation du président du Conseil à la réunion ministérielle des pays de l'ASEAN.
- Espagne, Portugal
  Rencontres multiples avec des dirigeants espagnols et portugais en vue des négociations sur l'adhésion.
- U.R.S.S.
  Contacts au niveau diplomatique, suite aux événements de Pologne.
- Amérique latine
  Nombreux contacts diplomatiques avec les pays d'Amérique latine pour limiter l'impact de la crise des Malouines sur les relations Europe-Amérique latine.
- Moyen-Orient
  La présidence belge a effectué une mission au Moyen-Orient, mission qui a contribué à l'établissement d'une position communautaire dans le cadre de la coopération politique.

Missions diplomatiques et présidence
Les missions diplomatiques belges ont reçu copie du programme d'action et ont été instruites de mettre en place les coordinations à Dix, tant dans le cadre commercial et économique que dans le cadre de la coopération politique. Les chefs de postes belges à l'étranger se sont acquittés de cette tâche qui vise à mettre d'une manière pragmatique les diplomaties des Dix en harmonie.

La présidence belge et les problèmes institutionnels
La présidence belge a assuré le suivi de l'initiative Genscher-Colombo. A cet effet, le ministre des Relations extérieures a chargé M. de Schoutheete de Tervarent, ambassadeur en Espagne et ancien chef de cabinet du précédent ministre des Affaires étrangères de présider le groupe ad hoc Genscher-Colombo. Sous la présidence belge, le texte original du projet Genscher-Colombo a été modifié. Le groupe a présenté un rapport intérimaire et a établi un avant-projet d'Acte européen, précédant la version approuvée lors du Conseil européen de Stuttgart de juin 1983.

ASPIRATIONS NATIONALES ET OBJECTIFS POUR LA PRESIDENCE

Comment les structures et les procédures en vigueur ont-elles résisté au poids de la présidence?

Les structures mises en place, tant au niveau des différents départements qu'au niveau de la Représentation permanente ou même au niveau politique, n'ont guère eu de difficultés à s'adapter aux charges que représente la présidence, si ce n'est un accroissement du travail et du temps consacré aux affaires européennes. Dans le cas belge, on constate que la plupart des agents qui s'occupent dans les différents départements ministériels des affaires européennes sont en place depuis longtemps et qu'ils en sont pratiquement tous à leur quatrième ou cinquième présidence du Conseil. Dès lors, il ne semble pas qu'il y ait des aménagements particuliers de structures qui soient rendus nécessaires par la présidence.

La Belgique n'a pas mis en place de systeme de formation spécifique pour les fonctionnaires chargés d'exercer les responsabilités de la présidence, ni pour ceux chargés de défendre la position des autorités belges. La formation des fonctionnaires se fait généralement 'sur le tas'. On veille à rappeler aux affaires européennes les fonctionnaires qui en ont déjà eu l'expérience. Il se crée ainsi un groupe de spécialistes des questions européennes, tant au département des Affaires étrangères que dans ceux de l'Agriculture, des Finances ou des Affaires économiques. Il ne semble pas qu'il y ait eu de difficultés particulières, compte tenu surtout du fait que les fonctionnaires sont aguerris aux questions européennes et que certains d'entre eux ont déjà vécu plusieurs présidences.

Si certains fonctionnaires se sont montrés quelque peu réticents à accepter la charge de porte-parole du point de vue belge, compte tenu du fait que le fonctionnaire de rang supérieur assumait la présidence, la pratique développée a permis de voir que ces porte-parole se tiraient très bien d'affaire. On peut donc considérer que la responsabilité de la présidence permet non seulement un recyclage général, car les fonctionnaires doivent prendre la dimension européenne des problèmes qui leur sont généralement posés dans un cadre national, mais elle donne aussi l'occasion à des fonctionnaires de rang subalterne de s'accoutumer à des responsabilités nouvelles.

Une présidence 'européenne'

Au niveau des procédures, tant au Coreper I qu'au Coreper II, le représentant permanent et le représentant permanent adjoint, confortés par la volonté de la Belgique d'agir dans l'intérêt de l'Europe, ont veillé pendant la période de la présidence à faire avancer les dossiers au niveau de leur intérêt européen. Les positions belges ont été défendues par un porte-parole provenant en général de la Représentation permanente, mais dans l'optique d'aboutir à un compromis bénéfique pour la Communauté européenne. On peut dire en ce sens que la présidence 'coûte' un prix certain à la défense des intérêts nationaux, mais il faut reconnaître que dans le cas de la Belgique, ces intérêts nationaux s'identifient souvent aux intérêts européens.

Cette volonté de progrès dans le domaine européen est certainement liée au degré assez grand de liberté laissé au président du Coreper I et Coreper II pour faire évoluer des choses vers la recherche d'un compromis; les instructions sont relativement moins strictes en période de présidence qu'en période normale.

Cette volonté d'aboutir à un compromis qui est reconnue à la Belgique permet à celle-ci de jouer dans un certain nombre de cas un rôle moteur. Il en a été ainsi, par exemple, lors de l'élaboration du trilogue budgétaire. L'analyse de ce cas exemplaire montre le rôle joué par la présidence, au niveau du Coreper 1ère partie, pour amener le Conseil Affaires générales à donner un mandat pour préparer ce trilogue entre les institutions. Après que les présidents des trois institutions - Conseil, Commission, Parlement se soient réunis à plusieurs reprises, réunions qui avaient d'ailleurs été préparées au plan technique par un groupe technique, une décision est intervenue en mars 1982. Suite à cette décision, l'influence de la présidence dans l'élaboration d'un compromis n'a cessé de grandir. La solution imaginée par le groupe technique est largement le fruit d'une collaboration exemplaire entre la présidence du Conseil et le Secrétariat général du Conseil. Le résultat a été acquis, notamment par le fait que la présidence du Conseil avait reçu en la matière un mandat clair de la part du Conseil (17).

La présidence dans le système institutionnel des Communautés

La présidence belge s'est fortement appuyée sur les services du Secrétariat général du Conseil. Celui-ci a été associé à la préparation de tous les Conseils Affaires étrangères; les services du Secrétariat du Conseil, particulièrement le service juridique, ont été souvent mis à contribution.

La présidence belge a également développé un grand degré de coopération avec la Commission, que ce soit à l'occasion de la préparation de la présidence ou à l'occasion de la recherche commune de compromis sur des dossiers politiques. Il en a été ainsi en particulier lors de la recherche d'un compromis en matière budgétaire à l'occasion des mesures spéciales prises au profit du Royaume-Uni à titre de compensation financière pour 1982. On a vu le président du Conseil et le président de la Commission faire au Conseil des propositions communes et effectuer des démarches auprès des capitales pour trouver une solution à cet épineux problème.

En ce qui concerne le Parlement, comme le président du Conseil l'avait promis lors de la rencontre Parlement/Conseil du 17 novembre 1981, M. Tindemans a suivi l'engagement pris d'assurer une présence régulière, au niveau ministériel, de la présidence aux sessions plénières et à certaines réunions des commissions parlementaires. De même, la présidence a pris soin d'informer le Parlement de l'évolution des discussions en matière de coopération politique; elle a pleinement associé le Parlement à la recherche d'un compromis en matière de trilogue budgétaire.

Quels problèmes sont apparus avant et pendant la présidence?

Le changement de gouvernement survenu le 17 décembre 1981, soit moins de quinze jours avant la prise en charge de la présidence, a certainement entraîné une modification du programme d'action dans le chef de certains nouveaux ministres. Il y a eu un réajustement des positions et une adaptation aux nouvelles charges. De même, le discours-programme du Conseil a été élaboré sous la responsabilité active et directe du ministre des Relations extérieures.

Il faut remarquer toutefois qu'il y a eu peu de changements d'orientation dans les faits par rapport à la préparation de la présidence qui avait été réalisée dans les derniers mois de 1981. On peut constater qu'en Belgique, les problèmes de choix politiques jouent moins que les éléments ayant trait aux personnes, tout au moins en ce qui concerne les questions européennes.

L'équilibre politique traditionnel, le système gouvernemental de coalition, l'adhésion implicite des partis politiques à l'idéal européen font qu'en Belgique, l'intégration européenne est une idée qui va de soi. En revanche, l'élément personnel joue certainement un rôle. La prise en charge de la présidence par M. Tindemans est significative à cet égard, car ce ministre a donné une orientation plus volontariste à son action que celle qu'auraient pu donner d'autres personnalités politiques moins averties des questions européennes.

Le changement de gouvernement a cependant entraîné un certain nombre de conséquences matérielles et administratives qui ont compliqué la tâche de la présidence dans les premiers jours de 1982. En effet, la nomination de tous les cabinets ministériels ne s'est pas faite très rapidement, ce qui rendait difficiles les contacts. Il y a eu des déménagements, des problèmes d'installation, notamment du service de presse et du porte-parole du ministre des Relations extérieures, qui ont influencé les relations avec la presse pendant les premiers jours du fonctionnement de la présidence. Mais les capacités d'adaptation ont été très rapidement éprouvées et le système d'information s'est mis très correctement en place comme le montre le fait que dès le 3 janvier, la presse a été correctement informée des réunions d'urgence qui se tenaient sur l'aide de la Communauté à la Pologne.

Bien que les différents responsables des questions européennes aient souligné que la présidence entraîne un accroissement de travail important, ils ont également relevé que le fait que les affaires européennes sont traitées par un nombre restreint de personnes facilite les contacts et la fluidité de l'information. En travaillant avec un nombre limité de personnes, on conserve une vue globale des choses et on parvient à établir des compromis politiques dans les affaires européennes. Il reste néanmoins que les matières à traiter deviennent de plus en plus compliquées et techniques et qu'il devient alors plus difficile de dégager une vue globale, laquelle, semble-t-il, était plus facile à trouver lors des présidences précédentes où l'on pouvait encore arriver à traiter les problèmes de façon ponctuelle et non liés les uns aux autres.

Opinions sur la présidence belge

Alors que certaines des personnes interviewées estimaient que les milieux académiques pouvaient offrir une aide utile à la réflexion, préalable aux tâches de la présidence, d'autres représentants ne croient pas que l'Université puisse être efficace dans ce domaine où l'expérience et le suivi au jour le jour des affaires européennes sont plus importants que la faculté d'analyse que peut apporter l'observation académique des phénomènes.

Il semble également qu'il serait dangereux de schématiser trop à l'avance la préparation de la présidence, car il est évident que l'on ne peut prévoir à l'avance les événements ni leur évolution.

Toutefois, en dépit de la grande expérience des fonctionnaires belges qui ont déjà plusieurs présidences à leur actif, on peut se demander si cette expérience n'amène pas un certain immobilisme dans les procédures. Il n'y a guère de procédures nouvelles qui aient été imaginées à l'occasion de l'exercice de la présidence, contrairement à d'autres pays membres où l'extension des responsabilités liées à la présidence est l'occasion de créer de nouvelles structures de décision et d'influence.

Il ne semble pas que la présidence pose des problèmes particuliers à la préparation des questions européennnes en Belgique, si ce n'est un sucroît de travail.

Il serait toutefois opportun de clarifier certaines dispositions de coordination, en particulier l'interférence que peut avoir dans le domaine européen, l'émergence des responsabilités au niveau régional. Mais ceci est un problème particulier à la situation belge et ne relève pas de l'analyse globale.

L'internationalisation et l'européanisation des politiques internes sont cependant des phénomènes constants dont il faudrait se préoccuper au niveau de l'organisation administrative.

Deux possibilités existent:

-   soit renforcer les services s'occupant des questions européennes au département des Affaires étrangères;
-   soit maintenir un tout petit groupe, comme actuellement, de responsables européens au département des Affaires étrangères, mais en précisant les tâches européennes dans les départements ministériels les plus intéressés.

Il faut toutefois se garder d'évoluer vers une structure bureaucratique. Le fonctionnement pragmatique et relativement informel actuel semble donner satisfaction et permet à la Belgique d'occuper sa place dans les débats européens.

NOTES ET REFERENCES

(1)　Avec la collaboration de M. Joël de Bry.

(2)　La Belgique et la Communauté européenne. Préface. Textes et documents. Collection 'Idées et Etudes'. Ministère des Affaires étrangères, du Commerce extérieur et de la Coopération au développement.

(3)　Voir la déclaration gouvernementale de M. Leo Tindemans. Annales parlementaires, séance du 7 juin 1977.

(4)　Le député Louis Van Velthoven a révélé lors d'une conférence de presse que l'on comptait en juin 1983, 2.735 membres pour les 56 cabinets que comptent le gouvernement, les Exécutifs flamand et wallon et la Communauté française. Conférence de presse du 29 juin 1983.

(5)　Citons notamment MM. Spaak, Tindemans, Simonet, Jean Rey, Dehousse, Davignon.

(6)　Voir à cet égard le rôle des représentants permanents de la Belgique auprès des Communautés européennes, en particulier le rôle du Baron Van der Meulen. Plus récemment, le rôle moteur du représentant permanent adjoint, Marc Lepoivre, dans la recherche de solutions pour l'amélioration de la procédure budgétaire.

(7)　Le rôle des Belges et de la Belgique dans l'édification européenne. Studia Diplomatica. Chronique de politique étrangère. IRRI, vol. XXIV, no. 1-4, 538 pages, Bruxelles.

(8)　Le CMCES a été créé par Arrêté Royal (AR du 26.8.1938) et modifié par AR du 1.5.1947, du 2.6.1961, du 25.8.1965 et du 12.4.1966.

(9)　CMPE - AR du 30.5.1974.

(10)　CRMEE - AR du 25.2.1982.

(11)　Composition:

- Le C.M.C.E.S. compte dans ses rangs les départements suivants: Commerce extérieur, Travaux publics, Agriculture, Affaires économiques, Finances, Classes moyennes, Emploi et Travail, Communications, services du Premier ministre, I-B-L-C.

- Le C.M.P.E.:
Relations extérieures, le Premier ministre, Défense nationale, Justice, Coopération au développement, Finances, Emploi et Travail, Agriculture, Affaires économiques, Commerce extérieur.

- Le C.M.R.E.E.:
Relations extérieures, Justice et réformes institutionnelles, Finances, Commerce extérieur, Intérieur et Fonction publique, Affaires économiques, Classes moyennes, Energie, Affaires européennes et Agriculture, Coopération au développement.

(12)　Loi du 16 novembre 1978 relative aux élections du Parlement européen. Moniteur Belge 23.12.78.

(13)　C.E.I. créé par AR du 26.8.1938 et modifié par AR du 14.8.1947 et par AR du 24.10.1962.

(14)　L. Defalque. Application du droit communautaire par les Etats membres. Le cas de la Belgique. W.P. Institut d'Etudes Européennes, ULB, 1982.

(15)　Note 81/88/a.h./56 du 23.11.1981. Direction générale de la Politique. Ministère des Affaires étrangères.

(16) G.E.P.E. - Les priorités de la présidence belge, février 1982. Bruxelles.

(17) Jean-Louis Dewost et Marc Lepoivre. La déclaration commune du Parlement européen, du Conseil et de la Commission relative à différentes mesures visant à assurer un meilleur déroulement de la procédure budgétaire, signée le 30 juin 1982. Revue du Marché Commun, no 261. Paris.

Chapter 3

THE PRESIDENCY OF THE COUNCIL OF MINISTERS OF THE
EUROPEAN COMMUNITIES: THE CASE OF DENMARK
Mr Jørgen Grønnegaard Christensen, Aarhus

INTRODUCTION

Due to different societal changes during the last twenty years Danish
central administration has been confronted with the massive need for
adaptation of both its institutional structures and its way of working.
Developments on the Danish scene as well as in the international
environment account for the adaptive measures taken.

In the perspective of the 1970s, it has been commonplace to point
to the needs for adaptation created by the Danish entry into the
European Communities in 1973. It is unquestionable that precisely this
event necessitated an administrative adjustment of unprecedented
scope. Yet, it must not be overlooked that this need for administrative
adaptation in several respects coincided with the kind of
administrative problems already experienced by national governments
as a consequence of the general growth of international organisations
after the conclusion of World War II (1).

This is especially true of Denmark. The very openness of the
Danish economy and society in itself triggered adaptive measures in
response to international developments. Furthermore, since the late
1940s, Denmark has taken part in international co-operation at the
universal, the European and the Nordic levels. Most of this
international co-operation has been limited in scope and intensity.
However its broad coverage of issue areas and sectors involved
domestic ministries in the handling of international relations at an
early point in time.

Of even greater importance was the fact that Denmark's early
dependence on established trade patterns within Western Europe had
involved civil servants from the Ministry of Foreign Affairs and the
Ministries of Agriculture and Trade and Industries as well as the
customs administration within the Ministry of Finance in dealing with
the consequences of the establishment of a European common market.
Apart from the experience acquired by Danish civil servants in dealing
with the problems of European integration, the establishment of EFTA
together with the first round of negotiations (1961-1963) aiming at
Danish entry into the European Communities, led to some
administrative adjustments within the ministries mentioned above,

directed towards the adaptation decisions made when Denmark actually joined the European Communities.

In two important respects, membership of the European Communities gave the problem of adaptation a new dimension. Firstly, the EC had the capacity to make decisions which were legally binding at the national level. Secondly, the very question of entry into the Communities constituted one of the most controversial issues in Danish politics since the conclusion of World War II. Both factors presented arguments for the more serious consideration of the problem of administrative adaptation. The former might be interpreted as an argument for setting up a more formalised system of interdepartmental coordination, while the latter could also be seen as an argument for considering the need for some centralised handling of the political aspects of EC affairs. This was especially true because of the tight procedures of parliamentary control of and information on governmental EC policy set up within the auspices of the Parliamentary Committee on European Market Affairs.

The lengthy prehistory of Danish entry into the European Communities did not reduce the process of administrative change to a pure problem of organisational engineering. However it eased administrative adaptation in other important ways, so the Danish government had no great difficulty in identifying the kind of administrative problems to be dealt with when Denmark actually entered the Communities. The problems were:

1) The distribution of competences relating to the EC among government departments, primarily between the Ministry of Foreign Affairs and domestic ministries;
2) The establishment of procedures for interdepartmental coordination;
3) The adaptation of the internal organisation of the ministries affected, including decisions as to the staffing of the ministries;
4) The organisation and competences of the Permanent Representation to the EC.

These problems were not specific to the Danish situation. In most respects the original six members of the EC had already met them even if they had chosen different solutions to them according to national circumstances (2). They also seem to be parallel to those of the other new entrants (3).

COPING WITH THE PRESIDENCY

Denmark entered the European Community on 1 January 1973. Six months later the Danish government had to take over the Presidency of the Council of Ministers. The implications were alarming. Denmark had not only to adapt its administrative structure and procedures as mentioned in Section 1, but it had at the same time to prepare its first period as Presidency of the Council of Ministers and therefore also to preside over the numerous committees and working parties set up by the Committee of Permanent Representatives. These narrow restrictions of time put a great deal of stress on the whole process of adaptation. The problem was to solve the general problem of administrative adaptation and to make sure that Denmark could run the Presidency in a smooth and efficient way, all more or less at the same time.

The challenge was even greater as the decision to apply for membership was highly controversial. Even if the adaptation of governmental bureaucracy could be planned well in advance, most implementative steps had to be postponed for political reasons until after 2 October 1972. On that date the electorate would, by means of a referendum, take the final decision on the membership issue. However after 2 October less than three months were left to put into operation the administrative changes deemed necessary.

Given these severe conditions, much was at stake for a number of top civil servants. The same was true for a handful of cabinet ministers who were more than peripherally involved in EC affairs. Nothing could be allowed to go wrong. In this perspective the impending responsibility to run the Presidency after merely six months' membership could be one burden too many for a small country with perhaps not exactly small, but nevertheless at least comparatively limited political and bureaucratic resources.

After all this 1 July 1973 arrived with Danish ministers and bureaucrats in the chair. They handled their six months in the presidential chair without causing any scandals or breakdowns which could have been attributed to poor planning, simple inexperience or inadequate resources.

Since 1973 Denmark has acted as President of the Council of Ministers on two further occasions, namely in the first half of 1978 and more recently in the first half of 1982. By the time these two later occasions had arrived, the EC Presidency had been reduced to its proper proportions, viz. an extra burden of limited duration to be dealt with according to the procedures set up in the past and the experiences gained during the first presidential term in 1973. What had once been a problem has been turned into a non-problem.

To phrase the general situation in these words may sound harsh and disrespectful considering the overloaded job conditions of many bureaucrats. However some of the characteristics often attributed to bureaucratic organisations should be brought to mind. One is that when bureaucratic organisations, and government departments belong to this category, meet new challenges they set up rules and procedures specifying how the challenge should be tackled. Another characteristic is that rules and procedures set up in one situation will be applied when the challenge is repeated. A third characteristic is that such rules and procedures are only changed if their previous application has been connected with problems or subjected to criticism. This of course does not imply that the rules and procedures need to have caused the problems. It means however that the standard political-bureaucratic response to all kinds of critical situations is to revise and strengthen the rules of the past.

DECIDING ON THE ADAPTATION ISSUE

Even if the identification of adaptation problems was comparatively easy, the problems to be dealt with were not reduced to technical matters. On the contrary, the political controversy regarding Danish entry into the EC and the vested interests of the ministries affected complicated decision-making and contributed to an extension of the deliberations already started in summer 1971.

Essentially the interests connected with the issue of administrative adaptation fell in three categories:

1) Since the late 1950s the politically unstable situation concerning the future of the EEC and the EFTA as well as their mutual relationships had given the economic division of the Ministry of Foreign Affairs and its Secretariat for European Market Affairs a powerful position within central government. The Secretariat had established itself as the place where information on European integration was gathered and analysed and, on this basis, also as the place where the general policy of the Danish government was prepared and coordinated. The position of the Secretariat was finally stressed by the appointment of a cabinet minister responsible for European market problems and foreign economic policy. The appearance of a more stable situation after entry into the EC endangered this position; domestic ministries argued that there would no longer be any need for a strongly centralised authority now that the uncertain period of entry negotiations would be replaced by co-operation within a well-known institutional framework. The future of the Secretariat for European Market Problems would therefore depend on its ability to gain political support for strong coordination procedures centered around itself.

2) Domestic ministries, especially the Ministry of Finance, the Ministry of Economic Affairs, and the Ministries of Agriculture and Industry and Commerce looked upon the Secretariat for European Market Affairs as an **ad hoc** organisation; as such it might have had an indispensable function as long as everything was in a state of flux. With the issue of Danish membership of the EC finally resolved, they saw no reason why the problems of EC co-operation could not be dealt with within a basically decentralised framework, following the pattern established, e.g., within the field of OECD co-operation.

3) Given the dominant position of the Common Agricultural Policy, it is also worth mentioning the interests of agricultural interest organisations. Even if the Common Agricultural Policy implies the transfer of policy-making competence to the EC, national authorities still retain the responsibility for the current administration of the common policy, e.g. market interventions and stockpiling of surplus products. The farmers' organisations, partially supported by the Ministry of Agriculture, showed a marked interest in the establishment of a semi-public market organisation at the national level, mainly controlled by the organisations themselves.

This brief presentation of the interests involved when the government had to decide on the issue of adaptation, demonstrates that the process of adaptation was not a general political issue, mobilising political parties in Parliament. It was an issue of bureaucratic politics, setting the different departments of central government against each other. When first raised in the late summer of 1971 by the Minister of European Market Affairs, it was even an issue which cabinet ministers found neither very relevant nor pressing. As the prospective date of entry came closer, and as the deliberations concerning the adaptation problems progressed at the level of the civil service, individual ministers lined up without reservation behind the demands put forward by their respective civil servants. In certain phases of the interdepartmental negotiations this implied domestic ministers taking comparatively firm positions against the Minister of European Market Affairs. It also implied some tough discussions between the Minister of Foreign Affairs and the Minister of European Market Affairs (4).

The decision-making process concerning the adaptation problems did not result in one general decision covering all aspects of the issue. Decisions were made in a piecemeal way ranging from May 1972 to spring 1973, when the remaining questions were settled. Since then the system has been surprisingly stable with only minor changes made within the general principles of the 1972-1973 decisions.

INTEGRATING THE EC IN THE NATIONAL ADMINISTRATION

According to the premise of the interdepartmental coordination system, civil servants from the ministries having jurisdiction over the subject matter on the domestic scene will normally represent Denmark in the EC. By implication, this means that a considerable number of civil servants have to go to Brussels on behalf of their ministers, representing the positions reached within the coordination committees. Based on the number of missions conducted by Danish civil servants between 1973 and 1978, Table 3.1 gives documentation of the rather wide-ranging administrative consequences of EC participation. ·

First, it can be seen that every year Danish civil servants have made 4-5000 missions to meetings within the EC institutions. To this participation by members of the Permanent Representation in Brussels should be added the participation by civil servants from the Ministry of Foreign Affairs in the foreign policy consultation between the members of the EC.

Secondly, Table 3.1 reveals how EC membership has given most ministries a considerable international role; so it can be seen that civil servants from the Ministry of Foreign Affairs, i.e. in most cases the Department of Foreign Economic Affairs, only account for some 10 per cent of the missions to negotiations at Community level.

Thirdly, it can also be seen that the really heavily involved ministries are the ones with political and administrative responsibility for matters related to the common market for industrial and agricultural products and to the common labour market. Civil servants from the Ministry of Agriculture accounted for 26 to 32 percent of all missions to EC negotiations. The corresponding figures for civil servants from the Ministry of Industry and Commerce are 16-19 per cent and for

Table 3.1
Representation at EC Negotiations by Type of Ministry. Percentages

	1973*	1974	1975	1976	1977	1978**
Ministry of Taxes and Tariffs	12	10	10	9	9	8
Ministry of the Environment	5	5	7	8	8	7
Ministry of Agriculture	27	32	30	28	26	27
Ministry of Industry and Commerce	19	16	16	17	17	17
Ministries of Fisheries Labour Housing	3	6	6	6	8	9
Ministry of Education	4	5	8	8	7	7
Other Ministries (Social Affairs, Public Works and Transport, Interior)	8	7	6	5	6	6
Ministry of Foreign Affairs	12	10	8	10	10	12
Ministries of Economics and Finance	7	7	7	7	6	5
Ministry of Justice, Legislative Coordination	3	2	2	2	2	2
Prime Minister's Office	-	-	-	-	1	-
N (= 100%)	1543	4010	4377	4587	4828	3214

*   Information only available for the latter half of 1973.
** Information only available for the first half of 1978.
General note: Not including the Ministry of Greenland and representation at the foreign policy consultations among the EC countries.

the Ministry of Taxes and Tariffs 8-12 per cent. Altogether civil servants from these ministries account for some 60 per cent of the Danish representation at negotiations within the EC. The ministries responsible for welfare policies and other public services such as the Ministry of Education, the Ministry of Social Affairs, and the Ministry of the Interior (health care) are on the other hand only marginally involved in EC relations. A close analysis of the kind of issues in which these ministries are representing Denmark in the Community reveals that these ministries are primarily involved in negotiations concerning the management of the common market for goods and labour, e.g. the right of establishment for health care personnel or the regulation of pharmaceutical production and commerce (5).

Important changes in the organisational structure were only made in the Ministry of Foreign Affairs and the Ministry of Agriculture. In the Ministry of Foreign Affairs decisive changes were made in the autumn of 1972, just after the referendum confirming the decision of entry. The Ministry of Foreign Affairs was divided into two separate departments, the Department of Foreign Affairs and the Department of Foreign Economic Affairs. However while the former deferred to the Minister of Foreign Affairs, in matters of personnel management and career planning, the Ministry was still considered as one organisation.

In some respects this reorganisation was a formalisation of a structure which had gained de facto existence during the 1960s. The background was the appointment in 1966 of a cabinet minister with special responsibility for European market affairs. This minister was advised by the Secretariat of European Market Affairs mentioned above.

In 1977 the post of Minister of European Market Affairs was dissolved, and the functions were transferred to the Minister of Foreign Affairs. Since then the Ministry of Foreign Affairs has gradually been reorganised. Although the organisation of the Ministry into two separate departments has been kept alive, steps have been taken in the direction of re-establishing the unity of the Ministry (6).

This development was first evidenced through the constitution of regular (weekly) coordination meetings where the top civil servants from both departments met under the chairmanship of the Director of the Ministry, who also acted as Permanent Secretary of the Department of Foreign Affairs. In 1980 this was followed up by the de facto appointment of a Permanent Secretary of this department; the implication being that the Director was established with responsibility for the coordination of the two departments of the Ministry, both led by a Permanent Secretary. Not until 1983 was this structure formalised through a revision of the Foreign Service Act.

The Ministry of Agriculture was also strongly affected by membership of the Communities. The Ministry took over the domestic administration of. the EC regulations of the common market for agricultural products. The Ministry was therefore reorganised; one division was made responsible for the general secretarial service to the Minister of Agriculture, connected with participation of the Minister in the negotiations of the Council of Ministers; the division also received the overall responsibility for policy-making concerning the economically vital market and price regulations of agricultural products. The other division of the department was primarily made responsible for policy-making concerning the structure of agriculture etc., an issue area more marginally affected by EC membership.

Secondly, to take care of the current execution of the EC market and price regulations, a new agency was placed below the department. This agency, called the Directorate of Market Regulations - or popularly the EC Directorate - was set up during the autumn of 1972 and was operating from the beginning of 1973.

Among the other ministries, the customs administration was also affected in important ways by entry into the EC. Even if EC membership had not provoked a general reorganisation of either the Department of Customs or the Directorate of Customs Administration, the administrative procedures of customs administration at both the central and local levels had to be modified significantly. One major consequence was that the more complicated customs procedures used by the EC necessitated the expansion of the personnel resources of the Danish customs administration.

Within other ministries, membership of the EC did not lead to profound changes in the administrative organisation. In retrospect however an interesting consequence of the increase in international co-operation has been that today nearly all domestic departments have established some kind of international affairs unit at the level of the department. The structure varies a great deal, from an international adviser working alone or assisted by a single junior civil servant at a bureau of international affairs to ministries like the Ministry of Agriculture, where the departmental organisation as a whole has been structured so as to take care of international relations, especially those arising from EC membership.

The establishment of a function as international adviser or a bureau of international affairs in no way implies that domestic ministries have specialised the international function. In all cases these units have a general coordinative function, managing the stream of communication to and from the ministries on international problems, and representing the ministry in committees within the interdepartmental coordination system and in negotiations within the EC and other international organisations.

To the contrary, as is seen from Table 3.2 on the representational patterns at EC negotiations in 1974 and 1977, the function as negotiator of Danish interests in relation to the EC is taken care of by civil servants at all hierarchical levels and from any type of organisation within the central administration. It is reasonable to expect a similar pattern as far as it concerns the handling of EC affairs on the domestic scene.

As to types of organisations being represented in the negotiating teams, Table 3.2 reveals a very stable pattern. The majority of negotiators are civil servants from the departments (some 60 per cent), while some 25 per cent are civil servants from the agencies or directorates placed below the departments. However it can also be seen how external expertise has been drawn into negotiation delegations by the ministries.

Table 3.2
Representational Patterns at EC Negotiations 1974 and 1977

	c.1*	c.2	c.3	c.4	c.5	c.6	c.7
Department							
1974	5	20	71	4	2511	63	59
1977	7	15	72	6	2947	61	57
Agency (Directorate)							
1974	6	8	22	64	975	25	27
1977	6	5	27	62	1155	24	27
Special Research Institute**							
1974	4	-	-	96	214	5	6
1977	5	-	-	95	290	6	7
University Institute							
1974	-	-	-	100	90	2	3
1977	-	-	-	100	157	3	3
Other Public Sector Position							
1974	-	3	17	80	191	5	5
1977	3	5	8	84	272	6	6
Total Row N (= 100%)							
1974	5	15	51	29		3981	3579
1977	6	10	51	33		4821	4308

*   Including Permanent Secretaries, Directors General, Agency Directors, and the Deputies of those three categories.
** Some ministries dispose of their own research institutes, e.g. the Ministry of Agriculture and the Ministry of the Environment.

Col. 1 = Top civil servants*
Col. 2 = Mid-level generalists
Col. 3 = Generalists - level of Principals
Col. 4 = Specialists
Col. 5 = Total Row N (= 100%)
Col. 6 = Total Column N (= 100%)
Col. 7 = Total column, Domestic Ministries only N (= 100%)

The composition of negotiation delegations is not quite as stable as far as it concerns the hierarchical level and degree of specialisation of negotiations. For both departments and agencies there seems to be a tendency towards using lower-level civil servants as negotiators, a fact that may be explained by the combined effect of the growing number of meetings and of the routinisation of the co-operation to Danish central administration. In parallel, there may be a tendency towards agencies being represented by generalist civil servants as opposed to specialists, e.g. engineers.

The spread of Danish EC negotiators across types of administrative organisation, hierarchical level and degree of specialisation leads to the assumption that handling EC matters either as a negotiator in Brussels or on the domestic scene has not been a specialised function within the central administration. Instead the responsibility for dealing with the EC is given, often on an ad hoc basis, to the civil servants working with the subject matter in question, whether it has an international aspect or not.

This assumption coming close to reality is confirmed by Table 3.3 which shows the number of travels to EC negotiations made by individual civil servants (and ministers) during the five years from 1 July 1972 to 30 June 1978.

Table 3.3

Number of Travels to Meetings Within the European Communities

1973-1978

Number of Travels	Number of Civil Servants*	Percentages
1	1083	40
2	345	13
3-5	456	17
6-10	323	12
11-30	361	13
31-50	88	3
51-100	62	2
101+	16	–
Total	2734	100

*Including ministers.

Of the some 5000 civil servants in central administration, about half had represented their ministry at some time at EC negotiations. Forty per cent of these had only acted in that capacity once and 70 per cent had represented their ministry only once up to five times at negotiations.

Because of the decentralised handling of EC affairs within the Danish central administration described above, it is not possible to tell, either in absolute or in relative terms, how many civil servants are occupied within this field. The figures referred to above however indicate that Danish participation in the EC occupies considerable resources in terms of administrative personnel.

Some idea of the importance of EC relations at the beginning of Danish EC membership can be gained from an answer given to Parliament by the Prime Minister in 1973. According to this information, EC related functions occupied a total of 585 full-time positions within central administration. To this has to be added a considerable, but unestimated use of personnel resources within the local offices of the customs administration.

Of the 585 positions estimated to be occupied by EC tasks, 367 were specially created because of the increased workload as a consequence of EC membership. Fifty-seven per cent of these new positions were created within the Ministry of Foreign Affairs and the Ministry of Agriculture. To this almost 300 positions created within the customs administration must be added.

Since the early days of Danish EC membership, more positions have been created on different occasions. According to the analysis given above, EC related functions are decentralised to all civil servants working on subject matters more or less affected by the co-operation among the EC countries, so an attempt to calculate the total number of administrative positions created with reference to the burden of being a member of the EC would not be justified. It would hardly form the basis for a fairly accurate estimate of the total personnel resources occupied by EC functions at the domestic level.

In view of the decentralised handling of EC affairs within central administration, it is not possible to speak of, for example, careers specially directed towards the functions related to participation within the Communities. Even within such heavily involved ministries such as Agriculture, Industry and Commerce as well as Foreign Affairs it is, at least until now, not possible to observe marked trends pointing in that direction. One exception to this impression may be the careers within the two departments of the Ministry of Foreign Affairs.

An important aspect of the adaptation problems concerned the internal organisation of the Permanent Representation to the European Communities and its relations with central government and its agencies in Copenhagen. The former issue gave rise to few problems. There was general acceptance of a scheme prepared by the Danish Ambassador to the EC in 1972. The principles laid down are still valid; currently, apart from the Permanent Representative and his deputy, the Representation has attachés with a diplomatic background and so-called special attachés temporarily placed at the Representation by their ministries. The domestic ministries with such special attachés at the Representation are Agriculture, Fisheries, Trade and Industry, Budget, Economic Affairs alternating with the National Bank of Denmark, Labour and Social Affairs, Justice, Environment, Transport, Customs (7).

The latter issue aroused some controversy between the Secretariat of European Market Affairs and the economic ministries. While the former argued in favour of the Permanent Representative's full control of all communication between the attachés and their home administration, the latter naturally spoke for a more flexible solution allowing for such direct interactions as might be deemed appropriate.

As the ministries involved finally reached agreement on the content of a general instruction to special attachés, the following principles were formally laid down, confirming the normally full hierarchical authority of the Permanent Representative over the special attachés:

1) The special attachés belong to the staff of the representation and are as such subject to the directions given by the Ambassador.

2) The reports drafted by the special attachés are included in the general reports made by the representation and therefore sent to the Ministry of Foreign Affairs. The reports are drafted on behalf of the Ambassador and on his responsibility.

3) Except for this main principle, the special attachés are authorised:
   - to give factual information to their ministry;
   - to transmit communications, documents, requests concerning specific information, etc. from the Commission and other EC institutions;
   - to transmit meeting agendas and meeting records;
   - to transmit publicly-available documents concerning EC affairs of interest to their ministry.

4) Special attachés may, depending on the authorisation of the Ambassador, be allowed under specific circumstances to give further written information within their field to the ministry.

5) They are generally authorised to give oral answers to questions from their ministers concerning the development within the EC in their field.

The elaborate content of the instruction was a logical consequence of the diverging views as to the appropriate place of the representation and its special attachés in relation to the domestic ministries. The 1973 instruction still constitutes the formal framework of the interaction between the representation and domestic ministries. Judging from the information available, it seems as if the changing staff of the representation have found a workable balance between the two kinds of interests on collision course in 1973, without questioning the need for hierarchical control or for flexible communication.

THE PRESIDENCY AS AN EXTENSION OF THE NORMAL PATTERN

In 1973, when Denmark planned its first Presidency, the task seemed formidable. Membership was still not routine for Danish civil servants and their ministers. In this situation they were obliged to take over a function governed by rules and procedures which they had not internalised. In addition to this came the simple problem of capacity; all at a time when the Presidency was forcing Denmark to double its representation at EC meetings, i.e. to place qualified people in the chair and still at the same time to be represented by national spokesmen who would be able to defend Danish interests effectively.

Table 3.4 gives an idea of the size of the task. In 1973 Denmark presided over 129 committees and working parties. In all these cases national spokesmen had also to be appointed. Since 1973 however the burden of the EC Presidency has increased. In 1978, during Denmark's second term in the chair, the number of committees etc. was about twice as high. In 255 cases chairmen and national spokesmen had to be appointed. Because of the international negotiations within GATT and within UNCTAD on trade in raw materials the number was extraordinarily high. During these negotiations in Geneva the Presidency had to act both as EC coordinator for 75 groups and to be represented by national spokesmen in the same groups.

Table 3.4
Presidential Posts 1973-1982

	1973		1978		1982	
	N	Pct.	N	Pct.	N	Pct.
Coreper/General Affairs	17	13	17	7	24	10
External Co-operation, (Global*)	8	6	91	36	52	21
External Co-operation, (bilateral and Regional)	20	16	20	8	21	9
Internal Co-operation	40	31	68	26	68	29
Agriculture	43	34	59	23	71	31
N (= 100%)	129		255		232	

Sources: Danish Presidency, Chairmen and National Spokesmen, Department of Foreign Economic Affairs 1973, 1978 and 1982.

* Including meetings in Geneva concerning international negotiations on trade in raw materials. At these meetings the Presidency had dual functions: that of being responsible for coordination within the EC and that of spokesman for the EC. In 1978, the number of chairmen for the different commodity groups in Geneva was 75 and in 1982 it was 31. Further the Presidency had of course to provide national spokesmen as well.

During the 1982 Presidency, the number of committees and working parties had decreased to 232 because of the less intensive activity within GATT and UNCTAD. Within the EC proper, the number of committees had stabilised at the 1978 level. The exception was the Common Agricultural Policy where, once again, the number of chairs to be filled had increased.

In the periods between the presidential terms Denmark is represented in Brussels by civil servants from the Permanent Representation, be they diplomats or special attachés seconded to the Representation by domestic ministries, by civil servants from the headquarters of the Ministry of Foreign Affairs and by civil servants from domestic departments. Exactly the same organisations provide the chairmen with personnel during the presidential terms. As is seen from Table 3.5, the pattern has changed since 1973. Domestic departments have an increasingly important part to play as the principal source of chairmen. This is seen most clearly if correction is made for the special circumstances during the Geneva negotiations in 1978.

Table 3.5
Organisational Origin of Danish Chairmen and National Representatives

| | a) | | | | | |
	b)	c)	d)	e)	f)	g)
Chairmen						
1973	24	6	19	50	1	129
1978	14	13	7	43*	23	253
1982	21	9	6	54*	10	227
National Represen- tatives						
1973	44	0	14	40	2	103
1978	14	7	27	46**	8	201
1982	15	5	9	66**	5	229

Sources: Cf. Table 3.3.
* = If representation at the UN Mission is omitted, the share of domestic ministries was 56% in 1978 and 61% in 1982.
** = If representation at the UN Mission is omitted, the share of domestic ministries was 51% in 1978 and 69% in 1982.
a) Permanent Representation
b) Foreign Office-Personnel   subdivisions of a)
c) Domestic Ministries
d) Ministry of Foreign Affairs
e) Domestic Ministries
f) UN Mission Geneva
g) N (= 100%)

In 1973 the diplomatic staff of the Permanent Representation still had the capacity to fill about one fourth of the chairs and at the same time to serve as national spokesmen in nearly half of the committees and working parties. Another fifth of the committees were provided with chairmen from the Foreign Affairs headquarters in Copenhagen. The reason for this policy was probably both the manageable size of the task and the fact that during the extended period of pre-entry negotiations with the EC, civil servants had built up a comparatively large group of personnel with sufficient knowledge of Community procedures.

With the 1978 Presidency the situation had however changed. Firstly, the staff of special attachés at the Permanent Representation had gained in experience and furthermore had been expanded in numbers; these people were therefore in a position to take over part of the job. Secondly, domestic departments now had civil servants with several years of EC experience. As these people were also in possession of the relevant policy expertise, domestic ministries from now on took the lion's share of the chair. Thirdly, it can be seen how diplomats from the UN Mission in Geneva were drawn upon as coordinators of Community policy in the numerous groups set up for different commodity groups during the GATT and UNCTAD negotiations. If allowance is made for the special circumstances of 1978, the pattern of the 1982 Presidency was very similar to that of 1978.

To some extent both the presidential function and the function of national representation have developed into specialised functions, e.g. Coreper is served by Foreign Affairs personnel from the staff of the Permanent Representation, a logical implication of the Minister of Foreign Affairs being the member of the General Council. No wonder that this pattern is also upheld during presidential terms. The same kind of logic comes into operation for the fields of internal co-operation and the Common Agricultural Policy: civil servants from the relevant domestic departments and their special attachés from the Permanent Representation have almost monopolised the presidential function and the function as national spokesmen in these fields. In other fields co-operation is practised between Foreign Affairs and the domestic departments, e.g. during the trade negotiations in Geneva, the Ministry of Foreign Affairs provided the chairmen through the Danish Mission at the UN in Geneva, while national spokesmen were taken from the relevant domestic ministries, in most cases Industry and Commerce plus Agriculture.

To preside over some 230-250 committees for even a limited period of six months puts a good deal of strain on the staff of government departments. One of the recurrent problems in the planning of the Presidency has therefore been where to find the resources. Should staff be transferred from other tasks? Or should the staff be at least temporarily expanded by either taking on outside experts as temporary support for the permanent staff, or should additional personnel be recruited? In practice a combined strategy has been followed.

Firstly, it has made sense to strengthen the staff of the Permanent Representation in the period before as well as during the presidential term. In this way the representation would be able to cope with some of the problems raised by the Presidency without constantly having to call upon **ad hoc** assistance from Copenhagen. These people sent to Brussels in temporary positions have, of course, without exception been civil servants with prior EC experience.

Secondly, as has been seen above, an increasing part of the presidential burden has been placed on the administrative headquarters in Copenhagen. They have been forced to either replace existing staff or to get access to additional resources. Normally, they have chosen the latter strategy. In 1973 about 40 positions as civil servants were created, half of them in the Ministry of Foreign Affairs. To this should be added an expansion of the clerical staff of the same size in the Ministry of Foreign Affairs. In 1978 a similar expansion took place related to the burden of the Presidency. Once again approximately half of the expansion took place in Foreign Affairs. In 1972 only the most involved domestic ministries (Agriculture, Fisheries, Customs, Labour and Environment) applied for a minor and temporary increase of their staff during the Presidency. Contrary to this, the Ministry of Foreign Affairs presented proposals for an even greater expansion of its staff than in 1973 and 1978, a surprising fact if the relatively decreased part of the Ministry in running the Presidency is considered (cf. Table 3.5 above.).

To be realistic these temporary expansions in administrative staff should not be seen only in the perspective of adding the personnel necessitated by the extra burden of the Presidency to existing staffs. It is open to discussion what kind of relief it is possible to get from recruiting young graduates directly from the university for periods of up to one year. One should view these expansions in staff, motivated by the extra work during the presidential term, as an example of how governmental organisations use any pretext to gain additional appropriations and additional staff. This has probably been the case to some extent, because experience tells governmental departments that temporary positions by deft bureaucratic manoeuvering can often be transformed into a permanent expansion. Much of the expansion of the Ministry of Foreign Affairs throughout the 1970s was based on this strategy. Both in connection with the 1973 and the 1978 Presidencies, the Ministry proved able to profit from it. In 1982 however, it seems as if a combination of critical press comments and political aversion against further expansion of the Ministry of Foreign Affairs on this basis blocked the repetition of the prior strategy. At any rate, the Ministry of Foreign Affairs had to accept a cut in its proposal for more positions, and also to accept that the temporary positions created with reference to the extraordinary burden of the Presidency would run out at the end of the period.

THE INTERDEPARTMENTAL COORDINATION SYSTEM

As the distribution of competences with regard to the EC was, with few exceptions, based on the existing structure of government, an overriding problem of adaptation was that of how and to what extent the EC policies of the different ministries should be coordinated. As seen above, the ministries had strongly diverging views on this point. Therefore it took a lot of bureaucratic horse-trading to reach agreement on the organisation of the coordination system.

The system which was finally established struck a delicate balance between the demand for centralisation made by the Secretariat of European Market Affairs and the demands for a decentralised structure put forward by the economic ministries. EC coordination was formalised to a much greater extent than is normal for Danish central administration. Probably there were two reasons for this:

1) The divergent interests of different ministries pulled decision-making towards a highly formalised organisational structure and minutiose written procedures. Only in this way was it possible to find a compromise trusted by the departments involved.

2) The decision to enter the European Communities represented one of the most contested political issues in Danish politics since the end of World War II. A considerable minority within Parliament and in the electorate doubted the viability of Danish national sovereignty within an integrated European Community. To the government it was important to establish coordination procedures which would guaranteee that Danish representatives would not take positions in EC negotiations that could raise doubt politically about the credibility of Denmark's officially reluctant attitudes towards further integrative policies.

The structure of the EC coordination system is shown in Figure 3.1. The system is organised at three levels with a Cabinet Committee, a Senior Civil Servants Committee, and a number of specialised committees organised at the middle or lower-level of civil servants. The system and its way of functioning is probably best understood from that shown in Figure 3.1.

In 1972, 18 specialised coordination committees were established. Later the number grew to some 25. The specialised coordination committees are chaired by a civil servant from the ministry having competence in the issue area at the domestic level; i.e. a civil servant from the Ministry of Agriculture presides over the committee of agriculture, and a civil servant from the Ministry of the Environment presides over the committee of environmental problems. The ministry from which the committee chairman comes also serves as secretariat for each specialised coordination committee. The members of the committees are recruited from ministries with neighbouring jurisdictions; the Department of Foreign Economic Affairs is represented in all specialised coordination committees and the Department of the Budget in all committees, with a few exceptions.

At the level above the specialised coordination committees, a General EC Coordination Committee has been established. This committee is presided over by the Permanent Secretary of the Department of Foreign Economic Affairs which also serves as secretariat for the committee. According to the original outline of the coordination system, the members of this committee were supposed to be top ranking civil servants from the most affected ministries, e.g. **skal det ikke vaere:** i.e. Permanent Secretaries or their deputies. In spite of occasional pressure to expand the membership of the committee to other

Figure 3.1
Formal Structure of the EC Coordination System

The Cabinet Committee of Common Market Affairs	The General EC Coordination Committee	The specialised EC coordination committees
a) Originally, the Minister of European Market Affairs, (1973-1975), and since 1977 the Minister of Foreign Affairs	The Permanent Secretary of the Department of Foreign Economic Affairs	Top or mid-level civil servant from the most affected ministry
b) The Prime Minister and (1980) the 7 most affected ministers	8 senior civil servants from the Prime Minister's Office and the most affected ministries	Civil servants from most affected ministries and, in all cases, the Department of Foreign Economic Affairs
c) The Department of Foreign Economic Affairs	The Department of Foreign Economic Affairs	The ministry having the chairmanship of the committee

a) = Chairmanship
b) = Members
c) = Secretariat

ministries, the membership has been restricted to the original 8-9 departments. The committee, however, has never succeeded in attracting the very top civil servants as members. Actually most ministries are represented at the level of assistant secretaries.

A Cabinet Committee of Common Market Affairs has been placed at the top of the coordination system. The history of the Committee goes back to the early sixties when Denmark first applied for membership of the Communities. Like the General EC Coordination Committee, the Cabinet Committee meets once a week except for the summer period. Until 1977, when the post as Minister of European Market Affairs was finally dissolved, this Minister presided over the committee meetings. Now the Minister of Foreign Affairs is chairman. The importance of the Committee is stressed by the membership of the Prime Minister as well as all other ministers with some current involvement in the handling of Community affairs. Unlike most other cabinet committees, negotiations within the Committee of Common

Market Affairs end up in final decisions which do not have to be confirmed by the Cabinet later on.

This three-level system of coordination is held together by an elaborate set of formal procedures. These procedures have three functions; they point out when the system has to be activated, and they determine the distribution of competences among the three hierarchical levels within the system. Finally they regulate the relationship between the Department of Foreign Economic Affairs and the domestic ministries.

The rules of procedure specify four different forms of co-operation within the Communities:

1) Participation in executive committees and working parties under the auspices of the Commission;
2) Participation in EC committees with coordination and/or information exchange functions, e.g. within the fields of economic and monetary policy;
3) Participation in legally binding co-operation under the auspices of the Commission and the Council;
4) Co-operation with the aim of taking up new fields of co-operation within the EC.

In situations 1 and 2, the coordination is supposed to be an affair for the specialised coordination committees exclusively; only in cases of disagreement within the relevant committee is the issue referred to the General EC Coordination Committee.

In situations 3 and 4, the issues are supposed to be put on the agenda of the EC Coordination Committee and, if necessary, on the agenda of the Cabinet Committee as soon as the Commission has transmitted a formal proposal to the Council of Ministers. Until this stage, the issue will be dealt with exclusively at the level of the specialised coordination committees.

When negotiations take place within Coreper or within a committee or working party set up by Coreper, the coordination procedure ends with the drafting of an instruction sent to the Permanent Representation. This instruction is drafted by the Department of Foreign Economic Affairs following the conclusions drawn in the General EC Coordination Committee or in the Cabinet Committee of Common Market Affairs.

The EC coordination system established in 1972 was based on a careful balance between the centralist claims of the Secretariat of European Market Affairs and the decentralist claims of domestic ministries. This balancing of bureaucratic interests probably had many important consequences for the functioning of the system and its further development. A timely hypothesis would be that the interaction of strongly opposed interests concerning the degree of centralisation accounts for the elaborate formalisation of the system of coordination. A high level of formalisation was the only way in which the different departments would be assured that other departments would not circumvent the procedures established.

Furthermore this balancing of interests has given a great deal of stability to the system of coordination. In the first years of EC membership the system was challenged on a few occasions by the Ministry of Economics and by the Ministry of Agriculture, both arguing that the procedures laid down for the coordination of Danish EC policy are unnecessarily heavy to allow for rapid and smooth decision-making. Such attacks on the system have been warded off, as it had to be recognised that the balance of interests could only be kept intact by not changing the basic principles of the system.

The system could, of course, be subjected to change without any explicit decisions. It could, for example, be imagined that the system would change if the different bureaucratic actors realised that in the course of time coordination problems do not necessitate current deliberations within a fixed network of coordination committees organised at different hierarchical levels. That is what often happens when coordination groups are set up within the Danish government. This however has not been the lot of the EC coordination system: my hypothesis would be that the high degree of formalisation of the system has made it some kind of self-perpetuating machine being automatically filled up with issues to be dealt with. Therefore the system, for good or bad, is not endangered by the same kind of semi-automatic adaptations which often mean that interdepartmental procedures set up under specific circumstances wither away as those circumstances change. So it is thought-provoking that the Cabinet Committee of Common Market Affairs is the only cabinet committee which has functioned over an extended period of time without many fluctuations in its level of activity. Due to the procedures established its agenda is filled up, maybe without any ministers wondering much about the continued validity of the reasoning behind it.

These factors may explain why the system has only been subject to marginal change. The most obvious deviation from the formal outline of the system concerns the relative position of the General EC Coordination Committee, which does not seem to have acquired the central position thought out for it. The general impression is that most problems, without severe conflicts, are solved at the level of the specialised coordination committees. In the few cases where this turns out to be impossible, the representatives of the ministries at this level are acting on instructions which have been confirmed by the upper levels of their ministries, often by their minister, so that the General EC Coordination Committee is in no better position to find a compromise. Therefore the diverging interests can only be settled through negotiation at the political level within the Cabinet Committee. Under these circumstances the General EC Coordination Committee acts more as a preparatory body for the Cabinet Committee than as a policy-making body. The Committee, however, may have established itself as a general monitor of the coordination system as a whole, evaluating the need for adjustments of the procedures established and for expansions in the numbers of specialised coordination committees.

One example of this function of the EC Coordination Committee has been the planning of the Presidency. For the three presidential terms the Committee has been responsible for setting up the official lists of chairmen. Even if the balance between the Department of Foreign

Economic Affairs and domestic departments has changed in favour of the latter, there is no evidence that this has caused any controversy between the departments involved. Planning the presidential terms and distributing posts as chairmen has been a matter of administrative convenience rather than a source of new department rivalries.

This points to the fundamental stability of the EC coordination system already mentioned. But it probably also points to the fact that many of the committees and working parties set up by Coreper are deemed as meeting places where common initiatives are discussed but where substantive results are rare and in some cases not worth the efforts. The potential influence following from the post as chairman over a committee within one of the Community's more marginal fields of co-operation is so minimal that it is not worth a fight. Perhaps a department would be better off if responsibility for chairing a committee could be shifted to a neighbouring department. This, for example, was the case in 1978 when the Ministries of Commerce and Industry, Labour and Environment among themselves had to decide which departments should bear the burden of chairing some Community committees set up to cope with technical trade barriers among the Member countries.

CONCLUSIONS: THE PRESIDENCY BEYOND REFORM

In the early history of the European Community it was generally assumed that the Presidency offered some possibilities of taking home some spoils for itself. The reasoning behind this assumption was that the Presidency could connect different issues in broader package deals. If these package deals were to have any chance of success they should, of course, be so well-balanced that no country could be the loser; rather, everybody would gain something and the presidential country would furthermore be able to take home an extra premium for itself.

In 1973 when Denmark entered the Community and planned its first term in the chair this assumption was still alive. This was also the case in 1978, when Denmark as President tried to launch a Community strategy for the solution of the economic and social crisis which had hit the Member countries (8). Even if the Presidency had been authorised to prepare a report on this common strategy, the initiative was abortive. The Community seems to be beyond the point in its development when a member country has any realistic chances of either setting its mark on EC policies or determining the agenda of the Community because for a period of six months it presides over the Council of Ministers.

In this chapter, the Presidency comes out as a burdensome routine giving very little influence to the incumbent, either at the national or at the Community level. The question could be raised whether it would be possible to alleviate the burden and/or increase the efficiency of the Presidency. At this point in time Danish civil servants have no ideas on the subject of reform. Not because reform is not needed, but rather because they have resigned themselves to not thinking about the idea of reform. Any initiative in this direction is deemed to be abortive. So why should they expend their efforts in doing something which will end up as nothing?

REFERENCES

(1) Max Beloff: New Dimensions in Foreign Policy, George Allen & Unwin, London 1981.

(2) - Pierre Gerbet & Daniel Pepy (eds): La décision dans les Communautés européennes, Presses Universitaires de Bruxelles, Bruxelles, 1969.
   - W.J.G. van der Meersch (ed): Institutions communautaires et institutions nationales dans le développement des Communautés, Institut de Sociologie de l'U.L.B., Bruxelles, 1968.
   - J. Grønnegaard Christensen: Integrationens indflydelse paa de nationale administrative strukturer i De europaeiske Faellesskaber, Nordisk Administrativt Tidsskrift, 1971, pp. 241 - 262.

(3) Colm O Nuallain: Membership of Supranational Bodies - Adaptation Implications for National Civil Services, OECD Co-operative Action Programme, Joint Activity of Public Management Improvement, Paris, 1980.

(4) - J. Grønnegaard Christensen: Da central administration blev international in: N. Amstrup & I. Faurby (eds.): Studier i dansk udenrigspolitik, Forlaget Politica, Aarhus, 1978, pp. 75 - 118.
   - K.B. Andersen: I alle de riger og lande, Glydendal, Copenhagen, 1983.

(5) J. Grønnegaard Christensen & C. Lehmann Sørensen: Fra formandskab til formandskab. Dansk centraladministrations deltagelse i EF's beslutningsproces 1973 - 78, Samfundwidenskabeligt Forlag, Copenhagen, 1981.

(6) Rapport fra arbejdsgruppen verdr. udenrigsministeriets struktur, Administrations-departementet, Copenhagen, 1979.

(7) op. cit., appendix 7.

(8) C. Lehmann Sørensen: EF - medlemskab, formandskab og makkerkab, in: N. Amstrup & I. Faurby (eds.) Studier i dansk udenrigspolitik, Forlaget Politica, Aarhus, 1978, pp. 119 - 152.

See also:

   - J. Grønnegaard Christensen: Blurring the International Domestic Politics Distinction, Danish Representation at EC Negotiations, Scandinavian Political Studies, vol. 4 n⁰ 3, 1981, pp. 191 - 208.
   - J. Grønnegaard Christensen: Centraladministrationen: Organisation og politisk plauring, Samfundsvidenskabeligt Forlag, Copenhagen, 1981.

Chapter 4

THE PRESIDENCY OF THE COUNCIL OF MINISTERS OF THE
EUROPEAN COMMUNITIES: NATIONAL PAPER ON THE FEDERAL
REPUBLIC OF GERMANY
Mrs Elfriede Regelsberger and Dr Wolfgang Wessels, Bonn

INTRODUCTION

German politicians and civil servants display a confusing pattern of
attitudes and behaviour **vis-à-vis** the Community. Official statements
such as the one by Chancellor Kohl before the German Federal Diet
(Bundestag) (4 May 1983) **(1)** reflects on the one hand the political
conviction that the Federal Republic needs a stable framework and a
reliable 'coalition' to exist in the international system. The historical
trauma of being isolated once again and the functional necessity to run
and administer all kind of policies together with other members of the
interdependent international system are two basic motives.

On the other hand, this positive attitude towards multilateral
policy-making does not necessarily lead to an overall and unconditional
Community orientated behaviour.

Doubts have existed from the 1950s up till now. Critical voices
have asked whether the Community of the Six, Ten or Twelve European
countries is the most useful arena for problem-solving. The western
'capitalistic' world's co-operation with the US or bilateral relations with
individual Community countries, especially France, were and, today
again, are quite often perceived as more useful for pursuing specific
German interests than an integrated Community. In recent years, this
sort of thinking has been shared by politicians and civil servants alike,
who are confronted with increasingly negative experiences in their daily
EC work. Germans do not like to be more and more isolated as the only
net contributors. They have difficulties in explaining to the German
public and to their colleagues, dealing with subjects outside the
Community framework, that savings in the Federal budget are of highest
priority, whereas the Community budget is constantly increasing. They
rate the political and administrative performance of some Community
bodies and some Member countries as rather low; in terms of economical
developments, they see the interest of the Federal Republic, integrated
in a world-wide trade system, increasingly threatened by intra-European
protectionistic attitudes.

This mixed pattern of support of the process of European
integration on the one side and scepticism about the functioning of EC
institutions and policies on the other are not evenly distributed over the

political circles and bureaucracies in the Federal government. Differences became apparent in the Genscher-Colombo initiative, which was regarded in the ministries outside the Ministry of Foreign Affairs with surprise, bewilderment and sometimes even suspicion.

The general picture of attitudes has become neither clear nor persistent over time. Though the basic attitudes are open (but critical) towards European integration, concrete behaviour in a given political situation and policies during the Presidency, will be the result of the struggle between different perceptions and interests. Often overall political interests are the dominant ones. These quite often lead to package deals which do not satisfy the ministers and civil servants responsible for specific policies. There seems to be some reluctance growing nowadays to give way to overall political goals due to various financial restrictions and general disillusionment about the progress of European policies. It is however difficult to predict this trend, as Bonn has already backed down quite often from seemingly 'tough' positions.

Interest groups are also participating in this struggle and these are well organised and have direct access to politicians and civil servants. Parliament and political parties, though less active, also contribute to this mixture of behavioural patterns in the Federal Republic.

The general political appeal of overall integration policies to the German public is of significance for the Presidency. The basic pro-integration attitude, which is linked with increasing scepticism about the Community as such (2), has been used especially by the Foreign Minister to underline his personal and his party's international and European vocation, perhaps to counterbalance the traditional East-European and global role of the Chancellor and his party (3). Since the end of the SPD/FDP government a slight change seems to be under way. More than his predecessors, the present Chancellor, Helmut Kohl, has shown greater interest in European affairs.

Another basic feature of administration must be added for the Presidency. It is a vital part of administrative culture (4) that a given 'job' be done at the least correctly, and many civil servants even take pride in good performance and will engage themselves in this way in Community business. The same is true for officials dealing with EPC questions: to them being in the chair for six months is seen as an intellectual challenge to do more than just manage the Presidency. They may also be helped by certain elements of German administrative culture, such as the search for consensus among the ministries involved, both on the national level and between Bonn and the Länder governments within the federal system, the freedom of the basic units to manoeuvre the long tradition of European involvement. On the other hand they may be hampered by other elements such as procedural rigidity, distance from other administrative cultures partly caused by lack of incentive to use languages and get additional experience outside the Federal Republic.

A special aspect of the administrative culture should be mentioned in relation to the 1983 Presidency. German civil servants normally pursue policies either for which they have been given some orders from the political top or political background, or which they deem to be in the broad framework of the political goals of the ministry. After the change of government from Schmidt to Kohl in autumn 1982 and during the election period until March 1983, this kind of political guidance and feed-back were reported to have been at least partly lacking as far as EC questions were concerned.

Decreasingly important for the attitudes of German civil servants vis-à-vis the Community are historical inhibitions which, in the first years, led Germans to a more modest position in defending their own national interests and to strong inclinations to follow French policies (5).

THE ROLE OF GOVERNMENT AND PARLIAMENT IN EUROPEAN AFFAIRS - ORGANISATIONAL STRUCTURES AND COORDINATION PROCEDURES

Policy-making in the Federal Republic is characterised first of all by constitutional regulations. According to the Basic Law each minister takes the sole responsibility for his policy, the Chancellor only having the right to give global directives. This competence is however seldom formally used. As one of the few examples, one could mention a letter in this respect by Adenauer to his ministers, in which responsibilities covering Community policy between the Ministry of Foreign Affairs and that of Economic Affairs were fixed. In general, the Chancellor is served in the Chancellery by his own services, which however rely for all routine operations in European affairs on the responsible ministries. The Chancellery does not and, according to officials, should not possess enlarged personnel and technical equipment. On the other hand, their own international and European contacts enable the civil servants in the Chancellery to broaden the perspectives of Bonn's foreign policy in a certain way. The same is true for the Chancellor himself. By his own regular contacts with other Heads of state and government (within the European Council, the Western Summitry, the European People's Party, the European Democratic Union and other forms of multiple bilateralism), he receives direct and personal information to enable him to form his own opinion and, at the same time, he has his own views and experiences at his disposal in the discussions within the cabinet and with his ministers.

The Ministry of Foreign Affairs takes a leading role in European affairs. Civil servants there describe their task as being the guardians of the process of European integration within the national administration, stressing the overall political and economic importance of the German membership of the EC. This comprehensive task has never been easy to fulfil and has provoked internal tensions due to the fact that other ministries became increasingly involved in Community policies, developing their own structures and procedures sometimes by means of a direct informal link bypassing the Ministry of Foreign Affairs. Bureaucratic struggles also arose due to perceptions in the other ministries which were based on specific sector-orientated interests reducing the general 'European' dimension given by the Ministry of Foreign Affairs. The debate can quite often be expressed in the words of a cost-benefit assesment: should we give up sound economic policies just for the sake of a European solution which will not solve the given problem. The Solemn Declaration of June 1983, the child of the Ministry of Foreign Affairs, is supposed to show some positive effects on the internal decision-making process within the Federal government and to stimulate a more coherent German policy. As far as European Political Co-operation (EPC) is concerned, the Ministry of Foreign Affairs, and within the administrative apparatus, the Political Division 2, are exclusively responsible.

The second 'pillar' dealing with EC questions within the government is the Ministry of Economic Affairs. Traditionally charged to push the economic integration process further, its European vocation has faded away over the years. There the advocates of European integration increasingly face the specific interests of colleagues from within their own ministry and from other ministries. External constraints like the evident national interests of EC partners, the restrictions of the budget at home or growing public demands to combat unemployment, or to manage the structural crisis of certain industries etc. do not facilitate a pro-European attitude. The Ministry of Economic Affairs is also the central agency for coordinating the different viewpoints on Community questions within the government and for the transmission of German positions to Brussels with all their technical implications.

Except for the Ministry of Defence and the Ministry of Intra-German Relations (Ministerium für Innerdeutsche Beziehungen), practically all other ministries are involved in Community policies in one way or the other. Besides the Ministry of Foreign Affairs and the Ministry of Economic Affairs, the Ministry of Finance, and Agriculture deal continuously with EC matters. Their bureaucratic structures are oriented towards the handling of European policies. Civil servants in crucial positions in these ministries are familiar with the day-to-day work of EC affairs having been in charge of it for many years (sometimes a decade or more)!

In the Federal Republic, all main political parties, including the 'Greens' to a certain degree, and interest groups are in favour of some kind of European integration. Their key argument is that there is no alternative to European integration, the Community being one of the basic pillars of German foreign policy aims. Different perceptions do of course exist on the shape and contents of Community policies, as well as on how to pursue sector policies or which ways should be followed to reach the common goal. Reports given to Parliament by the Chancellor or Foreign Minister on the meetings of the European Council traditionally do not therefore provoke controversies on EC membership as such. The same is true of the annual debates on the budget or other government declarations with reference to the EC. Aspects of Community policies are usually discussed in the various sector-oriented parliamentary committees. It is worth noting that with the signing of the Rome Treaties both parliamentary houses, the **Bundestag** and **Bundesrat**, were given by national law the right to be continuously informed by the Federal government about what is going on in the Council and to comment on directives drafted by the Commission. General political aspects of European integration, institutional questions or those dealing with EPC are sometimes on the agenda of the Committee of Foreign Affairs of the **Bundestag** (and the **Bundesrat**). The Genscher-Colombo

76

initiative, for example, was discussed at an early stage prior to the formal decision of the Cabinet in late 1981. Compared with other foreign policy issues - **Ostpolitik** or currently security policy and relations with the United States and Moscow - EC and EPC matters play however a minor role.

During the German Presidency in 1983 however, consultations in the Parliamentary Committee of Foreign Affairs did not take place until June due to the date for parliamentary elections being in March and the time needed for constituting the new committee. The first meeting (June 1983), which also comprised the members of the respective committee of the **Bundestag** (due to restrictions in the calendar of the Foreign Minister to hold a separate colloquium), was not devoted mainly to EC/EPC questions. Security policy and issues related to East-West policy in general prevailed.

Interest groups have various channels at their disposal for keeping informed directly about government positions in EC affairs. Access is guaranteed to all ministries and the Chancellery (except for EPC questions - which still seem to be **une quantité negligeable** for the federations of German industries and others) at the working level as well as at the political top. It can be characterised as a useful exchange of views of mutual interest, based on long-term personal contacts and confidentiality, although one should not forget that certain strong lobbies, like the farmers or the chambers of commerce, are able to push government positions in their direction.

1. In the case of Community policies (6)

Organisational charts reflect to a certain extent where questions relevant to European Affairs are settled within the bureaucratic apparatus of the Federal government. The Ministry of Foreign Affairs and the Ministry of Economic Affairs have specific departments for EC questions (Ministry of Foreign Affairs: Division 4; Ministry of Economic Affairs: Division E). In other ministries the competences for Community policies are spread and discussed in the various bureaucratic units oriented to issue areas. Civil servants in those ministries dealing constantly with EC affairs have their specific groups, councils and partners in the Commission and in other member countries. Ministries, and sometimes individual departments, each within one ministry, have their own ways of looking at EC problems; a situation which is natural and quite often makes sense as they represent different conditions and interests connected with EC policies. The problems arise when different approaches need to be coordinated and competing priorities and alternatives integrated.

In Brussels and other national capitals, German attempts to integrate different points of view into a coherent and consistent position are sometimes evaluated as being of limited success. Compared with French and British decision-making procedures, the Bonn process seems quite often to be more fragmentary and based less on a well-founded and evenly pursued national strategy. This image seems to be in contrast to a complex and smooth network of coordination mechanisms which has existed on different levels and with different actors from the very beginning of the Federal Republic's EC membership (7).

The Cabinet itself, although it deals with European questions and the intensity of discussions however vary according to the working style of the Chancellor, is seldom used as a compromise broker. This is also true for the period of the German Presidency during the first half of 1983. In preparation for assuming the chair, the cabinet did not function as a forum for discussions either. Due to the change in government in 1982, no time was left to talk about the programme of the German Presidency as had been envisaged before. In the first weeks of the Kohl/Genscher coalition (i.e. after elections in March, 1983), a broad exchange of views in one of the Cabinet meetings did not take place. Contrary to the Cabinet discussions held under Helmut Schmidt, which regularly covered the actual situation of Community policies, Helmut Kohl wishes only EC questions of crucial importance to be put on the agenda, the others are to be solved among the ministers and ministries concerned.

A special Cabinet Committee for European Politics, created in 1973, chaired by the Chancellor and comprising the Ministers of Foreign Affairs, Finance, Economic Affairs, Agriculture, Labour, Defence (including the participation of the President of the German Central Bank), does not play a role at all. In general, positions are harmonised in the so-called Committee of State Secretaries for European Affairs. If not, discussions on an informal basis between the respective ministers, often together with the Head of government, are said to be the appropriate way (these for example took place in preparation for the European Council in Athens (Dec. 1983) as well as in its follow-up). The Chancellor himself then quite often takes the initiative.

The Committee of State Secretaries for European Affairs is thus supposed to reach a consensus within the national system. This committee (established in 1963) as an informal group, is today chaired by the Parliamentary State Secretary, formally a State Minister and therefore a member of the Cabinet, of the Ministry of Foreign Affairs. It is worth noting that the Ministry of Foreign Affairs has double representation on the Committee: the view of the Ministry of Foreign Affairs on EC questions is given by the State Secretary responsible for Community policies and not by the State Minister. The secretariat work of this Committee is carried out however by the Ministry of Economic Affairs and not by the Ministry of Foreign Affairs. The role of the chairman of this group was actively pursued by some of its office holders, especially by Klaus von Dohnanyi during the German Presidency of 1978. State Secretaries of other ministries participate according to the topics on the agenda. The representatives of the Ministry of Foreign Affairs, the Ministry of Economic Affairs, Finance and Agriculture and of the Chancellery attend the meeting as permanent members. The Committee which is ranked at Cabinet level meets about twice a month and works on a consensus principle; its decisions are binding on the administration.

Each Tuesday civil servants of various ministries (the Ministries of Foreign Affairs, Economic Affairs, Finance and Agriculture being regularly represented, others according to the interests of the respective offices) meet under the chairmanship of the Ministry of Economic

Affairs (usually at working level i.e. the experts of the desks concerned) to work out the orders for the Permanent Representation in Brussels. According to the list of relevant subjects, the ministry which is responsible for a certain problem area, submits its position first, which is quite often already coordinated with the other ministries directly involved. In case different perceptions within one ministry continue to exist when the meeting is over, the responsible officials are asked to formulate a common line by means of direct contact and inform the Ministry of Economic Affairs again to transmit the German position to Brussels.

In addition to these weekly discussions, regular consultations on the level of Heads of Departments (and Deputies) are held to define German positions for each General Council meeting. In summarising the different levels of European policy-making in the Federal government, one should not however forget the various informal groupings of civil servants coordinating their views whenever demands are made. The form of discussions varies from telephone calls to fixed appointments and comprises the level of experts, heads of desks or departments according to a given subject.

In order to guarantee a broad interministerial flow of information about what is going on in the Community primarily for those who are outside the normal EC machinery, one civil servant in each ministry, usually at the rank of Deputy or Head of Department, is responsible for informing his colleagues within the ministry about European policies. Again the Ministry of Economic Affairs, and especially its EC department, functions as central agency in charge of distributing documents and relevant information to this European official (**Europabeauftragter**). From time to time (about every three months), they meet to have a general discussion on the main European questions.

The <u>Permanent Representation</u> in Brussels is fully integrated in this coordination process. Its personnel consists of diplomats and civil servants from the Ministry of Foreign Affairs (the present Permanent Representative is, as were all his predecessors, a career diplomat appointed by a Cabinet decision) and from the Ministry of Economic Affairs (the deputy of the mission always comes from this ministry - at present, a civil servant who has been doing the job for many years) and other ministries. They have constant contacts with Bonn. They report to the capital, give advice, accompany their ministers in the Council meetings and push the implementation of decisions. They are relied upon to a large degree.

This administrative structure and the behavioural patterns stemming from it have proved to be useful for the broad information of all concerned, for a thorough and careful analysis of proposals as well as for internal compromises; however, it is quite often too burdensome for forward-looking strategies, for flexible adaptations and for guaranteeing consistent policy. **(8)**. It reflects however major features of the administrative and political decision-making in Bonn.

2. In the case of European Political Co-operation (EPC)
The EPC apparatus within the Federal government is centralised in the two political departments within the Ministry of Foreign Affairs. Desk

200, responsible for European Integration and Political Co-operation; Council of Europe, non-governmental European organisations; WEU - non-military affairs - within the Political Department 2, can be described as the 'heart' and the coordinating committee for daily EPC work. It is responsible for COREU and interministerial distribution of Telex information. Usually the Desk comprises five diplomats, the head being the Political Correspondent. In the second half of 1982, one of the group assisted the Danish Presidency according to the troika model. He returned to Bonn for the following six months and then left for Athens to join the Greek EPC staff.

German participants in nearly all of the present 14 EPC working groups are either the heads of the respective (mainly regional oriented) desks within Political Department 2 (covering the countries of the Atlantic Alliance and the others of northern, southern and eastern Europe, the UN and questions of disarmament and arms control) and Political Department 3 (dealing with the countries of the Middle East, Africa, Latin America and Asia).

Communication between experts and the EPC Desk is well organised, which is not always true as far as co-operation between the Political and the Economic Department (Dep. 4) is concerned in cases where EPC issues touch EC responsibilities or overlap (Tindemans report, question of sanctions, Solemn Declaration). Some argue that such inter-departmental rivalries among the EC departments on one side and the EPC department on the other are not out of the ordinary as long as EPC and EC questions are handled in separate circles from the working level (desks) to the administrative top (State Secretaries). When different perceptions clash and both departments feel responsible for the same problem areas, especially in more comprehensive and global projects like the Tindemans report and the Genscher/Colombo initiative, it is said that the question has to be settled. Co-operation then takes place either on the basis of formal bureaucratic structures and/or in an informal way. Others who have been the 'Community Europeans' among German civil servants for years may fear an undermining of their competences and think little about EPC policy. The follow-up of the Genscher-Colombo initiative clearly reflected the daily bureaucratic struggle within the Ministry of Foreign Affairs. From the very beginning officials of the Political Department 2 of the Ministry of Foreign Affairs claimed to represent the Federal Republic in the coming consultation process with the other EC partners. Pressure from the EC department however led to the German proposal of building an **ad hoc** group of the Ten comprising two civil servants from each country: in the case of the Federal Republic, the personal deputy of the Foreign Minister (the Head of Department 2 (Political Director)) and the Head of sub-department 41 (economic section of the Ministry of Foreign Affairs, being responsible for EC issues).

Representation in the Political Committee is ensured by the Head of Political Department 2, the Political Director. He has direct access to the Foreign Minister.

EPC from the very beginning was and still is the domain of the Minister of Foreign Affairs. Neither Chancellor Brandt, nor Schmidt, nor currently Kohl have claimed to play a major permanent role in it. Their interest in international affairs has mainly focussed on issues outside EPC policy (**Ostpolitik**; international economic and monetary questions; security policy). To the extent that questions relevant to EPC arise (e.g. 'fireside chats' of the European Council) **(9)**, the Head of government takes the advice of the Ministry of Foreign Affairs. Both sides confirm that bureaucratic struggles in this respect do not exist. On the contrary, the staff of the foreign policy desks of the Chancellery is composed of civil servants from the Ministry of Foreign Affairs and leading civil servants of the foreign policy advisory staff of the Chancellor have been closely involved in EPC before they assumed the job in the Chancellery.

As far as the meetings of the Cabinet are concerned - under Schmidt each Wednesday, under Kohl flexible dates - EPC policy was on the agenda in the sense that when discussion focussed on international developments (usually reported by the Foreign Minister), the Ten's consultations and positions were referred to. In general, the Cabinet has no major impact either on the contents or on the procedures of EPC outlined by the Ministry of Foreign Affairs.

The Committee of State Secretaries for European Affairs makes no reference to questions relevant to Political Co-operation. The dossiers prepared by the EPC staff are neither on the agendas of this group nor on those of the levels below. In cases where topics relevant to Political Co-operation are planned to be discussed by the Foreign Ministers during their luncheons or on the fringes of Council meetings, the procedure is as follows: those within the administration who are charged with preparing the national dossiers related to EC questions (see above) only receive the information that the ministerial meeting will also deal with EPC. They, however, are not told what the contents of discussions and the German position will be.

Aimed primarily at coordinating the foreign policies of the EC Member States, EPC work is done in the national capital. Formalised coordination mechanisms between Bonn and the Permanent Representation in Brussels, which are used in the case of Community policies therefore do not exist in EPC. To the extent that meetings of the Ten touch EC responsibilities (sanctions), direct contact on an **ad hoc** basis is however sought from both sides, the members of the Permanent Representation and EPC officials. In these cases, the results of EPC consultations are directly transmitted to the Permanent Representation in Brussels.

One could raise the question whether only **ex-post** information is sufficient to make Europe's voice heard in world affairs or whether closer coordination on the national level at an earlier stage would be more appropriate. Some argue that the presence of Commission representatives, both at the ministerial and at directorial level and below, guarantees that EEC related aspects are taken into account in the Ten's consultations. Besides, the European Council and the Foreign Ministers themselves have brought about the interrelations between the EC and EPC matters. On the administrative level however the way of thinking in clear-cut divisions of responsibilities still prevails, with shortcomings in the flow of information and coordination of positions.

THE FUNCTIONING OF THE GERMAN PRESIDENCY

1. German Presidencies in their historical environment

The three German Presidencies since the first enlargement (1974, 1978, 1983) have all had their individual internal and external characteristics. All three were claimed to be relatively successful by German officials.

During the 1974 Presidency, Schmidt replaced Brandt and Genscher replaced Scheel. At the same time, Giscard d'Estaing was elected in France. These changes reduced the political field of manoeuvre.

In relation to Community policies, the Copenhagen crisis Summit of December 1973 was not successful in solving the major economic and energy problems; it even intensified the internal conflicts on the Regional Fund and on the next steps to be taken for the Economic and Monetary Union. Reactions, both slow and lacking coherence, vis-à-vis the energy crisis and Kissinger's 'Year of Europe' had left the Community in a weak position. The German government, engaged in overcoming the internal political changes, could only prepare dossiers for what were to become the decisions of the Paris Summit during the French Presidency of 1974. A new French-German understanding, this time developed by two former Finance Ministers, paved the way for the Paris package. The struggle about the concessions in relation to the Regional Fund (10) demonstrated some of the inherent weaknesses in the German procedures.

The German Presidency of 1974 is still known for two measures for strengthening the internal coherence of EPC; they are the holding of informal meetings of the Foreign Ministers and the improvement of contacts with the outside world. The 'Gymnich formula', as agreed by the Nine during their first informal meeting in Gymnich (a castle near Bonn), opened up a way of informing allied partners, especially the USA, on EPC matters. From the German Presidency 1974 onward, informal discussions of the Foreign Ministers (also called Gymnich-type meetings) became a permanent tradition.

The 1978 Presidency took place at the climax of the Schmidt/Genscher coalition. The Presidency was carefully planned by the administrative machinery and accompanied by political priorities set up before by Foreign Minister Genscher. Major areas of interest and occupation of the EC were enlargement and the negotiations with the Lomé countries; within EPC, relations with Africa were given priority (11).

The German Presidency was however dominated by the creation of the European Monetary System, which was not planned ahead of time by the Community machinery within the German bureaucracy, but by Schmidt and his closest advisors, especially Schulmann (12), who played the decisive roles together with their French counterparts leading up to the Brussels meeting of the European Council in December 1978. The creation of the EMS demonstrated the necessity for a combination of personnel engagement at the highest political level, flexible methods, and the normal Community procedures.

Equally important for the German Chancellor and closely related to his Community role was the Bonn Summit (of July 1978) of the seven western countries, which settled an economic package ('Locomotive theory') (13).

The Presidency in 1983 took place in a clearly deteriorated environment (14). The economic situation - also for the Federal Republic - had increased the problems of unemployment, lack of economic growth and competitiveness. The Community was directly affected by the different economic conceptions among the Member States on how to deal with these problems because they had led to increasing internal and external protectionism among other things. The 'home made' problems of the Community - especially the closely linked budgetary and agricultural issues - were approaching a situation in which solutions were needed and could no longer be postponed. In 1978, the German Presidency was in a better position to choose from among different areas of activities, whereas the 1983 Presidency had to be much more reactive to pressing needs.

As far as EC questions were concerned the 1983 Presidency was also atypical with regard to the procedure. The preparation on the working level from spring 1982 onwards was followed by hardly any setting of political priorities as the change of government in autumn and the subsequent election campaign up to March 1983 withdrew political attention from EC affairs (e.g. some meetings with EP committees had to be chaired by state secretaries). Although the new Kohl/Genscher government then gave European policies high priority, delays in the preparatory phase as well as during the first months of the German Presidency were visible due to the fact that some of the new political personnel needed more time to get accustomed to the Community procedures - time which was scarce as a result of the recently-held election and the formation of the new government. The ambitious programme of managing some of the key problems and strengthening the process of European integration needed intensive treatment, which was again made more difficult due to the British elections. Looking back however, one has to admit that the postponement of the Stuttgart Council finally led to a useful additional delay. The days before the meeting of the European Council in Stuttgart were characterised by the high engagement of the political leaders (e.g. the intense personal engagement of Genscher for the Genscher/Colombo initiative) and civil servants. The German proposal for a package based on a mission by State Secretary Lautenschlager (responsible for the Community, - Department 4 - within the Ministry of Foreign Affairs), and Kohl's negotiation skill during the discussions in Stuttgart finally helped towards reaching agreement at least on further procedures (the Stuttgart mandate) and on the Solemn Declaration.

2. The Presidency of 1983 and Community Policies
a) Management Functions

For the management of the Council business, the existing structure and the experiences with the last Presidencies were fully used (many actors were serving at least their second Presidency, though perhaps in different functions) . No major change was planned or installed.

In Bonn the existing personnel force was only marginally enlarged. Neither in the Ministry of Foreign Affairs nor in the other ministries were additional personnel employed (except for one civil servant in the EC department of the Ministry of Foreign Affairs, whose task was a mere technical-organisational one, i.e. collecting dossiers for the minister). The increased workload was absorbed by intensifying the work of the civil servants involved in Community affairs. The argument was the same everywhere: additional personnel do not really help us, as we spend more time acquainting new colleagues with the complex Community machinery instead of reducing our work load. As far as the pure administrative and technical work was concerned, no new personnel were needed either; the burden of these tasks was placed on the Council Secretariat and on the Permanent Representation in Brussels.

The logistical infrastructure of the Permanent Representation in Brussels was increased. Additional telephone lines and for the first time a tele-copying machine were installed. To guarantee a fast flow of information, daily couriers from Brussels to Bonn again proved to be indispensable. Within the Council Secretariat, one additional office (for typing) and a copy machine were at the disposal of the Presidency. Twelve teams of interpreters from the Commission services, which were eventually enlarged by two, were available.

Concerning the reinforcement of the diplomats and experts of other ministries working in the Permanent Representation, this staff grew by about 15 per cent, i.e. each division was enlarged by one or two civil servants delegated from the ministries in Bonn. Their work in Brussels practically coincided with the beginning of the EC chairmanship and they returned to Bonn after six months. Due to the need for a certain period of adjustment, proposals have been made that in future the stay of this additional personnel be extended to nine months, two before and one after the Presidency.

In addition to these structural adjustments, two coordinators already experienced in Community affairs (members of the Permanent Representation) were installed as in the preceding German Presidency. They had different tasks to fulfil. They were responsible for the internal coordination of discussions on the various levels of working groups and the flow of information to and from the Committee of the Permanent Representatives (Coreper - Part I and II). They coordinated top-level discussions of the General Council, Economic and Financial Council, and European Council. In addition they were the contact persons of the Presidency towards EC Member States, Commission, etc., in cases where meetings were chaired by officials coming from Bonn and thus not being permanently present in Brussels. If necessary, the coordinators were able to deputise at meetings on the working level in cases where the chairman was engaged in other meetings.

In relation to the timing, there were no shortcomings reported, for example like the one in 1978 when the Permanent Representative was supposed to be at three meetings at the same time. However, the purely physical and psychological stress on all involved was reported to have been reaching its limits. This might have been partly due to the broad programme of the German Presidency, partly to the rather late engagement of the political top (after the March elections) and partly to the self-proclaimed goals and external expectations.

The list of chairmen for about 150 permanent working groups was also established well in advance. On this list the name of the chairman, the spokesman of the German delegation and, in case both came from Bonn, a person responsible in the Permanent Mission (contact person) was named. The chairmen were instructed by letter from the Permanent Representation on their functions. About the performance of the chairmen, slightly differing evaluations seem to exist. In Bonn, the experience of the German civil servants in their subject matter and Community procedures was considered to be sufficient guarantee for adequate performances as chairmen, whereas Brussels would have liked to see more instruction for the chairmen in the procedure, so that all possibilities on the working group level could be exploited to the optimal degree. According to representatives of the Permanent Representation, some problems arose and led to discussions at the level of the Permanent Representatives at an inopportune time because of the lack of experience of German civil servants from Bonn. It was said that some guidelines and information at an early stage (before the Presidency) would have been useful. This leads to the general question of whether it is better to chair from Brussels or from the respective capital.

In terms of organising the numerous meetings (dates, rooms, etc.), close co-operation between the Permanent Representation and the respective services of the Council Secretariat ensured that there were no major problems. As far as the meetings of the European Council were concerned, the technical-organisational planning worked well. Besides the institutions mentioned above, the Ministry of Foreign Affairs in Bonn played a major role in organising the Stuttgart Summit. Besides 'Org.-200', the organisational unit created to run the German EPC Presidency (see point 3 below), the Protocol Department of the Ministry of Foreign Affairs was responsible for selecting the menus, the presents handed over by the Presidency to the participants in the European Council and for the reception of guests. In preparation for the Summit, the Chancellor himself visited Stuttgart to see where the Heads of State and government of the EC Member States would meet.

The programmatic work of the Presidency began nine months before the start of the Presidency by collecting the items and priorities for the German term-in-office. This work, called 'Operation Squirrel', took place in Brussels in contact with the Council Secretariat and the Commission as well as in Bonn in the network among the ministries. A long shopping list was set up, which served as agenda for all Council and expert meetings. Despite the fact that not all problems or the urgency of certain problems (like the Seveso scandal or the acid rain issue during the German Presidency) could be foreseen, other areas (like harmonisation and the internal market or the budget) would automatically be put on the agenda and would be of such a nature that they could be planned efficiently beforehand; besides a list of problems as complete as possible can always serve for contingency planning. The list of possible agenda points was then discussed in meetings of the Council Presidency with the Secretary General of the Council and with the Commission; the regular meetings of all responsible politicians and civil servants with their counterparts in other Community countries proved to be indispensable. At the end of 1982, four priorities were listed in the programme speech by Foreign Minister Genscher to the European Parliament (15). The priorities did not however serve as a straitjacket or as the ingredients for the global strategy of the Presidency. Nearly all officials involved developed some specific ambitions and tried to push their subject through the Council's channels. The programme set up during the preparatory period of 1982 was constantly revised due to new developments, especially tasks set by the European Council in Copenhagen in late 1982 and in Brussels in March 1983. A constant reappraisal procedure and regular progress report had been installed by State Minister Dohnanyi, then chairman of the Committee of State Secretaries, for the 1978 Presidency. This useful exercise was not repeated in the 1983 Presidency, partly due to the other political tasks of the State Minister in charge and partly due to another personal working style. Besides this comprehensive approach, individual civil servants had already started to prepare their programmatic work well before the Presidency.

The Permanent Mission was the key agency for the daily business. They worked in close contact with the Council Secretariat and with the Commission. In addition to normal business, there were weekly meetings between the Permanent Representative and the President of the Commission or his Chef de cabinet. Besides regular exchanges of views one should not forget to mention the various informal discussions on all levels of Community decision-making during the German Presidency. German officials in Brussels laid stress on the usefulness of contacting EC officials and members of the nine governments outside the Council or Working Group meetings. Being present not only to chair the meetings is said to have helped the respective President-in-Office to pave the way for reaching a consensus.

The normal working rhythm of the Permanent Representation was adjusted to the needs of running the Presidency. In the beginning the agendas of all meetings planned in the next days was discussed every Monday, later once a month. On the basis of reports submitted by the Ministry of Economic Affairs to the Permanent Representation, after having reached consensus in Bonn among the ministries involved in a given subject and including the statements of the Council Secretariat (so-called 'scenarios'), the final positions of the President-in-Office were defined in Brussels. According to the German officials there, the scenarios of the Council Secretariat proved to be of utmost importance in running the Presidency due to the expert knowledge and long-term familiarity of its staff with Community policies and the decision-making process in EC affairs. The role of the Secretary General, Mr N. Ersbøll, in developing certain strategies to promote European policies, was welcomed by the German Presidency. This more prominent and political role for the Secretary General of the Council had already been suggested by German politicians, especially Dohnanyi before the nomination of Mr Ersbøll.

A major problem to be managed was the timing of the six-months period which needed consideration at least one year before the Presidency, even though the dates had only to be presented seven months before. The calendar had to take into account different kinds of events such as:

- all regular monthly Council meetings (General Council, EcoFin-Council, Agricultural Council), the European Council meetings as well as the meetings of the Foreign Ministers in the framework of EPC;
- all other special Councils, including the informal ministerial meetings;
- international conferences (NATO, OECD, UN General Assembly, Western summitry);
- EC contacts with third countries on ministerial level (concerning enlargement, Association and Co-operation Councils);
- plenary sessions of the European Parliament;
- national holidays and regular Cabinet meetings in the Member States.

Due to the fact that Council meetings need careful preparation on the level of the Permanent Representatives (Part I and II) and the working groups, their calendars had to be taken into consideration at an early stage too.

- Coreper II (Permanent Representatives) usually met on Thursdays and Coreper I (Deputy Permanent Representatives) on Wednesdays, except in those weeks in which meetings of the General Council and the European Council were foreseen, then the Permanent Representatives and their Deputies met the other way around. This change was recommended by the Council Secretariat in order to win additional time to prepare the meetings of the political top.
- Simultaneous meetings of Coreper I and II should be the exception to the rule, at least during the first half of the presidential term, in order to secure participation of the Deputy Permanent Representative at the luncheons of Coreper II and to enable him to chair the German delegation in the meetings of the Permanent Representatives. According to the extent that consultations within both groups intensify - and this normally is the case during the second half of a Presidency - a person's physical strength reaches its limit, thus preventing the Deputy Permanent Representative from playing his role as spokesman any longer.

b) The Promotion of Political Initiatives

The German Presidency actively promoted initiatives in different ways and in several areas:

A global initiative was launched well in advance. The Genscher-Colombo plan for a European Act had already been developed two years before the German Presidency (cf. Foreign Minister Genscher's speech on behalf of his party's congress in 1981, traditionally held on 6 January each year). Although it was originally not intended to be part of the German Presidency, it soon became a realistic scenario that the German plan could reach its decisive phase during the German Presidency. With the promotion of this initiative, the German government wanted to underline that the Presidency means more than a management role, that it also includes conceptual guidance to open new ways for the integration process (16). In spite of many frustrations, Genscher spent considerable time and energy in achieving his goal before the Stuttgart European Council. Chancellor Kohl also contributed to the passing of the Solemn Declaration, especially by using his negotiating skill at the meeting in Stuttgart.

The German Presidency has also set priorities and enlarged the agenda of the Council (17). It introduced a Council on the Internal Market (which the French apparently want to abolish) and realised some points of the internal market programme set by the European Council in Copenhagen in December 1982. One of the four priority areas was declared to be the consolidation and stabilisation of the internal market (intense personal engagement of the Economics Minister, Lambsdorf). Some successes were achieved. The extraordinary number of seventeen directives were passed; the German Presidency pressed for the reform of the Social Fund (which was successful) and of the Regional Fund (which was not achieved).

By the reform of the Social Fund and by some declarations on vocational training, the German Presidency tried to fight youth unemployment, which the German government had also declared to be a priority area. It put the acid rain issue and other environmental questions on the agenda. The German Presidency also pressed the debate on technological questions. Two other priority areas were the southern enlargement and the solution of the budgetary problems. Both became part of the last-minute visits to the capitals by the State Secretary in the Ministry of Foreign Affairs, Lautenschlager, to prepare a package for the Stuttgart European Council. This initiative can also be seen as part of the brokerage function.

In institutional/procedural terms, the German Presidency initiated closer contacts with the European Parliament, especially consulting on the Genscher/Colombo initiative, by participating in emergency debates, by reporting about problems on the agenda of the Council and by letting a delegation of the EP participate in international conferences (CSCE, UNCTAD VI).

In general, the German Presidency tried to push forward a broad range of subjects. At the same time it downgraded certain areas like the second phase of the European Monetary System (which was actually a German creation) and the Middle East policy.

c) The German Presidency as a Package-Broker

The German Presidency fulfilled the role as package-broker and mediator in different ways and in several areas.

At the beginning of the German Presidency internal crisis management was necessary in the fishery policies. Genscher played a direct and personal part in mediating between different positions in March 1982. Crisis management was also necessary at the dramatic changes of parities in the EMS. In this matter the German Presidency was not only a mediator but a major party to the conflict. According to some observers, the conflict was settled partly due to the fact that the German Presidency was both a neutral operator as well as a major contributor to the package.

A major role as package-broker was played in preparing the Stuttgart package (Lautenschlager's **tour des capitales**). Again the German government was not only a neutral arbitrator, but a major partner to this dispute. Contrary to the assumption in Helen Wallace's paper that a strong vested interest might hurt the package-broker role, our argument is different, especially as the German government had a carrot (or stick) in the form of the financial resources in its hands. The power for setting a locomotive into motion to integrate diverging interests was stronger. Apparently there was no complaint that Kohl in Stuttgart or German representatives of other ministries misused the Presidency to pursue only their own national interests.

A mixture of initiative and brokerage function was performed for the Solemn Declaration. The strong interest by Genscher and at the same time the necessity to mediate led to **asterixes** expressing dissent - a procedure which was used for the first time for such an important document.

As mentioned in Helen Wallace's paper, the package-broker function also has a strong function inside a country's political system. In the case of the Federal government, the self-obligation of the German Presidency to achieve a European step forward, which was reinforced by the election campaign, played a major role in coming to a kind of internal, yet weak, consensus that the VAT might be increased if certain preconditions were met. Without the approaching Stuttgart Council which was supposed to conclude the German Presidency successfully, the Ministry of Foreign Affairs would have had less chance to move the Finance Ministry to this concession.

This internal dissent, which could only be overcome at the end of the Presidency, also explains the fact, perhaps not exclusively, that there was no advance political strategy as a package-broker. For observers the major elements of the Stuttgart Mandate had already been tabled for a long time and could thus be constituent parts of a constructive strategy right from the beginning of the Presidency. Such a strategy would however have presupposed a Presidency which would act in a consistent and planned way. Even without the election campaign it seems doubtful that the German government could have achieved this kind of package as goal of their strategy before the Presidency. This assessment does not imply that before the Presidency started no serious considerations were given to what should and could be achieved (see the part on the management and initiative function), but it puts up for debate whether the attempts to draw different areas together into a package deal in which the German offer would induce respective concessions from other countries were started rather late. This pattern of behaviour of not indicating possible concessions too early, so that they do not become accomplished facts too soon in the negotiations, is normal in the Community. However it makes life difficult for each Presidency.

Three levels of the political and administrative system were apparently needed both for the initiative as well as for the brokerage function:

-       the political top: Schmidt (in the case of the EMS), Genscher and Kohl for both the Solemn Declaration and the Stuttgart Mandate,

- a high-level civil servant who has the confidence of the political top and could deal permanently with the subject: Schulmann in the case of the EMS, Lautenschlager in the case of the Stuttgart Mandate,
- the normal bureaucratic machinery, both in Brussels and in the national capital, which prepares and implements decisions.

The necessary political leadership must be exercised both **vis-à-vis** the Community partner as well as **vis-à-vis** internal opponents. The role as Presidency might have helped Schmidt against the German Central Bank, Genscher against some of his colleagues within the Federal government.

d) Liaison with other Community Bodies

Besides the normal relationship with the Council Secretariat and the Commission described in the part on the management functions, the German Presidency paid special effort to establishing close links with the European Parliament.

For the first time ever, the German Presidency was present at each session of the European Parliament (EP) for two days. Chancellor Kohl visited the European Parliament twice. Again for the first time, there were two meetings between Council and the Bureau of the EP. Presidents of specific councils participated in plenary sessions of the EP eight times. Also the State Minister attended the security debate of the EP (13 January) and the human rights debate (17 May). He was also present at the EP-ACP meeting in Kingston and at the conference with Latin American Parliamentarians in Brussels. Three consultation procedures between Council and Parliament were concluded successfully.

As far as representation of the Presidency at meetings of EP committees was concerned, parliamentarians to a certain extent complained about the presence of state secretaries instead of ministers. Especially in the beginning of the Presidential term they had expected the political top to come and inform them about the priorities set for the next six months. Being fully engaged in the election campaign at home however, and being responsible for several parliamentary committees, a minister was not capable of fulfilling all these obligations at the same time. Thus the Parliamentary State Secretary, as his deputy, took over some of the work-load.

Four meetings took place jointly with the Presidents of the EP and the Commission. The President of the EP visited Bonn and Berlin before the Stuttgart European Council. Support was given by forty German embassies to delegations of the EP in third countries.

e) Contacts with Third Countries

Spectacular initiatives were not undertaken by the Community or by the Ten during the German Presidency, partly due to time problems, partly due to a lack of challenges (no major new crises, no start of Lomé negotiations etc.). The German Presidency presented Community views at the spring meeting of the OECD, at UNCTAD VI and twice to the

ASEAN countries and in preparing the Lomé III negotiations.

In bilateral talks with the US President and in his participation at the Western Summit in Williamsburg, Chancellor Kohl referred many times to his role as chairman of the European Council and to Community positions.

3. The Presidency of 1983 and European Political Co-operation (EPC) (18)

a) Management Functions

The Presidency in the EPC shows features clearly different from that of the EC, especially in the field of intellectual and organisational challenges (19). The differences are caused not only by the absence of institutions like the Council Secretariat and the Commission (which plays a different role in the EPC), but by the different nature of EPC issues and activities as well.

Contrary to the management of EC matters, EPC lacks a bureaucratic apparatus of its own. The country taking over the Presidency has therefore to install technical staff to organise all meetings taking place in the capital and to enlarge the group of national diplomats to prepare EPC consultations at all levels, to keep contacts with third countries and the European Parliament. In the preparation of the Presidency (about four months before), Desk 200 was reinforced by two top-level civil servants, one being predominantly occupied within the Solemn Declaration, the other holding intraministerial coordinating functions. Additional personnel (two civil servants) supported them in the daily EPC work. Besides this, two secretaries with an excellent knowledge of English and French were recruited. By the end of June 1983 all the additional staff was disbanded. As envisaged by the London Report of October 1981, the German Presidency was supported by diplomats of the preceding and succeeding Presidency. Those Danish and Greek diplomats (one of each country) left Bonn at the end of June after having assisted the staff of Desk 200 in their own office in the Ministry of Foreign Affairs with the daily EPC-work (rotating presence in all working groups, help in drafting reports and conclusions of the meetings). Notwithstanding some shortcomings, like problems with the German language, the troika formula proved of help to the Presidency.

In addition to Desk 200, a unit named 'Org. (Organisational Unit) 200' was established during the German Presidency (as in 1978) which was responsible for technical work (preparation of conference rooms and delegations' offices, luncheons, writing utensils, information booklets, etc.). It comprised eight people from the staff of the Ministry of Foreign Affairs (various levels), working from 1 September 1982 to 30 June 1983. This preparatory phase of four months was said to be long enough to make all the provisions necessary. Whereas the organisation of the working group meetings and those of the Political Committee and of the **ad hoc** group (Solemn Declaration) and the arrangements for consultations with third countries held in Bonn soon proved to be a routine job, the preparation of the ministerial meetings and that of the European Council in Stuttgart needed more attention. Although financed

91

by the Presidential budget of the Org. 200, decisions about menus, drinks, reception, etc. of these top-level discussions were in the end taken by the Protocol (Department 7) of the Ministry of Foreign Affairs. For all other EPC meetings, the Head of Org. 200 was responsible for choosing the luncheons, buffets, etc. One should not underestimate these organisational provisions of the Presidency because, as many EPC diplomats confirm, the atmosphere of meetings, including the meals, are of great importance for productive consultations.

As in 1978, the Palais Schaumburg, the former seat of the Federal Chancellery, served as conference building for the meetings of the Working Groups and those of the Political Directors. The Foreign Ministers held their discussions in the large conference room at the present Chancellery, which has enough room for the interpreters. Luncheon and buffet were again prepared at the Palais Schaumburg.

Contrary to the normal procedure, the consultations of the Presidency with the Political Affairs Committee of the European Parliament (twice in six months) were not held in the capital. It proved useful to let these conferences take place in Brussels in the framework of Genscher's endeavour to inform the parliamentarians about the Solemn Declaration. This meant a certain reduction of the organisational work load for the EPC staff in Bonn: two meetings (usually comprising more than 50 participants) which belong to the normal calendar of the Presidency dropped out of the list. According to budgetary calculations, about one million German marks were thought to be necessary for organising EPC meetings in the capital (not including the European Council in Stuttgart). In the end a quarter of the total amount of money was saved.

From January to June 1983 the Foreign Ministers met twice, in Bonn and in Gymnich (informal), to discuss EPC issues. Another meeting, planned to take place on the fringe of the Council meeting in Luxembourg, was cancelled due to the management of EC policies and the Solemn Declaration. Besides these meetings reserved exclusively for EPC questions during the German Presidency, no General Council meeting ended without touching on Political Co-operation. Is this an expression of growing EC/EPC interrelations or of the weight attributed to EPC in comparison to Community policies by the Foreign Minister?

On the level of Political Directors, seven sessions were held in Bonn, one more than usual. The frequency of working groups differed according to the subject (see Table 4.1).

Full participation of the Commission in the meetings was guaranteed. This also included the working luncheons of the Foreign Ministers and the Political Committee (20). Concerning the troika formula applied among others systems by the Ten in contacting third countries, the German Presidency launched the initiative of inviting officials of the Commission to attend these meetings.

Closer contacts than ever before were established with the European Parliament during the German Presidency. As far as EPC issues were concerned, one civil servant of Desk 200 was fully engaged in preparing the statements and answers to parliamentary questions. The various contacts of the Presidency with MEPs increased the awareness of German officials concerning the positions of the European Parliament on international developments. Direct dialogue related to the EP was intensified. Besides the normal procedure of two meetings of the Political Affairs Committee and the President-in-Office, the monthly question time and the programme speeches, the Presidency attended the debate on security policy (January), human rights (May) and held various consultations at different levels on the Genscher-Colombo Plan. The German Presidency also tried to draw the Ten's attention more frequently to the positions of the European Parliament. The real impact however seems to have remained marginal due to shortcomings in timing the discussion of questions relevant to Political Co-operation in the EP and to different conceptions among the EC Member States about the effective role of the EP in EPC.

Table 4.1

Working group	Number of meetings
United Nations	4
UN Disarmament	2
Non-proliferation	2
CSCE	2
Eastern Europe	4
Middle East	6
Mediterranean	-
Africa	3
Latin America	3
Asia	3
European Coordination Group for the Euro-Arab Dialog (EAD)	3
Protocol	1
Law of the Sea	1
Communications	3
Planning Staff	1

b) The Promotion of Political Initiatives (21)
Besides the respective chapters of the Solemn Declaration (more cohesion between EC and EPC; new element of political and economic aspects of security), Bonn intended to play an initiating function in intensifying the dialogue between the Ten and Washington on international developments (especially in the CSCE conference in Madrid and on the Middle East). Later priority was given to the whole range of

East-West relations (the strong personal endeavor of Genscher particularly in the CSCE framework in the Spanish capital) and to closer co-operation with Latin America.

Due to international developments, the situation in Lebanon, the Iran-Iraq War and Central America were all put on the agenda (as well as on those of the European Councils in Brussels and Stuttgart) together with other subjects which had been of interest to the Ten for years (e.g. South Africa, United Nations). In comparison to the Belgians one year before, the German Presidency was not confronted with new major international crises.

As in former Presidencies, the Federal Republic laid stress on strengthening the internal coherency of the Ten's consultations and on improving the external performance of EPC policies:

- for the first time the Heads of the Planning Staffs of the Ten met in Bonn to elaborate on longer-term perspectives of EPC activities;
- the Ten agreed to intensify co-operation in third countries to show an increasingly European profile as well as better technical-organisational coordination among the diplomatic missions of the Ten (e.g. health services);
- the Presidency was given some room to manoeuvre in answering the questions of Members of the European Parliament. In order to lessen the workload to a certain extent, the Presidency is now free to formulate the definite answers, after having consulted its partners via COREU on what are foreseen as the prime elements of the text.

As far as contacts with third countries are concerned, during the first half of 1983 consultations increased considerably both on the working level as well as at the political top.

- Under the chairmanship of Foreign Minister Genscher (troika formula), consultations were held with Japan for the first time. The Ten later responded favourably to the wish of the People's Republic of China at directorial level and in June the Political Director of the Ministry of Foreign Affairs had an exchange of views with the Chinese Ambassador accredited to Bonn. Again at directorial level the President-in-Office together with his Danish (preceding) and Greek (succeeding) colleagues held discussions with some members of the Council of Europe (i.e. the eleven non-EEC Members).
- The German Presidency declared relations with the United States to be of vital importance. Regular and close contacts had already existed between EPC officials in Bonn and the American Embassy, there and at the United Nations in New York. The same was true for consultations at ministerial level (German Presidency - Secretary of State and other high ranking personnel). Initiatives to formalise these contacts according to the troika system on directorial and ministerial level met with strong reservations in the EPC club. In the end, and in continuation of the procedure installed during the second half of 1982, the President-in-Office (Political

Director), together with the Danish and Greek representatives, met Assistant Secretary Burt to discuss international developments of mutual interest (e.g. Middle East; CSCE). Another meeting envisaged at ministerial level during the German Presidency failed however due to constraints in the calendar of the US Secretary of State.

c) The Presidency as a Compromise Broker

One characteristic of German EPC membership has been and still is that of holding even-handed positions, allowing shifts to one side or the other whenever a common line of the Ten seems to be achievable. EPC officials in Bonn stress the advantage of claiming no national outsider positions when sitting in the chair. Being in the middle of the line enabled the German Presidency to function as a compromise broker and consensus builder especially in the discussions on Latin and Central America. To reduce the growing heterogeneity among the Ten, steps were undertaken to convince the Greek partner of the value of common declarations and actions. These German initiatives proved however to be of very limited success. Some may argue that progress towards a common line was not achievable due to the outsider role Athens wanted to play. Others may say that consensus would have been reached in one case or the other if the Germans had chaired the meetings more skillfully and presented formulas for approval at the right moment.

d) Contacts with Third Countries

In addition to the contacts mentioned above, which were held for the first time or to which Bonn paid special importance, numerous consultations of the President-in-Office alone and, increasingly according to the troika formula together with his colleagues of the preceding and succeeding Presidencies, were held with third countries as well as with representatives of international organisations (e.g. the Secretary General of the Arab League). The procedures chosen varied according to the different interests and needs for contacts between the Ten and the partner in question. They ranged from specific approaches of German Ambassadors to the host governments (e.g. on human rights issues in Africa), to a broader exchange of views on the Ten's positions regarding international developments. The list of countries interested in closer contacts contained neighbouring ones (e.g. Norway) as well as countries far away from Europe (e.g. New Zealand, Australia). Institutionalised arrangements of special importance to the Ten existed with Turkey, Spain and Portugal. During the German Presidency meetings took place at directorial level (once for each country). The procedure envisaged with the candidate countries, i.e. top-level meetings of the Foreign Ministers of the Ten with their Spanish and Portuguese colleagues once each Presidency, was changed to the troika formula during the first half of 1983.

Unlike his predecessors Foreign Minister Genscher showed no inclination to go on a fact-finding mission in the name of the Ten. No spectacular engagement on the international arena should take place according to German officials. Stress was laid on using informal diplomatic channels provoking neither unrealistic hopes about Europe's international weight on behalf of third countries nor excessive fears in the American Administration. This is why Foreign Minister Genscher declined to visit the Middle East although he would have been encouraged to do so by his colleagues.

SOME CONCLUSIONS

The German Presidencies demonstrated a high degree of administrative and political engagement. They prepared their work carefully and were ambitious in pushing forward the work of the Community. The internal structures and procedures were efficient to such an extent that they distributed the necessary information back and forth from Brussels to Bonn. A mutual feedback was guaranteed. All actors who were responsible for matters touching on the Community were involved in the decision-making. For a business-like Presidency (23), these procedures and behavioural patterns are certainly sufficient. For a Community faced with crucial problems and, in the case of the German Presidency, for a Member State which wanted to achieve real success by contributing towards solving the crisis, the political strategy was however insufficient.

The programme of the German Presidency enumerated the goals and objectives to be pursued. It however did not reflect how they should and could be achieved to the necessary degree. The instruments and procedures for an overall political strategy were not adequately developed in advance. Package deals and especially the German inputs were not planned early enough. Shortcomings in the political performance of the Presidency reflects a general feature of German policy-making for the Community, which is due to several interconnected factors:

- there is no medium-term concept for the Community. Between declaratory support for an undefined European Union on the one side and pragmatic day-to-day work on the other, Bonn has no defined global framework for its Community policies. There are certainly clear medium-term positions on many separate subjects, but no overall concept for the eighties. This can be explained by the fact among others that the German government is not really challenged by other Community governments or political forces to do so. Given an unpredictable situation, German politicians apparently prefer piece-meal engineering;
- the internal structures and procedures are not geared to set clear priorities and guarantee a consistent and coherent policy. The decision-making among different perspectives, viewpoints and positions is mainly based on horizontal self-coordination principles and can lead to a negative coordination (24). The consensus quite often reflects the balances among political forces;
- the German Community procedures might be better prepared for horizontally linked decision-making (among respective ministries on the Community level) than for vertical decision-making in the capital the results of which are then transmitted to Brussels.

This feature of the German decision-making structure is seen by many as a weakness as Bonn lacks the dynamic strategy which others expect. To reform this procedure it has quite often been proposed that a Ministry for European Affairs be installed either in the Chancellery or with a staff of its own. This has not been implemented and, because of political and bureaucratic opposition, for good reasons. Either this minister would become a super-minister dominating other ministries (such as the Economic or Finance Ministry and the Ministry of Foreign Affairs), then additional political fights could be expected which would not serve a rational and effective Community policy and which could be akin to the Bonn tradition, or this minister would be a coordinator who would, at best, replace or reinforce existing coordination mechanisms but could not overcome the lack of political guidance. At worst, this minister would again complicate the whole coordination procedure as he might duplicate existing mechanisms and stir up bureaucratic in-fighting.

This sceptical assessment of chances for procedural reforms does not imply that changes in the procedure might not be useful. For example, the European Departments and Desks in the Ministry of Foreign Affairs could be better coordinated or even integrated into a single unit; or experiences of civil servants familiar with Community affairs from different perspectives could be augmented and/or put to better use. In addition, in the Permanent Representation in Brussels, a constant nucleus for the EPC could be installed to improve the day-to-day contacts among the Ten, reduce the burden of the Presidency and bring EPC and Community policies closer together thus strengthening Europe's international role (25).

Any overall political strategy will not be established by internal reforms but by external challenges. The task of a Presidency might help to create an initiative, but it will be not sufficient.

This assessment of some of the insuffiencies of the German internal structure is based on the assumption that the Federal government would act as such in a coherent and consistent way. It might however be argued that the present Community system needs more horizontal links reflecting the interdependencies of the European economies. Too strong a national position might lead to blockages inside the country and within the Community. The existing open system in which coalitions are partly built across frontiers, might be more effective for problem-solving in the Community. Such a system would however increase the burden of the Presidency as it would have to juggle on many internal and external levels at the same time. The German Presidency in 1983 might thus be a clear indicator of both the frameworks in which Presidencies have to work and the potential and limits which Presidencies are facing.

The German Presidency within the EC framework has shown that former administrative experiences can be adequately used to improve performance, especially as far as the management function contacts with other Community bodies and with third countries are concerned. Although the overall role of the Presidency in the Community framework looks perhaps rather defined (26) and fixed by various internal and external data, the German Presidency made some new marks. Some main actors of the Presidency, working in the fields of Community channels for a long time, came up with additional ideas and activities to get the machinery working more efficiently. There is apparently still room to improve the work of the Presidency in Brussels and in national capitals without major structural changes.

The experiences with the EPC Presidency also demonstrates that there is still some space for procedural developments, especially in the fields of planning and contacts with third countries. The trial-and-error process can and should be pursued.

Limits are however set by personal capacities. The Permanent Representative, the Political Director and the Political Correspondent as well as the Foreign Minister are being overloaded by the different functions they have to pursue which include an ever-increasing agenda of problems and intensified contacts with the European Parliament and with third countries. The German Presidency indicates this trend is still growing.

This constant increase of formal responsibilities might be detrimental to a more political role of the Presidency i.e. to develop substantial initiatives and political packages to keep the EC alive.

REFERENCES

(1)   See Press and Information Office of the Federal government, press material prepared for the European Council in Stuttgart, 17-19 June 1983.

(2)   See Elisabeth Noelle-Neumann/Gerhard Herdegen, Die Europäische Gemeinschaft in der öffentlichen Meinung: Informationsdefizite und enttäuschte Erwartungen, in: Integration, 3/83, Bonn, pp. 95-105.

(3)   See Reinhardt Rummel/ Wolfgang Wessels, Federal Republic of Germany: New responsibilities, old constraints, in: Christopher Hill (ed.), National Foreign Policies and European Political Co-operation, George Allen & Unwin, London 1983, pp. 34-55.

(4)   See for this term, Wolfgang Wessels, Community bureaucracy at crossroads? In: Wolfgang Wessels (ed.) The Community bureaucracy, proceedings of a Colloquium by the College of Europe in Bruges (to be published in 1984).

(5)   In the Ministry of Foreign Affairs, however, the following position formulated by a high civil servant seemed to have prevailed: Our partners do not want to be led by the Germans - even if it is the way to paradise.

(6)   The basic literature on this part is still Christoph Sasse, Regierungen, Parlamente, Ministerrat - Entscheidungsprozesse in der Europäischen Gemeinschaft, Bonn, 1975, p. 25. Published in English, as governments, Parliaments, and the Council of Ministers in Christoph Sasse et al., Decision Making in the European Community, Praeger, New York 1977.

(7)   See Hans-Peter Schwarz, Die Bundesregierung und die auswärtigen Beziehungen, in: Hans-Peter Schwarz (ed.), Handbuch der deutschen Aussenpolitik, München 1975, pp. 43-111.

(8)   One of the last moves of the German government in the Community framework - the Dohnanyi compromise in the Council on 30 May 1980 - was heavily criticised within the Federal government for having been an uncoordinated step.

(9)   See Wolfgang Wessels, Der Europäische Rat: Stabilisierung statt Integration? Geschichte, Entwicklung und Zukunft der EG-Gipfelkonferenzen, Europa-Union Verlag, Bonn 1980, pp. 69-74.

(10)   See for a report on this, Sasse, op. cit., pp. 36-39.

(11)   See Geoffrey Edwards, Helen Wallace, Die Präsidentschaft im Ministerrat: Eine zentrale Rolle im Entscheidungsprozess von EG und EPZ, Europa-Union Verlag, Bonn 1978, pp. 104-119.

(12)   See for this process Peter Ludlow, The Making of the European Monetary System, Butterworths, London 1982.

(13)   See Cesare Merlini (ed.), Economic Summits and Western Decision-Making, Croom Helm, London 1984.

(14)   See also Werner Ungerer, Europa-Politik unter deutscher Präsidentschaft, in: Aussenpolitik, 34. Jahrgang, 1/1983, pp. 4 - 11.

(15)   Cf. programme speech of Foreign Minister Genscher as President-in-Office to the European Parliament on Jan. 11, 1983, in: Press and Information Office of the Federal government, Bulletin No. 4, 13.1.1983

(16)   See Werner Ungerer, Europa-Politik, op. cit.

(17)   A broad overview on the list of priorities and the results of the German Presidency is given by: Werner Ungerer, Deutsche EG-Präsidentschaft im Rückblick, in: Aussenpolitik, 34. Jahrgang, 4/1983, pp. 332 - 347.

(18)   An excellent overview on EPC in general and on what happened during the German EPC Presidency was recently given by the German Political Director: Franz Pfeffer, Europa ist weiter, als viele annehmen, in: Frankfurter Allgemeine Zeitung, 24.8.1983, p. 7.

(19)   Cf. the remarks by the deputy Head of the EPC desk within the Ministry of Foreign Affairs in Bonn, Klaus-Peter Klaiber, during the Colloquium on 'The impact of European affairs on national administration - the case of the Presidency', 17/18.11.1983, Kerkrade (Castle Erenstein). Proceedings published as EIPA-Working Document 84/01.

(20)   according to Franz Pfeffer, op. cit.

(21)   Cf. the programme speech of Foreign Minister Genscher op. cit. (note 12).

(22)   This formula was used by one participant during the Colloquium on 'The impact of European affairs on national administrations - the case of the Presidency', 17/18.11.1983, Kerkrade (Castle Erenstein).

(23)   See the characterisation of the 1978 German Presidency by Edwards/Wallace, op. cit., pp. 104-119.

(24)   See Renate Mayntz, Fritz W. Scharpf, Policy-Making in the German Bureaucracy, Amsterdam, Oxford, New York, 1975, p. 147.

(25)   See for this proposal Hermann da Fonseca-Wollheim, Zehn Jahre Europäische Politische Zusammenarbeit (EPZ) in: Integration, Bonn 2/81, pp. 47-66.

(26)   See report by Helen Wallace in this volume.

Chapter 5

THE PRESIDENCY OF THE COUNCIL OF MINISTERS OF THE
EUROPEAN COMMUNITIES: NATIONAL PAPER ON GREECE
Mr Panos Tsakaloyannis, Athens

GREECE'S FIRST TERM IN THE PRESIDENCY OF THE EC:
A PRELIMINARY ASSESSMENT

Introduction:
Greece's assumption of the Presidency of the Council of Ministers of the
EC, in July 1983, aroused considerable interest and some commotion
both in Athens and in other Community capitals. Its limited experience
in Community affairs, its defective administrative machinery and varied
political and cultural traditions and, even more crucially, its
government's unsettled position regarding Greece's membership augured
a difficult debut.

It is true that the Greek government's initial reservations
concerning membership had been somewhat revised. Likewise, submission
of the Memorandum at the beginning of 1982 in which Greece called for
special treatment and certain exemptions from the Community, and the
latter's positive response helped to improve relations so that by the time
Greece assumed the Presidency a **modus operandi** had been reached.

Yet areas of uncertainty still remain. Even today there are
differing views within the government concerning Greece's future in the
Community. Furthermore, within the governing party there is a sizeable
anti-EC wing whose real strength is difficult to gauge, but whose
position the government cannot afford to ignore, at least not until a
satisfactory solution is reached in the negotiations of Greece's
Memorandum which are currently under way. In the meantime and during
Greece's Presidency, the present Greek government has had to steer a
very narrow political course between appeasing the Scylla of the anti-
marketeers at home and the Charybdis of appearing 'communautaire'
enough to get on with the task of the Presidency.

This, in conjunction with the fact that its Presidency had to be
conducted in the public glare, thanks to the sensationalism of most
Greek newspapers, did not help to create the ideal atmosphere for the
occasion. Consequently, any comments made in the other EC capitals
concerning Greece's effectiveness as President, however trivial, were
blown up beyond proportion and treated by the press as concerted moves
by outsiders to rob Greece of its inalienable right to take full control of
the Presidency (1). The above remarks are necessary to put Greece's

Presidency in its political context. One should hasten to add however that despite these political constraints, or perhaps thanks to them, the Greek government made a praiseworthy effort to organise the country's administrative machinery for a very difficult first Presidency. Greek pride, but also the government's sincere determination that any residual reservations it had had concerning Greek membership should not have spilled-over into administrative matters, were instrumental in provoking a strenuous response to prepare the country for the task.

GENERAL REMARKS CONCERNING THE GREEK PRESIDENCY

Expectations of a country's performance in the Presidency are pinned among other things on commitment to the EC, its domestic political and social conditions, its international economic and political standing, the quality of its civil service and also on its own and the other countries' perceptions concerning its influence in Community affairs (2). To give an example, the expectations of the German Presidency in the first half of 1983 were high because on all the above points Bonn scores high marks (3).

On the other hand Greece is in the unenviable (or could it be envious?) position of being flanked by the Community's two most influential and powerful countries, the Federal Republic of Germany and France, which also happen to share a special relationship between themselves within the Community. Furthermore, the administrative machineries of these two countries are renowned for their high standards and efficiency. Measured against these, Greece is a small and poor country with only a peripheral role in European affairs, uncertain of her world orientation, and burdened with a civil service in need of a profound shake up.

Greece's term in the Presidency was not devoid of some positive effects as the proximity of West Germany and France may have helped to cushion some of the structural weaknesses of Greece's term in the chair. This, of course, was more evident in EPC where the institution-alisation of the troika system leaves more room for a concerted Presidency. Similarly, the fact that the Greek administrative machinery had to measure itself against those of Germany or France and that it had to co-operate with Bonn and Paris on Community business prior to, during and after Greece's Presidency may have provided a stimulus for its improvement.

Another aspect of the Greek Presidency is its timing. Not only did it coincide with a time of uncertainty in relations between Athens and Brussels, but it also occurred during one of the most critical periods of the Community's own history, with some of its problems, such as future financing, Britain's budget contribution and enlargement, having reached breaking points. The range and complexity of the problems involved would have been taxing for the most experienced and qualified member, let alone Greece (4). The fact that the workload during Greece's Presidency could not have been satisfactorily carried out within an effective four and a half months in the chair (if one excludes summer holidays and Christmas breaks) was recognised in the Stuttgart European

Council meeting. There the Ten agreed to set in motion an emergency procedure whereby special Council sessions of Foreign, Finance and Agriculture Ministers were to be held once a month to try to solve the Community's financial difficulties. This was an extraordinary event in the Community's history (5). It was against this background that Greece had to prepare her administration for the task in hand.

PREPARATIONS FOR THE PRESIDENCY

The structure of the Greek EC machinery was reorganised by the present government soon after its advent to power in October 1981. In doing so, its objectives were to improve the coordination of the various ministries concerned, reorganise the Greek Permanent Representation to prepare the Greek administraton for the upcoming Presidency in the second half of 1983. Overall responsibility for coordinating Community affairs rests with the Ministry of Foreign Affairs, whose role as a filter of Community affairs has been strengthened under the present arrangement. Ultimate responsibility rests with the Foreign Minister but in practice the latter is in charge only of Political Co-operation whereas all 'technical' aspects, that is those which come under the provisions of the Treaties, are under the effective control of a Deputy Foreign Minister, a man with twenty years of experience in Community affairs, who is head of the Department of European Communities.

The Department of European Communities is divided into two sections, one in charge of finance, aid and other related economic issues, and the other responsible for administrative, political and institutional issues. The first consists of a pool of about forty experts mainly in Community and international trade issues; it is headed by a Special Adviser (6), who is a trained economist and it is not subdivided into smaller teams. During the Greek Presidency this section played an important role in assisting to define, together with other ministries, Greek priorities but otherwise its role in the actual running of the Presidency has been residual. This section dates back to the time of the Greek accession and it has continued to function after the Greek Presidency.

This was not so for the other section, an ad hoc department formed chiefly to meet the needs of the Greek Presidency. It was headed by another Special Adviser and subdivided into five groups with the following functions:

Group A: By far the most important and the largest with a team of five senior officials, most of them special advisers, and a supporting staff of fifteen, plus two secretaries. It was responsible for the organisation, preparation and the coordination of the Greek Presidency as well as for protocol.
Group B: Dealt with the institutional aspects of the Community. It had a staff of five.
Group C: Was responsible for the European Parliament, its functions being to carry out the preparatory work for the Foreign Minister when he addressed the EP or in answering oral questions. It also observed the

debates and developments in the EP and briefed Greek MEPs, if they so wished, on the government's position on major issues. This also had a staff of five.

Group D: Provided legal support and it had a team of ten legal experts.

Press Section: With one journalist in charge.

PREPARATIONS BEFORE THE PRESIDENCY

The second section of the Department of European Communities in the Ministry of Foreign Affairs, is better known as the Office for the Greek Presidency, and was set up in February 1982. Some problems which it faced demanded immediate attention. The most pressing was to find a suitable venue to host the Council meetings, the meetings of the Political Committee and in particular the European Council meeting. After consultations with the Council Secretariat, the main exhibition building of 'Zappeion' situated within the National Park in central Athens was singled out in August 1982 as the most appropriate place for this purpose. However this building was in need of extensive renovation in order to be made suitable for the occasion. A feasibility study was therefore undertaken under the auspices of the Ministry of Public Works in the autumn of 1982, and in March 1983 hectic construction, installation and renovation work began. The building was completed only days before 1 July and it cost about 4 million ECU's. Incidentally, this problem, which was a novel one, also preoccupied the Council's Secretariat, as one of its duties is to make sure that the necessary arrangements are made and basic facilities are available in the presiding country for the hosting of the European Council meeting (7).

Another major task of the section was to make up the list of Greek chairmen of the various working groups of the Council during the Greek Presidency. The compilation of this list was a product of the joint efforts of all the ministries concerned, but the Office for the Presidency coordinated the whole operation. At first however, the Office for the Presidency, after consultations with the Council and the Commission, had to decide the business calendar during the Greek Presidency. The agenda of the German Presidency and the mandate adopted at the Stuttgart European Council meeting provided the basic guidelines for the business in hand in the second half of 1983. Then there were new Commission proposals coming to the Council as well as working groups which had been inactive for some time, some of which the Greek side was keen to reactivate (8). In short, the task of the Presidency organisers in the Ministry of Foreign Affairs was first to make a list of all those working groups which were to be held during the Greek Presidency and then, in co-operation with the other Ministries, to define Greek priorities and objectives. Once the list of committee and working group meetings to be held in the second half of 1983 was finalised, the next step was to select the Greek chairmen. This required the co-operation of the various government departments. To simplify things the Presidency organisers asked each ministry to appoint a liaison between themselves and the Ministry of Foreign Affairs. In this way, direct contacts between the various ministries on organisational problems were secured. It also saved the organisers from having to trace individuals whose province covered a particular problem in the various ministries.

Another priority was to allocate the chairmanships of the working groups among the various government departments and decide which of them were to exercise their duties from the Permanent Representation in Brussels. Whether a chairman was to be based in Athens or in Brussels (Permanent Representation) was decided mainly on the volume of work of each working group. Those committees or working groups which were to meet at frequent intervals were accredited to the Permanent Representation, as the long distance between Athens and Brussels made it impracticable for the chairmen to operate from Athens. This factor determined to some extent the strength of the Greek Permanent Representation which, as we shall see below, assumed important tasks during Greece's Presidency.

Finally, the Presidency Office was also responsible for the training and briefing of the presidents of the Council committees and working groups and for contacts with the Secretariats of the Council of Ministers and the Commission, as well as for contacts with other governments. For instance, twenty prospective chairmen of working groups were sent to the European Institute of Public Administration in Maastricht (NL) for training in April 1983 and another twenty attended a one-week practical training course in the Commission. Some training was also done in the Ministry of Foreign Affairs and other ministries, notably in the Ministry of Agriculture.

INTERMINISTERIAL COORDINATION

As stated above, the Presidency Office in the Ministry of Foreign Affairs played the role of coordinator with other government departments on organisational matters before the Presidency, a function which it retained also during the Greek Presidency. Through the liaison personnel of the other ministries, it coordinated the day-to-day running. It also had a small office in Brussels through which it oversaw the organisational affairs of the Permanent Representation. The Presidency Office in Athens received the diplomatic bag from the Permanent Representation every day and then it distributed it to the other Ministries. For the coordination of more substantial issues there is an Interministerial Committee chaired by the Ministry of Foreign Affairs's Under-Secretary of State for Community Affairs. Its other members were the Heads of the Economic and the Political-Institutional Sections of the same Ministry, two Economic Advisers of the Prime Minister plus the Heads for Community aspects of the Ministries of National Economy, Finance, Agriculture and Trade. Representatives of other departments could also attend when necessary. It convened fortnightly although it had no fixed day. The authority of its chairman, plus the fact that all its members were political appointees of the governing party, helped to mitigate interministerial squabbling. On the other hand, the absence of civil servants in its midst had its negative aspects, some of which will be discussed at the end of this paper.

Differences not settled by the Interministerial Committee were referred to the Government Council (KYSYM). The latter convened once a week or fortnightly, although again there was no fixed day. Apart from the Prime Minister, who was its chairman, other members were the Ministers of National Economy, Finance, Interior, Public Works, Press and Information and the Prime Minister's Chief Economic Adviser, who also acted as Secretary. At a first glance it is obvious that KYSYM's composition was not ideal for settling outstanding differences concerning Community policy. For instance, key ministers such as the Foreign Minister or the Minister of Agriculture, were excluded from it. This meant that the Ministers of National Economy and Finance had a privileged position to influence the Prime Minister, who was the ultimate arbitrator. It should be noted however that the cases referred to the KYSYM were few, as most problems were settled in the Interministerial Committee.

Nevertheless, the arrangement was not completely sound, not only because key ministers engaged in Community business were not represented in KYSYM, but also because most of its members were not renowned for their pro-Community sympathies. There were considerable tensions in Greece between Community and national objectives, so KYSYM's role as umpire may have had an inhibiting effect on those ministers, such as the Minister of Agriculture or the Under-Secretary of State in the Ministry of Foreign Affairs, who made herculean efforts for a successful Presidency, as their endeavours may have been seen as excessive devotion to Brussels (9).

PREPARATIONS INSIDE THE MINISTRIES

Preparations for the Presidency inside the ministries varied considerably. One reason for this lack of uniformity was that some ministries, like Agriculture or the Ministry of Foreign Affairs had to shoulder a heavier burden than others, therefore force of circumstances, if nothing else, compelled them to act swiftly. However, apart from that, the depth and quality of preparatory work varied from ministry to ministry according to the predelictions and competence of the minister in charge and to a lesser extent to the traditions and the administrative standards of each ministry. Without doubt, the government's ambiguous stance **vis-à-vis** the EC, until the European Council meeting in Stuttgart, did not help planning at ministerial level. A 'free for all' situation pervaded whereby each minister responded to the task according to his own convictions regarding the EC and Greece's place in it. This explains to a large extent the apparent contrasts in official attitudes in the various ministries, some of which the present researcher had the opportunity to observe in the course of preparing this report.

In any case, apart from the Ministry of Foreign Affairs whose structure and role as interministerial coordinator in the Presidency have already been noted, the next one in importance was that of Agriculture, not only because it had to carry a heavy burden of duties, but also because its internal arrangements and procedures for coping with the challenge of the Presidency became a model for other ministries. Therefore a description of this ministry's Presidency arrangements and procedures before and during the Presidency can provide a useful illustration of the situation in other ministries, bearing in mind however that standards varied considerably and the fact that adjustments were made in each ministry to take account of particular needs.

The Ministry of Agriculture is one of the largest ministries in terms of personnel and one of the busiest. During the Presidency it was responsible for about one-third of the Community's committees and working groups. Under the previous government most Community business was handled by the ministry's Community section set up in 1980. At its peak it employed fifty experts plus secretarial staff. Similar departments existed, and still exist, in other ministries such as Finance, National Economy, Trade Technology, etc. However the policy of the present government has been to trim the scope of functions in these departments and confine them to the role of coordinators of Community affairs, with technical aspects being handed over to other vertical departments. The thinking behind this change was that the previous overgrown Community departments of the ministries were somewhat detached from the other departments of their ministries. National positions, it was thought, could be more vigorously defended by vertical departments as they have a more intimate knowledge of the problems at hand. Also this handing over of technical Community aspects to other departments was to serve another purpose, namely to reduce red tape and duplication of work. As a result of these changes the number of officials employed in Community sections of the Ministry of Agriculture was halved, from fifty at the beginning of 1982, to twenty-five by July 1983. Similar cuts in personnel were made in other ministries, the most impressive of all being that of the Ministry of National Economy whose Community Affairs' section was clipped from over sixty to twelve officials during the same period (10).

It is hard to appraise at this stage the effects these cuts had on the country's performance as President of the Council. However, one thing is almost certain, namely that they had only marginal effects on the calibre of the persons selected to chair the various working groups.

For the needs of the Presidency an office was set up in most ministries in the autumn of 1982. The largest and most active was that of the Ministry of Agriculture with a permanent staff of five. This ministry also had a Secretariat for the Presidency, of two well-qualified officials, attached to the Agricultural Section of the Greek Permanent Representation. The tasks of the Presidency Secretariats, before the commencement of the Greek Presidency, were to hold consultations with Commission and Council officials in order to decide the agenda during Greece's term. Another task was to determine which of the working groups were under their ministry's jurisdiction and then find their chairmen from the various departments of their ministries. Also some Presidency offices assisted in the chairmen's briefing and training. Finally they were responsible for contacts with other ministries. During the Greek Presidency, the Presidency offices retained the same functions plus the day-to-day running of the Presidency business, such as receiving the Permanent Representation mail-bag from the Ministry of Foreign Affairs and distributing it within their own ministry, making travel arrangements to Brussels for the chairmen of the working groups, finding replacements in case of indisposition, etc.

On a higher level, the less administrative and more political aspects of the Presidency were handled by special committees for Community affairs set up in many ministries. Their composition, procedures and agenda varied considerably. Some of these special committees were **ad hoc** and only met at irregular intervals to discuss certain problems which needed attention or to brief the ministers of current developments. This, for instance, was the character of the special committee of the Ministry of Trade, which was answerable to an Under-Secretary of State. On the other hand, the special policy committee for EC questions of the Ministry of Agriculture had more fixed procedures. It was chaired by the head of the Community department of the ministry; its other members were three ministerial advisors plus three ministry officials. It met daily and its task was to give to the other departments general guidelines of the ministry's policies. It was answerable directly to the Minister of Agriculture. Finally, as a rule, the heads of these special policy committees deputise for their ministries in the Interministerial Committee which convenes every fortnight.

THE ROLE OF THE PERMANENT REPRESENTATION

The Greek government attached particular significance to its Permanent Representation for the running of the Presidency. The distance between Athens and Brussels and insufficient air links between the two capitals was conducive to strengthening the Greek team of experts in the Permanent Representation during the Presidency. In fact the problem of distance received a lot of attention from the planners of the Greek Presidency both in Athens and Brussels. It is an almost exclusively Greek problem as all the other EC capitals, except perhaps Rome and Dublin, are in close proximity to Brussels. Therefore a Greek representative has to spend three working days in order to attend a one-day business session in Brussels if he/she travels from Athens. This is an enormous amount of wasted time, especially for a small country whose number of experts on Community affairs is severely restricted. The problem is so acute that the idea of hiring an aeroplane to transport all the Greek staff to and from Brussels during the Presidency was even contemplated, but dropped as too expensive and not altogether practical.

Apart from distance, a second reason for giving the Permanent Representation an enhanced role in the running of the Presidency was that only the Greek Permanent Representation could supply a pool of well-qualified experts with first-hand knowledge of the Community's institutions who, at the same time, were familiar with Community procedures and the personalities involved. Thus the Greek Permanent Representation became the second centre for the planning, coordination and management of the Presidency, the first being the Office for the Presidency in the Ministry of Foreign Affairs, the two centres working in unison.

The Greek Permanent Representation could not however perform these added duties with the previous material and human resources or without a major reorganisation of its structure. These changes are of particular interest for the present study. To meet these needs the Permanent Representation's manpower was strengthened from 65 to just over 100 people during the Presidency with most of the newcomers being clerical and supporting staff such as secretaries, typists, chauffeurs, telephonists, clerks, etc.. To accommodate this extra staff an extra floor was rented in the building housing the Greek Permanent Representation. Also the necessary provisions were made in office and telecommunication equipment.

Perhaps of even greater importance were the organisational changes of the Greek Permanent Representation. These changes, although long overdue, might not have been introduced had it not been for the pressures imposed by the Presidency. Under the previous regime, all the Permanent Representation's personnel were directly answerable to its Head and Deputy Head. This arrangement, also known as the 'solar model', although of some merit, was nevertheless becoming difficult to operate as it imposed considerable strains on the two Heads of the Permanent Representation who had to devote their attention to every question. Before Greece joined the Community, when her EC mission in Brussels was smaller and its duties more limited, the 'solar model' could work without serious problems. However, when the number of experts swelled to about sixty-five after Greece's accession, and the workload increased enormously, it was impossible for this system to work effectively. Under the new system the Greek Permanent Representation has been divided into ten sections, each with its own divisional head. The strength and composition of each section varies, with some, such as Agriculture, forming a section of their own, whereas other sections have been formed by merging related subjects. Five of the sections are under the overall control of the Permanent Representative whereas the other five are answerable to the Deputy Permanent Representative. The head of each section coordinates and directs the work of his department and makes sure that its policies are in harmony with those of the other sections. Each month the heads of the ten sections submit a report on the activities and the progress made in subjects under their jurisdiction. They are also responsible for personnel matters and for promoting a spirit of co-operation among their colleagues. Finally to coordinate the activities of the ten sections, their heads meet twice a week to discuss technical and organisational problems. At a higher level more substantive issues are handled by a committee whose members are the Head of the Greek Permanent Representation, his two deputies and the Heads of the Finance, Agriculture and Secretariat/Administrative sections.

The Greek Permanent Representation played a dual role during the Presidency. Its first role has already been mentioned, namely that of assisting Athens. During the Presidency, close contacts were maintained between the Permanent Representation and Athens mainly by telex, telephone or mail, but also by exchanges of visits. For instance, the heads of the ten sections went to Athens once a month to brief their ministries on the progress or the problems of the Presidency. Also the Head of the Permanent Representation made numerous trips to Athens for consultations. Finally a system of liaison was implemented, whereby each Greek chairman serving the Permanent Representation had also to observe developments in other related subjects, whose chairmen were based in Athens and keep the latter informed. Also, when officials from Athens went to Brussels to chair working groups, they were briefed by their colleagues in the Permanent Representation.

The second role of the Permanent Representation was to maintain contacts with Community institutions. Apart from the institutionalised weekly meetings at ambassadorial level, their deputies' meeting and the meeting of the various working groups, consultations with the Council's Secretariat were of great importance in sorting out practical problems, such as the booking of Council rooms for committee and working group meetings, arranging interpreting facilities etc.. Responsibility for these contacts with the Council was given to the administrative section of the Greek Permanent Representation. Although most contacts with the Council's Secretariat during the Greek Presidency were routine, there were however some discretionary powers exercised by the presiding country which were not devoid of political importance. For instance, the seemingly routine job of booking rooms for committee and working group meetings, especially during busy periods, gave it considerable leeway in deciding which business should receive priority and which should be delayed. Also the acute shortage of Greek interpreters in the Council and the Commission allowed the Greek organisers some freedom in the same direction. For instance, some working groups had to be postponed or had to take low priority, because there was either no room available in the Council or no Greek interpreter.

Apart from the administrative section, the agricultural section of the Greek Permanent Representation had its own Presidency office with a staff of two highly-qualified officials. Apart from its contacts with the Council, this office was active in cultivating contacts with other governments. For instance in the spring of 1983 one of its officials went to Bonn for one week to see how the German Ministry of Agriculture was coping with the Presidency (11). Yet a third channel of contacts was maintained by the section in the Permanent Representation responsible for the European Parliament, whose two-man staff was empowered to observe debates in the EP and, during the Presidency, to be in charge of relations between the Council and the EP.

It is impossible to give a more detailed description here of the Permanent Representation's tasks during the Presidency. The two points to be borne in mind are that it carried more tasks than its counterparts and that the Presidency acted as a catalyst for its reorganisation. Although it coped with its duties admirably, it is however not devoid of structural problems or shortcomings, some of which will be discussed in the last part of this paper.

THE PRESIDENCY AND POLITICAL CO-OPERATION

Most of the misgivings expressed by some of Greece's EC partners about its Presidency-in-Office were related to the government's manifest views on a range of international issues, from the Middle East to disarmament talks or to relations with Eastern Europe, the Third World, etc.. Seen from the point of view of Greece's partners, the question is not whether Greece or any other Community member holds minority views on certain international issues, but whether these differences are discussed in a positive spirit among the Ten, with an effort being made to stand together even where uniformity of views is wanting. What is resented is using the EPC platform to advertise national positions or for domestic consumption. On the other hand the Greek government insisted that its views on international issues had been endorsed by the electorate and, therefore, it should not lean over backwards to accommodate its EC partners by abandoning pre-electoral pledges. In any case, Athens argued, solidarity in EPC should be a two-way traffic and the record of Greece's partners on some international problems of vital concern to the Greeks, notably Cyprus, was far from impressive, as was shown in their UN voting on Cyprus.

It should be stressed however that some of the earlier misgivings concerning Greece's handling of political co-operation during its Presidency were somewhat dispelled partly as a result of Athens' evolving views, and also partly because of changing international circumstances. For instance, the signing of the agreement with the US government in July 1983 over the American bases in Greece helped improve Greece's image in the Community just before she was due to assume the Presidency. Also on the Middle East, Greece kept a low profile during her term in the chair, partly because of the complexities of the region but also partly because of a gradual reassessment of this government's position on the region (12). On the other hand, Athens' intention to place Cyprus on the Council of Minister's and the European Council's agendas initially raised some eyebrows in other Community capitals but, considering the complexities of the problem and the fact that certain proposals for a settlement by the Secretary General of the UN were on the table, it did not become a major source of friction among the Ten. On the contrary, the unilateral declaration of an independent Turkish-Cypriot 'state' in the occupied part of the island by Rauf Denktash in November 1983 helped promote a remarkable degree of solidarity among the Ten.

The same cannot however be said about Greece's other initiative; in the September meeting of the Council of Ministers' session on political co-operation, Athens proposed a six-month postponement in the siting of Cruise and Pershing missiles in Western Europe should the Soviet Union and the United States fail to reach an agreement in the Geneva talks by the end of 1983 (13). Putting aside the merits of this proposal, the way this affair was handled by Athens was bound to cast a shadow over its handling of political co-operation and to reinforce misgivings in other EC capitals about Greece's observance of the basic procedural principles. For not only was the Greek initiative taken without proper consultations, but the wide publicity given to it by Athens, far from improving the chances of it being adopted in the September Council meeting, helped to embarrass other Community capitals already committed to the siting of these missiles.

To complicate things even further the Greek Foreign Minister to the annoyance of his partners, dug in his heels in the same meeting and refused to discuss, let alone endorse, a Community response to the shooting down of the South Korean jumbo jet by the Soviet Union. Domestic considerations and the government's idiosyncratic policies vis-à-vis the Soviet Union were the main reasons for this uncompromising stance. Yet that contributed to creating tensions between the presiding country and most of its partners and sadly, to largely undermining Athens' credentials as a detached manager of EPC.

The above overview is, I think, necessary before we proceed to discuss the management of EPC by Greece. Political co-operation is under the domain of the Foreign Minister himself but, as with the other Community countries, day-to-day duties are exercised by the Political Director and a Secretariat for EPC, headed by an ambassador. This Secretariat did not escape unscathed from the change of government in October 1981 and for some time it only had a shadowy existence. It was given new life in view of the Greek Presidency at the end of 1982 and currently it has a small diplomatic staff of six, excluding the General Director - very small indeed for the running of the Presidency if compared with a staff of twenty diplomats employed by the other countries when they are in the chair. The only way the EPC Secretariat could cope with such a small team, was by being flexible; its staff had no well-defined duties, but they were expected to cope with a multitude of problems, or as the Political Director put it, borrowing a soccer term, they should be prepared to play the position of 'libero' (14). Whether this could be managed, without impairing Greece's capacity to preside over EPC, the Political Director declined to comment.

Likewise the size of the diplomatic service, together with its outlook and traditions, quite likely affected Greece's performance as President of EPC. Since this subject has received more elaborate treatment elsewhere (15), we shall confine ourselves to some basic relevant points. For instance Greece had no diplomatic presence in most Third World countries and in others it had only token representation (16). Consequently, as arranged, her duties in the Presidency had to be exercised, in those countries where Greece was not represented, by France, in accordance with the provisions of the Luxembourg and Copenhagen Reports and more specifically in the 1981 London Report on Political Co-operation (17). This arrangement worked remarkably well. In the case of Chad, for instance, Greece let France, with her intimate knowledge of the region, coordinate the Ten's position and represent the Community in N'djamena, in the absence of a Greek embassy. An important fact for the success of this arrangement was the traditionally close and excellent relations between Athens and Paris. This may however not be the case when Spain joins the Community; then Madrid and not Paris will succeed Greece in the chair, for the rotation will be Ellas-Espana-France. This is not because relations between Greece and Spain are not amicable, far from it, as Greece's support for Spain's entry testifies, but diplomatic exchanges and communications between Athens and Madrid are not as prolific as those between Athens and Paris. Also, although Spain could effectively look after the Ten's interests in those Latin American capitals to which no Greek diplomatic missions are accredited, this may not be the case for sub-Saharan or South East Asian countries where Spain's own diplomatic presence is not significantly stronger than Greece's.

For similar reasons, Greece also faced some difficulties in the chairing of certain working groups of EPC. Twelve of them were active during Greece's Presidency and they included those on Africa, Asia and Latin America. Finally the diplomatic representation of the Ten by Greece in some third countries, and above all in the United States, gave rise to some anxieties because of procedural complexities and the importance the Ten attach to their consultations with Washington. The fact that prior to and during Greece's term in the Presidency, there were persistent rumours of the resignation of the Greek Ambassador in Washington, did not help to quell these anxieties. However it should be emphasised that on the whole there were no serious mishaps; on the contrary the Greek diplomatic mission in Washington acted with exemplary swiftness in July 1983 in making representations to American officials on behalf of the Ten about America's protectionist measures.

GREEK EXPECTATIONS AND OBJECTIVES FOR THE PRESIDENCY

The complexity of the problems facing the Community, the shortness of time in the chair and Greece's limited resources and experience defined, to some extent, her expectations in the Presidency. At a bare minimum a smooth handling of the chair was, in itself, considered a success as it showed that, despite adverse conditions, the Greeks can do the job just as well as 'the Europeans'. Also the publicity received during those six months, especially at the European Council jamboree in Athens, and its enhanced international standing while in the chair, boosted the country's standing at home and abroad. One did not expect any major initiatives, either institutional or on policy issues. Greece had too much work on its plate even to contemplate this. It would have been miraculous if a major break had been made on any of the long-standing problems, such as the future financing of the Community or Britain's budget contribution or on enlargement.

It is rather unfortunate that the worst fears of the Cassandras were fulfilled and the Greek Presidency may be remembered for the disastrous European Council meeting in Athens in December 1983. Of course it would be naive to lay the blame on the Greeks for this failure. It was inevitable that some mistakes would be made through lack of experience but no serious mishaps occurred in Athens. Perhaps the Athens debacle may prove a blessing in disguise as all sides realised afterwards the magnitude of the Community's problems and that more imaginative ideas and more good will are required from its partners if they want to avoid a total collapse.

A disturbing aspect emerging from the Athens story was the fact that small members seem to offer a more convenient ground for the Community's battles to be fought out. The larger members particularly appear to have fewer problems in creating drama when Copenhagen, Dublin or Athens are in the chair than when Bonn, London or Paris are in charge. Of course these cases are too few to justify a complaint but should this pattern continue in the future it could be harmful to the Ten's cohesion. Of course the way the host country stages a European Council meeting is important for its success or failure, but its role should not be overstated. Generally thorough planning and the skill of the host Prime Minister are decisive for its success (18). Another important prerequisite for its success is the degree of rapport between the host Prime Minister and his nine counterparts. Finally, attention has been drawn in some recent literature to the language factor for a successful Presidency. As the only languages in the meetings of the Ten Heads of State and government are English and French, a Prime Minister who does not speak at least one of them with ease could be severely handicapped in his role as chairman (19). In the case of Greece however Papandreou's impeccable command of both was a bonus to his chairmanship.

Finally a few words about the handling of the setback of the Athens meeting by the Greek Prime Minister, its chairman. This is, I think, important as abortive European Council meetings are becoming more frequent and their management may prove more difficult for the Presidency than successful or routine meetings. After the Athens meeting had broken off, Papandreou as chairman briefed the reporters about the Ten's failure and he painted a bleak picture about the Community's future. Furthermore he refused to release to the Press the customary statement of the Ten on international and other wider issues which had been prepared by the Political Directors of the Foreign Ministries. This in itself was an unusual step for the practice of the past ten years (since the inception of the European Council meetings) has always been to issue such a statement regardless of the outcome of the meetings on domestic economic and trade issues.

Papandreou's action was no doubt partly motivated by party considerations, especially the forthcoming elections to the European Parliament (20). It was also in line with his government's attitude **vis-à-vis** the Community which lays more emphasis on bread-and-butter issues and less on international issues and political initiatives. It was also somewhat unexpected as the statement of the Ten on political and international questions unequivocally condemned the creation of an independent 'state' in Northern Cyprus. Nonetheless Papandreou's action was totally justified in the circumstances. For shock treatment may, in the long run, prove more therapeutic than keeping to the Community's rituals and releasing statements on a wide range of international subjects upon which the Ten lacked both the means and the will to act.

The economic priorities and strategies pursued by the Greek government during its Presidency were at some variance with those of its predecessor. This is hardly surprising given the fact that the economies of the two countries represent the two extremes of the Ten. Likewise different economic philosophies between Bonn and Athens, to some extent, determined their priorities. Hence Athens supported calls for an increased Community budget. It also promoted Community programmes of interest to Greece, such as current schemes for improving Mediterranean agriculture or youth employment schemes. Obviously closer to its heart was the Greek Memorandum on which Athens expected substantial progress while in the chair, at least on a technical level. However it recognised that the term in the Presidency was too short a time for spectacular successes, especially as the workload was so heavy.

Equally Athens strove to make the most of its term-in-office in domestic political terms, yet the best way of achieving this was hardly to wave the Presidency flag in international fora. Such cases as Athens' mishandled initiative on disarmament, or Papandreou's suggestion to speak on the Ten's behalf at a UN special meeting on the same subject, were also undoubtedly motivated by domestic considerations. However initiatives of this kind can certainly be what Geoffrey Edwards and Helen Wallace call 'a double-edged weapon' for the country in the chair 'since biased chairmanship is likely to provoke the active resentment of other governments' (21). This is particularly so if these initiatives are on extremely sensitive and domestically divisive issues, such as the siting of missiles in Western Europe. Likewise, ill-prepared initiatives of this kind may, no doubt, undermine the credibility of the country in the chair, especially of a small country like Greece. For as the Political Director of another small EC country, Denmark, aptly put it recently, the bigger members may sometimes use their economic and political weight as a substitute for quality but this option is not open to smaller countries (22). Consequently much of Greece's Presidency depended on how realistic her priorities and objectives were and whether enough preparatory background work had been done to ensure success.

CONCLUDING REMARKS

As this study was started prior to the completion of the first Greek Presidency, it can only provide general outlines of its organisational arrangements. The preliminary nature of this analysis has also put some constraints on its presentation. For instance, the Permanent Representation's role has been described at great length, whereas some other aspects of the Greek Presidency have only been touched upon. For example, the financial burden incurred in the running of the Presidency received scant attention, the reason being that the financial aspect seemed to be of little concern to those officials interviewed, not because they considered it to be negligible but because they were more engrossed, at the time the interviews were conducted, in more pressing problems. This however does not imply that the financial aspect was not a concern of the Greek Exchequer, far from it. Its precise cost, however, was only known after the completion of the Presidency. In the final estimate two kinds of expenses figured prominently. One was that of Zappeion and the other was for the running of the Permanent Representation.

A second important aspect of the Greek Presidency, not sufficiently mentioned, was the linguistic problem. Its immensity can hardly be overstated. All ministries interviewed mentioned it as one of the most worrying problems they encountered during the six months. This problem seemed to be more acute in so-called 'technical' ministries, such as Agriculture or Trade than in the Ministry of Foreign Affairs. Yet even in the Permanent Representation quite a few Greek nationals confided in the present writer their concern about the linguistic difficulties. The linguistic problem became so worrying in some ministries, such as Agriculture, in the preparatory stage of the Presidency that written requests were lodged with the Ministry of Foreign Affairs to press the Council to employ more Greek interpreters. Also many Greek officials responded wearily to the Council's suggestions that the reason for the Council's inadequate facilities had simply been that there were not enough qualified Greek nationals to fill vacancies.

A third feature, worthy of mention here, concerns the people involved in the running of the Greek Presidency. As pointed out above, in most departments, with the exception of Political Co-operation, the organisational and coordinating tasks of the Presidency were assigned to political appointees with little participation from civil servants. Of course this does not mean that the civil service was excluded. This would have been impossible and absurd anyway. It means, however, that its involvement was largely confined to an auxiliary role. Evidently their absence from the planning and coordinating of the Presidency must be regretted, because it did not help in the storing and tapping of the experience gained from it. On the contrary, little of what was learnt during Greece's first term-in-office will have been preserved by the time she is called upon again. It is a long time in any country's politics, let alone Greece's, to believe that in five or six years, if Spain and Portugal have joined by then, the same people will be called on again. Of course the Presidency Office in the Ministry of Foreign Affairs says that it intends to prepare a lengthy report on all the organisational aspects and the expenses incurred during those six months to be used by those who will have to do the job next time 'if Greece is still in the Community' **(23)**. This is by no means an ideal way of ensuring continuity.

This is only one example of how divergent Greece's structures and administrative practices can be from those of her partners. Another example, which illustrates even better the Greek civil service's subordinate position **vis-à-vis** the political masters - and this by no means applies to the present ones only - is the Permanent Representation which, despite the admirable organisational effort to cope with the task, is not free from these constraints. For example the absence of fixed tenure for its personnel, combined with enormous salary differentials between working in Athens and Brussels, gives rise to harmful political wheeling and dealing in order to prolong postings. The harmful effects of this situation need not be spelled out.

In brief, a better understanding of the relationship between the organisational aspects of the Greek Presidency and its decision-making procedures is unfortunately somewhat elusive at this stage. Perhaps some of the misgivings of Greece's partners prior to her assumption of the Presidency, while ill-founded may have arisen from an instinctive knowledge that Greece's means of problem-solving are less well-defined and are more idiosyncratic than those of her partners. What is certain, however, is that if her problems are not resolved not only Greece's future Presidencies but her ability to adjust to the Community's needs will be deficient.

NOTES AND REFERENCES

(1) For instance the Greek Prime Minister, at a Press Conference on 3rd May 1983, answering a question on persistant rumours of a contingency Community plan to overstep the Greek Presidency by putting it under the guidance of Bonn, answered that in such a hypothetical situation Greece 'would not be a party to such a plan but she would withdraw from the Community the very same day. Within twenty-four hours we would be outside the Community'. The same warning was given by the Greek government's spokesman ten days later. Elefterotypia, 4 May 1983 and 14 May 1983.

(2) A note of caution is necessary here. The criteria mentioned refer to perceptions, others' and one's own, about the prerequisites of a successful Presidency not to the actual criteria for an effective Presidency, which are discussed at length by Geoffrey Edwards and Helen Wallace in 'The Council of Ministers of the European Community and the President-in-office' Federal Trust, London, 1977, pp 69-71.

(3) As a student of the German Presidency pointed out, the FRG's Presidency raised high hopes because Bonn carries particular weight within the Community as it has been an avid protagonist of European integration; also because of its growing international status and its economic and political weight within the Community in terms of population, GNP and foreign exchange reserves. Werner Ungerer, 'European Policy under the German Presidency' Aussen Politik, vol. 34, no. 1, 1983, pp 3-4.

(4) As the Stuttgart mandate states, 'in the course of the six months a major negotiation will take place to tackle the most pressing problems facing the Community so as to provide a solid basis for the further dynamic development of the Community over the remainder of the present decade'. Agence Europe, no. 3632.

(5) Interview with Mr Fabri, Secretariat of the Council, 27 July 1983.

(6) 'Special Advisers' are political appointees brought into the various Ministries by the present government. Almost all the key functionaries in charge of the Presidency in the Ministry of Foreign Affairs are Special Advisers.

(7) Interview with Mr Fabri, Brussels, 27 July 1983.

(8) For instance in the agricultural sphere, Greece was reluctant to move 15 working groups but after consultations with the Commission, only 8 of them were excluded. Interview in Athens.

(9) In this respect, see Geoffrey Edwards and Helen Wallace, op. cit. p. 74.

(10) Interviews in Athens.

(11) Interviews in the Ministry of Agriculture, Athens and in the Permanent Representation, Brussels.

(12) For Greece's attitudes to the Middle East since 1974 see the author's 'Greece and the Arab Israeli Conflict' in Alfred Pijpers and David Allen (eds) European Foreign Policy Making and the Arab Israeli Conflict, Martinus Nijhoff, The Hague, 1984.

(13) The Greek proposal was immediately turned down by West Germany, Britain, Italy, Belgium and the Netherlands; that is by most

countries concerned.

(14) Interviews in Athens.

(15) Panos Tsakaloyannis, 'Greece: Old Problems, New Prospects' in William Wallace and Christopher Hill (eds) National Perspectives on EPC, George Allen and Unwin, London, 1983 esp. pp 130-131.

(16) Out of a total of about seventy Greek embassies about ten of them are in Arab countries and about another twenty in other Third World countries, half of which are in black Africa and the rest in Latin America and Asia.

(17) For instance the London Report stipulates that 'should he wish to do so, the President may delegate certain tasks to his successor; he may also request his predecessor to finish tasks which are close to completion when the Presidency is handed over'. Report on European Political Co-operation (London, 13 October 1981) point 10, paragraph 4.

(18) The amount of literature on the European Council is prolific and it is growing fast. Some of the most recent expositions include Leo Tindemans, 'Le Conseil Européen', (European Yearbook, vol. XXVIII, 1980, Martinus Nijhoff, The Hague, 1982 pp 3-15); also Christopher Bo Bramsen, 'Le Conseil Européen: Son fonctionnement et ses résultats de 1975 à 1981', Revue du Marché Commun, no. 262, December 1982, pp 624-42.

(19) Leo Tindemans, Ibid. pp. 7-9; C. Bo Bramsen, Ibid. p. 641.

(20) In October 1983 Papandreou in an interview with one of Greece's largest dailies stated that his party's strategy in the elections to the EP in 1984 would be decided upon the outcome of the Greek Presidency and in particular on the results of the European Council meeting in December. See Ta Nea, 25 October, 1983.

(21) 'The Council of Ministers ...', op. cit. p. 39.

(22) J. Ørstrøm Møller, 'Danish EC Decision-Making: an Insider's View', Journal of Common Market Studies, vol. XXI, no. 3, 1983, p. 249.

(23) Interviews in the Greek Ministry of Foreign Affairs.

Chapter 6

LA PRÉSIDENCE DU CONSEIL DES MINISTRES DES COMMUNAUTÉS EUROPÉENNES: RAPPORT NATIONAL SUR LA FRANCE
M. Philippe Moreau Defarges, Paris

INTRODUCTION

Depuis le premier élargissement (1er janvier 1973), la France a assumé à deux reprises la présidence du Conseil des Communautés, lors du deuxième semestre 1974, puis lors du premier semestre 1979. La France a été à nouveau présidente du Conseil pour six mois au cours du premier semestre 1984.

A. La France et les Communautés

Les relations entre le système communautaire et l'organisation politico-administrative française s'expliquent fondamentalement par la conception qu'a cet Etat de la construction européenne. Pour la France, deux impératifs ne cessent d'être affirmés:

Veiller à l'unité et à la cohérence de la diplomatie française.

Si l'Europe constitue l'un des champs privilégiés de l'action extérieure, elle ne saurait être un but en soi; au contraire, elle demeure l'un des axes d'une démarche d'ensemble, fondée sur une ambition globale (indépendance et concert des puissances, sous le général de Gaulle; dynamisme technologique et industriel, sous le président Pompidou; mondialisme du président Giscard d'Estaing; enfin, socialisme et nouvel ordre mondial du président Mitterrand). Cette préoccupation d'unité, de préservation d'un style diplomatique original se traduit dans les structures bureaucratiques qui, au lieu de promouvoir un traitement autonome des affaires européennes, rappellent leur insertion dans des enjeux plus vastes, économiques, politiques ....

Assurer, également, l'unité de la politique européenne de la France, tant dans son élaboration que dans son exécution.

Du point de vue français - en particulier du fait de la très forte empreinte gaullienne présente jusque dans les réactions administratives quotidiennes -, les multiples aspects de la construction communautaire, l'importance des travaux d'harmonisation ou de codification, ⸱⸱la prolifération des groupes et comités incitent les administrations et leurs agents à mener leur propre politique européenne, à lancer des initiatives plus ou moins mûries, parfois contradictoires. De là, la mise sur pied de procédures et d'un appareil visant à contrôler les prises de position, les allées et venues des fonctionnaires.

B. La France et la présidence du Conseil des Communautés

Ce double souci détermine l'approche française - essentiellement politique - de la présidence du Conseil des Communautés. D'un côté, les six mois de présidence peuvent permettre de 'boucler' des négociations essentielles. Dans cette perspective, la présidence, matérialisant, symbolisant la Communauté en tant que personne dotée d'une identité internationale, est regardée comme l'instrument diplomatique par excellence de l'Europe unie. Tout comme le Conseil européen, créé en 1974, à l'initiative de la France, doit être un Exécutif politique, son président deviendrait une ébauche de chef d'Etat de l'Europe.

D'un autre côté, la brièveté de la durée de la présidence, l'ampleur de l'intervalle entre deux mandats, le rôle d'abord technique de la fonction selon les Traités, enfin l'expérience, ces données se résument dans un enseignement simple: '... la présidence (...) est une présidence qu'elle (la France) exerce dans l'intérêt de la Communauté tout entière, c'est-à-dire pour permettre la solution des problèmes importants qui se posent aujourd'hui dans la Communauté' (1). Cette conclusion du président de la République souligne à la fois le sens bien précis du travail de la présidence et le poids des contraintes qui limitent sa marge d'action.

Dans ces conditions, même si la France, lors des deux semestres où elle assume la présidence, présente des programmes-catalogues aux très nombreux objectifs, les implications concrètes de cette présidence, notamment dans le système politico-administratif, se révèlent plutôt modestes et limitées. Les structures administratives dont s'est dotée la France pour l'examen des affaires européennes, garantissent un équilibre subtil entre les ministères concernés (Affaires étrangères, Finances, départements techniques ...); tout aménagement substantiel de ce compromis perturberait l'ensemble des relations tant entre services qu'entre fonctionnaires (2). Les exigences de la présidence doivent donc être assumées dans le cadre du dispositif existant.

LE RÔLE ET L'INTERVENTION DU GOUVERNEMENT ET DU PARLEMENT

La quasi-totalité des affaires européennes et surtout communautaires sont traitées par le seul Exécutif. L'intervention du Parlement garde un caractère exceptionnel.

Du point de vue français, les affaires européennes soit appartiennent aux domaines techniques les plus ésotériques (travaux d'harmonisation), soit relèvent de la pure diplomatie (coopération politique, délibérations du Conseil européen). Dans ces conditions, le gouvernement, en tant que collège, demeure en marge de ces travaux; il peut être informé des plus importants d'entre eux (des sessions interministérielles ou des réunions du Conseil européen), lors des communications du Conseil des Ministres, le mercredi matin. Ainsi seuls quelques membres de l'Exécutif sont directement concernés par ces affaires.

Le Conseil européen dépend du président de la République et du ministre des Affaires étrangères. Les ministres en charge des départements techniques (Agriculture, Travail, Transports, Environnement ...) participent aux sessions du Conseil des Communautés, portant sur les dossiers de leur compétence. Dans le fonctionnement quotidien de l'Europe, l'unité des vues gouvernementales est garantie:

- D'abord par le ministre des Affaires étrangères - depuis 1981, des Relations extérieures (3) - qui en règle générale représente la France aux sessions 'affaires générales'. Sous la présidence de M. Giscard d'Estaing, figurait en particulier, auprès du ministre des Affaires étrangères, un secrétaire d'Etat, recevant en fait pour tâche tout ce qui a trait à la gestion des Communautés (budget, notamment). Depuis 1981, M. Claude Cheysson a été assisté par un ministre chargé des affaires européennes, qui reste dans une position de subordination puisqu'il n'est que ministre délégué (M. André Chandernagor) (4). La nomination, le 18 décembre 1983, de M. Roland Dumas comme ministre des Affaires européennes, certes trop récente pour susciter des observations définitives, apporte deux 'signes' provisoires: l'importance spécifique des affaires européennes est affirmée, M. Dumas étant ministre dans le plein sens du terme et aussi, à la différence de son prédécesseur, participant au Conseil des Ministres; les dossiers européens appartiennent bien au domaine de l'attention directe du chef de l'Etat (M. Dumas est l'un des plus proches amis de M. Mitterrand).
- Ensuite par la préparation, pour chaque session du Conseil des Communautés, d'un dossier d'information et d'instructions, selon la procédure de coordination interministérielle. En outre, chaque ministre est accompagné d'une abondante délégation (membres de la Représentation permanente, agents du Quai d'Orsay (siège du ministère des Relations extérieures), fonctionnaires de la direction du Budget, responsables du ministère concerné ...), chacun surveillant ses moindres paroles.

Ces périodes de présidence n'entraînent aucune transformation fondamentale du dispositif. Lors des sessions du Conseil, des formules pragmatiques et changeantes sont mises au point pour faire face à la double charge de la représentation nationale et de la présidence. Par exemple, au cours des réunions 'Affaires générales', le ministre des Affaires étrangères (des Relations extérieures) assure la présidence, tandis que le secrétaire d'Etat (ou, depuis 1981, le ministre délégué; et, pour le premier semestre 1984, le ministre des Affaires européennes) ou le représentant permanent défendent la position française. La nomination d'au moins un secrétaire d'Etat auprès de la plupart des ministres autorise un même mode de répartition des rôles lors de sessions accueillant des ministres en charge de ministères techniques.

Alors que certains parlements nationaux reçoivent une information régulière et exercent un contrôle rigoureux sur les questions communautaires, l'intervention du Parlement français garde un caractère exceptionnel, la rareté de ces relations pouvant susciter d'ailleurs des réactions assez vives.

L'Assemblée nationale et le Sénat ne prennent connaissance et ne débattent vraiment de ces questions qu'à l'occasion de la soumission de textes (approbation de traités ou de conventions - par exemple, pour l'élection du Parlement européen au suffrage universel direct - ou examen de directives ayant des incidences financières). Ainsi, en décembre 1978, examinant la sixième directive d'harmonisation de la taxe sur la valeur ajoutée, l'Assemblée nationale, voulant donner 'un coup d'arrêt' aux atteintes à sa souveraineté fiscale, vote contre ce texte l'exception d'irrécevabilité (5). Le texte est finalement inséré par le gouvernement dans un collectif budgétaire et adopté!

LA COORDINATION INTERMINISTÉRIELLE POUR LES QUESTIONS RELATIVES AUX COMMUNAUTÉS EUROPÉENNES (6)

La coordination interministérielle pour les questions communautaires est, en France, ancienne et dotée de mécanismes rigoureux. Mais, comme tout dispositif rôdé par les années, ce système supporte mal les réformes, aussi réduites soient-elles.

En ce qui concerne les exigences spécifiques de la présidence, leur mise en oeuvre ne peut que s'insérer dans ce moule. Les six mois de la présidence, tout en déclenchant une mobilisation des moyens existants, n'entraînent aucun bouleversement de l'appareil politico-administratif, de ses circuits et méthodes. Plus précisément, la présidence ne donne lieu à aucune modification des structures; de même les effectifs restent identiques. Le surcroît de travail exigé peut et doit être assuré par les agents déjà en place, qui ont une solide habitude des dossiers. Cette optique s'explique largement par la conception que l'administration française a des dossiers communautaires: ceux-ci se définissent par leur technicité, leur ésotérisme, et leur maîtrise requiert un long apprentissage. Le recours de fonctionnaires n'ayant qu'une connaissance superficielle des questions constituerait non une aide, mais une gêne! En outre, pour ceux qui, dans l'administration, suivent les problèmes européens, il y a une sorte de domaine réservé, et les six mois de la présidence représentent l'occasion d'avoir une présence plus active. Bref, pour tous, les mécanismes existants doivent et peuvent supporter ce moment de surchauffe.

Comme toute structure bureaucratique, la coordination interministérielle repose sur une combinaison de procédures officielles, définies par des textes, et de pratiques, de liaisons informelles. Cette combinaison se traduit par des réseaux complexes d'information et de consultation, les liens personnels pouvant soit accélérer, soit freiner la prise de décision.

A. Structures
La coordination interministérielle est assurée par le Secrétariat général du 'Comité interministériel pour les questions de coopération économique européenne' (7). Ce dispositif naît en 1948 pour organiser 'la participation de la France au programme de relèvement européen' (8), au moment du lancement du Plan Marshall et donc, de la création de l'Organisation européenne de coopération économique (16 avril 1948).

L'instance-clef est en principe le Comité interministériel. Présidé jusqu'en 1981 par le Premier ministre ou, en son absence, par le ministre des Finances, il est aujourd'hui présidé par le ministre délégué chargé des affaires européennes, suppléant du Premier ministre. Participent aux réunions, le ministre des Relations extérieures et les ministres dans les attributions desquels figurent les questions de l'ordre du jour; y assistent également le commissaire général au Plan, le directeur des affaires économiques du Quai d'Orsay et le secrétaire général du gouvernement. Le rythme des réunions du comité est très irrégulier (au maximun cinq ou six par an); le comité n'intervient que sur des dossiers donnant lieu à de graves divergences entre administrations ou posant des questions de principes.

Dans la pratique, l'organisme essentiel est le Secrétariat général de ce Comité interministériel (S.G.C.I.). Par son statut, ses dimensions réduites et la souplesse de son fonctionnement, le S.G.C.I. demeure l'une des meilleures illustrations de ces structures parallèles - comme, par exemple, le Commissariat général au Plan ou la Délégation à l'Aménagement du Territoire - auxquelles depuis la fin de la Deuxième Guerre mondiale, le gouvernement français a recours pour faire face à des problèmes nouveaux et disposer d'une approche globale, surmontant le cloisonnement vertical des ministères.

Le statut du S.G.C.I. est fort peu orthodoxe (l'absence d'orthodoxie étant souvent un gage d'efficacité et peut-être aussi une source de prestige):

- Si le Secrétariat est rattaché au Premier ministre, son budget de fonctionnement s'insère dans celui du ministère des Finances (qui lui fournit aussi des locaux).
- A l'exception du secrétaire général (qui a la position de directeur d'administration centrale) et du conseiller juridique, les agents du S.G.C.I. - chefs de secteur, adjoints, secrétaires ... - sont mis à disposition, c'est-à-dire continuent d'être pris en charge et rémunérés par leurs corps ou administrations d'origine.
- Les postes d'autorité, soit ceux du secrétaire général, les deux secrétaires généraux adjoints et les sept ou huit chefs de secteur, font l'objet d'une répartition fort subtile entre les grands corps de l'Etat. Ainsi, jusqu'en 1978, seul un inspecteur des finances peut occuper la fonction de secrétaire général. De même, l'un des deux secrétaires généraux adjoints est toujours un ingénieur du corps des mines.

La coordination interministérielle se situe au carrefour d'attitudes et de préoccupations contradictoires:

- D'un côté, la tentation d'abord du ministère des Finances, mais aussi des départements techniques d'avoir leur propre politique européenne, de développer des contacts tant avec Bruxelles qu'avec les autres Etats membres et donc, d'échapper à toute contrainte interministérielle.
- De l'autre côté, le souci, notamment du ministère des Relations extérieures et du sommet de l'Etat, de maintenir une rigoureuse

unité de vues et d'instructions dans les affaires communautaires. Ces tensions imposent le rattachement du Secrétariat général au Premier ministre, auquel sa position confère un réel pouvoir d'arbitrage. Aussi, depuis 1981, la désignation d'un président suppléant, délégué auprès du ministre des Relations extérieures, affecte-t-elle l'autorité du S.G.C.I.. La nomination en décembre 1983 d'un ministre des Affaires européennes, au sens plein de terme, devrait contribuer à restaurer au moins partiellement cette autorité.

Les périodes de présidence n'entraînent ni modification de ces structures, ni accroissement des effectifs.

B. Procédures

L'efficacité quotidienne de toute coordination suppose l'imbrication de circuits officiels et de relations informelles et personnelles (notamment, contacts entre membres du service de coopération économique du ministère des Relations extérieures et agents de la Représentation permanente, les premiers et la plupart des seconds appartenant au corps diplomatique).

L'ensemble des procédures de coordination est soumis à une règle fondamentale: le Comité interministériel, ou plutôt, dans la pratique, le Secrétariat général (S.G.C.I.), 'élabore notamment les directives fixant la position française au sein des Conseils des Ministres des Communautés et des divers organes communs prévus par les traités ...' **(9)**. Ainsi les procédures de coordination s'identifient-elles aux fonctions du S.G.C.I.. Pour expliquer ces procédures, la plus claire démarche consiste à suivre le cheminement et les phases d'examen d'une proposition (de règlement, de directive du Conseil) au sein de l'administration francaise:

a) Information et diffusion:
   Toute proposition de texte, faite par la Commission, est transmise par la Représentation permanente au S.G.C.I.; celui-ci le communique tout de suite aux départements ministériels concernés pour examen.

b) Examen du texte et négociations:
   Alors s'engage, par l'envoi d'observations écrites des ministères et surtout par des réunions au S.G.C.I. - présidées soit par un chef de secteur, soit par l'un des secrétaires généraux adjoints -, l'étude du texte. Chaque réunion s'achève par un relevé de conclusions ou, plus souvent, par un projet de message d'instructions. Le texte 'tourne' dans les administrations concernées, afin de s'assurer que ne subsiste aucun point de désaccord **(10)**. L'accord de tous assuré, le message est expédié à la Représentation permanente! Toute négociation à Bruxelles se traduit par un va-et-vient d'instructions parisiennes et de télex de comptes rendus!

c) Divergences profondes entre administrations: conciliation ou arbitrage:
   Certains textes ou certaines négociations peuvent se heurter à des divergences de fond, notamment entre le ministère des Finances,

soucieux de limiter l'accroissement des dépenses communautaires, et tel ou tel ministère technique - Affaires sociales, Environnement, etc. ... - en quête d'actions européennes; également entre les préoccupations diplomatiques du Quai d'Orsay (siège du ministère des Relations extérieures) et celles financières de la Rue de Rivoli (siège du ministère des Finances). Dans ces hypothèses:

- Les divergences peuvent être discutées et résolues lors de la réunion d'information. Cette réunion hebdomadaire (11), présidée par le secrétaire général, et accueillant les fonctionnaires d'autorité exerçant des responsabilités directes en matière européenne (sous-directeurs, membres de cabinet ...), fait le point des travaux en cours (notamment, le bilan des sessions du Conseil), examine les plus importants messages d'instructions et surtout s'efforce de surmonter à l'amiable les oppositions interministérielles.

- Enfin, les questions en suspens peuvent être soumises à l'arbitrage ministériel. Avant juin 1981, la règle du jeu est bien établie et repose sur l'autorité du Premier ministre: le dossier litigieux, accompagné d'une note du S.G.C.I. résumant les enjeux et les points de vue en présence, est transmis au cabinet du Premier ministre, qui tranche. Afin d'éviter - ou au moins de limiter - des interprétations opposées, l'arbitrage fait l'objet d'instructions écrites, communiquées aux départements concernés. Depuis juin 1981, la remise du pouvoir d'arbitrage au ministre délégué chargé des affaires européennes soulève des réticences, d'abord de l'administration des Finances. Dans un Etat au sein duquel les Finances forment un bastion et se considèrent, par leur compétence et leur rôle, comme 'au-dessus' des autres ministères (dépensiers et quelque peu irresponsables), l'équilibre - et l'efficacité - de la coordination interministérielle dépendent d'une autorité claire.

La coordination ne saurait se réduire à un processus mécanique. Elle est conditionnée par les conceptions administratives dominantes, la manière dont chacun des ministères envisage les autres, ainsi qu'enfin, par les rapports personnels.

- Le ministère des Relations extérieures demeure le ministère politique. C'est à lui d'apprécier l'état des contraintes et opportunités politiques; son point de vue continue de prévaloir sur les questions de caractère juridique et institutionnel. De même le ministère des Relations extérieures est regardé comme le maître de la conduite des négociations. La signification exacte de ce rôle varie d'une négociation à l'autre. Souvent, elle permet aux Finances ou aux ministères techniques de conserver un droit permanent de critique! A l'inverse, le 'facteur diplomatique' fournit au Quai d'Orsay l'argument ultime pour conclure des discussions, paralysées par le refus de toute concession des autres administrations! Enfin, parallèlement aux dizaines de télex quotidiens entre le S.G.C.I. et la Représentation permanente, des télégrammes d'orientation politique sont envoyés à cette dernière par le ministère des Relations extérieures.

- Quant au ministère des Finances, en fait les directions du Budget et du Trésor, il ne cesse de rappeler sa responsabilité spécifique sur tout le domaine des dépenses, de leur accroissement et de leur contrôle. Cette attitude se traduit par des contacts directs entre ces directions et leurs homologues ouest-allemandes.
- L'efficacité de la coordination interministérielle, aussi bien organisée soit-elle, dépend de l'évolution même du système communautaire. Par exemple: avec le recours par la Commission à des groupes d'examen d'avant-projets des textes - avant leur dépôt sur la table du Conseil - les ministères techniques ont le sentiment de disposer ainsi de leur propre négociation, puisqu'il s'agit de discussions entre experts, n'engageant pas leur gouvernement.

De même, les caractères de telle ou telle structure créée à Bruxelles façonnent la pratique de la coordination interministérielle à Paris. Ainsi le Comité monétaire, enceinte à part, échappe-t-il à la coordination et relève-t-il, du côté français, de la seule direction du Trésor; les travaux du Comité - comme tous ceux portant sur les problèmes monétaires - sont entourés d'un épais secret!

Les périodes des présidences n'entraînent pas de transformation de ces procédures. Cependant, les réunions, les arbitrages et surtout les allées et venues entre Paris et Bruxelles se font beaucoup plus fréquents!

Surtout la présidence entraîne une mobilisation des moyens administratifs autour du S.G.C.I.:

Dans les mois qui précèdent la présidence, plusieurs réunions, associant toutes les administrations concernées, se tiennent au Secrétariat général.

- Elles arrêtent le programme de la présidence: recensement des problèmes en suspens; recueil des suggestions des ministères; fixation - plutôt floue - des priorités; enfin, établissement d'un document d'instructions d'une vingtaine de pages, véritable Charte pour l'ensemble de l'appareil politico-administratif tout au long des six mois de présidence (12).
- Ces réunions désignent les présidents et les porte-parole des comités et groupes du Conseil (dont le nombre dépasse 150). La présidence est confiée, en règle générale, à un agent de la Représentation permanente; le porte-parole est le plus souvent un fonctionnaire parisien. Etre porte-parole, c'est sortir de l'ombre, être enfin négociateur! Pour ce motif, la tâche de désignation des porte-parole revêt une grande importance psychologico-administrative: dans la distribution de ces postes, un équilibre doit être assuré entre le ministère des Relations extérieures, le ministère des Finances et les départements techniques.

Pendant les six mois de présidence, le travail de coordination, de surveillance des principales réunions doit être accompli avec un soin accru. D'où le rôle-clef de la réunion d'information dans cette phase.

A l'issue de la présidence, un bilan - évidemment décevant - est fait et donne lieu à un document interministériel substantiel. Ce document descriptif est largement diffusé dans tous les services concernés et fait l'objet d'une brève communication par le ministre des Affaires étrangères au Conseil des Ministres. Comme la plupart de ces rapports rétrospectifs, il est lu, commenté mais n'est guère utilisé, ne serait-ce que parce que plusieurs années s'écoulent entre deux semestres de présidence!

LES TRAVAUX DE PRÉPARATION AU SEIN DES MINISTÈRES

A. Structures

Face aux affaires communautaires, les ministères ont dans l'ensemble adopté deux types de comportements.

Pour le ministère des Relations extérieures et celui des Finances, préoccupés, semble-t-il, de garder une approche globale et horizontale des problèmes, la dimension européenne n'a pas à être isolée au sein d'une cellule spécifique (bureau ou service des affaires européennes), mais doit s'insérer dans les structures existantes.

-   Au ministère des Relations extérieures, les problèmes européens sont traités d'une part, par le service de coopération économique de la direction des Affaires économiques et financières (questions communautaires) et d'autre part, par la direction des Affaires politiques et la sous-direction d'Europe occidentale, direction d'Europe (coopération politique). La direction des Affaires juridiques assure la représentation de la France dans les contentieux devant la Cour de Justice des Communautés.
-   Au ministère des Finances, deux directions assument des responsabilités directes; la direction du Budget (budget communautaire, notamment) et la direction du Trésor (monnaie, coordination des politiques économiques). Au sein de chacune de ces deux directions, un bureau 'européen' non seulement suit les dossiers, mais participe aux discussions de Bruxelles.

En ce qui concerne les ministères techniques, les solutions retenues, tout en s'appuyant sur une structure spécialisée, n'en sont pas moins diverses:

-   Certains départements (Industrie, par exemple), qui ont un service des affaires internationales, s'en tiennent à des règles pragmatiques. Ainsi, pour le ministère de l'Industrie, le problème des aides amène les directions techniques - en liaison avec le S.G.C.I. - à nouer des contacts avec la Commission (direction générale de la Concurrence).
-   D'autres ministères (Agriculture, Affaires sociales, Transports, par exemple) disposent d'un service des affaires internationales qui, en principe, a seul la charge des questions européennes. En fait, l'évolution du domaine communautaire impose une grande diversité de structures:

-- A l'Agriculture et aux Transports, le caractère des problèmes (harmonisation de normes, fixation de quotas ou de prix) entraîne la participation étroite des directeurs techniques aux négociations bruxelloises.

-- Aux Affaires sociales, l'existence du Fonds social européen, l'élaboration des demandes d'aides réclament la mise sur pied d'une cellule du Fonds social européen (13).

Dans ces ministères, le service des affaires internationales a le statut de sous-direction. Les effectifs sont restreints: outre le sous-directeur, deux ou trois agents ayant rang d'attachés d'administration. Les tâches de gestion (par exemple, préparation et instruction de dossiers d'aides pour le Commission) relèvent de cellules spécifiques (cellule du Fonds social, dirigée par un chef de bureau, et comprenant deux agents d'exécution; à la Délégation à l'Aménagement du Territoire-D.A.T.A.R., bureau chargé des demandes auprès du F.E.D.E.R.).

Pour les ministères techniques, il est indispensable d'être présent directement dans les affaires européennes. D'un côté, il y a le désir de mener une politique autonome. De l'autre, les ministères, conscients de la complexité des procédures communautaires, quelque peu désarmés devant elles, savent qu'ils ne peuvent se soustraire à la coordination interministérielle, qu'il s'agisse de l'élaboration des textes communautaires ou de tâches de gestion.

B. Procédures

Le cloisonnement entre les services au sein d'une même administration se révèle encore plus fort que celui entre les ministères: les directions d'un même département ne font en général guère d'effort pour coordonner leur approche des questions communautaires!

- Aux Relations extérieures, les compétences sont bien réparties: au service de coopération économique, le domaine communautaire; au directeur des Affaires politiques et à la sous-direction d'Europe occidentale, la coopération politique! Si les télégrammes des ambassades et de la Représentation permanente permettent à chacun d'être au courant de l'ensemble des affaires, il ne saurait être question de pénétrer dans le champ de l'autre. Toutefois, une coordination ad hoc, temporaire, peut être instaurée: par exemple, pour l'examen du Plan Colombo-Genscher (novembre 1981-juin 1983), des réunions régulières associent la direction des Affaires politiques, celle d'Europe, celle des Affaires juridiques et le service de coopération économique, afin de définir la position française au fur et à mesure de la progression des travaux (14).
- Aux Finances, la monnaie 'appartient' à la direction du Trésor, le budget communautaire à la direction du Budget. Ce partage ne saurait provoquer un début de contestation.
- Au sein des ministères techniques, les questions européennes se trouvent centralisées par le service des affaires internationales.

Les procédures demeurent très empiriques. A cet égard, une distinction s'impose:
-- s'il s'agit de définir la position française face à des textes - propositions de règlements ou de directives - en discussion à Bruxelles, le S.G.C.I. organise et guide la totalité du travail. Il arrive que le Secrétariat général surmonte les oppositions entre directions d'un même département,
-- si se trouvent en cause des relations de gestion (demandes de soutien financier, contrôle des aides, information de la Commission...), le S.G.C.I. intervient plutôt comme organe de conseil ou tout simplement comme boîte aux lettres, toute correspondance officielle engageant le gouvernement français, passant par le Secrétariat général et la Représentation permanente.

LE RÔLE DE LA REPRÉSENTATION PERMANENTE ET LES RELATIONS AVEC LES INSTITUTIONS COMMUNAUTAIRES

A. Fonctions de la Représentation permanente
La Représentation permanente de la France auprès des Communautés européennes a en principe le monopole des relations avec la Commission et le Conseil: toutes les lettres entre ces institutions et le gouvernement français sont transmises par la Représentation; en outre, celle-ci représente la France dans la plupart des groupes.

Conformément aux habitudes de tout système bureaucratique, le travail de la Représentation est double:

- officiel: notification à Paris des réunions; réception et exécution des messages d'instructions et envoi de comptes rendus - soit des dizaines de télex.
- informel: contacts téléphoniques avec les administrations parisiennes. Au cours de toute négociation essentielle, l'agent négociateur participe aux réunions parisiennes de coordination, afin d'expliquer le climat des travaux, de faire sentir les points de blocage. Cet agent a par conséquent une tâche multiforme de liaison avec les fonctionnaires de la Commission, ainsi qu'avec ceux des autres délégations.

La Représentation permanente est formée:

- du représentant permanent,
- du représentant permanent adjoint,
- de plusieurs conseillers et secrétaires des Affaires étrangères,
- d'agents de divers ministères:
  -- un conseiller commercial,
  -- un conseiller financier (budget communautaire),
  -- un conseiller pour les questions agricoles,
  -- un conseiller pour les affaires sociales,
  -- un conseiller pour les problèmes de transport.

B. Périodes de présidence

C'est la Représentation permanente qui subit de la manière la plus marquée le 'choc' de la présidence. Ses moyens en personnel - une douzaine de fonctionnaires de reponsabilité - ne sont pas augmentés. Afin d'assumer les tâches de la présidence, agents de la Représentation et fonctionnaires parisiens procèdent entre eux à une répartition empirique des travaux, les seconds accomplissant des séjours plus fréquents à Bruxelles. De manière tout aussi pragmatique, le stagiaire, affecté pour neuf mois à la Représentation permanente par l'Ecole Nationale d'Administration, est mobilisé.

Les agents de la Représentation permanente se reposent donc sur le Secrétariat général du Conseil: pour ces agents, l'apport de cette logistique bien équipée, parfaitement rôdée, modifie profondément leurs conditions de travail.

La Représentation permanente appréhende la présidence dans une perspective politique:

- Le président, qu'il s'agisse du Coreper ou d'un groupe, doit faire progresser les dossiers et créer les conditions favorables à un compromis. D'où une recherche constante de contacts et de patientes tractations de couloir... L'illustration la plus frappante de cette démarche apparaît lors des travaux préparatoires de la Convention Lomé II (premier semestre 1979). Le président dispose d'une position centrale: il négocie au nom de la Communauté, allant et venant entre ses collègues européens et les ambassadeurs des pays ACP. Ainsi le représentant de la France - M. de La Barre De Nanteuil -, assisté d'un de ses collaborateurs - M. Blanchemaison, conseiller -, entretient des relations étroites avec quelques ambassadeurs africains à l'autorité incontestée. Derrière la lourdeur des mécanismes officiels, se mettent en place des conversations, plus franches, plus directes, entre les 'personnages-clefs'. Cependant, la présidence française s'achève avant que tout soit au point; et le gouvernement français sollicite de ses partenaires le droit de signer tout de même la Convention comme président - ce qui lui est refusé!
- La présidence affecte donc les relations entre Paris et la Représentation permanente. Celle-ci doit encore mieux exposer ce qu'il est possible d'obtenir et ce qui rencontre un obstacle insurmontable. Pour la Représentation permanente, la tâche pédagogique d'explication, et parfois de persuasion, se fait plus pressante.

LA PRÉSIDENCE ET LA COOPÉRATION POLITIQUE EUROPÉENNE

A. La France et la coopération politique

Toute réflexion sur l'attitude de l'appareil politico-administratif français face à la coopération politique européenne ne peut que partir de la conception qu'a la France de sa diplomatie. L'empreinte gaullienne demeure: la politique étrangère conserve les mêmes axes, les mêmes principes (indépendance, détente et coopération, ouverture vers le Tiers-

Monde...) La politique européenne de la France s'inscrit dans ce cadre: orientation essentielle, elle doit néanmoins s'harmoniser avec les autres choix de la France.

Cette vision détermine l'approche de la coopération politique européenne:

1) Alors que les questions communautaires sont examinées par des procédures interministérielles, la coopération politique relève exclusivement du ministère des Relations extérieures.

2) Au sein de ce ministère:

- d'une part, la coopération politique, placée sous l'autorité du directeur des Affaires politiques, est traitée par une sous-direction géographique, la sous-direction d'Europe occidentale qui a également dans son portefeuille, les rapports bilatéraux avec les pays ouest-européens (Grande-Bretagne, Pays-Bas, Scandinavie...),

- d'autre part, dans les directions ou sous-directions gógraphiques (Europe orientale, Afrique du Nord-Levant, Asie...), existent des correspondants, qui éventuellement participent, pour les dossiers de leur compétence, aux groupes d'experts de la coopération politique. Ce monopole des Relations extérieures est admis et reconnu, la coopération politique ne portant jusqu'à présent que sur la diplomatie pure, c'est-à-dire l'établissement de principes et de procédures face à des crises internationales.

Il est probable que l'interpénétration progressive et croissante des deux types de problèmes, ceux des Communautés et ceux de la coopération politique, pèsera sur l'organisation administrative française et remettra en cause le cloisonnement actuel, qui restera possible aussi longtemps que l'Europe n'aura pas une véritable politique étrangère.

B. La France et la présidence de la coopération politique

Les six mois de présidence sont aussi l'affaire de la direction politique. La démarche est bien sûr tout à fait différente de celle employée pour les dossiers communautaires. Ces derniers sont absorbés par le système interministériel, tandis que pour la coopération politique, les seuls circuits du ministère des Relations extérieures sont utilisés (15):

- Tout comme les problèmes communautaires donnent lieu à un document global d'instructions, la coopération politique fait l'objet d'un texte analogue, passant en revue les travaux de la douzaine de groupes d'experts. A propos de chaque groupe, le document d'instructions comprend quatre points: rappel de l'état du débat; recensement des rapports déjà établis au sein du groupe; problèmes de fond débattus; directives pratiques (calendrier des réunions, présence et rôle de la Commission; éventuellement initiatives de la présidence ....)

En 1979, quatre types de groupes sont distingués:

1) Les groupes à objectif limité - concernant l'Asie, l'Amérique latine, les Nations Unies et l'Europe de l'Est. Ces groupes appellent essentiellement une information réciproque.

2) Les groupes traitant d'une question substantielle et délicate - Afrique, Méditerranée ... - mettent en cause des intérêts ou des préoccupations majeures de certains Etats (et notamment de la France).
Ainsi le groupe Afrique discute de l'Afrique australe, le groupe Méditerranée surtout de Chypre. D'où des directives d'observation et de prudence ....

3) Les groupes présentant un intérêt particulier pour la France, C.S.C.E., O.N.U. - Désarmement, Moyen-Orient, évoquent des questions pouvant réclamer une initiative. D'où, éventuellement, la fixation d'objectifs (en ce qui concerne la C.S.C.E., préparation des travaux de Madrid et définition des thèmes ....).

4) Enfin, les groupes posant un problème spécifique - espace judiciaire européen, dialogue euro-arabe.... - donnent lieu à des instructions de négociation, et notamment à la définition des tâches des différents groupes politico-administratifs.

Ce document constitue donc l'instrument de référence pour l'ensemble des fonctionnaires chargés de la coopération politique. Les annexes rappellent le rythme de réunions, indiquent les noms des responsables, etc.

- De même, parallèlement aux instructions adressées pour les affaires communautaires, des directives relatives à la coopération politique parviennent, par télégrammes circulaires, à l'ensemble des ambassades françaises dans les pays tiers ainsi qu'aux représentations permanentes auprès des organisations internationales. On procède à des échanges de vues périodiques entre ambassades des Dix (16) et à l'élaboration de rapports communs ainsi qu'à des démarches éventuelles, etc.

Dans les pays tiers, la mission principale de la coopération politique est l'échange d'informations auquel procèdent soit les ambassadeurs, soit d'autres agents. A l'occasion de ces conversations, l'écart de situation entre 'grands' et 'petits' pays est souvent ressenti, les premiers apportant les renseignements, la plupart des seconds écoutant, recevant.

PRÉOCCUPATIONS NATIONALES ET OBJECTIFS DE LA PRÉSIDENCE DE COMMUNAUTÉS

Face à la présidence des Communautés, à ce qu'elle est et signifie, l'attitude française est dominée par deux sentiments quelque peu contradictoires:

1) La volonté d'utiliser la présidence dans une perspective politique.

Le meilleur - peut-être le seul - exemple de cette approche reste la négociation de la Convention Lomé II (premier semestre 1979). La combinaison de plusieurs éléments, tous aussi importants - nature des problèmes, état des discussions, intérêts particuliers de la France, réseaux de relations entre le représentant français, ses collègues européens et les ambassadeurs africains -, permet une utilisation efficace de la présidence.

2) La conscience de plus en plus claire des contraintes et limites de la présidence, bien cernée par un ministre des Relations extérieures: 'Toute présidence, au début de son bref mandat, est pleine d'ambitions. Celle qui vient de commencer l'est comme les autres et elle déploiera le maximum d'efforts pour atteindre les objectifs qu'elle s'est fixés. Et si ceux-ci ne sont pas atteints, elle sera satisfaite d'avoir fait avancer les dossiers. L'essentiel, par delà les bilans semestriels, c'est que l'Europe progresse' (M. Jean-François Poncet, janvier 1979) (17).

Même si, au moment où elle aborde ses six mois de présidence, la France met sur pied un programme de travail très ambitieux, son attente est en définitive limitée pour trois raisons majeures:

1) Le calendrier politico-administratif français.
Ce calendrier détermine, rythme les initiatives européennes de la France, la considération selon laquelle la présidence constituerait un moment privilégié n'intervenant guère.
Ainsi les initiatives françaises s'expriment-elles en général par des mémorandums. Ceux-ci sont de deux sortes: les plus importants émanent du gouvernement lui-même et recensent, dans un document, les souhaits de la France à une date donnée (le dernier mémorandum de ce genre est celui du gouvernement Mauroy, en octobre 1981); d'autres mémorandums, plus modestes, rassemblent les préoccupations françaises dans un domaine précis (politique sociale, politique industrielle, environnement...)
Or le moment auquel un tel document est élaboré et remis à Bruxelles, est dicté par les contraintes de la politique intérieure française: accès au pouvoir d'un nouveau gouvernement, soucieux d'affirmer son attachement à l'Europe; volonté d'un nouveau ministre de se forger une image d'Européen...

2) La lourdeur des affaires communautaires et la charge en résultant pour la présidence.
La complexité de certains dossiers - et d'abord de la procédure budgétaire, qui tend à s'étaler sur toute l'année et déclenche des crises périodiques -, l'existence de débats jamais clos, sans cesse repris - telle l'affaire de la contribution britannique -, la lenteur des discussions accaparent de plus en plus l'attention de la présidence dont la mission n'est certes plus de dégager des orientations d'ensemble, mais de concilier, de chercher sans cesse des compromis.
L'une des meilleures illustrations de cette contrainte communautaire a été le budget pour 1979. Au moment où, le 1er janvier 1979, la France accède à la présidence, la procédure est

133

dans l'impasse: il est reproché à l'Assemblée d'avoir voté une augmentation des dépenses au-delà du taux maximum. Le litige risque d'aller devant la Cour de Justice de Luxembourg. Dans ce conflit entre Assemblée et Etats membres, la France se place dans le camp des 'durs' pour lesquels l'Assemblée a outrepassé ses pouvoirs et par conséquent, doit se soumettre.

Cependant, la logique de la présidence, sa fonction conciliatrice amènent la France à assouplir sa position, à rechercher, puis à trouver un compromis sur l'accroissement des crédits du FEDER. Par ailleurs, la France obtient que huit Etats membres sur neuf (à l'exception des Pays-Bas) conviennent d'une procédure interne au sein du Conseil, afin d'éviter que ne se reproduise une crise identique à celle de la fin de 1978 (18). Il n'en demeure pas moins qu'une nouvelle crise budgétaire (ayant, certes, un point de départ différent) éclate sur le budget pour 1980! Et le processus se répète à propos des budgets suivants!

3) L'intervention de plus en plus décisive de la diplomatie bilatérale.

Par sa position, la présidence attire, concentre les faiblesses, les difficultés du système communautaire. La paralysie relative de ce dernier atteint nécessairement le 'sommet', à son tour privé de toute capacité d'impulsion. Le pouvoir d'initiative des institutions communautaires n'a cessé de décliner; perte de prestige de la Commission, enlisement des débats du Conseil...

D'où un déplacement partiel de l'initiative des instances européennes vers des enceintes parallèles, fondées sur la concertation bilatérale. Tant en 1974 qu'en 1979, le système communautaire n'intervient dans plusieurs négociations majeures que lorsque l'essentiel est réglé de façon informelle entre chefs d'Etat ou de gouvernement (par exemple, naissance du Conseil européen, ou mise sur pied du Système monétaire européen (19)). L'importance donnée - notamment par le président Giscard d'Estaing, de 1974 à 1981 - aux contacts informels - en particulier avec M. Helmut Schmidt, chancelier de l'Allemagne fédérale pendant la même période - tend à rejeter dans l'ombre la fonction même de présidence. Les innovations majeures réalisées alors sont mûries par de longues et discrètes tractations. Les liens entre MM. Giscard d'Estaing et Schmidt, au pouvoir tant en 1974 qu'en 1979, fournissent le fondement politique indispensable à la réalisation de projets comme le Conseil européen ou le Système monétaire européen.

Il s'agit là d'une évolution qui se situe au-delà des personnes et qui apparaît liée à l'usure, la sclérose de l'organisation communautaire.

Le système communautaire et l'administration française chargée des questions européennes apparaissent aujourd'hui prisonniers de leurs procédures et de leurs pratiques.

L'appareil bruxellois offre une image paradoxale: comprenant à peine plus de douze mille agents - nombre bien faible, par comparaison avec les effectifs de n'importe quelle fonction publique nationale -, l'administration communautaire présente déjà la lourdeur et le byzantinisme de toute bureaucratie ancienne.

Quant à l'administration française, elle montre vis-à-vis de l'Europe ses qualités et/ou défauts classiques: centralisation, préoccupation prioritaire de cohérence, difficulté à établir des priorités, rigidité des positions... Le comportement face à la construction européenne de chaque administration nationale, qu'elle soit allemande ou italienne, britannique ou danoise, irlandaise ou française, résume, illustre - parfois jusqu'à la caricature - ses traditions ou même ses tics.

De ce point de vue, l'entreprise européenne, au lieu de pousser les Etats à réformer, aménager leurs structures, les incite peut-être - inconsciemment? consciemment? - à se figer dans des réactions stéréotypées. Dans cette perspective, le moment de la présidence, s'il encourage en apparence l'imagination, impose en fait à l'administration française un exercice quelque peu contradictoire: il s'agit, en principe, d'essayer de faire prévaloir ses thèses mais, en fait, de favoriser la conclusion de compromis. Affirmation d'une vision propre de l'Europe, quête de solutions pragmatiques, tels sont les deux pôles entre lesquels oscille toute présidence. En définitive, la conception française de la présidence connaît une évolution parallèle à l'approche française de l'Europe: d'abord, l'enthousiasme et l'idéalisme; puis, un réalisme parfois brutal; enfin, l'adaptation à une Europe diverse, hétérogène...

NOTES ET RÉFÉRENCES

(1) Déclaration du président Giscard d'Estaing, à l'issue du déjeuner avec les quatre présidents, 1er février 1979 - La Politique étrangère de la France, 1er trimestre 1979, page 48.

(2) Ainsi, par le décret no 81-655 du 12 juin 1981 (Textes et documents de la politique étrangère de la France - juin 1981 - page 31), le ministre délégué chargé des affaires européennes (M. André Chandernagor) 'assure la suppléance du Premier ministre à la présidence du Comité interministériel pour les questions de coopération économique européenne'. Cette simple modification dans la présidence du comité entraîne un amoindrissement de l'autorité du Secrétariat général du Comité (S.G.C.I.) et ainsi de son pouvoir effectif de coordination!

(3) Décret no 81-631 du 28 mai 1981 relatif aux attributions du ministre des Relations extérieures (Textes et documents de la politique étrangère de la France - mai 1981 - page 10).

(4) Voir note 2 ci-dessus.

(5) Patrick Frances - Un 'coup d'arrêt' des députés aux pratiques communautaires européennes - Le Monde du 2 décembre 1978.

(6) Tout ce qui a trait à la coopération politique est traité aux pages 130-132.

(7) Décret no 48-1029 du 25 juin 1948, portant organisation des services français en ce qui concerne la participation de la France au programme de relèvement européen, modifié par le décret no 52-1016 du 3 septembre 1952, et par le décret no 58-344 du 3 avril 1958 portant attribution de compétences pour l'application des traités instituant les Communautés européennes.

(8) Membre de phrase extrait du titre du décret no 48.1029 du 25 juin 1948.

(9) Extrait de l'article 1er du décret no 58-344 du 3 avril 1958.

(10) Alors que les convocations aux réunions du S.G.C.I. se font sur des feuilles roses, les projets d'instructions parviennent aux administrations sous des bordereaux de couleur bleue. Les instructions, approuvées et envoyées à Bruxelles, sont reproduites sur le papier blanc.

(11) La réunion se tient le mercredi matin, entre les sessions du Conseil, se déroulant les lundis et mardis, et les réunions du Coreper no 1 et 2.

(12) Un document analogue est mis au point pour la coopération politique. Ce point est étudié aux pages 130-131.

(13) De même, à la DATAR (Délégation à l'Aménagement du Territoire et à l'Action Régionale), existe un service ayant pour mission la confection des dossiers destinés au FEDER.

(14) Bien sûr, le cabinet du ministre est tenu informé par les comptes rendus des réunions du groupe ad hoc. En outre, dès que surgit une question d'importance politique, elle est soumise au cabinet.

(15) Depuis l'instauration de la troïka, associant à la présidence en place celle qui la précède et celle qui la suit, les diplomates (grec, irlandais) invités pour ce motif à Paris sont installés dans les bureaux de la direction politique du Quai d'Orsay.

(16) Rapport de Luxembourg du 27 octobre 1970.

(17) Discours de M. Jean-François Poncet, ministre français des

Affaires étrangères, président du Conseil des Communautés, devant l'Assemblée parlementaire européenne à Strasbourg, le 17 janvier 1979 (Textes et documents de la politique étrangère de la France, premier semestre 1979, page 30).

(18) Cette crise naît de l'incroyable complexité des règles budgétaires communautaires. D'un côté, l'Assemblée vote l'accroissement des crédits du Fonds régional - ce qu'elle est en droit de faire - et ainsi dépasse le taux maximal d'augmentation des dépenses - en violation des dispositions des Traités. Mais, de l'autre côté, le Conseil ne parvient pas à dégager en son sein une majorité qualifiée, permettant de rejeter l'amendement parlementaire!

(19) Peter Ludlow - The making of the European Monetary System, Butterworths European Studies, London, 1982.

Chapter 7

THE PRESIDENCY OF THE COUNCIL OF MINISTERS OF THE EUROPEAN COMMUNITIES: IRELAND AND ITS EC MEMBERSHIP
Ms Marian O'Leary, Maastricht

INTRODUCTION

In order to understand Ireland and its attitude to the EEC, it is necessary to take into account a major factor in Irish history which continues to have an effect on many aspects of Irish life. This is the prolonged involvement of Britain in Irish affairs which has left its mark not only on the administrative system but also on the complex relations between the two countries which have remained close after Ireland's independence in 1922. At independence Ireland inherited an administrative structure which was based on the British model as it had been applied to the country before independence. The first parliament of the new state chose to retain the basic political institutional system of the United Kingdom - a parliamentary democracy with a cabinet system of government, with the structure of ministerial departments and administration, both central and local, based on the British system. Indeed many of the senior civil servants who joined the administration after the founding of the state had already been in senior positions in the British civil service, and therefore had unusually close contacts with colleagues in Whitehall (1).

Traditionally Ireland had very close economic links with Britain and these were retained in the new state. Many sectors of the economy were geared towards Britain, and areas such as banking, insurance, trade and industry were predominantly British-oriented. For many years Britain remained Ireland's main market and main supplier. However this pattern has changed significantly in the past 20 years and in particular since Ireland's accession to the European Communities in 1973. The change in pattern is particularly evident in relation to exports. (In 1972 the United Kingdom was the market for 61 per cent of Irish exports, while other EC Member States imported 16 per cent of Ireland's total exports. In 1982 the figures were 39 per cent and 32 per cent respectively). There has been a less marked change in respect of imports. (In 1972 Ireland imported 51 per cent of its supplies from the United Kingdom and 18 per cent from other EC Member States. In 1982 the figures had changed to 48 per cent and 22 per cent respectively) (2).

Up to the end of the 1950s, economic development in Ireland had been limited. Based on the policy of self-sufficiency introduced by the first Fianna Fáil government, which came to office in 1932, the Irish economy was extremely protectionist and had not become part of the increasingly liberalised trade system which emerged at the end of World War II. The government had perceived its role as the creation of an environment in which economic development could take place, but had not been active in instigating measures to promote economic development. The absence of positive government intervention to promote economic development was the subject of comment by Basil Chubb in a review article on 'Treasury Control and Economic Planning', published in 1956, in which he said that it was 'high time that we paid conscious attention to the development of our economic planning and coordinated arrangements.' (3).

Beginning in 1957 and inspired by its Secretary, Mr. T.K. Whitaker, the Department of Finance perceived the need for it to do 'some thinking. . . about the future economic development of the country' (4). Mr Whitaker, and his colleagues prepared a study for the government entitled 'Economic Development'. The study aimed '(a) to highlight the main deficiencies and potentialities of the economy, and (b) to suggest the principles to be followed to correct the deficiencies and realise the opportunities indicating a number of specific forms of productive development which appear to offer good long-term prospects'. The introduction specifically stated that 'Economic Development' did not aim 'to draw up a detailed five or ten-year plan of national development' (5). It then went on to explore all development possibilities and incorporated proposals for the promotion of development with the assistance of the World Bank, of which Ireland became a member in 1957. Many of the proposals outlined in 'Economic Development' were taken up in a White Paper published in 1958 under the title 'Programme for Economic Expansion' (6). This document stated that 'it should be read as an outline of the more important contributions, direct and indirect, which the government propose to make to economic development in the years immediately ahead'. From 1957 onwards, the Department of Finance assumed the responsibility for the elaboration of proposals to hasten the country's economic development. These proposals included the promotion of an external trade policy, which would be based on a move away from protectionism towards free trade. This move was perceived as an essential precondition for economic development and led the Department of Finance to argue for Ireland's membership of the GATT as a means of ensuring access for Irish agricultural exports to the markets of industrialised countries.

The Department of Finance, because of what it saw as 'its central position in the administration and its prime responsibility for future economic development' (7), was also the initiator of the debate on whether Ireland should join the EEC. In 1960 it recommended that British membership should be a pre-condition for Irish membership based on the fact that Britain, recipient of 74 per cent of Ireland's total exports in 1960, was considered an essential market for the export of Irish agricultural produce. In 1961, when it became clear that Britain would apply for EEC membership, the department proposed that Ireland should also apply for full membership of the EEC. Following the suspension of the EEC accession negotiations in 1963, attention was concentrated on

Ireland's accession to the GATT and on the negotiation of the Anglo-Irish Free Trade Agreement of 1965.

The reasons for Ireland's application for EEC membership were therefore primarily economic. Accession was seen as an opportunity to expand the market for Irish exports, which were predominantly agricultural, and as a spur to economic development. Although the application of the United Kingdom was seen as a pre-condition for Irish accession, membership was perceived also as a confirmation of the country's independence and the challenge of participating as an equal partner in such a European venture was widely appreciated. Once the decision in principle to apply for Community membership had been taken, the government's commitment to it remained firm. There was also the realisation that once a member, Ireland would remain so and would be committed to work for its objectives within the EEC. As the then Prime Minister, Mr Seán Lemass, said in 1962 'When we join the EEC, there will be no drawing out again. We cannot keep one foot outside the door ready to pull back if we do not like what we find inside' (8).

Following the conclusion of the accession negotiations and the signature of the Treaty of Accession in January 1972, it was necessary for the government to seek the approval of the Dáil (elected assembly) to the terms of the treaty and to hold a referendum to amend the Constitution to allow Ireland to undertake the obligations arising from Community membership. The referendum campaign on Ireland's accession to the European Communities was centred largely on economic issues, with the government in its White Paper underlining the economic benefits of membership and the existence of 'no realistic alternative to membership of an enlarged Community which is compatible with the national objectives of increasing employment and improving the standard of living' (9). The White Paper pointed out that the treaties 'are concerned solely with economic, commercial and related social matters. There are no specific provisions in the treaties on political matters involving political obligations as such. However it is clear that, in establishing the Communities, the founder members were motivated by aspirations that went beyond the purely economic, commercial or social. . . . The founder members of the EEC declared themselves in the preamble to that treaty as determined to establish an ever-closer union among the European peoples and resolved to strengthen the safeguards of peace and liberty.' (10). It was recognised that accession was therefore not simply an economic matter, but that it also had a political dimension. The accession of Ireland to the European Communities was supported by the two main political parties, Fianna Fáil and Fine Gael, and the campaign was therefore one in which the main participants argued in favour of membership. The opposition to EEC membership was led by the Labour Party, in loose coalition with a number of other parties and groupings such as the trade union movement and extreme nationalist groups, including Official Sinn Féin. The latter emphasised the issues of Irish neutrality and loss of sovereignty, but did not have much success in moving these issues to the centre of the debate.

The referendum resulted in an overwhelming victory for the supporters of membership. In a 70 per cent poll, 83 per cent voted in favour. The referendum effectively marked the end of the debate about

Ireland's accession to the EEC. The Labour Party accepted the vote of the Irish people as being decisive and when it entered a coalition government with Fine Gael only four months after Ireland's accession, the question of Ireland's membership of the EEC was not an issue in the discussion of the terms of coalition. In addition there had been no division within the major political parties on the question of membership and consequently, following accession, there was no further debate in Parliament on the issue of EEC membership.

Another element of the 1972 referendum on Ireland's accession to the European Communities was that it approved the amendment of the Irish Constitution to allow laws adopted by the Communities to have 'the force of law in the state'. In the previous text of the Constitution, Article 29.6, stated that 'no international agreement shall be part of the domestic law of the state save as may be determined by the Oireachtas (Parliament)'. Following this enabling amendment the European Communities Act (1972) provided that 'the treaties governing the European Communities and the existing and future acts adopted by the institutions of those Communities shall be binding on the state and shall be part of the domestic law thereof'. This major change in Irish administrative law, whereby Community law was enacted into Irish domestic law, was not the subject of any particular attention during the referendum campaign. It did not give rise to a heightened interest of parliamentarians in the evolution of policy, nor in any concerted attempt by them to influence the positions taken by Ireland in negotiations within the EEC.

THE ROLE AND INTERVENTION OF GOVERNMENT AND PARLIAMENT

In Ireland both government and Parliament have in practice played a relatively limited role in relation to foreign policy. This has been due in part to the circumscribed role which a small country like Ireland can expect to play on the international stage, but also to the fact that for many years the main issue in Ireland's international relations has been the bilateral relationship with Britain, in particular in respect of policy on Northern Ireland. This issue has been of such national importance that it has been handled by the Prime Minister himself, rather than by the Minister for Foreign Affairs, and has been the subject of heated debate in Parliament on many occasions.

While history, and in particular the legacy of the Civil War of 1922-23, have ensured that parliamentarians have an active interest in issues arising from Ireland's bilateral relations with the UK, other aspects of foreign policy have not been subject to the same treatment. With Ireland's entry to the United Nations in 1955, the horizons of foreign policy were broadened and Ireland began what has been described as a period of 'tentative internationalism' (11). However, this did not lead to any substantial increase in the involvement of government and Parliament in the discussion of foreign policy issues. This was due in part to the fact that the then Minister for External Affairs, Mr Frank Aiken, was a very senior member of his own party and held the department almost as his own fief. In addition the declaratory nature of many of the activities of the United Nations meant that the global concerns it dealt with did not impinge to any great extent on the exchequer or on sectional interests and were therefore not amenable to exploitation by politicians more familiar with a constituency-oriented system of politics.

Accession to the European Communities represented an important change in the way in which Ireland was involved with the world. Prior to accession there was some public interest in the problem of legislative control over the Brussels machine. Parliamentarians, and indeed others, were faced with the problems resulting from the fact that the EEC straddles the boundary between domestic policy and foreign policy. In common with parliamentarians of other EC Member States, Irish parliamentarians found it difficult to adapt to this phenomenon. In addition, the methods of decision-making and the quantity and complexity of the documentation on issues under discussion made it very difficult for them to keep abreast of developments in the Community (12).

Many countries have established a system of parliamentary committees which are set up to cover the main areas of national policy including policy towards the EEC. These committees consider government, and other suggested, policy initiatives and also make their own proposals. The Irish Parliament has not had a tradition of parliamentary committees. However, following Ireland's accession to the European Communities, a Joint Committee of both Houses of Parliament on the secondary legislation of the EC was established. Its mandate allowed the committee to consider and report on Community laws at every stage of the policy-making process, but did not give it any form of control over on-going negotiations. Up to 1975 the committee worked with the considerable handicap of having a very small secretariat which seriously limited its capacity to cope with the volume of business within its mandate. In order to increase the flow of information available to the committee, civil servants have since 1975 been allowed to attend its meetings and to provide it with information of a factual nature. In 1977 the terms of reference of the committee were extended to allow it to examine and report on Commission memoranda and communications that may serve as the basis for future legislation. However, as its 55th Report pointed out, the committee is debarred from raising questions of policy with civil servants who come to brief its sub-committees. The same report expressed the hope that it would be able to discuss the issues with the ministers responsible (13).

The relationship of the Joint Committee with both Houses of Parliament has been the subject of some considerable frustration to its members. Neither house has arranged a regular procedure for the discussion of its reports, which have so far been set aside without debate. However, this situation may change significantly in the near future. In June 1983 a total of 16 parliamentary committees were established to look at developments in a wide range of subjects including public expenditure, womens' rights, crime, drug abuse, marital breakdown, legislation and development co-operation. These committees are innovative not only by virtue of the range of subjects which will be considered but also because of the procedures which have been adopted for the preparation of their reports. In a number of cases the committees will hold public hearings and will include a report on these in their reports to Parliament.

The absence of real debate which has been such a feature in relation to reports of the Joint Committee has also characterised the reports on the developments in the European Communities. These reports are submitted to Parliament by the government twice a year under the terms of the European Communities Act (1972). In fact, the debate on these reports is frequently negligible. The reports are not considered regularly, and one debate often covers several reports. The other mechanism by which members of Parliament can seek information from ministers on government policy and its effects, the Parliamentary question, has not been exploited to any significant extent to further the debate on issues arising within the EEC. While this is obviously due in part to lack of familiarity with the workings of the EEC and of the details of EEC policy, it is also a consequence of the importance of constituency politics in the Irish political system. This has led to a situation where parliamentary questions have frequently centred on issues of administrative rather than of legislative policy. As one commentator has remarked, Irish parliamentarians have shown 'traditional willingness to give the government considerable initiative and control over policy and administration' (14).

Under the Irish Constitution the 'sole and exclusive power of making laws for the state' resides with the Houses of Parliament. However, in practice Parliament has played a relatively limited role in the elaboration of laws. The executive powers of the state are exercised by, or on the authority of, the government, which acts as a body and is collectively responsible for the conduct of the affairs of the state. In practice it is of course not possible for the Cabinet to meet to consider each and every decision. The policy guidelines are agreed by the government as a whole and individual ministers then take decisions on questions arising within or in relation to the department for which they have responsibility.

On questions relating to the European Communities, cabinet discussion usually takes place at the initiative of individual ministers, most frequently the Minister for Foreign Affairs, whose departments prepare memoranda for the government which outline the background to the particular question and suggest possible policy directions. In the period 1973-1977, a cabinet sub-committee was established to deal with EEC affairs. However, this sub-committee was not considered to be very effective either as a source of policy initiatives or as a forum for broader discussion of matters arising from EEC business and it has not been reinstated since 1977. One commentator has suggested that 'neither the cabinet committee nor the full Cabinet is an important source of policy initiatives, for in so far as initiatives stem from ministers, this is usually through departmental channels' (15). The committee was seen by the same writer as a 'court of appeal ... to reconcile departmental differences in which the policy options have already been drastically reduced' (16).

INTERMINISTERIAL COORDINATION

The formal mechanism for interministerial coordination on questions arising from Ireland's membership of the European Communities is the interdepartmental European Communities committee. This committee is composed of high-level officials of the Departments of Foreign Affairs, Prime Minister, Finance, Agriculture and Fisheries, Trade, Commerce and Tourism and Industry and Energy. The Permanent Representative to the EEC attends on a regular basis while high-level officials of other departments are invited to attend when issues of importance to them are being discussed. The European Communities committee meets under the chairmanship of the Secretary of the Department of Foreign Affairs approximately once a month. Its function is to consider overall policy in relation to the European Communities; it is not involved in day-to-day coordination and does not seek to define a position in respect of issues as they arise. The committee acts as the coordination mechanism for the submission of periodic reports to the government on developments in the European Communities and it also prepares proposals on overall policy issues for submission to the Cabinet. In particular cases it may consider strategy for negotiations, but this is not its main activity.

At the time of Ireland's initial application for membership of the European Communities in 1961, the Department of Finance assumed the leading role in coordinating the preparation of material for the negotiations and was responsible for the organisation of interdepartmental committees to perform this function. However, at the time when the accession negotiations resumed in 1970, the Minister for Foreign Affairs was given the responsibility for conducting the negotiations. Following accession, the responsibility for overall coordination of work relating to Ireland's membership of the European Communities was assigned to the Department of Foreign Affairs, while individual departments retain primary responsibility for their own subject areas.

The transfer of the role of coordinator on European Community issues from the Department of Finance to the Department of Foreign Affairs did not take place without an administrative struggle. The Department of Finance had viewed Irish membership of the Community as a matter of economic and commercial policy, but by 1970 it had become clear that it had much wider implications of a political, economic and social character. The solution of the conflict was seen by some as a question of central importance affecting 'the allocation of prime responsibility for European affairs, and also the status, influence and role of the departments within the administrative hierarchy and the decision-making process' (17). The increase in the role of the Department of Foreign Affairs was also due in part to the dynamic attitude towards the EEC taken by the Minister for Foreign Affairs, Dr Garret FitzGerald, who assumed office shortly after accession in 1973 and took on the duties of the 1975 Presidency with considerable enthusiasm. His term of office ended in 1977, but by then he had succeeded in using EEC membership as the means through which to revitalise the department, and to increase its standing within the administration. At the same time other departments, which previously had little or no international experience, have undergone significant changes in response to the demands of EEC membership. For many line departments, much of their work is now related to questions arising from Ireland's membership of the European Communities rather than to internal or bilateral issues. Other departments face demands to fulfil obligations directly arising from membership; for example, the revenue commissioners are responsible for a compilation of all VAT receipts required to calculate the 1 per cent payable by Ireland to the Community budget. Most officials of the Department of Agriculture now work on the elaboration of Community rather than national policies, and on the implementation of legislation and the supervision of European Agricultural Guidance and Guarantee Fund (EAGGF) spending.

The Department of Foreign Affairs acts as the channel for communications between the Permanent Representation and the departments in Dublin, a function which is carried out by its economic division. It is responsible for ensuring that the departments receive all information of interest to them in connection with developments in the European Communities including documentation, draft decisions etc.. It also coordinates the transmission of instructions for Coreper meetings and compiles briefing material for meetings of the Foreign Affairs Council and on 'A' points for other Council meetings ('A' points are those on which agreement has already been reached at official level and on which the assent of Ministers is required.). Departments whose minister is attending a Council meeting have the responsibility for the coordination of the briefing material on 'B' points (items on which there will be substantive discussion). In this case the material is prepared by the department primarily concerned.

The members of the staff of the Permanent Representation also ensure that relevant information is transmitted to the appropriate departments in Dublin. As the staff includes representatives from the main departments involved in EEC affairs, direct contact between them and their parent department in relation to on-going Community business is frequent. In the light of the very nature of Community business, such contact is of necessity pragmatic, and the emphasis is on effective and efficient handling of business rather than on formal adherence to tightly controlled procedures.

Interdepartmental coordination on day-to-day aspects of Community business is conducted either by means of special meetings convened to discuss a particular issue or by informal contacts between officials of different departments. Because of the small size of the Irish administration and the relatively small number of officials involved in dealing with Community business, contacts are frequently informal. Departments have retained primary responsibility for questions arising in their traditional area of competence and the lead department arranges for representation at meetings of Council and at Coreper working groups. It may consult other departments about this representation and is expected to agree with them the line it proposes to take at the meeting on aspects of policy which are of interest to them. The position to be taken by the Irish delegate at the meeting is frequently agreed in informal consultations between departments, but may be the subject of a special interdepartmental meeting if several departments are involved.

Conflicts of interest among departments are relatively rare. Where they do occur, officials usually endeavour to resolve them by informal consultation. Should this prove unsuccessful, an interested department may request a coordination meeting at which all the departments concerned can be represented. In all cases the Department of Foreign Affairs is advised of the request for a coordination meeting and in many cases it arranges for such a meeting to be held. In other cases direct discussions between those primarily interested can lead to a solution of the problem and thus obviate the need for a formal meeting. Should it not be possible to resolve conflicts of interest at the day-to-day working level by informal contacts or at a coordination meeting among officials, these problems are brought to the attention of the European Communities committee. In cases where it is not possible to find a solution in this committee, the conflict can be submitted to the government for decision. In other cases it may be resolved in direct contact between the ministers concerned or in direct consultations between their highest level officials.

PREPARATION OF POSITIONS WITHIN MINISTRIES

The relatively informal nature of the Irish administrative system, aided by frequent and direct contacts between the small number of senior officials involved in EEC affairs, has led to a pragmatic approach being adopted to deal with problems as they arise and also influences the way in which an Irish position is defined on a particular subject or dossier. Contacts between officials are often informal and consultation is frequently oral. Occasionally formal meetings are convened to allow discussion of a particular issue or number of issues, but this type of coordination is the exception rather than the rule.

The initial processing of a dossier is frequently done by a relatively junior administrative official (administrative officer or third secretary), whose responsibility includes the identification of the major issues raised by the dossier in question and possible problems it may cause for Ireland. Decisions on whether to bring questions to the political level for advice from the Minister or Minister of State are frequently determined by the extent to which the particular problem is one of domestic political interest or whether it has wider implications for other issues under discussion at Community level. In the Irish administrative system, ministers have traditionally not been surrounded by their own 'cabinet'. In some cases they have one or two special advisers, but in most cases they have relied on officials within their department to advise them on questions of policy. This system has meant that officials, whether they are senior or middle-level, when dealing with a particular dossier are in direct contact with the minister and will have a certain amount of access to him.

In general terms a distinction can be drawn between the treatment of issues which fall under the treaties, and those which are in the field of European Political Co-operation (EPC). For issues falling under the treaties, interministerial coordination is frequently required, as many of the subjects which are dealt with in this context are not within the

147

exclusive competence of one department. On the other hand, questions which arise in the framework of European Political Co-operation are almost always under the exclusive purview of the Department of Foreign Affairs and, in almost all cases, consultations take place exclusively within that department.

Issues which fall under the Treaties remain the primary responsibility of the department which has competence for the question at the domestic policy level. The departments which have a sustained involvement and interest in Community affairs have one or more members of their staff assigned to the Permanent Representation in Brussels. These officials attend meetings of working groups of the Council which are convened to consider issues within the competence of their parent department. Briefing for delegates to these meetings is frequently prepared by the delegate himself, in consultation with his parent department. This consultation may be channelled through the Department of Foreign Affairs or may be direct. Should a particular problem arise covering issues of concern to more than one department, interdepartmental consultation will take place either formally or informally. Opportunities for consultation are taken up as they arise; for example, problems may be discussed between officials of several departments in the corridors at meetings which they are attending in Brussels.

Briefing material for Coreper is coordinated by the Department of Foreign Affairs. However, the Permanent Representative and his Deputy also receive reports directly from the members of the staff of the Permanent Representation who have attended the previous discussions at the level of the working group. Further advice may be sought from or through the Department of Foreign Affairs on the preferred Irish position on the basis of this briefing. Through this procedure the Permanent Representative becomes aware of differences of appreciation between departments and thus may become the informal arbiter in seeking to establish a common view.

The written briefing material for ministers attending Council meetings is prepared both by the Department of Foreign Affairs and by the minister's own department. The Department of Foreign Affairs prepares the material on 'A' points, the minister's own department coordinates the preparation of material on 'B' points. An essential element in the briefing of ministers for Council is the delegation meeting which has taken place following the minister's arrival at the venue for Council, in Brussels or Luxembourg. This meeting provides a supplement to the written briefing and is attended by the members of the delegation who have accompanied the minister from Dublin and the Permanent Representative and officials of the Permanent Representation who have normally followed the discussions at the working group. The delegation meeting allows the minister to be provided with the latest information available on the discussions to date and on the likely positions of other EEC Member States, and allows any remaining problems in his briefing to be resolved.

Questions which arise in the framework of European Political Co-operation naturally receive a different treatment. These questions are normally handled exclusively by the Department of Foreign Affairs, and coordination on them takes place within the department itself. The Political Director is head of the political division and the European correspondent is a senior member of the staff of that division. They assume the primary responsibility for the handling of questions which arise in the framework of European Political Co-operation and for the definition of the national position in relation to these questions. In many cases the policy adopted will be approved by the minister and, in some cases, consultation with other divisions of the department will take place on aspects of wider interest within the department. On issues which have implications of a wider kind or which may impinge on other aspects of national policy, the suggested position may be referred to the Prime Minister for his approval.

THE ROLE OF THE PERMANENT REPRESENTATION AND RELATIONS WITH THE EC INSTITUTIONS

The Permanent Representation naturally plays a central role in Ireland's on-going relation with the EC institutions and in relations with other Member States in the framework of the meetings which take place continually at Community level. It maintains contacts with officials of the Community institutions at all levels and with representatives of other Member States through contacts with other Permanent Representations and with officials from their capitals attending meetings in Brussels. It advises on the likely time-table for the consideration of Commission proposals and services many of the Council and Commission working groups.

The Permanent Representation has a staff of 25 diplomatic officers. Of these 11 are members of the Department of Foreign Affairs while the remaining 14 are from other departments but seconded to the Department of Foreign Affairs for the duration of their assignment to the Permanent Representation. The breakdown of the staff is as follows:

- Permanent Representative, Deputy Permanent Representative and nine other officials from the Department of Foreign Affairs;
- two officials from the Department of Agriculture;
- three officials from the Department of Finance (one of whom is specifically charged with the responsibility of being the link with the Department of the Public Service);
- four officials from the Department of Trade, Commerce and Tourism;
- one official from the Department of Industry and Energy;
- one official from the Department of Transport;
- one official from the Department of the Environment;
- one official from the Department of Labour;
- one official from the Department of Social Welfare.

For further details see Table 7.1.

In addition to the Permanent Representative and Deputy Permanent Representative there are eight counsellors, twelve first secretaries and three third secretaries. Staff of departments other than Foreign Affairs who are assigned to the Permanent Representation are seconded to Foreign Affairs at the corresponding diplomatic grade (see Table 7.2). The average length of assignment for all staff at the Permanent Representation is three or four years, regardless of their department of origin.

The division of responsibilities among the staff of the Permanent Representation follows the distribution of competences between departments on Community issues. Officials from the Department of Foreign Affairs assume responsibility for external relations, for general coordination and for general affairs, including relations with the European Parliament and other institutional questions. The Permanent Representative and the Deputy Permanent Representative have overall responsibilities, while most of the other members of staff have specific sectoral duties.

Contacts between the Permanent Representation and the National Administration

Contacts between the Permanent Representation and the national administration are maintained at all levels, and for many members of the staff of the Permanent Representation take place almost daily. These contacts include reporting from the Permanent Representation on developments in Brussels, both during meetings and in other less formal gatherings, consultations on positions to be taken by the national delegate at forthcoming meetings, provision of briefing material for officials in Dublin, etc. Some of the contacts will be formal, by the provision of written reports or requests for instructions. In many other cases consultations will be informal, particularly by telephone or through personal contacts with Dublin-based officials attending meetings in Brussels.

On a more formal level, the Permanent Representative attends meetings of the European Communities committee. Other members of the Permanent Representation are occasionally recalled for briefing or consultation, in particular in advance of Council meetings which their minister will attend. In some cases they will attend discussions in which policy is reviewed. Although regular contact is maintained, no fixed rules apply and the frequency of contact depends to a large extent on the department to which the individual official belongs. In recent times budgetary constraints have contributed to a reduction in the number of meetings which members of the staff of the Permanent Representation attend in Dublin.

Before the Presidency

Because of its central role in Ireland's relations with the European Community and its Member States, the Permanent Representation plays a very important part in the substantive preparation of the Presidency. The Permanent Representation prepares the initial paper on the major issues likely to arise during the Presidency and suggests possible objectives for the Irish chairmanship. It makes suggestions concerning the provision of chairmen of the various Council working groups which are expected to be active during the Presidency and, together with the Department of Foreign Affairs, ensures that other departments will be in a position to provide chairmen for groups for which they have primary responsibility.

During the Presidency

The Permanent Representation assumed a crucial role in Ireland's first two presidencies, in 1975 and 1979. It was responsible for the day-to-day handling of the Presidency in light of the general objectives for the Presidency approved by the government. As the members of the diplomatic staff of the Permanent Representation normally assumed the chairmanship of the groups which they had been attending as national delegates prior to the Presidency, the work of the Permanent Representation became almost exclusively presidency-oriented and the Permanent Representation provided the chairmen for many of the working groups. Other chairmen remained based in Dublin and travelled to Brussels as required. In cases where the chairmen were based at the Permanent Representation, national delegates, mostly travelling from Dublin for the meeting, were expected to assume the duties normally connected with the work of a national delegate to free the Brussels-based chairmen for presidency duties.

For those officials attached to the Permanent Representation the methods of preparation for the Presidency, in relation to the specific issues which would be before them as chairmen, were mainly of an on-the-job character. For the most part, officials designated to assume responsibilities as chairmen of working groups or committees meeting regularly were assigned to the Permanent Representation at least six to twelve months in advance of the Presidency. They became national delegates to working groups which they would be called upon to chair during the Presidency, and were expected to make the contacts which they considered necessary for their effective chairmanship. They were encouraged to establish close contacts with relevant officials in the Commission and in the Council Secretariat, with a view to working in collaboration with them during the Presidency.

A training programme was organised for many of the Dublin-based officials who would assume responsibilities as chairmen during the Presidency. They followed a special course run by the Institute of Public Administration which covered the following topics:

1)   the background to the EEC policies of other Member States;
2)   the role and functions of the Community institutions;
3)   role of the Presidency;
4)   committee rules and procedures;
5)   the technical and other functions of the chairman;
6)   skills of chairmanship.

The duration of these courses was of up to 10 working days, and was organised in modules spread over a period of 6 months.

For the 1979 Presidency, the staff of the Permanent Representation was increased by five diplomatic officers and by four executive officers. The executive officers were assigned to act as desk officers and, in particular, to ensure liaison between chairmen and departments in Dublin on issues as they arose. In general it was considered desirable to keep the increase in the staff of the Permanent Representation to the minimum necessary to perform the tasks of the Presidency, in order to avoid too many changes in working procedures.

Another feature of adaptation to the demands of the Presidency period was the tightening of the internal coordination mechanisms within the Permanent Representation itself. The Permanent Representative was fully informed of all the main issues under discussion and, in particular, on issues of importance for the overall management of the Presidency. The Irish representative in the Antici group was assigned the role of coordinator within the Permanent Representation and was responsible for planning many of the practical aspects of the Presidency. (The Antici group is an informal group composed of the personal assistants to the Permanent Representatives. Since its establishment in 1975, the group has become responsible for the preparation and coordination of arrangements and agenda for Coreper II and the Foreign Affairs Council. The members of the group are points of contact for the Council Secretariat, the Commission and other Member States. They are also responsible for coordination between Brussels and European Political Co-operation). An assistant to the Antici group member was appointed to work in a similar function for issues arising at Coreper I to ensure the tighest possible coordination within the Representation. Reports to Dublin were oriented towards the Presidency and towards issues which would have an impact on the organisation of meetings, while responsibility for substantive reports on meetings as they affected national perceptions and interests was left to the national delegate.

During the six months of the Presidency contacts between the staff of the Permanent Representation and the Council Secretariat were close and frequent, in particular in relation to the planning of programmes and timetables. Chairmen made use of the briefing provided by the staff of the Council Secretariat for them and took advantage of the advice provided on problems which arose during meetings.

The Irish perception is that the Commission has a vital role to play in the drawing-up of the Presidency programme and timetable. Before the first Irish Presidency in 1975, the Irish Foreign Minister met the members of the Commission to discuss issues which were likely to arise for the Community during the following six months. This practice was innovative. Up to then it had been the custom for incoming Presidents of the Council to call on the President of the Commission but not to meet all the members of the Commission. This practice was taken up by other countries and was repeated before the second Irish Presidency in 1979. The purpose of the meeting is considered to be to provide an opportunity for the in-coming President to be informed directly of issues of particular concern to the Commission and to allow the Commission and President to discuss together the organisation of Community business for the period of the Presidency.

THE PRESIDENCY AND EUROPEAN POLITICAL CO-OPERATION

Ireland's accession to the European Communities in 1973 led to a considerable increase in the scope and content of issues facing Ireland in international relations. Up to 1973 the United Nations had been the main focus of Ireland's activities at the multilateral level. Ireland had remained outside many of the more important developments in Europe and her involvement in regional international politics had been limited. This was in part a consequence of history and of the particular relationship with Britain, but was also due to the location of Ireland. Having remained neutral during the Second World War, the country did not become a member of NATO, at its establishment in 1949, largely for bilateral reasons. Ireland also remained aloof from the original movements towards European integration in the 1950s. In addition the number of Ireland's diplomatic offices abroad (26 in 1972, including 18 embassies, 5 consulates, 2 missions to the UN and the Permanent Representation to the European Communities) and their limited geographic distribution, with only four of the offices situated outside Europe and North America, (Buenos Aires, Canberra, New Delhi and Lagos) had resulted in a very limited number of direct contacts between Ireland and other countries except in multilateral fora such as at the United Nations.

Participation in European Political Co-operation has led to a significant change in the manner of Ireland's involvement in international relations. Because of the nature of EPC, it is no longer possible for Ireland to choose the issues with which it wishes to become involved. In EPC, 'each Member State is no longer in a position to confine its diplomatic activity to issues impinging on its own immediate interests, or to pick and choose in accordance with its own priorities the questions on which it wishes to be active or for which it feels a particular affinity' (18). To allow Ireland to cope with the demands arising from EPC, there has been a considerable expansion and extensive reorganisation of the Political Division of the Department of Foreign Affairs which assumed the responsibilities arising from Ireland's participation in European Political Co-operation. In 1972 there had been 12 officials of diplomatic rank working in the Political and Cultural Division. Following accession, this Political Division was reorganised on the basis of a 'desk' system, with the 'desks' divided geographically, and corresponding to a considerable degree to the working groups of European Political Co-operation. In 1983 the division has a staff of 23 diplomatic officers. The number of resident embassies has risen to 29, and 3 development co-operation offices have been opened. In addition Ireland now has ambassadors accredited to a further 26 countries on a non-residential basis. The new arrangements have taken account of the need for the Irish administration to be able to respond to the demands placed on it by its participation in European Political Co-operation.

During the Presidency
The administration of the machinery of European Political Co-operation and the organisation of meetings held within this framework is one of

the more onerous tasks of the Presidency. As William Wallace has commented, in Political Co-operation 'national governments themselves provide the role which in the Community is played by the Commission and the Council Secretariat in Brussels' (19). He adds that 'the Presidency, rotating among the member governments every six months is thus the key element in Political Co-operation' (20). It is the country holding the Presidency which assumes direct responsibility for convening meetings of Political Co-operation (now 60 to 80 meetings per term of office), and for consultations held in third countries and in delegations to international organisations, especially the United Nations. In addition the Presidency takes over the responsibility for the operation of the COREU network, and thus for communications between the foreign ministries of the Ten. All of this places a very significant burden on the national administration, in particular a small one. Fortunately policy coordination within a small administration can be somewhat more flexible than in larger ones. It has been said that 'it is largely through this type of flexibility and intimacy that an administration of such limited resources can cope with the demands of the Presidency' (21).

The Irish administration has depended largely on normal staffing arrangements to cope with the burdens of the Presidency period. Staff increases are kept to a minimum and officials are expected to take on an extra workload to enable the tasks of the Presidency to be carried out. At the end of 1978, the staff of the Political Division was 21 (1 deputy secretary, 4 counsellors, 8 first secretaries and 8 third secretaries). For the duration of Ireland's second Presidency in the second half of 1979, the staff of the division was increased by one first secretary and one third secretary who were assigned to cope with the organisational matters arising from the Presidency. They dealt in particular with arrangements for meetings held in Dublin, including those of the Political Directors, Foreign Ministers and the European Council. The number of support staff was increased by 16, including five French language typists and three translators.

In order to improve coordination within the Department of Foreign Affairs, the usual weekly meeting of the secretary, deputy secretary and assistant secretaries was expanded to include counsellors and first secretaries. These meetings discussed the agenda for the week and the administrative problems likely to arise in connection with the management of the Presidency. The discussion focussed on the issues likely to arise at meetings in Brussels and the administrative and organisational implications of meetings to be held in Ireland, especially meetings of European Political Co-operation. The Permanent Representation, with the assistance of the Council Secretariat, was responsible for the coordination of arrangements for meetings in Brussels. Prior to the Presidency, two other groups had been involved in the material planning of the Presidency. These were a committee to discuss physical arrangements for meetings including representatives of the Departments of the Prime Minister, Finance, Foreign Affairs and the Office of Public Works (responsible for provision of rooms and facilities). A committee within the Department of Foreign Affairs had brought together representatives of the different divisions to make the necessary arrangements for the hosting of meetings, including the provision of hospitality and the setting-up of the necessary material facilities.

In line with the agreement of the Ten to improve coordination between out-going and in-coming presidencies, Ireland has joined in the arrangement whereby staff from the preceding and succeeding presidencies are assigned to the Foreign Ministry of the country holding the Presidency. Under this arrangement officials from the Foreign Ministries of France and Italy were assigned to the Political Division to assist in the management of European Political Co-operation.

External Relations and the Presidency

Another aspect of the Presidency which puts a considerable burden on the administration and on the Minister for Foreign Affairs himself is the external representation of the Community by the Presidency alone or by the Presidency in conjunction with the Commission. This external representation gives a small country a much more prominent position in international affairs than it has at other times. During the first Irish Presidency in 1975, the then Foreign Minister, Dr Garret FitzGerald, visited Washington, Lisbon, Athens, Ankara, Tel Aviv and four Arab capitals in his capacity as President-in-Office of the EC. It was the first visit of an Irish Foreign Minister to several of these. The fact that Dr FitzGerald was speaking as the representative of the Community and not simply as Irish Foreign Minister increased the weight given to the views he expressed and enhanced the importance attached to his visit. There are other less demanding tasks which fall to the President-in-Office, such as the reception of credentials of ambassadors from third countries accredited to the Community and the signature of a large number of routine documents. These tasks are less onerous in terms of time and preparation and were frequently performed by the Irish Foreign Minister in conjunction with a visit to Brussels to preside over a Foreign Affairs Council meeting.

For the administration, the tasks of coordinating the position of the Community and speaking on behalf of the EC and its Member States at meetings of international organisations, such as the United Nations General Assembly, were particularly demanding in terms of time and effort. The work associated with the elaboration of the positions of the EC Member States and the reflection of these positions in a common statement delivered by a representative of the Presidency was especially onerous. To allow the delegation to the General Assembly to cope with the responsibilities of the Presidency, together with the task of representing Ireland at the session, the delegation in 1979 was twice that of the previous year. The increase of staff was achieved by the temporary transfer of staff from offices, in most cases embassies, which were considered to have few responsibilities in relation to the Presidency, or which were thought to have enough staff to cope with these responsibilities.

The embassies of the country holding the Presidency also assume a particular role during the Presidency. In capitals other than those of the other EC Member States they become the channel for official communications between the Presidency and the host country. They also host the monthly meetings of EC ambassadors and other EC meetings, such as those of economic counsellors. Because of the small number of countries in which Ireland has a resident ambassador (29 at present) the representations made by Irish ambassadors on behalf of the Community are relatively few. However, any approach agreed by the Ten necessitates urgent and specific instructions to the relevant embassy, in line with the established procedures of European Political Co-operation. Where possible any approach to the authorities of a country to which Ireland has accredited a non-resident ambassador is also made by the Irish ambassador.

NATIONAL EXPECTATIONS AND OBJECTIVES FOR THE PRESIDENCY

As indicated earlier in this study, Ireland's accession to the European Communities opened up a new horizon in her relations with the outside world. Accession had been supported by the vast majority of the Irish people and membership of the EC had been heralded with enthusiasm. By the time of Ireland's first term in the Presidency in 1975, this optimism still remained. The financial benefits of EC membership were obvious, in particular in the agricultural sector and the net receipts from the EC were of the order of £ 106 million over the two-year period 1973-'74 (22). In 1975 one commentator wrote that 'Irish membership in the Community has fulfilled the expectations of the overwhelming majority of Irish people who voted, in May 1972, to enter the EEC' (23).

Under the leadership of the Foreign Minister, Dr Garret FitzGerald, the Presidency was welcomed as an opportunity to play a role on the international stage and to contribute in a meaningful way to the progress of the Community. As Helen Wallace has written, 'for a small country this six-month period offers the opportunity of playing a genuinely mediatory role while at the same time gaining in national prestige' (24). The challenge of the Presidency was seen by many in terms of an occasion on which to prove that small countries can also perform the tasks of the Presidency with success. The significance of the role as a means of broadening the scope of national foreign policy was not lost on observers. As William Wallace has commented, 'for the Irish government, its assumption of the Presidency in January 1975 opened up a new dimension in its foreign policy, with Garret FitzGerald, its Foreign Minister, convincing a sceptical Dr Kissinger that a small country was capable of managing the United States' consultative relationship with the Nine, and conducting a successful tour of Middle Eastern countries which had previously had only the most indirect of relations with his country' (25).

Within the Community also the period of the Irish Presidency was one of optimism. The Paris Summit of December 1974 had unblocked a number of issues which had been hampering progress, and the outcome augured well for the evolution of Community institutions and political co-operation. In addition the Summit had gone some way towards narrowing the gap between the U.K. and France on the revision of the terms of Britain's entry to the Community. It fell to Dr FitzGerald to announce the achievements of the Summit to the European Parliament in his first statement as President of the Council of Ministers on 19

February 1975. By then he was also able to announce the successful conclusion of negotiations between the EEC and the ACP countries, thus giving a rather positive view of Ireland's initial month as President-in-Office.

One of the concerns of the Irish Presidency in 1975 was to improve in a concrete manner the relations between the Council and other Community institutions. In his speech to the European Parliament on 19 February, Dr FitzGerald stressed this as one of the main objectives of the Presidency. He reported that he had met the Commission as a whole in December 1974 to discuss the programme of work for the coming semester. In addition he expressed his hope of achieving closer relations between the Council and Parliament, and between the Council and the Economic and Social Committee. Throughout the Presidency, Dr FitzGerald sought to live up to the intentions outlined in this speech, and expressed his belief that direct elections to the European Parliament should be accompanied by an extension of its powers.

By the time of the second Irish Presidency beginning in July 1979, the situation in Ireland and in the Community had become more serious with the European Council of 21 and 22 June concentrating on the world energy situation and the need for a consolidated Community approach to it, both in the short and longer term. As the Irish Foreign Minister, Mr Michael O'Kennedy commented: 'We saw the danger of large-scale economic and social crisis and this underpinned our determined resolve to maintain our oil imports at the 1978 level until 1985' (26). On the same occasion he stated that the Irish Presidency would endeavour' to ensure that the Community is united and consistent in its efforts to tackle the major problems facing it'.

The second Irish Presidency, like the first one, included in its objectives the improvement of relations between the Council and the European Parliament and the harmonisation of their respective roles. The 1979 Presidency, which came into office shortly after the direct elections to the Parliament, was obviously facing a new Assembly anxious to establish its credibility and to assert itself. In his speech to the Parliament on 19 July 1979, Mr O'Kennedy promised to ensure that 'under the Irish Presidency due weight and gravity should be seen to attach to the Parliament's salient role'. However, it proved difficult for the Presidency to satisfy the demands of the newly-elected Assembly for greater attention by the Council to its resolutions and for increasing the number and quality of the reports made by ministers on developments in the Council.

Within the administration the task of the Presidency is perceived above all as the responsibility for the management, and to a certain extent the organisation, of the day-to-day business of the Community. However, it is also seen as the duty of the Presidency to seek to advance the discussions at all levels within the Community and in relations between the Community and other countries or groups of countries. Irish officials approach their six-month term as President with the aim of conducting Community business during the period as efficiently and effectively as possible. In establishing the objectives for the Presidency there is a consciousness that six months is a short time in which to play a motor role in furthering developments in the Community, and in particular, that any new initiative is unlikely to come to fruition during the period. In addition certain issues require the attention of the country holding the Presidency e.g. the negotiation of the Community budget takes place during the second semester and has to be dealt with by the Presidency-in-Office, and a number of items of on-going business are automatically inherited from the outgoing Presidency. The identification of specific objectives for the Presidency is therefore carried out in a spirit of realism rather than one of innovation, and attempts are made to avoid the setting of over-ambitious targets. Nevertheless, the objectives for the Presidency will normally include the improvement of existing procedures within the EEC and the strengthening of interinstitutional coordination and consultation. In addition a number of issues will be highlighted for special attention and effort and the Presidency will attempt to make significant progress on a certain number of files during Ireland's tenure of office.

The structures adopted for the first Irish Presidency of the European Communities in 1975 were modified only slightly for the 1979 Presidency and it is anticipated that there will be no fundamental changes for the next Irish Presidency in 1984. From an administrative point of view there is little modification for periods of Presidency of the basic structures which have been adopted do deal with EEC issues in general and with interdepartmental coordination on Community issues (27). The impact of the Presidency is therefore perceived more in terms of the quality and nature of the work associated with the performance of the tasks which fall to the country holding the Presidency rather than the adjustment of the structures to cope with these tasks.

REFERENCES:

(1)   For a general introduction to the Irish political system and its background see B. Chubb, The Government and Politics of Ireland. Stanford University Press, second edition 1982, Chap. I, pp. 5-23.

(2)   Statistics for 1972 from Historical Statistics of Foreign Trade, OECD Paris 1982 pp 66-67. Statistics for 1982 from OECD Economic Surveys - Ireland, OECD Paris 1983.

(3)   Basil Chubb, 'Treasury Control and Economic Planning' in Administration vol. 4, no. 3 (1956), Institute of Public Administration, Dublin.

(4)   R. Fanning, The Irish Department of Finance 1922-58, Institute of Public Administration, Dublin 1978, p. 509.

(5)   T.K. Whitaker Economic Development, Stationery Office, Dublin, 1958, Pr. 4803.

(6)   Programme for Economic Expansion, Stationary Office, Dublin, 1958, Pr 4796.

(7)   Cited in R. Fanning, The Irish Department of Finance 1922-58, Institute of Public Administration, Dublin 1978, p. 609.

(8)   S. Lemass 'The Task of Reorganisation', Address to the fourth conference on higher administrative studies at Killarney on 26 April 1962 in Administration vol. 10, no 1 (1962), Institute of Public Administration, Dublin p. 4.

(9)   The accession of Ireland to the European Communities, Stationery Office, Dublin 1972, Prl. 2064, p. 66.

(10)   Ibid, p. 55.

(11)   P. Keating 'Ireland and The World 1957-82' in Administration, vol. 30, nrs 2 and 3, Institute of Public Administration, Dublin 1983, p. 226.

(12)   For a general discussion on this point see D. Coombes, The Role of National Parliaments in Christoph Sasse (et al), Decision-Making in the European Community, Praeger Publishers, New York 1977, pp. 310-331.

(13)   Fifty-fifth Report of the Joint Committee on the Secondary Legislation of the European Communities, Stationery Office, Dublin, 1977, Prl. 6169.

(14)   B. Chubb, The Government and Politics of Ireland, Stanford University Press, second edition 1982, p. 197.

(15)   P. Keating, A Place among the Nations, Institute of Public Administration, Dublin 1978, p. 219.

(16)   Ibid, p. 219.

(17)   B. Burns and T. Salmon, 'Policy-making coordination in Ireland on European Community issues' in Journal of Common Market Studies, Oxford 1977, vol. XV, p. 278.

(18)   'Ireland and European Political Co-operation'. Paper presented by P. MacKernan, Assistant Secretary and Political Director, Department of Foreign Affairs, to the fourth annual conference of the National Committee for the Study of International Affairs, Royal Irish Academy, Dublin, 20 November 1981.

(19)   William Wallace 'Introduction: Co-operation and Convergence in European Foreign Policy' in C. Hill (ed.). National Foreign Policies and

European Political Co-operation, George Allen and Unwin, London 1983, p. 3.

(20) Idem, p. 3.

(21) P. Keatinge 'Ireland: neutrality inside EPC' in C. Hill (ed), National Foreign Policies and European Political Co-operation, George Allen and Unwin, London 1983, p. 148.

(22) Figure cited in E. Moxon Browne 'Ireland in the EEC', The World To-day, vol. 31 no. 10, 1975, p. 309.

(23) Idem, p. 425.

(24) Helen Wallace 'Holding the ring: the EEC Presidency', The World To-day, vol. 31 no. 8, 1975, p. 309.

(25) William Wallace, op. cit. p. 5.

(26) M. O'Kennedy. Speech to the European Parliament, 19 July 1979.

(27) For a general description, see D. Scott 'EEC Membership and the Irish Administrative System', Administration, Institute of Public Administration, Dublin, vol. 31, no. 2, 14-199.

TABLE 7.1

Permanent Representation of Ireland to the European Communities
Summer 1983

Permanent Representative:	His Excellency A. O'Rourke
Deputy Permanent Representative:	Mr John Swift

Sections:

Agriculture	1 Counsellor 1 First Secretary
Environment	1 First Secretary
External Relations	2 Counsellors 2 First Secretaries 1 Third Secretary
Finance	1 Counsellor 2 First Secretaries
Trade, Commerce and Tourism	1 Counsellor 2 First Secretaries 1 Third Secretary
Industry and Energy	1 Counsellor
Labour	1 First Secretary
Press and Information	1 First Secretary
Social Welfare	1 First Secretary
Transport	1 Counsellor
General Affairs and Administration	1 Counsellor
General co-ordination	1 First Secretary 1 Third Secretary

TABLE 7.2

Decision-making structure in Irish Government Departments

General service   Department of
                                                   Foreign Affairs
                                                   equivalent

Minister
Minister of State
Secretary
Deputy Secretary
Assistant Secretary

Principal   Counsellor
Assistant Principal   First Secretary
Administrative Officer
Higher Executive Officer   Third Secretary

Chapter 8

LA PRESIDENCE DU CONSEIL DES MINISTRES DES COMMUNAUTES
EUROPEENNES: RAPPORT NATIONAL SUR L'ITALIE
Prof. Antonio Papisca, Padova

INTRODUCTION

L'impact de la présidence du Conseil des Ministres de la Communauté et
des structures de la coopération politique européenne sur l'administration
publique italienne s'avère être actuellement un impact tout à fait
'normal'.

En effet, l'exercice de la présidence est considéré comme une
tâche supplémentaire qui, en dehors du fait qu'elle implique un certain
type de mobilisation de ressources **ad hoc,** ne provoque aucune pression
sur la structure de l'administration nationale.

Selon les fonctionnaires publics, il n'existe en Italie aucun 'traumatisme'
particulier découlant de la présidence des affaires européennes.

Comme on le verra plus en détail dans les pages qui suivent, il existe
trois attitudes différentes de l'administration publique vis-à-vis de la
présidence, mais peut-être est-il plus exact de parler de nuances ou
d'approches complémentaires. On peut affirmer que l'opinion la plus
largement répandue dans les milieux de l'administration publique est que
l'exercice de la présidence, outre qu'il s'agit d'une dimension acquise du
processus de l'intégration européenne, est en soi un fait positif, une
occasion et une chance de plus de développer le système communautaire
et l'intégration en général.

Il ressort très clairement des entrevues avec des hauts
fonctionnaires de l'administration publique qu'ils n'éprouvent aucune gêne
ou indifférence en ce qui concerne le semestre de présidence. Leur
attitude est celle d'une attente plutôt positive, favorable, et on peut dire
qu'il existe un bon degré de disponibilité.

Quoiqu'à la direction générale des affaires économiques du ministère des
Affaires étrangères, on fasse remarquer avec insistance que l'exercice de
la présidence est une série d'actions techniques accomplies au jour le
jour, l'attitude beaucoup plus politisée de la direction générale des
affaires politiques du même ministère n'est pas critiquée. Tout au
contraire, cette attitude est acceptée et justifiée par le reste de
l'administration publique.

L'attitude positive qu'a l'administration italienne vis-à-vis de la
présidence des affaires européennes entre tout à fait dans la ligne de la
politique européenne, au sens communautaire et supranational du terme,

menée traditionnellement par l'Italie. Et pourtant, cette attitude fait ressortir les contradictions qui existent entre cette tradition et les nombreuses difficultés que l'exécution des actes communautaires rencontre à l'intérieur du sous-système gouvernemental et bureaucratique italien.

A cet égard, il faut souligner que la faute ne doit pas être imputée entièrement à l'administration publique. Bien sûr, à l'exception de l'élite des fonctionnaires de la carrière diplomatique et des autres fonctionnaires plus directement engagés dans les affaires communautaires, élite sur laquelle repose le poids de l'exercice de la présidence, il existe à la base de l'administration publique italienne un assez faible degré de préparation en la matière. La responsabilité principale de cette situation revient à la classe politique (partis politiques, membres du parlement national) qui n'a pas encore démontré, au-delà d'une rhétorique européiste parfois ennuyeuse, qu'elle a la capacité et la volonté de créer les prémisses institutionnelles et organisationnelles capables d'assurer une coordination efficace entre le fonctionnement du système communautaire et l'adaptation administrative du système italien.

Grâce à des initiatives intelligentes et efficaces, on a pu créer de facto les bases d'une pratique en matière soit de coordination interne, soit d'exercice (et surtout de préparation à l'exercice) de la présidence. Ces initiatives ont été imaginées et mises en oeuvre par des personnalités de l'administration publique, notamment du ministère des Affaires étrangères. Dans cette entreprise, les hauts fonctionnaires ont su exercer avec doigté et compétence une certaine pression sur les politiciens dans le but d'obtenir la légitimation de cette pratique grâce à leur appui ou, pour le moins, à leur non-opposition. Il est peut-être surprenant de constater qu'à l'intérieur de la philosophie européenne de l'administration publique, le principe primordial est celui de la primauté du 'politique' sur 'l'administratif', alors que les hommes politiques font preuve d'un haut degré d'impréparation et d'insensibilité vis-à-vis des problèmes européens. Il suffit de rappeler à cet égard que les membres du parlement national, en grande majorité, ne lisent pas même le rapport que l'Exécutif leur présente annuellement en matière communautaire.

Dans l'engagement particulier des hauts fonctionnaires de l'administration publique, on pourrait naturellement voir l'ambition de profiter de l'exercice de rôles bureaucratiques qui sont, dans une certaine mesure, encore extraordinaires, aux fins de réaliser une sorte d'auto-promotion de leur statut. Peut-être! D'ailleurs, il ne s'agirait pas d'une stratégie illégitime. En tout cas, une chose est claire: face à une telle attitude, il nous faut développer une pratique qui permette de parer, même dans une mesure incomplète, aux manques et au peu de préparation en matières internationale et européenne de la majorité des membres de la classe politique italienne.

LA STRUCTURE DE L'ADMINISTRATION PUBLIQUE ITALIENNE CONCERNANT LES AFFAIRES COMMUNAUTAIRES ET LA COOPÉRATION POLITIQUE EUROPÉENNE. PRINCIPES ET CRITÈRES.

Pour ce qui concerne les affaires européennes - communautaires **stricto sensu** et coopération politique (CPE) - l'administration publique italienne se structure et agit sur la base des principes et des critères suivants, critères qui peuvent être considérés comme étant définitivement acquis dans la pratique ordinaire:

1) la primauté du 'politique' par rapport à l'"administratif'.

Ceci signifie que les questions communautaires européennes en tant que telles sont considérées du point de vue officiel, soit formel, soit informel, comme ayant un rang et une importance différente et même supérieure par rapport à d'autres questions de politique étrangère. Autrement dit, la gestion des affaires communautaires, même dans leur dimension administrative et bureaucratique, est perçue dans une optique de tension et de développement continus, c'est-à-dire, dans une optique de 'haute politique'.

Que l'on s'adresse soit à des hommes politiques, soit à des fonctionnaires de la carrière diplomatique ou de la carrière dite ordinaire, il ressort qu'en Italie, on continue d'attribuer une importance tout à fait fondamentale et prioritaire au choix européen.

Cette attitude se retrouve régulièrement confirmée dans les programmes des différents cabinets: l'Italie est toujours favorable à l'élargissement ainsi qu'à l'approfondissement de l'intégration européenne, même si dans les milieux les plus responsables, on reconnaît que l'administration publique - mais il faut ajouter le parlement national - n'est pas en mesure d'accomplir les lourdes tâches qui lui sont imposées par le fonctionnement du système politique de la Communauté et des structures de la CPE. On admet donc qu'il n'existe pas de synchronisme entre le fonctionnement du système communautaire et l'adaptation administrative (et tout d'abord législative: il suffit de penser à la question des directives) du système italien.

2) Conformément au principe de la primauté du politique sur l'administratif, le ministère des Affaires étrangères (MAE) garde un rôle principal, voire exclusif, d'orientation et de coordination en matière communautaire et, bien sûr, de CPE.

Basée sur le principe de primauté du politique, la position des Affaires étrangères est justifiée, compte tenu du fait que la politique italienne en matière communautaire, même dans ses aspects routiniers, continue à être considérée comme une partie tout à fait fondamentale de la politique étrangère.

D'autres explications découlent du fait que la présidence du Conseil des Ministres italien (ou, plus exactement, le Premier ministre) n'exerce pas, sinon de façon épisodique et dans une optique de médiation inter-partis, son rôle constitutionnel de coordination des différents éléments de la politique étrangère; ce qui renforce, également dans le domaine des affaires communautaires, le rôle traditionnel d'acteur principal - et donc la primauté non plus seulement administrative - du ministère des Affaires étrangères. Afin d'expliquer cette situation, on admet également dans les milieux de l'administration publique que beaucoup de fonctionnaires n'ont pas une préparation adéquate dans les affaires communautaires et internationales en général. De son côté, l'Ecole Supérieure d'Administration Publique a essayé d'insérer dans ses programmes, un enseignement visant à donner une formation européenne et internationale, surtout du point de vue juridique, mais elle n'a pas encore été en mesure de réaliser de véritables cours de spécialisation multidisciplinaire.

3) La compétence de l'administration publique italienne en matière communautaire est une compétence qu'on peut appeler diffuse, dans le sens qu'elle n'appartient pas à une seule structure spécialisée, mais qu'elle est répartie dans différents ministères et autres institutions publiques (Banca d'Italia, par exemple).

Même à l'intérieur du ministère des Affaires étrangères, il n'existe pas de structure unique ou d'unité administrative qui soit chargée des affaires européennes (communautaires et de CPE), bien que la coordination générale soit faite, en matière spécifiquement communautaire, par la direction générale des Affaires économiques, (la DGAE). Au sein du ministère des Affaires étrangères, la compétence en matière communautaire est opérationnellement partagée entre les directions générales des Affaires économiques, des Affaires politiques, des Affaires sociales et de l'Emigration, avec la collaboration technique d'autres structures, tel par exemple le service du contentieux diplomatique, traités et affaires administratives.

On explique et on justifie le caractère thématique de cette répartition en disant qu'elle permet, entre autres, de faire face plus aisément aux lourdes et coûteuses mobilisations ad hoc qu'implique la gestion de la présidence des institutions communautaires et des structures de la CPE.

Il faut quand même reconnaître que la division du travail à l'intérieur même du ministère des Affaires étrangères n'est pas toujours claire et rationnelle (du moins du point de vue strictement théorique): ainsi par exemple, les travaux concernant la loi sur les élections européennes en vue de la première élection directe du Parlement européen ont été presque complètement effectués par la direction générale de l'Emigration et des Affaires sociales, la préoccupation principale étant évidemment la question du vote des Italiens à l'étranger, et non pas par les directions générales des Affaires économiques ou des Affaires politiques.

4) On a déjà remarqué l'incapacité du cabinet et du Premier ministre à promouvoir et à assurer une coordination continue et efficace entre les différents ministères en matière de politiques communautaires.

Il existe de nombreux éléments qui expliquent cet état de choses: il suffit de rappeler que la présidence du Conseil des Ministres italien n'a pas encore été réglementée dans le sens prévu par la

Constitution; que les cabinets italiens sont, en règle générale, des cabinets de coalition et que le Premier ministre est forcé de réaliser une harmonisation, surtout en matière de politique interne, qui est essentiellement une médiation politique entre les positions des différents partis représentés par les différents ministres.

5) Néanmoins, il existe en Italie une problématique quant à la coordination des affaires communautaires, qui devient de plus en plus pressante. Les fonctionnaires sont les plus sensibles à ces problèmes, les hommes politiques semblant quant à eux moins intéressés à trouver une solution opérationnelle. De toute façon, la coordination se présente comme divisée en deux parties, aspects ou niveaux. Il y a en effet une coordination externe qui est fonction de la définition de la position de l'Italie par rapport aux différentes questions communautaires, ainsi que de la manière dont cette position est représentée et négociée à l'intérieur des processus décisionnels communautaires; et il y a une coordination interne, qui est fonction de l'application des actes communautaires à l'intérieur du système italien. On parle aussi à cet égard d'une phase de pré-negociation et d'une phase de mise en oeuvre (A. Massai). Il faut répéter qu'il ne s'agit pas seulement d'une théorie, mais de la pratique d'une certaine division du travail administratif - et même politique - mise en oeuvre à l'intérieur de l'administration publique italienne.

Dès 1980, cette distinction a trouvé une sorte d'arrangement formel.

De toute façon, une plus grande concentration de ressources a été exigée, et en bonne mesure réalisée de façon flexible en fonction de la coordination qu'on appelle externe.

Encore faut-il remarquer que la coordination interne a presqu'entièrement pour but d'éliminer le retard dans l'application des directives communautaires et de réduire le volume du contentieux communautaire concernant l'Italie.

6) Les relations entre les deux types ou niveaux de coordination ne sont pas encore systématisées et de toute façon, elles se déroulent sur un plan d'inégalité objective. A la lumière des données empiriques qu'on possède en cette matière, il semble que l'unité officiellement chargée de la coordination interne joue un plus grand rôle lorsque le ministre sans portefeuille qui en a la responsabilité politique, est membre d'un parti politique différent de celui du titulaire du ministère des Affaires étrangères. Cette pratique est en tout cas très récente et il est difficile de distinguer entre les actions personnelles du ministre sans portefeuille et l'activité administrative concrète de l'unité bureaucratique placée sous sa direction.

LA COORDINATION EXTERNE

a) Domaine communautaire au sens strict.
La coordination interministérielle est assurée dans ce domaine par la direction générale des affaires économiques (DGAE) du ministère des

Affaires étrangères dont les bureaux 1 et 5 sont spécifiquement chargés des affaires communautaires, le secteur des relations externes étant confié au bureau 5.

Grâce à ces deux bureaux, le ministère des Affaires étrangères garde des contacts directs avec la délégation permanente italienne à Bruxelles et il prend l'initiative de la grande majorité des réunions interministérielles en vue de définir la position italienne qui devra être défendue et négociée dans les processus décisionnels communautaires.

L'approche qui régit la coordination interministérielle est que toute communication entre l'Italie et Bruxelles relève de la compétence principale, sinon exclusive dans la pratique, du ministère des Affaires étrangères, tandis que toute communication de Bruxelles à Rome relève aussi de la compétence du département pour la coordination des politiques communautaires et donc, du ministre sans portefeuille qui en est le chef politique, ainsi que d'autres ministères 'techniques' (notamment Agriculture, Trésor, Commerce extérieur). C'est là une approche pratique et opérationnelle.

Du point de vue strictement institutionnel, la ligne frontière entre la compétence du ministère des Affaires étrangères et celle d'autres structures internes n'est pas exactement tracée. En tout cas, il subsiste une volonté précise du ministère des Affaires étrangères d'assurer de façon autonome la définition et plus encore, la négociation de la position italienne dans les processus décisionnels de la Communauté et de la CPE.

D'un autre côté, l'ambition du ministre sans portefeuille pour la coordination des politiques communautaires, qui est de voir ses compétences élargies à tout ce qui concerne la pré-négociation de la position italienne, ce qui impliquerait des contacts directs avec la délégation permanente à Bruxelles, n'a pas été satisfaite jusqu'à présent.

Au sein de la direction générale des Affaires économiques du ministère des Affaires étrangères, la coordination des deux bureaux déjà mentionnés est assurée par un haut fonctionnaire de la carrière diplomatique (ayant actuellement le rang de conseiller d'ambassade), qui exerce une sorte de supra-fonction, assez atypique dans la pratique administrative ordinaire, par rapport aux fonctions exercées par les deux chefs des bureaux en question.

Le bureau 1 est compétent pour les questions communautaires générales, tandis que le bureau 5 est compétent pour les relations externes. Le bureau 1 se compose de quatre fonctionnaires de la carrière diplomatique (y compris le chef du bureau), trois fonctionnaires techniques détachés d'autres ministères (Agriculture, Industrie, Transports), un expert chargé du secteur 'directives' ainsi que de neuf secrétaires et employés divers.

Le bureau 5 se compose de trois fonctionnaires de la carrière diplomatique (y compris le chef du bureau) et de trois secrétaires et employés.

La situation organisationnelle et fonctionnelle actuelle de la coordination externe, qui doit être considérée comme presque définitivement acquise par la pratique, est le résultat d'une longue évolution qui commença à la veille de la signature du Traité de Rome et qui a comme inspirateur, tenace et concret, l'ambassadeur Cesidio Guazzaroni.

A la fin des années '50, un Comité interministériel fut mis en place; il se composait des ministres des Affaires étrangères, de l'Agriculture, de l'Industrie et des Finances (notamment MM. Segni, Rumor, Colombo, Russo), et était assisté par une vingtaine de directeurs généraux de différents ministères. Ce comité assurait les liaisons entre ministères et remplissait des fonctions consultatives et d'expertise pour le cabinet et le Premier ministre. En 1960, le Premier ministre, M. A. Fanfani créa un Comité de ministres, qui était chargé de la coordination de la politique économique internationale (affaires communautaires comprises), et était placé sous la présidence du Premier ministre. Ce Comité de ministres se composait fondamentalement des ministres des Affaires étrangères, de l'Agriculture, de l'Industrie, du Travail, du Trésor et des Finances, d'autres ministres pouvent s'ajouter le cas échéant. Un sous-comité de directeurs généraux, présidé par le sous-secrétaire d'Etat aux Affaires étrangères, fonctionnait alors en tant qu'organe de travail permanent: un rôle tout à fait particulier y était joué par le directeur général de la DGAE du ministère des Affaires étrangères. En raison de turbulences politiques, le Comité de ministres créé en 1960 espaça ses réunions et c'est à ce moment que se manifesta activement le sous-comité des directeurs généraux (appelé 'Comité Guazzaroni') et que se développa la pratique de la coordination externe conduite par la direction générale des Affaires économiques du ministère des Affaires étrangères. Au début, il y eut une certaine résistance, notamment de la part du ministère du Budget, ainsi qu'un manque d'homogénéité, vu que le Comité interministériel pour la programmation économique (le CIPE) - un organisme 'technique' qui n'a jamais sérieusement fonctionné - revendiquait la discussion de certaines questions de politique économique communautaire.

Graduellement, la DGAE du ministère des Affaires étrangères réussit à faire accepter sa primauté. Quand il s'agissait de questions ayant un caractère politique marqué et donc potentiellement conflictuel, le Comité des directeurs sollicitait la convocation de l'ancien Comité de ministres. Si même de cette façon, aucune solution ne pouvait être trouvée au conflit, on s'adressait alors directement au Premier ministre, ce qui arrivait une ou deux fois par an. La pratique actuelle, solidement gérée par la DGAE, engage les hauts fonctionnaires dans des réunions interministérielles n'ayant pas une périodicité bien définie. Il faut remarquer que ces hauts fonctionnaires ne sont plus, comme dans la procédure normale, les directeurs généraux. Les réunions avec la participation directe des directeurs généraux sont devenues moins fréquentes qu'à l'époque du 'Comité Guazzaroni'. Il n'y a pas, en ce domaine, de réunions régulières de cabinet avec la participation de ministres sous la présidence du Premier ministre. Les réunions au niveau des ministres doivent être considérées comme tout à fait exceptionnelles (dans le cas récent de la question sidérugique, il y en a eu deux ou trois en une seule semaine).

Les réunions entre fonctionnaires sont convoquées par le coordonnateur de la DGAE lorsqu'il estime qu'il y a une nécessité réelle: par exemple, la présentation d'une nouvelle proposition ou d'un rapport important de la Commission au Conseil des Ministres de la Communauté.

Lorsqu'il s'agit de questions qui sont clairement de la compétence des ministères techniques (notamment Agriculture, Trésor, Commerce extérieur), l'initiative, au plan institutionnel, de la convocation de ces réunions est confiée exceptionnellement aux bureaux des ministères compétents. Pour ce qui est des questions monétaires, il faut noter le rôle important qu'y jouent le directeur général du Trésor et la Banque centrale (Banca d'Italia). Cette dernière compte en effet plusieurs fonctionnaires chargés particulièrement des affaires communautaires.

La DGAE du ministère des Affaires étrangères accepte avec réalisme et confiance ce principe du déplacement de l'initiative de la convocation; de toute façon, elle participe activement à ces réunions techniques de coordination externe. De plus, sa confiance est basée sur le fait qu'une liaison étroite est maintenue avec la délégation permanente à Bruxelles, que beaucoup de fonctionnaires techniques ont reçu une bonne préparation 'sur le tas' et qu'enfin, il s'agit là de la discussion de questions relevant de la compétence de comités communautaires qui, tels le Comité monétaire ou le Comité spécial agricole, sont en fait autant d'organes spécialisés **ratione materiae**, d'un rang équivalent à celui du Coreper.

Les réunions convoquées au titre de la coordination externe se déroulent dans un contexte de consultations permanentes entre les fonctionnaires des divers ministères, ainsi qu'avec les groupes d'intérêt (associations professionnelles, syndicales et patronales, experts, etc.).

Il faut remarquer que dans le cercle des fonctionnaires chargés des questions communautaires, il s'est développé un processus de socialisation - la variable indépendante étant la spécialisation européenne - qui dépasse les aspects purement bureaucratiques et formels de leurs fonctions respectives. C'est une élite bureaucratique qui a sa propre culture, en plus de ses propres règles du jeu, et qui vise à renforcer une identité professionnelle tout à fait différente de celle traditionnelle de l'administration publique italienne.

b) Coopération politique européenne (CPE).

Les affaires concernant la CPE sont traitées par un bureau **ad hoc**, le Bureau 1 appelé 'Ufficio Europa', de la direction générale des Affaires politiques (DGAP) du ministère des Affaires étrangères. Il est dirigé par un fonctionnaire (présentement, un conseiller d'ambassade) ayant le titre de 'correspondant'. Les compétences de ce bureau sont très larges et il est prévu qu'elles s'élargiront davantage encore.

Le bureau s'est spécialement occupé ces dernières années de l'élaboration et de la mise à point du plan Genscher-Colombo.

Les relations de l'Ufficio Europa avec les deux bureaux de la direction générale des Affaires économiques sont très bonnes; il y a en effet une division précise du travail qui est pleinement acceptée par les deux directions générales.

L'organisation du bureau 'Europe' est quand même faible et tout à fait insuffisante, compte tenu des tâches non seulement bureaucratiques mais aussi, dans une certaine mesure, d'initiative politique, que ce bureau doit accomplir.

Le bureau se compose de deux fonctionnaires de la carrière diplomatique (le 'correspondant' et le diplomate chargé des questions relatives au Conseil de l'Europe, à l'UEO, aux organisations et mouvements fédéralistes), plus trois personnes, employés et secrétaires. Le fait que ce bureau compte peu de personnel est encore plus marquant, si l'on pense que le premier principe de l'approche italienne de l'intégration européenne est celui de la primauté du politique sur l'administratif et que le bureau 'Europe' doit s'intéresser aussi à des questions européennes autres que celles de la CPE.

c) La Représentation permanente.

La délégation permanente italienne à Bruxelles vit en symbiose avec le ministère des Affaires étrangères, notamment avec la direction générale des Affaires économiques et avec celle des Affaires politiques. Les fonctionnaires de ces directions se déclarent tout à fait satisfaits des rapports avec leurs collègues de la délégation. Ils remarquent en particulier la rapidité et la précision des communications. Le ministère des Affaires étrangères est relié à la délégation permanente par des lignes téléphoniques internes: ainsi les informations circulent en temps réel.

Au ministère des Affaires étrangères, on tient aussi à remarquer qu'il existe une division du travail tout à fait rationnelle et efficace, entre les bureaux à Rome et la délégation à Bruxelles. Aucun double emploi n'est constaté, et au contraire, le large degré de complémentarité est relevé.

La délégation est une structure assez importante quant au nombre du personnel qui la compose: 16 fonctionnaires de la carrière diplomatique (qui pourraient passer à 18 en vue de la prochaine présidence italienne en 1985) et 16 fonctionnaires et experts détachés d'autres ministères (Agriculture: 3, Trésor: 2, ministère de l'Intérieur: 1, Transports: 1, Industrie: 3, Commerce extérieur: 2, Marine marchande: 1, Santé publique: 1, 'Cassa per il Mezzogiorno': 1, Banca d'Italia: 1). Il faut y ajouter une trentaine de personnes, employés, secrétaires et autres engagées sur place, ainsi qu'un conseiller juridique.

La nomination de ce dernier est à mettre en rapport avec, d'une part, les problèmes que pose l'initiative du Parlement européen visant à modifier les Traités communautaires, et d'autre part les problèmes de contentieux que rencontre l'Italie notamment en matière de directives et de concurrence.

LA COORDINATION INTERNE.

La constatation selon laquelle le ministère des Affaires étrangères n'est pas en mesure d'accomplir de façon adéquate la lourde tâche de la coordination interne, a rendu nécessaire la création d'une structure administrative spécifiquement chargée d'exécuter ou de promouvoir l'exécution des actes communautaires à l'intérieur du système italien.

En ce qui concerne la transposition des directives communautaires, il faut dire qu'en Italie, la procédure est devenue très lente, voire pénible, nécessitant nombre d'actes spécifiques qui doivent être arrêtés par le parlement national. Pendant les deux premières étapes de réalisation du Traité de Rome, c'était la direction générale des Affaires économiques du ministère des Affaires étrangères qui se chargeait de convoquer périodiquement une commission parlementaire composée de 24 membres: 12 sénateurs et 12 députés. La DGAE exerçait, par l'entremise de son directeur, une remarquable pression sur cette structure parlementaire extraordinaire en vue justement d'accélérer la procédure législative d'application. On sait que ce groupe parlementaire suivait fidèlement les recommandations de la DGAE.

Au fur et à mesure que le système de la Communauté se développe dans sa structure et dans ses fonctions - le rapport des Trois Sages en arrive à parler de 'lourdeur' dans l'organisation et la procédure -, les difficultés de la coordination interne en Italie augmentent de façon exponentielle et rendent pratiquement inutilisable la 'procédure Guazzaroni'.

Il faut remarquer à ce propos que:

1) la structure de l'administration publique italienne est complexe et lourde (124 directions générales, 830 divisions);
2) les régions jouissent d'un grand degré d'autonomie (en matière d'agriculture, notamment), ce qui pose des problèmes de coordination des politiques communautaires entre les différents ministères de l'Etat, et entre ceux-ci et les diverses administrations régionales;
3) qu'il peut y avoir cinq, et même plus, ministères engagés dans l'application d'une même directive.

En Italie, le pouvoir d'orientation et de coordination quant à la mise en oeuvre des politiques communautaires relève de la compétence du Premier ministre et du cabinet en tant que tel. On a vu que dans la pratique, ce pouvoir a été exercé jusqu'aux années '70 par le ministère des Affaires étrangères.

Dans l'attente de l'adoption d'une loi qui puisse organiser la structure et les fonctions de la présidence du Conseil des Ministres, et étant donné l'urgence réelle d'améliorer le mécanisme de la coordination interministérielle, un poste de ministre sans portefeuille pour la coordination des politiques communautaires a été créé en 1980, lors de la formation du deuxième cabinet Cossiga. Ainsi, le ministre Scotti fut-il investi de pouvoirs délégués par le Premier ministre pour l'exercice des fonctions de coordination définies dans le décret de délégation. On a mis à sa disposition une très petite structure administrative.

Tandis que la délégation de pouvoirs ad hoc continuait à être pratiquée (le dernier décret concerne le ministre sans portefeuille Biondi), ce qui contribue à personnaliser dans une certaine mesure et à rendre provisoires les fonctions du ministre en question, un premier décret d'organisation du cabinet fut arrêté en septembre 1980 par le Premier ministre. Ce décret attribuait entre autres, un caractère plus homogène - disons, une identité propre du point de vue de l'organisation ainsi que des fonctions - à la structure administrative mise à la disposition du ministre sans portefeuille en l'appelant 'département

La Présidence des CE: Rapport national sur l'Italie

pour la coordination des politiques communautaires'.

Ce département demeurait intégré dans la structure de la présidence du Conseil des Ministres, mais il bénéficiait d'une large autonomie fonctionnelle, étant donné qu'il était organisé et coordonné non pas directement par le chef de cabinet du Premier ministre, comme c'est le cas pour d'autres unités administratives à l'intérieur de la présidence du Conseil, mais directement par le ministre sans portefeuille, en accord avec le président du Conseil des Ministres.

Aussi les compétences du département apparaissaient-elles assez larges, allant jusqu'à inclure des contacts directs avec les institutions communautaires et la délégation permanente à Bruxelles, ce qui introduisait évidemment la possibilité de participer aux procédures de la coordination externe. Dans le décret de 1980, on lit notamment: 'Le département pour les affaires communautaires est chargé de la coordination avec les institutions communautaires'.

Mais pour toute une série de raisons, la nouvelle structure ne réussit pas. Ces raisons vont de l'opposition du ministère des Affaires étrangères, inquiet d'une telle perte de compétences, au manque presque total de ressources humaines et financières pour accomplir ces fonctions de coordination externe.

En mai 1982, le Premier ministre arrête une deuxième version du décret d'organisation du cabinet. La disposition relative aux fonctions qu'on vient de mentionner est tout simplement biffée, tandis qu'on confie au département la tâche, entre autres, d'"assurer et coordonner les relations entre les régions et les institutions communautaires'. S'agirait-il d'une forme spéciale de coordination externe? On note ici une contradiction évidente entre l'incapacité de garder, en règle générale, des contacts directs avec les institutions communautaires et la tâche d'assurer les contacts entre les régions et Bruxelles.

Les fonctions arrêtées dans le décret de délégation de pouvoirs **ad hoc** au ministre sans portefeuille Biondi, le 2 décembre 1982, paraissent clairement privilégier l'aspect interne de la coordination, bien qu'il soit prévu que le ministre sans portefeuille participe aux processus qui définissent, à l'intérieur du système italien, la position nationale vis-à-vis des initiatives communautaires. Les fonctions du ministre sans portefeuille sont les suivantes:

1) contribuer à élaborer, dans le respect des compétences du ministère des Affaires étrangères, la position italienne par rapport aux initiatives 'législatives' de la Communauté, en collaborant avec chacune des administrations intéressées, régions comprises;
2) informer les ministères et autres institutions publiques et privées sur les projets de directives, établir des contacts particuliers avec les organisations syndicales et informer le ministère des Affaires étrangères des résultats;
3) surveiller l'exécution des actes communautaires et proposer les mesures aptes à résoudre les conflits découlant d'une éventuel manque de coordination des procédures internes;
4) favoriser la coordination entre le gouvernement central de l'Etat et les régions dans le domaine des affaires communautaires;

173

5) recueillir et diffuser informations et analyses en la matière;
6) surveiller la gestion des régimes d'aides communautaires et faciliter le dépassement des obstacles qui existent en ce domaine;
7) examiner les projets de loi qui sont de l'initiative du gouvernement central aussi bien que des régions afin d'en assurer la compatibilité avec le droit communautaire;
8) promouvoir et développer les relations du gouvernement (cabinet en tant que tel et ministères particuliers) avec les membres italiens du Parlement européen.

Bien que les compétences déléguées puissent paraître assez larges et même dans une certaine mesure, originales pour la pratique italienne (par exemple, la promotion de relations avec les membres italiens du Parlement européen), beaucoup de limites entravent l'exercice des fonctions de la structure administrative chargée de la coordination interne.

Tout d'abord, il faut remarquer que le ministre qui y est préposé est 'sans portefeuille', c'est-à-dire qu'il exerce une fonction provisoire et qu'il ne dispose pas de ressources appropriées (par exemple, son budget ne prévoit que 15 millions de lires italiennes pour les missions à l'étranger!).

Le département se compose de 33 personnes qui sont des fonctionnaires et des employés détachés des différents ministères, ce qui veut dire qu'au départ, ces personnes ont des expériences de travail tout à fait différentes. L'organisation du département, décidée par le ministre sans portefeuille en accord avec le Premier ministre sur la base des ordres de service de ce dernier, datés du 13 août 1981 et du 29 avril 1982, est la suivante:

- Secteur I : Affaires générales;
- Secteur II : Affaires juridiques et législatives;
- Secteur III : Etudes et informations sur les politiques communautaires;
- Secteur IV : Définition et réalisation des politiques communautaires.

Le personnel est réparti de la façon suivante:

- huit personnes (fonctionnaires, employés et secrétaires) pour le bureau du ministre sans portefeuille;
- pour le reste du département proprement dit: trois fonctionnaires de rang supérieur, dix autres fonctionnaires, douze employés et secrétaires.

La distinction entre le bureau du ministre et le reste du département est importante, car le travail le plus professionnel, voire dans une certaine mesure, spécialisé en matière communautaire, est assuré par le personnel de ce dernier.

Le ministre sans portefeuille a récemment demandé au Premier ministre d'augmenter le nombre du personnel permanent ainsi que le budget du département, mais la réponse a été négative (le problème de la réduction des dépenses publiques se pose ici aussi).

Il faut remarquer en passant qu'au sein du département, il n'existe pas de bibliothèque spécialisée, ni de centre de documentation approprié en matière communautaire. De même, il n'y a pas en ce moment de possibilité de mettre sur pied des groupes de recherche ou de consultation.

Les fonctionnaires du département admettent (peut-être avec un peu de masochisme) que leur préparation, sauf quelques exceptions, n'est pas suffisamment spécialisée. Ils souhaitent qu'il soit possible de recruter une vingtaine d'experts qui puissent dialoguer sur le même plan avec les experts des différents ministères.

Pour ce qui concerne les relations avec les groupes d'intérêt, des contacts continus sont assurés et assez fréquemment, le ministre y participe.

Les contacts de type interministériel sont assurés grâce à des réunions (souvent) convoquées directement par le ministre. S'il existe de graves conflits entre ministères, le ministre sollicite l'intervention du Premier ministre.

Le département s'occupe de l'envoi de documents et de dossiers aux fonctionnaires des différents ministères.

Les contacts informels sont la règle.

Les contacts avec la délégation permanente à Bruxelles sont évidemment moins organisés que ceux qui sont assurés par la DGAE du ministère des Affaires étrangères, mais ils existent quand même.

Il faut souligner le caractère de coordination au sens propre, et non pas de gestion, des fonctions exercées par le département.

La coordination a été jusqu'à présent réalisée en grande partie en vue de rattraper le retard pris dans l'adoption des directives communautaires (en 1980, il y en avait 200 en attente; au début de 1983 il en restait 97: presqu'un succès!).

Un autre secteur qui occupe de façon directe le département est celui du contentieux communautaire, particulièrement en ce qui concerne les mesures d'exécution des nombreux arrêts de la Cour de Justice des Communautés européennes concernant l'Italie.

En cas de conflits 'normaux' entre ministères, les procédures employées par le département sont celles de la négociation aux différents niveaux (fonctionnaires, experts, plus rarement ministres) et de la médiation politique (un rôle qui est en principe exercé personnellement par le ministre sans portefeuille).

L'exercice des fonctions du département est perturbé par la succession rapide des cabinets de coalition et par les fréquents conflits qui jaillissent en leur sein sur les questions de politique économique et financière, de réduction des dépenses publiques, etc. . . Si les conflits touchent le domaine communautaire, c'est l'éventuelle influence du ministre sans portefeuille (plus encore que celle du Premier ministre) qui peut jouer un rôle essentiel. Le travail du petit département pour la coordination interne s'avère important aussi aux fins d'évaluer et même de mesurer avec une certaine précision, la situation économique et sociale interne dans son ensemble. En effet, l'exécution des actes communautaires met en relief les divergences et les contradictions inhérentes au système italien.

Quant à l'avenir du département et particulièrement en ce qui concerne le rôle du ministre sans portefeuille, d'influentes personnalités du monde politique, diplomatique et administratif écartent, dans leur majorité, l'idée de la création d'un ministère pour les Affaires européennes, lequel remplacerait le ministère des Affaires étrangères pour ce qui est de la coordination interne dans son ensemble et, dans une certaine mesure aussi, pour la coordination externe. Il est à noter que les fonctionnaires du département expriment un avis différent.

On suggère que la tâche principale, à court et moyen terme, du ministre sans portefeuille devrait être de rendre plus réguliers et efficaces, voire plus informés, les rapports entre le cabinet (et évidemment, les différents ministres et ministères) et le parlement national, afin de sensibiliser et encourager ce dernier à accomplir ses fonctions en matière communautaire de façon systématique, surtout en ce qui concerne l'adoption des décrets législatifs de mise en oeuvre des directives.

Plus précisément, on suggère que le département devrait obtenir de la part du Parlement une délégation **ad hoc**, quoique renouvelable dans le temps, pour l'exécution des directives.

Une autre tâche du département devrait être de réduire le décalage chronologique et fonctionnel qui existe entre le fonctionnement de l'administration communautaire et celui de l'administration publique nationale.

Une haute personnalité du monde diplomatique en vient à proposer que le ministre sans portefeuille se consacre personnellement et complètement - une véritable 'mission' politique - à accomplir la double tâche d'obtenir à bref délai du parlement national, l'adoption de toutes les directives demeurant en attente et d'engager sérieusement les différents ministères (et personnellement leur ministre respectif) dans l'utilisation des fonds communautaires qui sont à la disposition de l'Italie (parfois depuis 8 ans!) et qui demeurent bloqués.

Pour ce qui concerne l'organisation interne du département, il est clair qu'il faut augmenter les ressources humaines et financières et qu'il faut assurer une coordination, voire une collaboration, plus étroite entre la structure du cabinet du ministre sans portefeuille et les divers secteurs du département proprement dit.

Une certaine évolution paraît s'amorcer à la suite de la formation du cabinet de coalition présidé par M. Bettino Craxi (août 1983). L'évolution va dans le sens d'un élargissement des compétences et des fonctions du ministre sans portefeuille et du département.

Le décret arrêtant la composition du cabinet ne spécifie pas la fonction de coordination des politiques communautaires par l'adjectif 'interne' (qui a donc disparu du texte). Bien qu'il n'existe pas encore (décembre 1983) de décret de délégation de pouvoirs **ad hoc** au nouveau ministre sans portefeuille, le successeur de M. Biondi, à savoir M. Francesco Forte (socialiste, ancien conseiller économique de M.Craxi) participe activement aux réunions du Conseil des Ministres de la Communauté, notamment celles ayant une nature financière et celles concernant la révision et le développement des politiques communes. En particulier, il a participé aux réunions préparatoires du Conseil européen d'Athènes. De même les fonctionnaires du département ont-ils commencé à se déplacer hors d'Italie.

Il y a donc une mobilité nouvelle qui dépasse largement le cadre traditionnel d'action du département et qui est jugée de façon positive par les membres de la délégation permanente à Bruxelles. Ceux-ci tiennent à remarquer que, de cette façon, la contribution apportée à la préparation de la position italienne au sein des processus décisionnels communautaires, est plus fonctionnelle et plus importante. En effet, il faut relever que le département fait partie de la structure administrative du cabinet, bien qu'il soit autonome du point de vue fonctionnel.

Le peu de données empiriques dont on dispose ne permettent pas d'avancer des prévisions quant à l'institutionnalisation définitive d'une telle pratique. Une donnée peut pourtant être considérée comme acquise, à savoir la consolidation du département dont le personnel vient d'être augmenté de quelques fonctionnaires et employés, notamment d'un conseiller diplomatique dont la tâche est d'aider ses collègues des ministères techniques à mieux se préparer en vue de leur participation directe à telle ou telle réunion externe.

LE ROLE DE LA PRESIDENCE DE LA REPUBLIQUE DANS LES AFFAIRES DE LA COMMUNAUTE EUROPEENNE

Pour la première fois dans la pratique administrative et politique italienne, le président de la République italienne, M. Sandro Pertini, a nommé, à côté des conseillers diplomatique et militaire traditionnels, un conseiller pour les questions communautaires et européennes en la personne de l'ambassadeur Guazzaroni, ancien directeur général des affaires économiques au ministère des Affaires étrangères. Ce geste souligne l'importance que le président de la République accorde à l'intégration européenne et au fonctionnement du système de la Communauté: c'est un signal que le président a voulu expressément donner dans son premier message au parlement national.

Comme chacun le sait, le président de la République italienne ne peut pas exercer, en vertu de la Constitution, un rôle politique actif: il n'est pas politiquement responsable des actes du cabinet. **De facto**, le président actuel intervient plus ou moins directement, mais toujours concrètement, dans les affaires européennes sur la base des informations et des suggestions que lui fournit son conseiller en la matière. Ainsi par exemple, le président convoque tel ou tel ministre pour discuter spécialement de telle ou telle question communautaire.

Dans une première phase, à savoir pendant les années 1979-1982, le rôle du conseiller a été particulièrement actif.

Un cas exemplaire est celui de la loi électorale italienne en vue des élections directes du Parlement européen en 1979. A cette occasion, il y avait du retard dans la procédure d'approbation du projet de loi par le Sénat, les groupes politiques ne paraissant pas être en mesure de trouver un accord sur certains points. Le conseiller du président de la République intervint auprès du président de la commission des Affaires étrangères du Sénat et les choses s'éclaircirent rapidement. Toujours en matière électorale européenne, la question très délicate du vote des Italiens à l'étranger se posait; question qui pour la première fois aurait dû être réglée par une loi du Parlement. Le problème présentait des aspects de politique étrangère: il s'agissait par exemple, d'obtenir l'accord des autres pays membres de la Communauté pour fournir des locaux, l'assistance de la police, etc... Le conseiller du président de la République reçut mandat de la part du Premier ministre pour faire un tour des capitales des pays de la Communauté et pour en référer ensuite à la sous-commission de la commission Affaires étrangères de la Chambre des Députés.

Donc, on se trouve ici en présence d'exemples qui montrent comment s'exerce une fonction de coordination à la fois interne et externe au plus haut niveau des institutions italiennes.

Pour ce qui concerne particulièrement la présidence italienne des institutions communautaires et des structures de la CPE en 1980, il faut remarquer le caractère continu des consultations qui ont eu lieu entre le conseiller du président de la République et les différents ministres et hauts fonctionnaires engagés dans l'accomplissement de cette tâche.

Le rôle du conseiller pour les questions communautaires est actuellement un rôle qu'on peut appeler intermittent. Le président de la République le consulte lorsqu'il le juge opportun, notamment en ce qui concerne l'évolution institutionnelle de la construction européenne par rapport à l'initiative du Parlement européen.

La pratique actuelle de la 'présidence Pertini' est que le chef de l'Etat a des contacts directs et assez fréquents avec les différents ministres, avec quelques membres du Parlement européen, ainsi qu'avec tel ou tel membre de la Commission de la Communauté.

LA PRÉSIDENCE ITALIENNE DU CONSEIL DES MINISTRES DE LA COMMUNAUTÉ ET DES STRUCTURES DE LA CPE

On a déjà remarqué qu'en Italie, le caractère diffus des compétences en matière communautaire est aussi considéré comme un élément utile pour la gestion de la présidence du Conseil des Ministres de la Communauté.

La conviction profonde et largement partagée au ministère des Affaires étrangères ou dans d'autres ministères techniques, est que la présidence du Conseil des Ministres, des groupes de travail ainsi que des structures de la CPE est un fait dont l'importance augmente au fur et à mesure que les problèmes de la construction européenne se multiplient et se diversifient. On remarque qu'au début et jusqu'à la fin des années '60, la présidence était une charge de présidence ordinaire. L'aide et l'assistance techniques du personnel du Secrétariat du Conseil étaient suffisantes pour assurer l'exercice de cette fonction. Le rôle de proposition et de médiation, voire d'initiative, était assuré exclusivement ou en tout cas, principalement, par la Commission. Les rares sommets intergouvernementaux restaient des 'sommets', c'est-à-dire des consultations diplomatiques épisodiques et non pas des structures ni, moins encore, des institutions.

Cette situation change rapidement lorsque surgissent des problèmes qui entraînent plus directement les gouvernements nationaux sur le plan de l'initiative diplomatique et de la négociation politique.

Citons quelques exemples: la question des règlements financiers agricoles, la question des ressources propres, la négociation pour l'élargissement de la Communauté, le démarrage du système Davignon, le lancement de l'idée d'Union européenne, la négociation de l'Acte final d'Helsinki, la participation à la Conférence Nord-Sud de Paris, etc.

Dans cette phase d'involution du système politique communautaire et d'évolution du système parallèle de la CPE, le rôle jadis central de la Commission s'affaiblit, alors qu'augmente parallèllement le rôle des gouvernements nationaux et par conséquent, celui des institutions européennes ayant un caractère essentiellement intergouvernemental.

Dès lors, étant donné la nécessaire, ou plus exactement, l'inévitable prépondérance des gouvernements et des administrations nationales, la présidence acquiert une dimension tout à fait fondamentale: elle n'a plus un rôle de simple gestion, mais au contraire, une fonction d'initiative, de médiation et de proposition.

En plus de ces rôles politiques internes exercés sur le double plan des affaires communautaires et de la CPE, il y a une augmentation graduelle du rôle externe de représentation de la position et des intérêts communs des Dix, ainsi que de la CEE, vis-à-vis des pays tiers et des organisations internationales.

L'exercice de la présidence qui était au début, un souci presque exclusif de quelques ministres et sous-secrétaires d'Etat, ainsi que des diplomates et experts de la délégation permanente à Bruxelles, devient une affaire qui concerne un nombre croissant et diversifié d'institutions politiques et bureaucratiques: ministères, banque centrale, ambassades dans les pays tiers, délégations permanentes auprès des organisations internationales, etc. Même les conseillers commerciaux des ambassades du pays exerçant la présidence sont mobilisés pour la préparation de dizaines de rapports.

Dans le domaine spécifique de la CPE, le rôle externe de la présidence se développe de façon encore plus évidente et délicate.

La complexité croissante du rôle de la présidence entraîne automatiquement l'augmentation des exigences de la communication à l'intérieur du système européen, et ce, au double niveau communautaire et CPE, ce qui oblige les différentes administrations nationales à rendre plus fonctionnels les canaux existants et à en rechercher d'autres. Sur ce plan aussi, il y a une remarquable mobilisation de ressources techniques et financières. Il faut remarquer que cette mobilisation contribue dans une bonne mesure à moderniser la structure technologique des administrations intéressées.

La présidence italienne de 1975 se situe justement dans cette phase d'évolution-involution. La réponse italienne à l'engagement plus grand que requièrent les multiples processus de décision et de négociation aux différents niveaux et dans les différentes enceintes de la construction européenne, se caractérise par l'action passionnée de certains ministres (il suffit de rappeler Aldo Moro) et directeurs généraux. Cette réponse se traduit fondamentalement par un renforcement de l'organisation de la délégation permanente à Bruxelles (c'est un acquis qui restera pour les années suivantes). Une loi spécifique pour la contribution financière nécessaire à l'exercice du rôle de la présidence (surtout pour les frais des réunions convoquées en Italie au titre de la CPE) est adoptée, on

179

mobilise un bon nombre de hauts fonctionnaires du ministère des Affaires étrangères et d'autres ministères, on renforce le système des communications entre le ministère des Affaires étrangères et la délégation permanente (dans ce domaine, il y aura aussi un 'acquis' pour le ministère).

Durant cette période, il faut remarquer entre autres, le rôle tout à fait fondamental joué par M. Aldo Moro lors du Conseil européen. Il faut aussi rappeler que l'ambassadeur Guazzaroni reçut mandat du gouvernement français afin de présider la délégation communautaire aux réunions préparatoires de la Conférence Nord-Sud.

En ce qui concerne la présidence italienne de 1980, la pratique suivie fut celle mise en oeuvre en 1975: adoption d'une loi spécifique pour la contribution aux frais, renforcement de la délégation permanente, détachement d'un fonctionnaire du ministère des Affaires étrangères pendant trois mois à Dublin (capitale du pays qui exerçait la présidence immédiatement avant l'Italie). Ainsi le ministère des Affaires étrangères, notamment la direction générale des Affaires économiques, mobilisa 173 fonctionnaires (notamment de la carrière diplomatique, mais provenant aussi d'autres ministères) pour la présidence des groupes de travail.

APPROCHES ITALIENNES DE L'EXERCICE DE LA PRÉSIDENCE

On peut distinguer trois approches ou attitudes fondamentales concernant la gestion de la présidence du Conseil des Ministres et des structures CPE:

- l'approche de la direction générale des Affaires économiques (DGAE) du ministère des Affaires étrangères;
- l'approche de la direction générale des Affaires politiques (bureau 'Europe') du même ministère;
- l'approche du département pour la coordination (interne) des politiques communautaires.

Il faut cependant souligner qu'il n'y a pas de grandes contradictions entre les trois, bien que la distinction ne soit pas purement analytique. Les trois approches, surtout les deux premières, doivent plutôt être considérées comme autant de prémisses, axiologiques et pratiques, d'une véritable division du travail dans la gestion de la présidence.

a) L'approche de la direction générale des Affaires économiques du ministère des Affaires étrangères se caractérise davantage par le souci des aspects organisationnels, techniques et de procédure, autrement dit de la gestion au jour le jour de la présidence, tout en appréciant l'attitude et les efforts de haut niveau du bureau 'Europe'. Les hauts fonctionnaires contactés tiennent à souligner l'existence d'une pratique de la présidence désormais claire et solide qui ne provoque aucun traumatisme. Bref, on est satisfait des lignes directrices existantes et on a une grande confiance d'une part dans les capacités professionnelles de la délégation permanente, d'autre part dans l'esprit de collaboration, ainsi que dans les capacités techniques du personnel du

Secrétariat du Conseil des Ministres de la Communauté.

b) L'approche du bureau 'Europe' de la DGAP du ministère des Affaires étrangères est beaucoup plus politique. Le temps de la présidence est vu comme l'occasion de lancer et de faire avancer des initiatives concernant le développement de l'intégration européenne suivant la méthode communautaire: donc, développement politique du système de la Communauté, approfondissement de l'acquis communautaire, élargissement des compétences, amélioration du système de consultation et de négociation au sein de la CPE. Cette attitude met l'accent sur les aspects politiques et créatifs de la présidence par rapport aux aspects technico-économiques (sans toutefois sous-évaluer ces derniers).

L'opinion des hauts fonctionnaires contactés est que pendant les six mois d'exercice de la présidence, on ne peut pas résoudre les problèmes qui n'ont pu être résolus lors du précédent semestre et qu'il faut en tout cas, profiter de ce pouvoir en plus que donne la gestion de la présidence pour promouvoir des initiatives nouvelles.

En effet, on considère la présidence (surtout des structures CPE) comme une recherche continue de nouvelles frontières pour le système de l'intégration supranationale: autrement dit, c'est la recherche et la mise au point quotidienne de l'Europe politique. Il s'agit clairement d'une 'approche CPE', c'est-à-dire d'une approche hautement politisée qui vise à privilégier l'initiative par rapport à la gestion. Mais la tâche du bureau 'Europe' est justement de profiter de la flexibilité des structures de la CPE pour les orienter et les engager dans un sens décidément européen.

c) L'approche du département pour la coordination (interne) des politiques communautaires se caractérise par une absence relative d'implication: pour tout ce qui concerne la gestion de la présidence, on fait référence au ministère des Affaires étrangères et on répète que les ressources dont le département dispose ne lui permettront jamais de faire face à des tâches extraordinaires.

Il semble que la raison fondamentale de cette absence d'engagement est le manque de compétences institutionnelles en ce qui concerne la coordination externe.

Pourtant l'évolution **de facto** qui vient de se dégager lors de la formation du cabinet présidé par M. Craxi, paraît aussi impliquer un changement graduel d'attitude quant au rôle que le département pourrait jouer dans la gestion de la présidence.

LA PRÉPARATION DE LA PRÉSIDENCE

La préparation de la présidence mobilise les bureaux intéressés pour une période d'un an et demi (quelques mois avant et quelques mois après le semestre de présidence effective).

On crée pour cette période, une délégation **ad hoc** composée de deux ou trois fonctionnaires du ministère des Affaires étrangères, de deux ou trois experts, plus un certain nombre de secrétaires et d'interprètes. La direction de cette délégation **ad hoc** est confiée à un ambassadeur qui est directement responsable devant le ministre des Affaires étrangères.

La tâche de la délégation, telle qu'elle a été expérimentée en 1980, est d'assurer entre autres, un soutien logistique approprié à la présidence, surtout pour les réunions convoquées au titre de la CPE. De même, la délégation est compétente pour la préparation du projet de loi portant sur le financement de la présidence: pour 1985, on prévoit que la requête portera sur 5 à 7 milliards de lires italiennes.

Pour la préparation du projet de loi, des réunions sont prévues avec la participation de fonctionnaires de la direction générale des Affaires économiques, de la direction générale des Affaires politiques, du cabinet du ministre, de la direction générale du Personnel et, surtout, du service du Protocole du ministère des Affaires étrangères. Le texte du projet est concrètement rédigé par le service du contentieux du ministère des Affaires étrangères. Un mécanisme permettant d'éviter que le Parlement ne doive à chaque fois approuver une acte législatif, est à l'étude.

Deux ou trois mois avant le début du semestre de présidence, des réunions sont convoquées par le coordonnateur du ministère des Affaires étrangères afin de désigner les fonctionnaires qui agiront comme présidents des groupes de travail. En général, on préfère les fonctionnaires qui ont déjà eu une expérience professionnelle directement à Bruxelles. Si les fonctionnaires appartiennent à l'administration publique centrale de Rome, ils doivent en tout cas avoir eu des contacts avec l'administration communautaire.

La plus grande part du travail est confiée aux membres de la délégation permanente à Bruxelles (fonctionnaires de la carrière diplomatique, fonctionnaires et experts d'autres ministères).

Deux aspects sont à relever:

1) la préparation, bien que faite par la DGAE du ministère des Affaires étrangères, associe de façon directe le ministère de l'Agriculture (groupes et comités agricoles) et le ministère du Commerce extérieur (Comité 113);

2) l'ordre du jour des réunions préparatoires demeure limité aux questions purement organisationnelles, sans déborder sur la substance même des politiques communautaires.

En janvier 1983, le bureau 'Europe' de la DGAP du ministère des Affaires étrangères - celui qui privilégie l'approche de haute politique pour la présidence - a préparé un document de travail concernant les problèmes organisationnels pour la présidence italienne en 1985.

Dans ce document, on demande de détacher auprès de ce bureau quatre fonctionnaires en plus des deux actuels. Ce personnel devrait être détaché, avec un rôle de liaison, à Dublin de janvier à mai 1985, sur la base de l'expérience personnelle déjà vécue en 1979 par le directeur actuel du bureau. On demande aussi six secrétaires, deux machines à photocopier, un poste télex (en liaison directe avec le Parlement européen) et un télécopieur (en liaison directe avec la délégation permanente à Bruxelles).

Quant aux aspects logistiques, on demande de pouvoir disposer de cinq à six salles pour les réunions à Rome.

La structure de la délégation permanente est généralement jugée apte à accomplir les fonctions requises par la gestion de la présidence.

On prévoit pourtant, en vue de la présidence de 1985, de la renforcer davantage en envoyant à Bruxelles deux fonctionnaires de la carrière diplomatique en plus des seize qui font actuellement partie de la délégation. En ce qui concerne les fonctionnaires des autres administrations, la délégation permanente prévoit (et espère) qu'un expert scientifique sera bientôt détaché à Bruxelles.

L'impact de l'exercice de la présidence sur l'opinion publique italienne est jugé important et positif par les fonctionnaires du ministère des Affaires étrangères, moins important par les fonctionnaires d'autres structures de l'administration publique.

Les fonctionnaires du ministère des Affaires étrangères tiennent à souligner que la presse et les mass media en général consacrent un plus grand espace aux questions européennes; ce qui implique, à l'avis même de ces fonctionnaires, une plus grande attention de la part de l'opinion publique pour ce sujet.

A cet égard, il n'existe pas de données statistiques spécifiques. Sur la base de ce qu'on a pu constater en lisant un certain nombre de journaux parus à l'époque des deux dernières présidences italiennes, l'espace réservé aux affaires communautaires et européennes est en effet plus large qu'en période normale (sans toutefois trop insister sur le 'plus'. . .). Mais l'attention des mass media se tourne surtout vers les questions de CPE, c'est-à-dire vers les problèmes de politique étrangère. A cette occasion, les mass media voient le gouvernement italien dans un rôle plus ou moins formel de protagoniste. Au ministère des Affaires étrangères, on relève à ce propos la fonction de porte-parole du système européen dans le monde entier, remplie par le pays qui a la charge de la présidence. Quant à l'intérêt éventuellement plus grand de l'opinion publique, en l'absence de données statistiques, il est difficile de dire quelque chose de précis: l'avis optimiste des fonctionnaires du ministère des Affaires étrangères pourrait aussi être interprété comme le souhait d'une réalité qui n'existe pas (encore). Ce qui est certain, c'est qu'il y a un plus haut degré de prépondérance, institutionnelle aussi bien que personnelle, des élites politiques et bureaucratiques à l'intérieur du système politique national.

L'AVENIR DE LA PRÉSIDENCE

Dans les pages qui précèdent, on a eu l'occasion de remarquer, sur la base d'une opinion largement partagée par les fonctionnaires des différents ministères, que l'évolution objective de l'intégration européenne a contribué à donner une importance croissante au rôle de la présidence.

C'est une constatation qui doit être interprétée à la lumière de l'approche italienne traditionnelle de l'intégration européenne, approche qui privilégie depuis toujours tout ce qui contribue à valoriser les aspects véritablement communautaires par rapport à ceux qui sont, plus ou moins explicitement de nature intergouvernementale.

Dans les milieux de l'administration publique italienne, on souhaite que la Commission recouvre, d'une façon ou d'une autre, ses pouvoirs d'initiative, selon la méthode communautaire la plus orthodoxe.

Rebus sic stantibus, étant donné la complexité des problèmes et des procédures (voir les règles du jeu aux divers niveaux de la construction européenne), l'opinion des diplomates et des fonctionnaires de l'administration publique est que la présidence, telle qu'elle a évolué, c'est-à-dire en tant qu'exercice de rôles de gestion administrative et de procédure en même temps que d'initiative et de médiation politiques, doit être désormais considérée comme un acquis à garder et à exercer avec tout l'engagement nécessaire, sans pourtant lui attribuer de structure organisationnelle qui soit différente et autonome par rapport à celle périodiquement assurée par les différents pays membres de la CEE. Donc, pas de 'secrétariat permanent' de la présidence en tant que tel.

Le Secrétariat général du Conseil des Ministres est jugé par les Italiens comme étant tout à fait fonctionnel et suffisant par rapport aux exigences de la présidence. A cet égard, on a déjà remarqué combien les Italiens apprécient le travail d'aide technique que le Secrétariat fournit à la présidence, ainsi que la collaboration 'politique' consistant à signaler à la présidence telle ou telle question délicate nécessitant l'exercice du rôle d'initiative ou de médiation.

L'attitude traditionnellement pro-communautaire de l'Italie n'empêche pas que les fonctionnaires de l'administration publique, surtout ceux de la carrière diplomatique, attribuent une importance particulière au domaine de la coopération politique européenne.

La CPE et la présidence de ses structures sont vues comme des instruments et des occasions pour élargir, approfondir et donc faire avancer le processus de l'intégration supranationale.

En général, la période de six mois est considérée comme tout à fait suffisante pour l'exercice de la présidence, surtout si la pratique de la troïka s'améliore et se renforce, ce que les Italiens souhaitent vivement. Les Italiens sont opposés à un éventuel prolongement de la période de présidence, car selon eux, le système actuel de rotation est à même d'assurer un bon dynamisme à l'exercice de fonctions de la présidence. On remarque que celle-ci doit être exercée par dix (et peut-être sous peu, douze) gouvernements et que son éventuel prolongement pourrait faire naître la tentation d'un leadership institutionnalisé et favoriser un exercice de la présidence subordonné exclusivement à l'intérêt national, et ce, de façon beaucoup plus accentuée que ce qui peut se passer actuellement.

Garder la rotation semestrielle permet, entre autres, de limiter les dépenses en ressources humaines et financières que l'exercice de la présidence entraîne pour chaque administration publique nationale.

Il faut ajouter que la rotation semestrielle peut favoriser un esprit d'émulation entre les différents gouvernements, ce qui ne peut qu'être utile à l'efficacité de l'exercice de la présidence.

Les fonctionnaires italiens, ainsi que les hommes politiques, souhaitent qu'il y ait un rapport plus intense et plus sincère, voire moins formel et routinier, entre la présidence et le Parlement européen dans le double but de développer le contrôle démocratique au niveau européen et de favoriser une coordination plus efficace et rationnelle entre les différentes institutions communautaires d'une part, et entre le système politique de la Communauté en tant que telle et les structures de la CPE d'autre part.

Ainsi les principales variables indépendantes que les Italiens paraissent adopter pour évaluer la qualité d'une présidence sont les deux suivantes:

1)   capacité (et engagement) d'organisation;
2)   originalité (et cohérence) des programmes.

REMERCIEMENTS

Vifs remerciements aux fonctionnaires et aux personnalités qui ont accepté d'être interviewés, notamment à M. l'ambassadeur Cesidio Guazzaroni, à M. Paolo Janni ('coordonnateur' au sein du ministère des Affaires étrangères), à M. Fernando Laj ('correspondant' au sein du même ministère), à M. Romano Lazzareschi (du département pour la coordination des politiques communautaires), à M. Avogadro (de la délégation permanente italienne auprès des Communautés), à M. Nelli Feroci (de la direction générale des affaires économiques du ministère des Affaires étrangères).

Un remerciement tout particulier aux collaborateurs de la recherche: Ferruccio Pinotti et Guido Garavoglia.

REFERENCES

M. Capurso,   'Il Ministro per gli Affari europei', in Parlamento, Rivista di vita politica e parlamentare, XXVI, nn.5-6-7, maggio-luglio 1980, pp. 13-15.

A. Massai,   'Il coordinamento interno delle politiche comunitarie', in Quaderni Costituzionali, II, n.2, agosto 1982, pp. 481-489.

A. Papisca,   'The Dynamic of European Community Institutions in a Future Context of Political Development', in Lo Spettatore Internazionale, XV, July-September 1980, pp. 223-248.

Chapter 9

LA PRESIDENCE DU CONSEIL DES MINISTRES DES COMMUNAUTES
EUROPEENNES: LES PRESIDENCES DU G.D. DE LUXEMBOURG
M. J-M. Hoscheit, Maastricht

INTRODUCTION

La conscience de sa propre faiblesse a conduit très tôt le Luxembourg à
s'intégrer à des espaces économiques plus larges, effort dont
l'implication dans l'intégration européenne est un aspect majeur. Comme
on l'a constaté récemment:

> 'l'économie est la principale variable indépendante dans la
> formulation de la politique étrangère. L'extrême petitesse du
> marché national - en termes de territoire - démontre l'impossibilité
> de toute politique économique purement nationale. La théorie
> économique est très explicite sur la seule solution permettant dans
> ces conditions la survie et la prospérité économiques: ces buts
> peuvent être atteints soit par une zone de libre échange, soit par
> une union douanière, soit par un marché commun' (1).

Une telle attitude ne saurait étonner de la part d'un pays dont les
exportations et importations contribuent pour 80 pourcent au Produit
national brut. La participation du G.D. de Luxembourg à la création de la
C.E.C.A. et puis de la Communauté économique européenne démontre
une conscience aiguë du fait que la contradiction entre les exigences de
la rationalité économique et les nécessités de la souveraineté ne peut
être résolue que dans un cadre plus large. Ainsi la C.E. permet aux petits
Etats, poussés par la 'logique de l'intégration', de se 'dégager dans une
large mesure de leurs faiblesses structurelles, inhérentes à leurs faibles
dimensions et d'acquérir une stature hors de proportion avec leur
dimension réelle' (2).

La participation à la Communauté européenne permet au
Luxembourg de profiter d'instruments juridiques, politiques et de
procédure qui, fonctionnant dans un cadre multinational et échappant
ainsi aux dangers du bilatéralisme, rendent possible une participation
effective aux processus de décision. Outre un statut international accru,
le Luxembourg a pu tirer un certain nombre d'avantages matériels de sa
participation au processus d'intégration européenne, p.ex. dans le
domaine agricole ou industriel. De même l'implantation de certaines
institutions européennes à Luxembourg (Cour de Justice, services de la

Commission, Cour des Comptes, Secrétariat du Parlement européen), revêt une importance politique et économique tout à fait centrale.

Etroitement dépendant du maintien d'un climat favorable au libre-échange, le Grand-Duché a adopté dès les années 50 une politique résolument pro-européenne. En général, le Luxembourg prend dans les négociations communautaires le point de vue d'une stricte orthodoxie communautaire, respectant et la lettre et l'esprit des actes juridiques européens et soutenant bien souvent une position de conciliation moyenne, plutôt favorable aux propositions de la Commission. Néanmoins, la diplomatie luxembourgeoise prend des positions fortes dans quelques domaines considérés comme d'intérêt vital pour la survie de l'entité nationale: la question du siège des institutions, les problèmes relatifs à la restructuration de la sidérurgie, les discussions touchant au droit des sociétés et à la législation bancaire sont quelques uns de ces thèmes mobilisateurs.

Ainsi la politique d'intégration est une donnée permanente de la politique étrangère luxembourgeoise, donnée qui n'est plus remise en cause, ni par la population, ni par les principaux partis politiques. Ceci permet aux fonctionnaires et diplomates luxembourgeois de situer leur action dans un cadre de référence clair et largement intériorisé.

Petit par le nombre de ses habitants et la dimension de son territoire, le Luxembourg s'est doté d'une structure administrative adaptée à cette situation.

Ainsi 'pour faire face à l'augmentation des tâches que comportait cette nouvelle politique (de présence internationale), il a fallu trouver un compromis entre la nécessité d'assurer l'accomplissement satisfaisant des travaux supplémentaires et d'autre part, l'impossibilité de gonfler proportionnellement les effectifs administratifs. C'est ainsi que le gouvernement a été amené à se préoccuper du bon rendement de ses services plutôt que de l'application stricte des textes répartissant les compétences' (3). Ces caractéristiques politiques et administratives expliquent dans une large mesure les positions du Grand-Duché de Luxembourg au sein des institutions communautaires, aussi bien en temps normal qu'en temps de présidence.

I. L'INTERVENTION DES AUTORITES POLITIQUES

L'intérêt des membres du gouvernement pour les affaires communautaires est naturellement variable selon le degré d'intégration du domaine concerné. Cet intérêt est souvent à la fois grand et petit: grand à cause de l'importance primordiale de la dimension européenne pour un petit pays dépendant de ses exportations, petit à cause du nombre limité d'intérêts spécifiquement luxembourgeois.

Tant par leur fonction que par la personnalité des titulaires, les ministres des Affaires étrangères ont été plus directement touchés par l'état d'avancement de l'intégration européenne.

Les grandes divergences entre les ministres et leur appareil administratif sont rares. Normalement, les données fondamentales des problèmes sont généralement connues et intériorisées, et la marge de manoeuvre disponible s'en dégage implicitement. Cette tendance est encore renforcée d'une part, par la facilité de contact entre le ministre et son personnel et d'autre part, par la grande permanence des fonctionnaires luxembourgeois, qui sont le plus souvent chargés de suivre un domaine particulier pendant des années. A ceci s'ajoute que le Luxembourg ne connaît que dans une mesure restreinte, le système du cabinet ministériel qui peut former écran entre le ministre et son département. Le ministre est normalement saisi d'un dossier qui, selon le jugement du fonctionnaire, dépasse les simples mesures d'ordre technique et nécessite des décisions politiques quant à l'attitude à adopter.

La préparation des sessions du Conseil des Ministres s'effectue, d'après l'ordre du jour, entre les fonctionnaires supérieurs chargés des dossiers et le ministre, selon les lignes générales de la politique européenne du Luxembourg. Un très grand rôle dans cette préparation est joué par le représentant permanent qui, du fait de sa longue expérience, connaît le mieux les différents intérêts en jeu. De même, les représentants du Secrétariat du Conseil ont un grand poids dans la préparation des ministres concernés.

La Chambre des Députés luxembourgeoise n'a jusqu'à présent fait preuve que d'un intérêt limité pour les affaires européennes, l'ensemble du débat en ce domaine ayant lieu une fois par an lors de la discussion budgétaire. L'attention portée à l'intégration européenne se situe davantage au niveau des principes généraux qu'à celui des questions techniques. Un échange plus actif entre le gouvernement et le parlement se déroule au sein de la commission des Affaires étrangères (4).

Bien évidemment, le temps de la présidence impose des contraintes spécifiques sur les hommes politiques qui sont souvent engagés de longue date dans les négociations européennes. Une préparation plus intensive de l'ensemble des dossiers s'impose afin que le président du Conseil des Ministres, connaissant les diverses positions nationales, puisse formuler des propositions de compromis valables. Les ministres doivent pouvoir remplir les cinq fonctions de la présidence identifiées par Wallace et Edwards (5):

-   la gestion du travail du Conseil;
-   l'élaboration d'initiatives politiques;
-   le rôle de médiateur lors des négociations;
-   les contacts avec les institutions communautaires;
-   la représentation de la Communauté dans les relations extérieures.

L'opinion générale qui s'est cristallisée est qu'un pays comme le Luxembourg n'a que des moyens restreints pour jouer un rôle actif dans la politique européenne et que l'aspect 'technique' de la présidence est prioritaire.

La charge de travail représentée par la préparation, les réunions elles-mêmes et les événements liés à la présidence (visites à des pays tiers, O.N.U.) est lourde et peut absorber, p.ex. pour le ministre des Affaires étrangères, jusqu'aux trois quarts de son temps disponible. Ainsi G. Thorn, ministre des Affaires étrangères, a visité durant les six mois de la présidence de 1976, une dizaine de capitales et en 1980, une vingtaine, en particulier en relation avec sa mission au Proche-Orient. De plus et surtout, les sept ministres impliqués dans le présidence de

1980 ont dû présider 32 sessions du Conseil des Ministres, occupant à elles seules 43 journées de travail.

Les fonctionnaires interrogés se sont accordés pour reconnaître qu'une des principales qualités nécessaires, hormis une bonne connaissance des dossiers, est la faculté d'élaborer des propositions de compromis consistantes. Ceci se combine avec le rôle traditionnel 'd'honnête courtier' qu'essaye de jouer le Luxembourg dans les relations internationales.

On est généralement conscient des moyens dont dispose le président pour bloquer ou retarder un dossier qui risque de porter atteinte à un intérêt national, notamment par le contrôle de la convocation des réunions et par la fixation de l'ordre du jour. Néanmoins le recours à ces techniques est estimé à la fois limité et dangereux: limité car la plupart des problèmes discutés sont sur la table depuis un certain temps déjà et ont souvent une dynamique propre; limité aussi à cause du contrôle des autres Etats membres. L'usage des techniques de retardement est dangereux en ce sens que la présidence risque de détruire son propre prestige et son image de neutralité, aspect essentiel de sa fonction. De plus, cette attitude peut provoquer un 'effet boomerang', les mêmes méthodes pouvant être utilisées contre le pays lors de présidences ultérieures. Les personnes interrogées se sont montrées très soucieuses de relever que les présidences luxembourgeoises ont toujours été d'une grande modération, reconnue selon eux par la plupart des Etat membres et les institutions.

Il est évident que la personnalité du ministre et son engagement dans certains domaines ont une influence certaine sur le déroulement de la présidence et l'avancement de quelques dossiers choisis. Ainsi p.ex. le grand poids mis en 1976 par le ministre des Affaires étrangères, Gaston Thorn, bien connu pour ses prises de position en faveur de l'intégration européenne, sur l'élection au suffrage universel du Parlement européen. La préparation des ministres pour leur tâche de président consiste davantage dans l'expérience accumulée lors de leur vie politique et lors de négociations communautaires antérieures que dans une préparation spécifiquement orientée vers la période de présidence.

II. LA COORDINATION INTERMINISTERIELLE

Il est évident que les caractéristiques de la culture administrative luxembourgeoise se retrouvent dans une certaine mesure dans les relations entre les divers départements. C'est le ministère des Affaires étrangères qui a la compétence de principe dans le domaine communautaire (6). Les dossiers à traiter sont transmis pour étude et commentaires aux ministères spécialisés concernés. Ces observations sont communiquées, avec ou sans avis spécial du ministre des Affaires étrangères, à la Représentation permanente et elles constituent la position de négociation luxembourgeoise. Lorsque des approches divergentes sur un point particulier se font jour, une négociation ad hoc entre les ministères et au niveau des fonctionnaires se met en place. Lorsqu'aucun accord ne peut être trouvé ou lorsque l'affaire touche à des intérêts nationaux importants, le dossier est évoqué au Conseil des Ministres.

La présidence des CE: Les présidences luxembourgeoises

Comme le constate très justement Ch. Sasse:

> Cette absence relative de conflits est, bien sûr, liée très étroitement à certaines données naturelles du Grand-Duché de Luxembourg et ne peut pas être recréée à volonté dans d'autres conditions. La faible dimension de l'appareil administratif luxembourgeois, qui permet de fréquents contacts informels entre les services ministériels et les hommes politiques responsables, prévaut à cet égard au même titre que le fait que le Luxembourg ne poursuit que rarement, au sein de la Communauté européenne, des intérêts nationaux marqués **(7).**

Ceci explique que contrairement à d'autres pays, le Luxembourg n'a pas créé de système institutionnalisé de comités interministériels, sauf en ce qui concerne certains intérêts particuliers du Luxembourg, p.ex. le siège des institutions européennes à Luxembourg.

L'essentiel des affaires se traite de manière informelle entre agents se connaissant personnellement la plupart du temps, instaurant ainsi un système de coopération très souple entre fonctionnaires et départements.

Un équilibre stable s'est développé entre les Affaires étrangères qui se concentrent sur les aspects politiques des dossiers et les ministères techniques dont les représentants dans les divers groupes jouissent d'une assez large liberté d'action. Ce **modus vivendi** imposé par des contraintes externes est jugé satisfaisant par la plupart des fonctionnaires interrogés qui mentionnent que d'une part, les problèmes majeurs sont rares et que d'autre part, il n'y a pas vraiment d'alternatives à cet état des choses.

L'initiative pour la mise en oeuvre du dispositif en vue de la présidence provient de la Représentation permanente en collaboration avec le ministère des Affaires étrangères. Le schéma d'organisation provisoire est discuté entre les Affaires étrangères, qui assurent la coordination matérielle du dispositif, et les départements. A l'issue de ces négociations, le schéma d'organisation est finalisé et communiqué aux personnes chargées de présider les groupes de travail. En outre une réunion de tous les fonctionnaires engagés dans la présidence et du ministre des Affaires étrangères est organisée quelques mois avant le début de la présidence. Telle est en principe la seule réunion de coordination organisée à Luxembourg, les réunions préparatoires **ad hoc** ayant lieu, le cas échéant, à la Représentation permanente à Bruxelles. Il est certain que ce dispositif très décentralisé comporte certains risques et quelques cas de positions contradictoires ont pu exister. Néanmoins ce danger a pu être limité grâce au rôle de filtre que joue le représentant permanent présidant le Coreper.

Ceci mis à part, il n'y a pas de changements majeurs dans les structures et procédures de coordination interministérielle en vue de la présidence, cet aspect restant plutôt à l'arrière-plan au vu des nécessités primordiales imposées par la présidence des groupes. Un minimum de coordination s'effectue, dans la mesure du possible, à la Représentation permanente. Quant aux canaux de communication, il se dégage des entrevues qu'il s'agit surtout de communications orales, la circulation de l'information sous forme de rapports écrits sur les activités des divers groupes étant plutôt réduite.

Cette structure de coordination extrêmement légère a permis, grâce à son caractère informel et peu formaliste, de concentrer toutes les énergies disponibles sur l'exercice des fonctions essentielles de la présidence. Les rares critiques concernant l'insuffisance de la coordination et de la circulation de l'information proviennent plutôt des Affaires étrangères et de la Représentation permanente que des ministères techniques.

III. LA PREPARATION A L'INTERIEUR DES MINISTERES

Le Luxembourg est membre fondateur des différentes Communautés européennes. Ceci implique qu'un certain capital d'expérience s'est accumulé au cours des années au sein des divers ministères concernés par les activités communautaires. Fonctionnant avec un personnel réduit en nombre - on compte environ 150 fonctionnaires de la carrière supérieure pour l'ensemble de l'administration luxembourgeoise - les ministères ne disposent en général pas de fonctionnaires suivant à plein temps et au jour le jour les affaires européennes. D'autre part, un certain nombre de charges résultant des obligations communautaires sont réparties entre des fonctionnaires qui, bien souvent, assurent le suivi dans un domaine spécialisé, et ce, sur des périodes assez prolongées. Les départements ministériels traitant des dossiers communautaires sont, à des degrés d'intensité variable, les ministères des Affaires étrangères, de l'Agriculture, de l'Economie, des Finances, de l'Environnement, de la Justice et enfin, de l'Energie.

Pour comprendre le caractère pragmatique et informel du processus administratif luxembourgeois, il faut voir que les distances hiérarchiques sont plus réduites que dans d'autres pays. La prise de contact avec le ministre à propos de problèmes ayant une incidence politique, est directe, alors que d'autre part, les fonctionnaires de la carrière moyenne sont parfois chargés de dossiers importants. Les procédures de décision à l'intérieur des départements ministériels sont réduites, étant donné que l'essentiel se déroule directement entre le fonctionnaire qui suit l'affaire et le ministre. Les consultations nécessaires sont effectuées de manière peu formelle par contact direct ou par téléphone. Au sein de chaque ministère technique, un nombre limité de fonctionnaires constituent les points de contact pour la Commission ou les organisations représentatives. Ainsi en ce qui concerne le ministère de l'Agriculture, l'un des ministères le plus intensément engagé dans l'élaboration des politiques européennes, on peut évaluer à une vingtaine le nombre des personnes partiellement concernées par les négociations communautaires. Ce nombre est encore plus réduit pour les autres ministères spécialisés.

En raison même de son étendue limitée, l'administration luxembourgeoise a dû favoriser l'apparition de généralistes dont la caractéristique est une grande polyvalence, au détriment des experts spécialisés dans certains domaines. 'Au sein des autorités gouvernementales, l'organisation du travail et la répartition des tâches se sont faites en fonction des nécessités ou possibilités pratiques, plutôt que selon une stricte observance des textes réglementaires' **(8)**. L'avantage de cette solution est évidemment de favoriser une certaine flexibilité au niveau administratif.

Cette flexibilité est encore accentuée par l'autonomie poussée dont dispose chaque ministère dans sa pratique au niveau communautaire. Ainsi, à partir de données de principe bien connues, les divers ministères techniques sont assez libres de développer leur politique communautaire, ceci n'aboutissant d'ailleurs généralement pas à des positions contradictoires. C'est pourquoi des domaines comme l'agriculture, l'énergie ou encore les problèmes économiques spécifiques échappent dans une mesure variable au département des Affaires étrangères. Ce système n'est viable que dans la mesure où des contacts étroits sont possibles entre les fonctionnaires des ministères concernés.

Etant donné que le Luxembourg n'a des intérêts nationaux spécifiques que dans un nombre limité de domaines, les départements ministériels expriment lors des négociations, une position générale favorable aux solutions communautaires, tout en essayant de jouer le rôle d' 'honnête courtier' entre des intérêts nationaux divergents.

Le ministère des Affaires étrangères continue néanmoins à jouer un rôle important dans la préparation des positions politiques. En raison de la technicité croissante de nombreuses négociations communautaires, il a été amené à affirmer son rôle de coordination aux dépens de tout essai de contrôler le déroulement concret des discussions. Selon le schéma d'organisation, environ 185 groupes ont fonctionné à Bruxelles lors de la présidence de 1980. La présidence a été assurée par une centaine de personnes. Le Luxembourg a rempli ses fonctions dans 169 groupes. Seize groupes ont été présidés par la Belgique et les Pays-Bas. Au sein du ministère des Affaires étrangères, c'est la direction II: relations économiques internationales et coopération, qui est chargée des dossiers C.E.E. (voir tableau 9.2 en annexe). Cette direction comprend moins d'une douzaine de fonctionnaires de la carrière diplomatique. Elle s'occupe de même de l'Union économique belgo-luxembourgeoise, du Benelux etc. En principe, le ministère des Affaires étrangères est le point de passage obligatoire pour toutes les communications entre les départements ministériels et les institutions communautaires, en particulier en ce qui concerne la correspondance écrite. Néanmoins, ce principe semble être souvent battu en brèche soit pour des raisons objectives (pression du temps etc.), soit à cause de certaines réticences du côté des ministères techniques.

Au plan de l'organisation interne des ministères spécialisés, on peut constater le maintien et l'intensification des arrangements antérieurs à la présidence. Les fonctionnaires qui sont présents, souvent depuis longtemps, dans certains groupes effectuent la transition sans problèmes majeurs, 'ils continuent tout en présidant' selon la formule utilisée par l'une des personnes interrogées. Ces fonctionnaires sont en outre chargés de couvrir d'autres groupes dans leur domaine de compétence. Les groupes restants sont présidés soit par des fonctionnaires n'ayant pas encore participé aux travaux des groupes concernés, soit par des diplomates de la Représentation permanente. En dernier recours, un nombre limité de groupes sont présidés par des fonctionnaires belges ou néerlandais.

En général, il n'y a pas d'accroissement important du personnel en vue et pour la présidence, chaque ministère étant censé accomplir sa tâche par ses propres moyens. Néanmoins, diverses mesures permettent de renforcer le personnel: ainsi les mises à la retraite intervenant normalement juste avant ou lors de la présidence sont retardées; de même en 1976 et 1980, certains fonctionnaires ont été rappelés au service actif pour la durée de la présidence; enfin, un certain nombre de fonctionnaires non directement liés aux ministères concernés sont appelés en renfort (Commissariat aux Banques; Caisse d'Epargne). En ce qui concerne le ministère des Affaires étrangères, des mouvements de personnels plus importants s'effectuent. Une dizaine de diplomates en poste dans des ambassades luxembourgeoises à l'étranger ont été rappelés en 1976 et 1980 pour être attachés temporairement soit aux représentations permanentes à Bruxelles, New York ou Genève, soit au ministère lui-même, p.ex. dans le cadre de la coopération politique.

Mis à part ces quelques renforcements temporaires, des changements dans l'organisation et la procédure sont rares. Certaines adaptations d'une présidence à l'autre sont dues plus à l'évolution du rôle de la présidence (9) qu'à un changement du style administratif luxembourgeois (p.ex. renforcement des moyens techniques de communication).

Il est évident que dans une administration aussi réduite, l'impact de la présidence sur la vie normale de l'institution est important et un certain nombre d'activités sont au ralenti: ainsi s'explique p.ex. que pendant la période de la présidence, très peu de conventions internationales sont soumises à la ratification de la Chambre des Députés.

La détermination des présidents des groupes de travail s'effectue en négociation (parfois difficile) entre le ministère des Affaires étrangères et le département visé au regard des activités passées des fonctionnaires et des moyens personnels disponibles. Normalement les marges de manoeuvre sont très réduites et les fonctionnaires sont fermement invités à contribuer au succès de la présidence luxembourgeoise. Il faut noter qu'une indemnité spéciale est accordée à chacun des participants, alors que d'autre part, les réglementations sur les frais de route et de séjour ont dû être adaptées et allégées en raison des circonstances exceptionnelles.

La préparation de la présidence dans les groupes de travail est essentiellement une préparation 'sur le tas', les futurs présidents étant invités, dans la mesure où ils ne le font pas déjà, à participer à l'avance aux activités des groupes dont ils sont chargés, et ce, au moins quatre mois à l'avance. Aucune activité de formation n'a eu lieu en 1976 et 1980. Cette confiance dans un apprentissage pratique pour les nouveaux venus sur la scène européenne explique pourquoi on essaye d'établir assez longtemps à l'avance la liste des groupes à couvrir et la liste des personnes prenant en charge ces groupes.

Alors que des premières évaluations des besoins en personnel s'effectuent en partie déjà plus d'une année à l'avance, les choses passent à un stade critique environ six mois à l'avance avec la détermination d'un schéma d'organisation. Cette préparation précoce n'exclut bien entendu pas les surprises en dernière minute (désistements, maladies) qui, en raison des effectifs limités, ne peuvent être que difficilement amorties, les réserves disponibles étant très réduites. Ce dernier point est ressenti pour quelques interlocuteurs comme un problème sérieux pour les prochaines présidences luxembourgeoises.

Lorsque le Luxembourg prend la présidence d'un groupe de travail, il n'est plus, en règle générale, représenté par une délégation propre. Ceci empêche évidemment tout conflit entre la délégation nationale et le président. Bien entendu, il peut s'avérer parfois difficile de combiner la casquette nationale et la casquette communautaire. Dans ces situations, beaucoup dépend de la personnalité du président. Plusieurs interlocuteurs ont confirmé que dans une mesure plus ou moins réduite, un président habile peut avoir un effet temporisateur sur certains dossiers. Néanmoins les dangers d'une telle approche sont clairement perçus (cf. point I).

Au niveau de la pratique des présidences de 1976 et de 1980, un jugement globalement positif sur la préparation et la mise en oeuvre des présidences luxembourgeoises s'est dégagé, et ce, dans l'ensemble des ministères couverts par l'enquête. Selon les personnes interrogées, la plus grande partie du 'stress' a pu être absorbée sans accrocs majeurs, confirmant ainsi les jugements du ministre des Affaires étrangères que 'nous nous sommes tirés de ce long défi plus qu'honorablement' (10). (1976). Sur le plan individuel, la lourde charge physique et nerveuse pesant sur les présidents désignés a été plusieurs fois relevée, ce qui conforte la constatation que 'lors de la dernière présidence, la corde était vraiment tendue à l'extrême' (11).

IV. LE ROLE DE LA REPRESENTATION PERMANENTE ET LES CONTACTS AVEC LES INSTITUTIONS COMMUNAUTAIRES

Pièce centrale du dispositif communautaire luxembourgeois, la Représentation permanente remplit selon la formule d'un fonctionnaire, 'davantage le rôle d'une direction externe du ministère des Affaires étrangères que celui d'une ambassade'. En temps normal, une grande partie de l'activité communautaire se concentre à la Représentation permanente, qui jouit d'un statut élevé au sein de l'administration luxembourgeoise. Les rapports oraux et écrits provenant de l'ambassade auprès des C.E. ont un impact direct sur la formulation des positions luxembourgeoises, 'le poids des appréciations de la mission est un facteur d'influence important qui amènera plus d'une fois la capitale à entériner les suggestions de la Représentation' (12).

Au vu des fonctions importantes que remplit la mission permanente dans le contexte luxembourgeois, il est étonnant de voir qu'en temps normal, l'ensemble des dossiers sont traités par quatre à cinq fonctionnaires. Ils proviennent sans exception du ministère des Affaires étrangères.

Une grande partie de la coordination entre les représentants dans les groupes, de même que les contacts avec les institutions communautaires passe par la Représentation permanente qui est ainsi souvent en contact direct avec les ministères techniques.

Le rôle important joué par la mission auprès de la C.E.E. provient aussi de l'expérience accumulée au cours des années dans les matières européennes par les diplomates affectés à Bruxelles. Ceci se vérifie au niveau du représentant permanent lui-même. Alors que l'ambassadeur A. Borschette est resté en poste pendant 12 ans, le représentant permanent Jean Dondelinger a fait partie de la délégation luxembourgeoise de 1961 à 1984, soit pendant vingt-trois ans! Cette stabilité permet bien sûr une pénétration accrue dans les réseaux communautaires d'information et une connaissance approfondie des dossiers. Ceci se traduit surtout par les contacts intensifs qu'entretient la Représentation permanente avec le Secrétariat du Conseil et la Commission. Ce facteur de durée et de permanence n'est pas négligeable pour la compréhension de la place du représentant permanent dans le processus d'élaboration des positions luxembourgeoises. Ceci se concrétise par des fréquents séjours dans la capitale du Luxembourg et par des contacts directs quasi quotidiens avec le ministre des Affaires étrangères.

La délégation luxembourgeoise jouit d'une assez large autonomie d'action. Lors de négociations, elle est le plus souvent tenue à observer des instructions assez générales laissant le champ libre à l'appréciation du négociateur. Pour les domaines où le Luxembourg n'a pas d'intérêts spécifiques, le représentant permanent ne doit se tenir qu'aux orientations générales de la politique européenne luxembourgeoise. Un problème peut se poser du fait d'une attitude trop passive de certains ministères techniques qui ne suivent pas au jour le jour les problèmes européens qui les concernent.

Un certain changement s'effectue en vue de la présidence pour laquelle la représentation permanente est l'élément moteur. Plus d'une année à l'avance, l'ambassadeur, en collaboration avec le Secrétariat du Conseil, établit une liste des groupes à pourvoir ainsi qu'une estimation des besoins en personnel. Son influence sur la désignation des présidents de groupes n'est pas négligeable. C'est à la Représentation permanente que sont établis le schéma d'organisation, le calendrier et le projet de programme de la présidence luxembourgeoise, ces documents étant par la suite discutés et approuvés par les départements ministériels. Il en est de même pour la fixation des objectifs des comités essentiels.

Autre aspect de la préparation, le représentant permanent est chargé de négocier avec ses homologues belge et néerlandais la manière dont ces deux Etats pourront prendre en charge certaines fonctions de la présidence. La règle communautaire lorsqu'un Etat ne préside pas un groupe, est que c'est la prochaine présidence qui s'en occupe; c'est-à-dire dans le cas luxembourgeois, les Pays-Bas. Néanmoins du fait du Traité d'Union économique belgo-luxembourgeoise (U.E.B.L.), la Belgique est en principe compétente pour représenter le Luxembourg dans certains domaines. On peut estimer qu'en raison des positions tranchées des Pays-Bas sur certains dossiers (transports, énergie, aide au développement), il n'est peut-être pas de bonne politique de déséquilibrer par trop les données des négociations. Voilà pourquoi une discussion cas par cas se déroule à la Représentation permanente, permettant de répartir les groupes non couverts par des présidents luxembourgeois. En règle générale, les groupes plutôt politiques sont attribués aux Pays-Bas, alors que les dossiers économiques sont traités par la Belgique, sans que le partage selon ce critère soit absolu, ne serait-ce qu'en raison de la nature hybride de nombreux problèmes. En vue de la présidence, la mission à Bruxelles est renforcée par le détachement à Bruxelles de diplomates en poste dans d'autres ambassades ou au ministère des Affaires étrangères. En 1980, trois diplomates des ambassades de Paris, Londres et Bruxelles ont été envoyées pour sept mois à Bruxelles. Néanmoins, la possibilité existait déjà auparavant d'assurer la présence de ces personnes pour des réunions de groupes de travail.

Les méthodes de travail au sein de la mission ne changent pas fondamentalement à l'approche de la présidence. En dehors des fréquentes réunions de service avec l'ambassadeur, aucun autre mécanisme de coordination n'est prévu, l'essentiel de l'information étant échangé de manière informelle. Toutes les personnes interrogées qui ont participé à l'activité de la Représentation permanente lors d'une présidence luxembourgeoise ont relevé la grande pression physique et nerveuse que représente cet exercice. Toutes ont estimé que la dotation en personnel est insuffisante pour faire face aux exigences croissantes de la fonction présidentielle. Même si des crises majeures ont pu être évitées dans le passé, il n'en reste pas moins, selon ces personnes, que la mission permanente ne dispose pas de réserves suffisantes pour faire face à des situations imprévues (maladies, réunion de nouveaux groupes, etc.).

La présidence se traduit aussi par une intensification des contacts tant avec le niveau politique qu'avec les administrations nationales.

Afin de permettre une meilleure communication entre Luxembourg et Bruxelles, les moyens techniques disponibles (télex, téléphone) ont été renforcés et complétés (télécopieur).

Sur le plan des contacts avec les institutions communautaires, il faut noter que l'importance du Secrétariat du Conseil est unanimement relevée. Dans une très large mesure, le Luxembourg utilise les services du Secrétariat pour préparer les négociations. Des échanges réguliers ont lieu entre le secrétaire général et le représentant permanent pour préparer les discussions du Coreper. De même, tous les présidents des groupes de travail sont vivement encouragés à prendre contact avec les fonctionnaires du Secrétariat. La qualité des avis de cet organe est reconnue et un large usage de son appui matériel et intellectuel semble être commun aux représentants de tous les ministères concernés. 'Le Luxembourg est certainement le pays qui utilise le mieux le Secrétariat du Conseil selon les buts pour lesquels il a été institué', commente l'une des personnes interrogées. Ce jugement a aussi été confirmé par des agents du Secrétariat. Cette présence du Secrétariat se marque à plusieurs niveaux: élaboration de notes de synthèse, de compromis du président et de rapports, briefing des ministres, participation à l'élaboration du discours-programme devant le Parlement européen, rédaction de projets de réponse aux questions parlementaires, etc. L'importance des services rendus par le Secrétariat a été mis en évidence lors de la grève qui a bloqué cet organe à la fin de 1980.

En raison de l'attitude de principe favorable du Grand-Duché envers la Commission, il n'y a pas d'obstacle majeur à une intensification des contacts, même si la densité et la fréquence restent inférieures à celles des échanges avec le Secrétariat du Conseil. La réunion du ministre des Affaires étrangères, futur président du Conseil, et des membres de la Commission se situe largement à un niveau protocolaire, même si un certain nombre de points concernant le programme de la présidence y sont discutés. Cette rencontre est préparée par le représentant permanent en collaboration avec le secrétariat général de la Commission.

Traditionnellement le Luxembourg a pris des positions favorables au Parlement européen (élection directe, pouvoirs accrus). Cette attitude n'a pas été démentie lors des présidences 1976 et 1980. Un diplomate attaché à la Représentation permanente avait été spécialement chargé des relations avec l'Assemblée et participait aux sessions à Strasbourg et Luxembourg. Au niveau ministériel, une grande attention a été consacrée à une information étendue du Parlement. Ainsi sous la présidence de 1976, la possibilité de questions parlementaires orales portant sur des questions relevant de la coopération politique européenne a été introduite. Outre le discours-programme en début de présidence, les occasions de contacts entre les ministres et les parlementaires se sont multipliées (comptes rendus des sessions du Conseil, réponses aux questions parlementaires; procédure de concertation, trialogue budgétaire, colloques dans le cadre de la coopération politique, etc.).

En conclusion, la place centrale de la Représentation permanente dans l'élaboration de la politique communautaire luxembourgeoise est constatée par l'ensemble des interlocuteurs. Ce rôle s'intensifie encore à l'approche de la présidence. D'autre part, le terme de 'symbiose' a été utilisé pour décrire les relations avec le Secrétariat du Conseil, ce qui montre bien que le jugement de Wallace/Edwards selon lequel 'la capacité des gouvernements de gérer la charge de travail liée à la présidence dépend en partie de l'usage qu'ils font du Secrétariat du Conseil' (13), est particulièrement adéquat dans le contexte luxembourgeois.

V. LA PRESIDENCE ET LA COOPERATION POLITIQUE EUROPEENNE

Le développement de la coopération politique européenne à partir des rapports de Luxembourg et de Copenhague est un des faits marquants de ces dernières années. Non seulement la présidence des divers groupes de travail, la préparation de certaines réunions des ministres des Affaires étrangères et des chefs d'Etat et de gouvernement reposent sur l'Etat qui assume la présidence, mais de plus, l'organisation matérielle et le secrétariat des réunions dépendent de lui seul. Enfin les théâtres d'action sont multiples: Nations Unies et organes spécialisés, pays tiers, réunions internationales, etc.

De plus en plus la présidence de la coopération politique est considérée comme la principale charge de travail avec laquelle un Etat est confrontée lors de ces six mois. En effet,

la présidence, qui est transmise à tour de rôle tous les six mois à un des Etats membres, est l'élément-clé de la coopération politique.

Elle donne dans une large mesure le dynamisme dont la Commission était investie initialement par les Traités dans le cadre communautaire: prise d'initiatives, organisation de réunions, établissement de l'ordre du jour, élaboration de compromis, porte-parole des Dix, gestion et conduite des consultations avec les pays tiers et, pour autant que cela soit nécessaire, mise en oeuvre des décisions prises (14).

On peut estimer entre 60 et 80 le nombre de réunions rien que dans la capitale. Ceci montre qu' 'il existe une limite physique au nombre de tâches que l'on peut confier à la présidence de la coopération politique, sans lui fournir aucune structure administrative propre sur laquelle elle puisse s'appuyer.

Cette limite est sans doute plus évidente lorsque la présidence est exercée par les plus petits pays de la Communauté dont les moyens, notamment en personnel, sont limités' (15).

En temps normal, c'est la direction 1: affaires politiques et culturelles, composée d'une demi-douzaine de diplomates, qui prépare les discussions de la coopération politique aux divers niveaux (ministres, directeurs politiques, correspondants, groupes de travail) (voir tableau 9.2 en annexe). Lors de la présidence de 1980, ce département a été renforcé par deux diplomates. En outre, le personnel administratif a été renforcé, notamment en vue de la gestion du réseau télex Coreu.

Ces quelques données expliquent que p. ex., un seul fonctionnaire ait présidé toutes les réunions des quatre groupes régionaux: pays de l'Est, Afrique, Asie et Amérique latine. De même, l'effort nécessaire pour établir des projets de réponse à un nombre croissant de questions parlementaires (autour de 150) a dû être fourni quasiment par une seule personne.

Alors que le Luxembourg n'a pas voulu reprendre en 1976 le secrétariat informel créé sous la présidence irlandaise, il semble que la formule de la 'troïka', c'est-à-dire de la collaboration entre l'ancienne, nouvelle et la prochaine présidence, gagne du terrain. Elle a été mise en oeuvre en 1980, notamment dans le contexte du dialogue euro-arabe, avec la participation de diplomates italiens et néerlandais.

Un des problèmes de la présidence luxembourgeoise est certainement l'absence d'un réseau diplomatique étendu, le Luxembourg ne disposant que de onze ambassades et de huit représentations permanentes à l'étranger. C'est la raison pour laquelle en vertu du traité néerlando-luxembourgeois du 24 mars 1964, les intérêts luxembourgeois sont représentés dans les autres pays par les ambassades des Pays-Bas. Cet arrangement peut être la cause de difficultés, notamment protocolaires, lorsque la délimitation avec les compétences de représentation de la Belgique au titre de l'U.E.B.L. n'est pas clairement définie.

L'absence d'ambassades propres est un facteur négatif, d'une part en raison de la carence d'information de première main disponible, d'autre part en raison de la confusion qui peut en résulter lors de la présentation de positions communautaires dans un pays tiers. Ce problème est considéré comme un obstacle majeur pour la mise en oeuvre d'initiatives diplomatiques sérieuses par certains observateurs (16).

En général, l'activité diplomatique par les canaux belges et néerlandais est jugée satisfaisante, même si quelques problèmes ont pu se présenter. Il faut encore mentionner le surcroît de travail résultant, pour les ambassades luxembourgeoises dans des pays tiers, de l'organisation des réunions de coordination sur place, notamment à Washington (17). Il est certain que l'exercice de ces responsabilités est une source de gains de prestige, surtout pour un petit pays.

Une fonction importante revient à la mission permanente de l'Etat assumant la présidence auprès de l'Organisation des Nations Unies et de ses organes spécialisés tant à New York qu'à Genève, qu'à Vienne (18). En effet, le Luxembourg a été confronté pour la première fois pendant la seconde moitié de 1980, avec l'obligation de présider un certain nombre de groupes dans le contexte de l'Assemblée générale des Nations Unies. La gestion des diverses procédures de coordination (entre Etats membres de la C.E.E., entre les pays industrialisés, avec les pays non-alignés, etc.) a posé des problèmes énormes pour une mission qui est passée, pour les besoins de la cause, de un à quatre fonctionnaires à temps plein. De plus, certains diplomates y ont participé à temps partiel, notamment en raison de la réunion à New York des ministres des Affaires étrangères au titre de la coopération politique. La représentation luxembourgeoise à Genève a de même été légèrement renforcée (trois fonctionnaires).

Malgré ces renforts en personnel et en matériel (surtout à New York), la charge de la présidence n'a pu être remplie de façon satisfaisante que grâce à plusieurs facteurs externes:

-   l'appui de la Commission, présenté à des titres divers (présidence bicéphale);
-   la couverture de quelques commissions par la Belgique et les Pays-Bas;
-   la coopération, qualifiée de franche et substantielle, de quelques Etats membres.

Dans ce contexte, la facilité du point de vue linguistique a été citée comme un grand avantage lors des négociations et des contacts informels.

Grâce à ces quelques facteurs favorables et grâce à l'engagement physique de ses représentants, 'le Luxembourg a pu mener à bien l'essentiel de ces tâches présidentielles, infirmant ainsi un certain scepticisme initial' (interview). Néanmoins, on s'est accordé à constater que la gestion de la coopération politique sur les lieux de travail des Nations Unies est un point faible qu'il s'agira de renforcer lors de la prochaine présidence.

Toujours dans le cadre de la coopération politique européenne, la représentation de la position communautaire dans le cadre de conférences internationales comme le Dialogue Nord-Sud ou encore la Conférence sur la Sécurité et la Coopération en Europe (CSCE) a constitué un élément majeur des présidences de 1976 et 1980. Ainsi, malgré des effectifs limités, le Luxembourg a réussi à présider les quatre groupes de travail constitués dans le contexte de la conférence de Paris.

Un grand moment de la présidence de 1980 a été la mission diplomatique de M. Gaston Thorn au Proche-Orient. Cette mission qui a été entièrement préparée par le ministère des Affaires étrangères est considérée par certains comme le 'moment-phare' de la dernière présidence. A cette occasion, la diplomatie luxembourgeoise a pu faire preuve de sa capacité de mettre sur pied et de conduire une mission d'une durée de plusieurs semaines, se déroulant dans une dizaine de pays, et ce, dans un contexte international délicat et complexe. On a relevé le volume de travail matériel énorme et inaccoutumé que cela a imposé aux personnes impliquées. A cette occasion a été mentionné, exception-nellement, le problème des gros coûts financiers qu'implique la conduite d'une opération diplomatique d'une telle envergure, et ce, en dépit du support logistique apporté par le réseau diplomatique néerlandais et les Forces aériennes belges.

Enfin, dernier aspect qui entre en partie sous la coopération politique, la préparation du Conseil européen à Luxembourg. Cet événement politique majeur a été préparé en grande partie par la Représentation permanente à Bruxelles. Il a été l'occasion pour le Grand-Duché de Luxembourg d'affirmer sa présence sur la scène internationale, même si la part qu'il peut jouer lors des discussions mêmes est plus modeste. Un grand effort a été entrepris à cette occasion pour améliorer l'infrastructure matérielle (logements, moyens de communication, centre de presse etc.). L'ensemble des interlocuteurs se sont accordés à relever l'importance d'une bonne préparation intellectuelle et matérielle du Conseil européen, tout succès ou échec formant un élément important du jugement d'ensemble porté à l'issue des six mois sur la présidence luxembourgeoise.

En conclusion, il convient de tirer un bilan nuancé des présidences luxembourgeoises de la coopération politique européenne. Confrontée à une charge de travail grandissante, le ministère des Affaires étrangères a réussi, au prix d'une mobilisation de toutes ses ressources, à faire face aux exigences imposées par le fonctionnement des mécanismes de coordination et l'évolution rapide de l'agenda international. Ainsi, il a été reconnu que 'même le Luxembourg avec les ressources en personnel les plus réduites a pu non seulement gérer de façon satisfaisante la pléthore de réunions, mais aussi permettre à Gaston Thorn de se libérer pour sa mission itinérante au Moyen-Orient' (19).

Cette capacité d'assumer les obligations de la présidence, même en utilisant divers mécanismes de soutien (troika, utilisation des services diplomatiques des Pays-Bas et de la Belgique etc.), revêt une importance centrale pour la diplomatie luxembourgeoise qui peut ainsi faire preuve de sa présence, modeste mais réelle, dans le cadre de la C.P.E.

Comme pour tous les pays, la présidence de la C.P.E. est une source de prestige international pour le Luxembourg, car par elle:

les petits et moyens Etats ont acquis une importance dans le monde de la diplomatie internationale qu'ils n'auraient jamais eue autrement: tous les quatre ans et demi lorsque leurs pays ont la présidence, Luxembourg et Dublin, Copenhague et La Haye deviennent des capitales européennes majeures. Les Etats ont aussi obtenu un poids diplomatique à la fois en relation avec les autres Etats membres et aussi avec les pays tiers, car ceux-ci ne peuvent jamais être sûrs de la contribution que même le plus petit Etat pourrait avoir sur ce qui pourrait devenir une position européenne unifiée **(20)**.

Si la présidence est l'occasion pour un petit Etat de profiter d'un surplus de présence, de statut international et d'information, et par contrecoup, de développer une sensibilité accrue à la nécessité de développer une identité nationale propre sur le plan international **(21)**, il ne faut pas se faire d'illusion sur les possibilités réelles d'influence sur les position prises dans le cadre de la C.P.E. A cet égard, il est révélateur que dans un livre récent consacré aux liens entre les politiques étrangères nationales et la C.P.E., on ait cru bon de diviser l'ouvrage en deux parties, l'une consacrée aux grands Etats, l'autre aux petits Etats, cette division étant censée refléter une réalité fondamentale de la coopération politique.

Même si le gouvernement luxembourgeois affirme avec force le principe de l'égalité des Etats membres, la réalité de cet état de fait est implicitement et dans la plupart des cas, reconnue et une attitude pragmatique et réaliste est adoptée, l'ambition majeure restant de réaliser une présidence efficace sur le plan administratif et organisationnel.

VI. L'ATTITUDE NATIONALE ENVERS LA PRESIDENCE

Les fonctionnaires rencontrés ont, dans l'ensemble, surtout relevé le rapide développement des fonctions présidentielles, développement qu'ils relient au problème général des processus décisionnels de la Communauté (statut amoindri de la Commission, problème du vote au Conseil des Ministres, ...). Le rôle de la présidence est considéré comme une donnée sur laquelle le Luxembourg n'a que peu prise. D'un avis unanime, la charge de travail s'est considérablement alourdie entre 1976 et 1980, en raison surtout de l'extension de la coopération politique.

Le temps de la présidence est ressenti comme un défi, comme l'occasion pour l'Etat luxembourgeois de faire la preuve qu'il est un membre à part entière de la Communauté européenne et qu'il peut 'observer les règles du club' (interview). Ou pour reprendre la formule de M. Paul Helminger, secrétaire d'Etat aux Affaires étrangères, 'il nous faut accepter ce défi, car l'exercice de la présidence devra fournir la démonstration de notre capacité à préserver dans la Communauté notre existence d'Etat membre égal en droits et obligations'.

De plus, l'exercice de la présidence est l'occasion pour le Luxembourg de jouer un rôle politique sur la scène internationale, car:

> quand un petit pays comme le Luxembourg assume sa présidence, il parle au nom de la Communauté dans son ensemble. Dans un monde tourmenté où les relations se mesurent en rapports de force, la voix de la Communauté européenne compte. Grâce à sa structure institutionnelle, celle du Luxembourg aussi **(22)**.

Cette attitude explique en partie l'atmosphère de mobilisation générale qui semble régner à l'approche de la présidence. Cette attitude explique aussi le rejet absolu et inconditionnel des propositions visant à réduire le rôle de quelques petits Etats (proposition d'une présidence Benelux), l'argument étant que la preuve est loin d'être faite que les présidences des petits Etats sont moins efficaces quant à l'avancement des dossiers que celles des grands Etats. D'autre part, la proposition du rapport Tindemans d'une présidence de douze mois est rejetée comme irréalisable du fait des problèmes politiques et organisationnels que cela risque de poser dans une Communauté de dix, et bientôt de douze Etats membres.

La possibilité pour la présidence luxembourgeoise d'apporter une contribution substantielle à l'intégration européenne est vue avec scepticisme, tant en raison du fonctionnement effectif des procédures de prise de décisions communautaires qu'à cause du faible poids politique dans la balance. D'où ce jugement du ministre des Affaires étrangères:

> Dans ces conditions, si la présidence luxembourgeoise n'a pas été à même de réaliser entièrement le programme de travail qu'elle s'était fixé et si elle a dû essuyer plusieurs échecs, il faut en rechercher la cause dans la constellation politique et économique européenne voire mondiale et non pas dans un défaut de volonté et de détermination des ministres et fonctionnaires luxembourgeois qui, pendant six mois, ont assumé la direction des affaires communautaires (23).

Cette interprétation ne saurait cacher le fait qu'un certain seuil semble avoir été atteint en 1980 en ce qui concerne les aspects organisationnels et administratifs de la présidence.

A preuve le jugement suivant de Mme Colette Flesch, ministre des Affaires étrangères:

> la présidence du Conseil des Communautés européennes qui revient régulièrement, à tour de rôle, à chacun des Etats membres pour une durée de 6 mois, constitue pour chaque délégation une tâche particulièrement lourde et ardue. Que dire de l'effort exigé d'un petit pays dont les effectifs totaux au ministère sont inférieurs à ceux de certaines représentations permanentes? Aux Affaires étrangères à Luxembourg, nous avons l'impression que lors de la présidence luxembourgeoise au cours du second semestre de 1980, nous avons littéralement atteint le point de rupture. Si nous voulons, au cours du deuxième semestre de 1985, assumer pleinement nos obligations communautaires, force sera de renforcer nos effectifs (24).

Les mesures proposées afin de réduire le 'stress' de la prochaine présidence vont d'une augmentation substantielle du personnel à un renforcement des procédures d'information mutuelle entre ministères, en passant par une préparation à plus long terme.

L'expérience de la présidence a été jugée à la fois éprouvante sur le plan physique et psychique, et enrichissante de par les contacts et expériences rassemblés à cette occasion. Il a été remarqué à plusieurs reprises qu'il existe toujours une certaine réticence dans quelques

ministères techniques à s'engager à fond dans ce qui été appelé
'l'aventure de la présidence' et une certaine passivité a été critiquée.

En résumé, on peut identifier les éléments suivants composant
l'attitude luxembourgeoise envers la présidence (25):

- des possibilités accrues de jouer le rôle d'intermédiaire discret,
  ('honnête courtier');
- l'occasion de présenter des propositions de solution acceptables
  pour toutes les parties;
- une chance additionnelle pour le Luxembourg de jouer un certain
  rôle sur le plan mondial.

D'une manière générale, les fonctionnaires interrogés ont exprimé
leur conviction que la gestion de la présidence pour un petit pays comme
le Luxembourg, ne disposant que d'un appareil administratif réduit, n'est
possible que si une grande mobilité et flexibilité dans les structures et
procédures est maintenue. Ce n'est que dans la mesure où le Luxembourg
parvient à remplir correctement les obligations matérielles résultant de
la présidence, qu'une certaine marge de manoeuvre s'ouvre pour quelques
initiatives politiques allant dans le sens d'une intégration européenne
accrue.

REFERENCES:

(1)   P.L. Lorenz, Luxembourg: the upgrading of foreign policy p. 154 in Ch. Hill (ed.): National Foreign Policies and European Political Cooperation, R11A/George Allen & Unwin, London, 1983 (traduction par l'IEAP).

(2)   M. Hirsch, Die Logik der Integration, - Uberlegungen zu den Aussenbeziehungen westeuropäischer Kleinstaaten, Europa-Archiv, 13/1974, 447-456.

(3)   G. de Muyser, La préparation de la décision communautaire au niveau national luxembourgeois p. 230, in: P. Gerbet/D. Pepy (eds): La décision dans les Communautés européennes, Presses Universitaires de Bruxelles, Bruxelles, 1969.

(4)   Ch. Sasse, Le processus de décision dans la Communauté européenne, P.U.F., Limoges, 1977, pp. 61-62; voir aussi: N. Niblock: The EEC: National Parliaments in Community Decision-making, Chatham House: PEP, London, 1971.

(5)   H. Wallace & G. Edwards, The Council of Ministers of the European Community and the President-in-Office, Federal Trust, London, 1977. Voir aussi H. Wallace dans ce volume chap. 1.

(6)   voir sur le ministère des Affaires Etrangères: G. Trausch: The Ministry of Foreign Affairs in the Grand Duchy, in: The Times Survey of Foreign Ministries of the World, London, Times Books, London, 1982, 345-361.

(7)   voir Ch. Sasse, Le processus de décision dans la Communauté européenne, P.U.F., Limoges, 1977, pp. 30-31.

(8)   op.cit. p. 230.

(9)   H. Wallace & G. Edwards, European Community: The Evolving Role of the Presidency of the Council, International Affairs vol. 52, 1976, no. 4.

(10) G. Thorn, Discours budgétaire, 1976 p.1.

(11) idem p. 38.

(12) G. de Muyser op. cit. p. 233. Voir aussi: E. Ruppert; La Représentation permanente du Luxembourg auprès des Communautés européennes, in La Fraternelle luxembourgeoise de Bruxelles, 65e anniversaire, 1971.

(13) H. Wallace & G. Edwards, The Council of Ministers of the European Community and the President-in-Office, Federal Trust, London, 1977, p. 25.

(14) W. Wallace, Cooperation and Convergence in European foreign policy in: Ch. Hill (ed.) op.cit. p. 3. (traduction par l'IEAP).

(15) Ph. de Schoutheete, La coopération politique européenne, p. 127, Labor, Bruxelles, 1980.
voir aussi en général:
-   D. Allen, A. Rummel, W. Wessels (eds.), European Political Cooperation: towards a foreign policy for Western Europe, Butterworths, London, 1982
-   W. Wallace, Political Cooperation: Integration through Intergovern-mentalism in: H. Wallace, W. Wallace & C. Webb, Policy-Making in the European Community, Wiley, London, 1983, p. 373-402.

(16) P.H. Lorenz: op.cit. p. 162.

(17) voir en général: Ph. Taylor, Political Cooperation in Washington, International Affairs, vol. 57, no. 3, Summer 1981.

(18) voir: B. Lindemann, EG-Staaten und Vereinte Nationen - Die politische Zusammenarbeit der Neun in den U.N.-Hauptorganen, R. Oldenbourg, München, 1978.

(19) Ch. Hill: National interests - the insuperable obstacles in: CH. Hill (ed) op.cit. p. 130.

(20) P. Taylor: The Limits of European Integration, Columbia University Press, New York, 1983, p. 84.

(21) voir à cet égard les commentaires lucides de P.H. Lorenz dans l'article cité (surtout les pages 158-161).

(22) G. Thorn, Un petit pays dans le processus d'intégration, in: Le Luxembourg et la C.E.E., un bilan politique, Cahiers de la B.I.L., 1982/3.

(23) G. Thorn, Discours budgétaire 1977 p. 31.

(24) C. Flesch, La diplomatie luxembourgeoise: nécessité, réalité et défi. Conférence prononcée à l'Institut Royal des Relations Internationales (25.1.83), publié dans Studia diplomatica 36(2), 1983, 145-162.

(25) G. Thorn, La politique étrangère du G.D. de Luxembourg.

TABLEAU 9.1

NOMBRE DE SESSIONS DU CONSEIL DES MINISTRES LORS DES PRESIDENCES LUXEMBOURGEOISES

	1972 (1er sem.)	1976 (1er sem.)	1980 (2ème sem.)
Type de réunion			
Affaires générales	6	7	7
Agriculture	8	7	6
Finances	3	3	4
Budget	-	1	4
Energie	-	1	1
Affaires sociales	1	1	1
Transport	1	-	1
Recherche	-	1	-
Développement et Coopération	-	1	1
Environnement	-	-	1
Education	-	-	1
Fiscalité	-	-	1
Justice	-	-	-
Brevet européen	-	-	-
Divers (Pêche)	2	-	4
TOTAL	21	22	32
Conseils d'Association	5	3	?
Coopération politique	1	4	?
Conseils européens	-	1	1

Sources: Bulletin des Communautés européennes, Rapports du Secrétariat du Conseil, Rapports des gouvernements aux parlements nationaux (tableau repris et complété de Wallace / Edwards 1977).

TABLEAU 9.2

LUXEMBOURG
ORGANIGRAMME DU MINISTERE DES AFFAIRES ETRANGERES

MINISTRE DES AFFAIRES ETRANGERES

Chef de Cabinet
Cabinet du Ministre

Secrétaire d'Etat

Secrétaire général/
Secrétariat général

Direction I:	Direction II:	Direction III:	Services généraux
Affaires politiques et culturelles	Relations économiques internationales et Coopération Office des Licences	Protocole, Administration et Affaires juridiques; Service des passeports, des visas et des légalisations	

Source: Tableau repris et adapté de G. Trausch: The Ministry of Foreign Affairs in the Grand Duchy. The Times survey of Foreign Ministries of the World, Selected and edited by J. Steiner, Times Books, London, 1982.

208

Chapter 10

THE PRESIDENCY OF THE COUNCIL OF MINISTERS OF THE
EUROPEAN COMMUNITIES: THE DUTCH AND THE PRESIDENCY
Mr Max Jansen, Amsterdam (1)

INTRODUCTION

The prevailing view among Dutch civil servants as to what the
Presidency means, what it is, and what it is not, is based on an article of
faith in Dutch politics: the EC was devised as a supranational
organisation and therefore we must support all initiatives to strengthen
its supranational character and resist all attempts to upgrade
intergovernmental aspects. Perceived in this way the European
Commission is and must be the central institution; the Council of
Ministers has its proper role to play, and no more. Consequently the task
of the Presidency is to ensure that the Council can do its work properly
and smoothly; this is no mean task, but it is definitely less than being
charged with running the Communities as a whole.

There is no doubt in the minds of Dutch civil servants that the
Council has not been operating effectively for many years. They agree
that the decision-making is cumbersome and that the failure to make the
necessary decisions makes the Council at least co-responsible for the
virtual stagnation in the integration process. This, they point out, is not
the Commission's fault, nor is it caused by a lack of devotion on the part
of the Council presidents; it is rather the consequence of the Council's
unwillingness to adhere to the provisions of the Rome Treaty. If the
Council would resort to majority voting, the Community would be able to
make real progress. It is clear from this perspective that the Presidency
of the Council is of secondary importance. Any measures to enhance the
position of the President in order to improve the effectiveness of the
Council is, in the Dutch view, definitely the wrong answer to the
problem. As a matter of principle such (indirect) reinforcement of the
Council has to be rejected because it would be detrimental to the
position of the Commission.

This general attitude explains why the Dutch are disinclined to
attach too much importance to the Presidency. The task of acting as
President is an interesting one, but it is not of such overwhelming
importance that many special arrangements have to be made. Existing
permanent arrangements are used in the preparation and discharge of the
Presidency; permanent staff work extra hours, but hardly any additional
manpower is made available. The civil servants involved in Community

affairs do not think that it should be otherwise; they find the way in which the various ministries prepare and coordinate their EC policy quite satisfactory. Moreover they possess the knowledge and information required for dealing with the Presidency; to recruit non-experts from other quarters would only complicate matters.

EC policies are in the hands of a few dozen civil servants, working in five ministries. They have frequent institutionalised and informal contacts, they know each other, and each other's views. It was this relatively small group which handled the Presidency, treating it as normal business with some extra duties. In dealing with the Presidency they were confident that they had the skill and the means to accomplish what could be reasonably expected from them; they relied heavily on information provided by the Secretariat of the Council; they were convinced that the room for initiatives was indeed very limited and that a great deal of improvisation would be required to cope with unexpected developments. Such developments also imply that very detailed planning of a programme for the Presidency is not realistic. Too ambitious a platform is considered counterproductive, as it is bound to disappoint those who take it seriously.

With regard to the Presidency, and in line with Dutch policy, a strict distinction is made between the European Communities and European Political Co-operation (EPC). Since the latter lacks a permanent office, its Presidency involves all the organisational and administrative work that, in the case of the EC, can be left to the European Commission and the Secretariat of the Council. Logically, those in charge of the Presidency of EPC considered it a much heavier burden than that of the EC. The European Council, treated as an extension of the Council of Ministers, is viewed by the people from the Ministry of Foreign Affairs as an important event, from which new impulses for integration may arise; other Ministries are more inclined to see it as little more than an over-exposed meeting of prime ministers who can hardly be expected to solve any problem.

In bureaucratic terms, EC affairs and EPC are strictly separated; only at the very top, i.e. with the minister, do the two meet. EPC is almost exclusively the domain of the Ministry of Foreign Affairs, whereas EC policy is very much an interdepartmental affair. An effective coordination mechanism has been developed to deal with EC matters in which all ministries may participate; the hard core consists of the Ministries of Foreign Affairs, Economic Affairs, Agriculture and Finance. In addition, representatives of the Ministries of Employment and Social Security, and of Transport, as well as a member of the Prime Minister's staff, frequently attend coordination meetings.

In the Netherlands, European integration is not a controversial issue; the European policy of the Dutch is very stable indeed and changes in government have never caused any basic shift in the pro-integration attitude of the country. This continuity provides a clear frame of reference to the civil servants who have to translate policy-principles into policy-decisions. Within this framework, policy-making is largely left to the responsible officials; ministers become involved when interdepartmental controversies cannot be resolved by the civil servants; when officials judge it advisable to involve their minister at an early stage because of the politically sensitive nature of the issue at stake; when the Cabinet has to take a formal decision; and in questions which are so loaded with political implications that the coordinating bodies of civil servants leave the substantial decision-making to the Cabinet.

In preparing this report on the Dutch and the EC Presidency, interviews were held with officials from six ministries, from the Permanent Representation in Brussels, and with members of the government-in-office during the Dutch Presidency in 1981. There appeared to be general agreement on what the Dutch position is **vis-à-vis** the Community and its Presidency. Shades of difference may well be more attributable to temperament rather than to fundamentally different opinions. Consensus could be reached with regard to the following conclusions:

- As a small country, the Netherlands is better served by a strong and independent Commission.
- The Council of Ministers should not be strengthened at the expense of the European Commission.
- The Presidency of the Council should not be upgraded if this would mean a weakening of the position of the Commission.
- Proposals aimed at enhancing the Presidency are not to be supported.
- The Presidency is a burden in terms of more work and extra financial costs, but both are bearable.
- The Presidency requires some sacrifices, as the country in the chair may need to subordinate its national interest in order to solve a problem.
- A successful Presidency yields prestige, but no concrete benefits in specific policy areas.
- The Presidency has no lasting effect on the national administration.

ROLE AND INVOLVEMENT OF GOVERNMENT AND PARLIAMENT IN POLICY-MAKING

The Dutch view on integration can be summarised in a few words: 'European integration is good for the Netherlands and therefore it should be promoted and supported'. This view, based primarily on economic interests (trade), is widely held but a closer look reveals different priorities and approaches. The political integration of Western Europe and the embedding in it of the German Federal Republic have been consistently defended as major aims of Dutch foreign policy. The economic and political view on integration led, in the early stages of the process, to a major controversy on the question of its real scope and meaning. Were we engaged in the development of a new and unique relationship with neighbouring countries? Was it another form of intensifying our economic and trade relations with other countries? Were we dealing with medium-term trade relations or with the long-term political unification of Europe?

The answer to these questions was to have a direct bearing upon ministerial competences and responsibility for integration issues. Who was to be in charge: the Ministry of Foreign Affairs or the Ministry of Economic Affairs? The former claimed prime responsibility for European integration as part of Dutch foreign policy; the latter contested this claim, stressing the economic character of the European Communities. After long discussions Foreign Affairs carried the day as its minister was to be the coordinating member of government. His scope for action was limited, however, by an elaborate system of consultation and coordination which was to be applied to all decision-making regarding EC matters. The result has been a fair balance between two approaches: the Ministry of Foreign Affairs approach, pleading for a long-term policy in which the promotion of economic and political integration prevails over short-term economic interests, and the approach of other departments, where actions can be more easily assessed in terms of economic costs and benefits. It is typical, and not only of Dutch politics, that the reluctance to accept integration grows when the costs involved become more apparent. Parliament is also more likely to question ministers on the concrete consequences of economic integration than on the, as yet unknown if not unpredictable political effects. Consequently the ministers of the 'technical' departments have good reason to be concerned about the short-term effect of their policies.

This tension between politics and economics is still a permanent feature in the interministerial discussions on EC matters; a situation which is likely to last as long as the state of the economy makes it difficult for any government to pay an economic price for long-term political integration.

On the basis of their involvement in EC policies, the ministries could be divided into four categories:

A)   Foreign Affairs, Finance.
B)   Economic Affairs, Agriculture.
C)   Employment and Social Security, Transport.
D)   General Affairs (Prime Minister), Justice, Education, Environment, Development Co-operation, etc.

Category A consists of the two ministries directly and continuously dealing with all EC affairs; the other ministries are only involved in part of the Community affairs. For the ministries of category B this means quite intensive involvement, for category D it is only a marginal task, whereas category C takes an intermediate position. The number of officials more or less engaged full-time in policy-making in relation to the EC is relatively small, with the exception of Agriculture. In the Ministry of Foreign Affairs, the number is approximately 20 out of 300; in Economic Affairs, less than 10 per cent of the officials deal with EC questions, but only a very few of them are full-time. In the Ministry of Finance, it is less than 2 per cent, with only a handful of people more than marginally involved. Understandably the proportion is quite different in Agriculture, where two-thirds of the civil servants have at least something, and often much more to do with Community policies. In the ministries of categories C and D, the number of people dealing with EC questions is very small indeed.

Parliament's role in the making of European policy is modest, to say the least, marginal. Twice a year a general debate is held, in which most of the party-spokesmen repeat what they have been saying for years: they are worried because of a lack of progress in integration, the European Parliament must be granted more powers, the Council should embrace the principle of majority voting, and candidate Member States must be admitted. European integration is hardly a partisan affair and consequently there are no substantial conflicts between the government and the large majority in Parliament as far as the European Communities are concerned. Parliament wants to be informed on how the Dutch government approaches the Community's problems; it does not try to dictate to the government what its policy **vis-à-vis** specific issues is to be. It should be added that only in very exceptional cases the government would accept such binding instructions; in discussions and negotiations in Brussels, the Dutch government acts according to its own view. Only at a later stage will the government defend its attitude before the Dutch Parliament, if summoned to do so.

A regular exchange of views between the Minister of Foreign Affairs and the Commission for Foreign Affairs of the Second Chamber of Parliament guarantees that Parliament stays informed. It takes place before every meeting of the General Council of Ministers of the EC; all major items on the Council's agenda are then discussed, apparently sometimes rather thoroughly.

The influence of interest groups in policy-making in the Netherlands is probably not very different from that in other Member States. The Ministries of Agriculture, Economic Affairs, Employment and Social Security, and to a lesser extent also Finance, all acknowledged regular, necessary and useful contacts with interest groups; the Ministry of Foreign Affairs is hardly ever approached by economic interest groups on Community matters, but occasionally there is an exchange of views with top-level business managers and trade-union leaders.

Regular institutionalised consultations between representatives of interest groups and civil servants from all relevant ministries also take place in the Commission for International Social and Economic Affairs (ISEA) of the Social and Economic Council (SER), the highest advisory council on social and economic policy.

INTERMINISTERIAL COORDINATION

To make sure that the involvement of so many policy-makers does not lead to incoherence and contradictions, coordination is provided for at various levels:

- A weekly meeting to draw up instructions for the Permanent Representative; in this meeting, chaired by an official of the Ministry of Foreign Affairs, representatives of Economic Affairs, Agriculture and Finance participate, as well as other departments if they wish to do so.
- Meetings of the permanent Coordination Commission (CoCo), held almost weekly, in which the ministries of categories A, B and C

participate as well as those of category D which cannot resist the temptation to do so. The chairman is the State Secretary for European Affairs, the vice-chairman is the Minister of Economic Affairs. The Permanent Representative is also present at these meetings.

- Occasional meetings of the Council for European Affairs (REZ), chaired by the Prime Minister. Members are eight ministers, two state secretaries, seven top civil servants and the Permanent Representative.
- Discussions in the Cabinet to decide on which position Dutch ministers are to take in the EC Council of Ministers.

Apart from bilateral consultations, which can take place at all levels and in all stages of the policy-making process, informal discussions are sometimes held between the responsible Directors General of the ministries of categories A and B, to clear the path either for CoCo or for REZ.

The various stages of coordination reflect the stages of decision-making in the Council of the EC, i.e. the working groups, Coreper and the Council itself. In the working groups, the Netherlands is in 80 per cent of the cases represented by a member of the Permanent Representation. The staff members stay in close contact with their own ministry; when they represent the Netherlands in a working group dealing with issues falling within the field of their own ministry, they are used to receiving their instructions directly from their own ministry. These instructions are supposed to take the general Dutch view into account in respect of integration matters. There are no institutionalised interdepartmental consultations at this stage, but in many cases the matter will be discussed with colleagues from other departments before a spokesman in a working group announces the Dutch position. An unwritten rule is that on new topics no Dutch standpoint is expressed in a working group unless it has been the subject of interministerial consultation. In fact, such consultations do take place frequently, and also regularly, with regard to some fields of action, such as development co-operation, environmental issues, harmonisation of company law and others. In many cases the initiative for these consultations is taken by the Directorate-General for European Co-operation (Ministry of Foreign Affairs) or the Directorate General for External Economic Relations (Ministry of Economic Affairs).

When the outcome of the work of the groups comes up for discussion in Coreper, the Permanent Representative receives instructions from The Hague regarding the position he has to take in the discussion. A weekly meeting is held in The Hague for this purpose and instructions are formulated at this meeting for all items on the agenda of Coreper for the coming week. It is a form of obligatory coordination, in which Foreign Affairs, Finance, Economic Affairs and Agriculture participate, as well as any other department involved in specific questions. In these 'instruction-meetings', decisions are made by consensus; if agreement cannot be reached, there are three possible solutions:

1. The instruction is phrased rather vaguely, leaving the matter to the discretion of the Permanent Representative.
2. The question is settled at a higher level (directors general).
3. When fundamental differences are at stake, the matter is referred to CoCo.

The Permanent Representative is not present at these weekly instruction meetings, but through his written reports, which may contain indications for the course to be pursued by the Netherlands, he has indirect influence on the decision-making. It should be stressed that it is possible for this coordination group to come to a decision which deviates from the position up until then defended by the Dutch representative in a working group on instructions from his own department. To avoid embarrassing situations, most officials will first consult their colleagues in other departments in order to ensure that the position they intend to take in the working group will be upheld at a later stage.

When Coreper has completed its work and a topic is ripe for discussion and decision in the Council of Ministers, the Dutch position is discussed in CoCo, mainly consisting of high-ranking officials from all departments concerned. CoCo's task is to advise the Cabinet on all matters to be decided upon in the Council; proposals for the Dutch standpoint in the Council discussion can only be submitted to the Cabinet through CoCo. The aim of the discussions in CoCo is to reach consensus; when this proves impossible, the directors general may again step in and try to solve the problem. They may also find it wiser to involve their ministers in the discussion; for this purpose the REZ has been formed, a noteworthy body including both ministers and civil servants **(2)**.

Its task is to facilitate the decision-making in the Cabinet; it cannot take policy decisions itself, but it is evident that agreement in the REZ means agreement in the Cabinet **(3)**. The final decision on the Dutch attitude in the Council of Ministers is made by the Cabinet; this is the only instance in which voting may take place. For all European affairs, the Minister of Foreign Affairs acts as coordination minister. Formally it is he who decides whether or not a REZ meeting is to be held; in fact, however, much depends upon the availability of the Prime Minister and this availability seems to be directly related to the Prime Minister's interest in European questions. Den Uyl (Prime Minister 1973-1977) took a lively interest in social and economic questions and had the REZ meet, on average, at least once every two weeks. His successor, Van Agt (1978-1982) had so much confidence in his colleagues that he was satisfied with only a few REZ meetings per year. The present Prime Minister Lubbers seems to have settled for one meeting every month. Dates for these meetings are set well in advance, which indicates that REZ is becoming part of the normal decision-making process, its meetings no longer being primarily dependent on whether or not the Prime Minister can arrange to be free at short notice.

In the majority of cases, ministers are only involved in the decision-making process in the Cabinet meetings. This is not to say that they hardly know what they are talking about. A summary of the discussions and conclusions in CoCo, prepared by the Ministry of Foreign Affairs, is sent to all ministries. Each minister receives it together with

Table 10.1: The Interministerial Coordination System

Corresponding EC level	Coordination gremium	Approx. frequency	Participants	Function
Working groups	Interminist- erial contacts	frequently	civil servants	consultation
Coreper	'Instruction meeting'	weekly	chair: official Min. For. Affairs - civil servants	To draw up in- struction for the Permanent Representation
Council	Coordination Commission (CoCo)	almost weekly	chair: State Secr. for Eur. Affairs - senior civil servants - Perm. Representative	To advise Cabinet on items on Council agenda
	Council for European Affairs (REZ)	monthly	chair: Prime Minister - 8 ministers - 2 State Secretaries - 7 top civil servants - Perm. Representative	To pave the way for Cabinet decisions
	Cabinet	almost weekly	chair: Prime Minister - all ministers - State Secretary for European Affairs	Decision on Dutch stance in EC Council

Scheme of interministerial coordination

——— = obligatory   ·············· = non-obligatory

additional comments from his own staff. So he knows what the issues are and what his own staff thinks of them; it goes without saying that in matters for which his own department bears prime responsibility, he has been informed by his staff at a much earlier stage.

In summary, coordination in EC matters takes place almost weekly on all issues on the agenda of Coreper and of the Council; positions to be taken in working groups are quite often the subject of interministerial consultations, but these are not institutionalised. Coordination is the responsibility of the Ministry of Foreign Affairs; the State Secretary for European Affairs is the political coordinator, but political responsibility rests with the Minister of Foreign Affairs.

In relation to the European Council and European Political Co-operation, the need for coordination is less evident. The Dutch position in the European Council is prepared by CoCo, the REZ and the Cabinet, similar to the procedure used for Council of Minister meetings. EPC is the exclusive responsibility of the Ministry of Foreign Affairs; other departments may be consulted on specific issues, just as they may be consulted on any other matter not related to the EPC.

INFLUENCE

As to the role various departments and groups play in the policy-making process, the coordinating role of the Ministry of Foreign Affairs is generally acknowledged. The part it plays in determining the contents of policy decisions is more modest, technical aspects being largely determined by the ministry most directly concerned. Yet, as it is the foreign ministry's task to ensure that a decision is taken, it can be quite active in hammering out compromises when two or more ministries disagree on what the Dutch policy should be in relation to a specific issue. Serious disagreements are always brought up for solution in the Coordination Commission. As the State Secretary for European Affairs chairs these meetings, his ability to a great extent determines the outcome and the foreign ministry's share in it. It has been said, with some exaggeration, that the foreign ministry's influence varies with the caliber of its State Secretary for European Affairs. More generally, civil servants have pointed out that their strength in interministerial discussions is directly dependent on the weight their minister carries among his colleagues. A minister with a forceful personality rather than one who is somewhat irresolute is more likely to have his views accepted by the Cabinet. Civil servants can quite easily predict the outcome of a discussion in the Cabinet and when they anticipate the vindication of their own minister, they are rather reluctant to give in to representatives of a minister who will lose in the end anyway. The personality of politicians is, indeed, considered a factor of some importance.

Generally speaking, the ministries are not inclined to encroach upon each other's territory; as a result the obligatory consultations are not experienced as a threat. There is no fear of being overruled by others who do not bear prime responsibility for the policy area concerned. If no agreement can be reached, the issue is ultimately decided in the Cabinet, the only institution where voting takes place. Therefore, no one ministry, nor minister holds a dominant position. Yet the prevailing equality is that of 'Animal Farm', the Ministry of Finance being a little more equal than the others. Nowhere has it been said that Finance could actually block a decision regarding the Dutch policy **vis-à-vis** the Communities, but neither has anyone denied that this ministry's influence in the decision-making process is very real. Officials of the ministry acknowledge that Finance actively participates in discussions on all levels and that it is 'satisfied' with the way in which other ministries take Finance's views into account. At the Ministry of Foreign Affairs it was argued that the influence of Finance has grown with the deteriorating state of the Dutch economy; in fundamental matters, such as 'the one per cent question', the Ministry of Finance comes very close to having veto-power, according to a Foreign Affairs official.

A special role, but certainly not a dominant one, is played by the Permanent Representative. In policy-making he acts as an advisor, counselling the administration on the Brussels scene on what may be considered reasonable propositions, and on how others are likely to react. His influence in policy-making is judged to be considerable, probably greater than that of any other single official; his weekly meetings with the State Secretary for European Affairs, his frequent contacts with the ministers involved in Community matters and his geographic proximity make him an integral part of the Dutch policy-making machinery.

The general opinion among civil servants and politicians is that the coordination system works well. It requires a certain amount of flexibility in the discussions; this flexibility is possible because the participants represent small groups and sectors in their respective departments, rather than large and more bureaucratic bodies. Together they form a small circle, knowing each other quite well as they meet regularly and frequently. Their co-operation is facilitated by a basic agreement on the need for more integration and the Dutch interest in it; this, in turn, induces them to leave those with prime responsibility for specific questions ample room to do their job.

PREPARATION FOR THE PRESIDENCY

A. Structures and Programme
Satisfaction with existing structures and procedures makes it understandable that no special measures were considered when the Dutch had to prepare themselves for the Presidency. The general approach was that of EC business as usual, albeit more and more intensive. There was no reason to fear that what was normally quite adequate would fail when problems of the EC Presidency were to be coped with.

It seems that if the Dutch ministries had to restrict their preparations for the Presidency to contacts with only one institution, they would all opt for the Secretariat of the Council. Invariably the Council Secretariat was mentioned as the chief source of information for the presidents-to-be. For the work in the working groups, preparatory talks with the Commission were considered useful and necessary. Since members of the staff of the Permanent Representation were to preside over most of the working groups, the Permanent Representation seemed more inclined to seek the advice of the Commission rather than the ministries in The Hague. Of the latter, only the Ministry of Economic Affairs mentioned direct preparatory contacts with Commission officials.

In The Hague, the Ministry of Foreign Affairs is the coordinating and stimulating body. It invites other departments to submit plans and proposals for the Dutch Presidency and it drafts a general outline of a programme. Once this programme has been discussed in the Coordination Commission and adopted by the Cabinet, it is sent to the Dutch Parliament; a debate is held some months before the Netherlands assumes the Presidency, giving Parliament ample opportunity to let the government know what it should really try to accomplish during the six months in the chair.

On contacts with the President-in-Office, opinions varied somewhat without anybody being strongly in favour of the idea. One line of reasoning stipulated that the Netherlands assist the Luxembourg Presidency in a number of sectors, so that direct contacts already exist. Others argued that the Council Secretariat is much better equipped to provide all necessary information and that talks with Luxembourg would not add much to their insight. Other sceptics pointed out that Member States know quite well what they want to do and neither need nor want the advice of the outgoing President.

A somewhat deviating view was expressed in the Ministry of Finance. There it was argued that, in most cases, six months is too short a period to have new ideas and proposals accepted. Therefore it is necessary to start working on them already well before one takes over the Presidency. For this purpose it could be useful to entertain close contacts with the President-in-Office, soliciting his co-operation in preparing the ground for effective action. Actually, this is what the British did during the Dutch Presidency. Apparently the Dutch found it a useful initiative, since it gave them an opportunity to plead with their successors for the continuation of certain issues the Dutch had been dealing with. However this is more a matter of after-care than of preparation.

Organisational preparations for the EC Presidency start approximately 12 months in advance with the fixing of dates for the Council meetings. The time schedule for the Presidency is the prime responsibility of the Permanent Representative, who co-operates closely with the Commission in this matter. The Permanent Representative also plays a prominent role in the discussion on who is to chair which group - a question that has to be solved not later than six months before the beginning of the presidential period. Around this time, the various Ministries begin to prepare their programme.

There is widespread agreement that programmatic planning is needed. It is not enough to let others or circumstances decide which activities will be developed during the upcoming Presidency. The Presidency gives a Member State the chance to make an extra effort to solve certain problems in the interest of the Community or the Member State itself. Yet a great deal of scepticism exists among Dutch officials about what a country can really do.

The Presidency of the EC: The Dutch Presidency

A President is dependent on:

- the Commission's proposals;
- the Member States' willingness to co-operate;
- deadlines set in the treaty or by previous decisions.

In the Dutch case, the steel crisis was not a Dutch hobby-horse; it had to be given priority irrespective of Dutch interests. A favoured topic of the Dutch, the entry negotiations with Spain and Portugal, could hardly be worked on due to the French presidential election. Moreover, the question of EC civil servants' salaries and the strike which accompanied this conflict - not wanted nor foreseen by the Dutch Presidency - forced it to spend considerable time on its solution.

Ambitious planning, the Dutch believe, is bound to lead to disillusion and an impression of failure, since only under extraordinarily favourable circumstances can such a programme be carried out to any extent. Modest programming, on the other hand, brings reproach about being too timid to risk anything and of not being ready to accept the challenge of the Presidency. In other words, the need to plan one's Presidency with regard to content inevitably leads to a denunciation, either at the beginning or at the end. It is therefore not surprising that in the preparation for the Presidency the Dutch tend to put more time into organisation than into breathtaking policy-initiatives. In the Dutch view, taking over the Presidency is like taking over a running train; its direction cannot be changed at will; if it is running behind schedule, the engine driver may try to make up for lost time, but there are no short cuts to the final destination.

What has been said in this paragraph refers to the Presidency of the Council of Ministers and its sub-organs. In comparison, the preparation for the European Council is a relatively simple affair. The President does not have to be recruited; the agenda is more a matter of prevailing circumstances rather than the preferences and priorities of the Netherlands. Only the logistics side made the European Council meeting into a major problem for quite a few people. The decision on the location was taken by the Prime Minister and was certainly not the outcome of interdepartmental consultations. A task group was formed of some officials from the Prime Minister's Cabinet and the Ministry of Foreign Affairs. The organisational work started more than one year before the meeting actually took place. Special problems arose from the task of accommodating the hundreds of media people and the security of the participants. This made the European Council the most expensive activity during the Dutch Presidency; the costs could however have been kept considerably lower if the meeting had been held in The Hague instead of Maastricht.

During the preparations for the discussions in the European Council, all bodies and institutions involved in policy-making at national and European level were consulted.: in The Hague, the Coordination Commission, the Council for European Affairs and the Cabinet; in Brussels, the European Commission, the Secretariat of the Council and Coreper, and for the EPC, the Political Committee.

B. Personnel

Preparing for the Presidency means, first and foremost, putting the right people in the right spot. Both in the ministries and in the Permanent Representation the selection of chairmen for the numerous groups was singled out as of vital importance for the success of the Presidency. Chairmen must have personality, be familiar with Brussels and have a good knowledge of languages; in addition, they must be capable of summarising the essence of debates and good at detecting chances for compromise. They must be technically-able chairmen, but not necessarily experts in the problems discussed. The debates are seen, at all levels, as negotiations between representatives of states; political compromises are the outcome.

The great importance attached to the quality of the chairmen would make one expect that the search for qualified people had been a laborious process. In practice this was not so. Most groups were chaired by members of the Permanent Representation, who by their very function were considered to be qualified for the job. This arrangement made it certainly easier for the Permanent Representative to coordinate the work of the numerous groups in Brussels. In a number of cases, some twenty out of a total of over one hundred, The Hague preferred a chairman from one of the ministries. This often proved to be a difficult decision, although in the majority of cases, the person selected was the official responsible for the subject matter in his ministry.

THE ROLE OF THE PERMANENT REPRESENTATION

In the making and implementation of Dutch policies related to the EC, the Permanent Representation plays a key role. Consequently the Permanent Representation is mentioned frequently throughout this chapter. In this paragraph it may suffice to briefly mention its main features.

Apart from the Ambassador and his Deputy, the staff of the Permanent Representation consists of nine officials from the Ministry of Foreign Affairs, four from Finance, three from Economic Affairs, two from Transport and one from Employment and Social Security. The great majority of them stay for two to four years; consequently only few staff members experience more than one Dutch Presidency.

As far as representing the Dutch Government in Coreper I and Coreper II is concerned, no distinction is made between the Permanent Representative and his Deputy. The latter participates in coordination meetings and acts as President of Coreper I, as if he were the Permanent Representative. Thus, whenever 'the Permanent Representative' is mentioned here, it should be understood as 'the Permanent Representative or the Deputy Permanent Representative'. The Permanent Representation is the eyes, the ears and in many cases also the voice of the Netherlands in Community affairs. More than the Dutch ministries (notable exception: Agriculture), the Permanent Representation entertains close and frequent contacts with the European Commission (members and staff). This is a logical consequence of the Permanent Representation representing the Dutch government in most of the working groups. As for contacts between the Dutch ministries and the Commission, the Permanent Representation wants to act as intermediary. In general, it insists that contacts between The Hague and the Council Secretariat, the Commission and the other Community institutions run through the Permanent Representation. Formal contacts are indeed dealt with in this way, but informal contacts (phone calls, 'dropping in just to say hello') are beyond the reach of the Permanent Representation. To remain fully aware of what is going on, the Permanent Representation insists on being informed about any substantial contacts between Dutch officials and Commission or Council staff.

Governments of Member States are in most cases approached through the Permanent Representation; relatively little use is made of the embassies in the various capitals.

As has been described in the paragraph on 'Interministerial Coordination', the Permanent Representative plays an important role in the shaping of Dutch standpoints in all EC matters. The weekly instructions that he receives through the Ministry of Foreign Affairs are largely based on his own suggestions for standpoints to be adopted by the Netherlands in upcoming Coreper or working group meetings.

When the Netherlands holds the EC Presidency, the Permanent Representation is the centre of activities. Many officials in the various Dutch ministries experience the additional pressure of work that comes with the Presidency; quite often they are able to cope with this extra workload by delegating some of their other work to assistants or by postponing less pressing matters to a later stage. Neither solution is available to the Permanent Representation, where the work has to be finished according to schedule. The organisational line ends here; whatever has to be done, must be done here. Or, as a sign on President Truman's desk put it: 'The buck stops here'.

THE PRESIDENCY OF EUROPEAN POLITICAL CO-OPERATION

According to some officials close to the EPC circuit, the Presidency of the European Communities would be a rather easy task, except for the EPC. Economic Community matters are largely taken care of by the Council Secretariat, whereas the European Council is an over-publicised event and should be treated as such. Being in charge of the EPC, on the other hand, means that one has to perform all the tasks ranging from organising lunches to representing the Ten in distant countries. All the functions which the Council Secretariat performs for the Council of Ministers and which makes it absolutely indispensable for any President of the Council, have in the case of EPC to be carried out by the President's staff. All meetings have to be organised by the President-in-Office in his own capital and this requires careful planning.

Work started 18 months before the Presidency was taken over from Luxembourg. A major problem turned out to be a lack of suitable conference locations in The Hague and housing for the delegations from the Member States. A working group would meet every week; the Ministers of Foreign Affairs were to have one meeting in The Hague and one more of the Gymnich-type, to be held in Venlo. The latter turned out to be a costly affair because of the required security measures. Finally, the EPC component of the European Council had to be prepared.

In the Ministry of Foreign Affairs, the permanent staff dealing with EPC is very small indeed. Basically it is the concern of two officials only: the Director General Political Affairs, who represents the Netherlands in the Political Committee, and the Correspondent, the only official who is more or less engaged full-time in EPC affairs. The Correspondent was the central figure in the organisational preparations for the EPC Presidency. One extra man was added for communications, whereas an additional staff member spent most of his time dealing with questions from the European Parliament. The chairmen of the working groups, of course, had to carry their share of the extra work. They were selected with great care; in some cases the head of the department dealing with the subject matter was designated; for other groups, 'outsiders' from inside the ministry were recruited. Whereas, for the Council, it was judged undesirable that a chairman should also act as spokesman for the Netherlands, such a combination of functions was deemed acceptable within the EPC framework.

Although international developments would determine **ad hoc** actions of the Ten, the Dutch wanted to present a programme of activities related to the issues with a quasi-permanent character. To prepare for it, the ambassadors of the other Member States were invited to discuss various proposals with the Minister of Foreign Affairs some six months in advance of the Dutch Presidency. Elaboration of these ideas was the task of the departments in the foreign ministry. For this purpose and because of the need to provide a chairman for the related EPC working group, these departments were temporarily reinforced with one official, often recruited from the Foreign Service. Since, as a rule, diplomatic personnel when stationed in the ministry stay there for a least two years, the necessary transfer of people was consequently for a longer period than that of the Presidency.

In the preparatory stage there were hardly any contacts with the Luxembourg Presidency; in principle, however, the Dutch favour co-operation between successive Presidents to facilitate a smooth transfer and continuity. The British were invited to The Hague one month before they were to take over the Presidency.

In a way it could be said that EPC is a framework for co-operation between Ministries of Foreign Affairs, rather than between states or governments. The COREU network links the ministries and their various departments in a more direct way than secretariats of international organisations used to do. In this respect the lack of a permanent secretariat could be considered an asset to EPC. The directness of the interministerial connections enabled the Dutch Presidency to contact the governments of the other Member States without involving the Dutch embassies; in third countries Dutch embassies were, of course, used to transmitting messages on behalf of the Ten.

The President can have considerable influence on the work of EPC, by deciding the order of the agenda, by ruling a matter not ripe for decision and by referring an issue to a subordinate body. His powers are limited however by three factors beyond his control: he is dependent on the co-operation of the other Member States, he may have to wait for reports from working groups and international political events may force him to deviate from his course. Only seldom do entirely new problems present themselves for solution or action in EPC; in most cases it is a matter of pushing the discussion on a long-standing problem, or of postponing such discussion until better times.

In the case of the Dutch Presidency, apparently no topics were put on the agenda simply because they were attractive to the Netherlands. According to one source, the Dutch used all their skill to prevent a meeting of the Euro-Arab Dialogue under a Dutch Presidency, since such a happening would be difficult to sell in the Netherlands, where the traditional pro-Israel mentality had lost some of its vigour, but was not yet to be ignored. Others deny any particular Dutch effort in this respect; no European state wanted a meeting at a time when the Arabs were rather divided amongst themselves. At the same time it is worth noting that the Dutch Minister of Foreign Affairs spent a great deal of his time, as EPC President, on a mission to the Middle East; he testified himself that this was a most positive aspect of his Presidency, because next to presenting the European position, it had provided him with the opportunity to demonstrate to the Arabs the even-handedness of the Dutch Middle East policy.

Those people involved in the Dutch EPC Presidency showed themselves reasonably satisfied with the quality of their work. Their workload was very considerable, lasting a full two years, as preparations were started early. The hard core consisted of a very small number of people, but for the working groups they could count on the active co-operation of many departments inside the ministry. The quality of their accomplishment was the result of careful and timely planning, hard work and the ambition to do a good job.

THE PRESIDENCY: DUTCH ATTITUDES AND OBJECTIVES

In November 1980, the Dutch government sent a note to Parliament informing it of the government's views on and plans for the EC Presidency during the first half of 1981. In the note, four tasks for the Presidency were distinguished:

-   The first, and perhaps most important, task of the Presidency is of an organisational nature. It is the President's responsibility to make the complicated and troublesome decision-making structure of the Community function as efficiently as possible.
-   The second task is that of mediation in the solution of conflicts and controversies. This task is one of a more improvising character, as it is difficult to predict in advance which differences of opinion will become so acute that the President can successfully suggest a compromise solution.
-   A third task of the Presidency includes taking or promoting certain initiatives, of course with due regard to the European Commission's right of initiative. Compared with the two foregoing functions, this one is more an exception than the rule. Except for very specific

cases, it is hardly possible for individual Member States to launch their own initiative; in such cases the Presidency is a handicap rather than an advantage.

- Finally, there is the aspect of promoting the national interests of the presiding state itself. In this respect the opportunities provided by the Presidency should not be overestimated, as its influence on the course of events remains rather limited.

These four tasks may be summarised as taking care of the decision-making machinery and of mediating in the decision-making process. What was to be discussed depended primarily on the European Commission. The Netherlands have not tried to keep any topic off the agenda; they only insisted on having a Jumbo Council, although there was considerable doubt among other Member States whether this would be a useful experiment **(4)**.

In general, the agenda of the Council of Ministers was drawn up in close consultation with the Council Secretariat and the European Commission; specific Dutch interests played no role whatsoever.

Of course the bulk of the work was not done by the Council but in the numerous working groups. Their chairmen were left free to organise their own work, the only limitation being the time reserved for meetings of their group. The time-table of the Dutch Presidency was firmly in the hands of the Permanent Representative, who, by granting extra time to a group, could try to speed up its work. In running the shop this was an important element, as it linked the activities of the groups, Coreper and the Council. The coordination of group meetings was certainly facilitated by the principle that working groups are presided over by staff of the Permanent Representation.

Independence of the chairmen was enhanced by the appointment of a second delegate, usually from one of the ministries, as spokesman for the Netherlands. He was to represent Dutch interests and for that purpose received instructions from The Hague; the chairmen of the groups did not receive instructions from anyone. Indeed the proper situation, in the Dutch view, on the relationship between the chairman and the national delegate, is that of the Dutch helping the President, rather than the President helping the Dutch.

These principles are also applied to Coreper and the Council. The President does not speak for his own country; this is done either by the State Secretary or the Permanent Representative. Since in the Dutch context the presiding minister is the superior of the spokesman for the Netherlands, one may rightfully doubt whether the spokesman is really in a position to resist the President's pleas to accept the compromise solution he proposes. As one of the participants observed: 'We went to Brussels as two Presidents, rather than as two Dutchmen.' This indeed was one of the cost-aspects of the Presidency.

Few people would deny that the Presidency carries an additional workload for all involved. For ministers, it means that they have to travel more, and that they have to spend more time studying the files under discussion in the Council. Preparatory consultations with the Council Secretariat and the Commission also take time. Explicitly mentioned as time-consuming were the relations with the European

225

Parliament. In line with the Dutch view that the position of the EP should be strengthened, the Dutch Presidency decided that ministers should attend important debates in the EP. In addition, more elaborate reports were to be made to the Parliament on Council meetings, whereas parliamentary questions should be dealt with seriously. The preparation of ministers for question hour in the EP proved to be no sinecure. Their performance in Parliament was sometimes rather frustrating because of poor attendance on the part of the Members of Parliament, the non-committal answers the minister had to give on behalf of the Council, and the preference of Parliament to discuss political issues rather than EC business.

Ministers can cope with the extra work, making time for it by delegating some of their routine activities to their staff. This staff in most cases did not experience the additional work as an unbearable load, as it could be spread amongst a number of people well-acquainted with the subject matter. One of their main concerns was the preparation of their minister for Council meetings; they had to inform him thoroughly on the position taken by other Member States, as well as on the specific Dutch interests involved. The information on other Member States was provided by the Council Secretariat, whereas the Permanent Representative advised the minister on the opportunities for compromise. The Dutch dimension was added to indicate to the minister how far he could go in sacrificing Dutch interests for the sake of reaching agreement in the Council.

Those civil servants who were to chair a working group had to prepare themselves for the task, assisted again by the Council Secretariat. A third category experiencing the blessings of the Presidency consisted of the Dutch embassies in the EC Member States. They were occasionally used to inform the governments of Dutch initiatives, either when time was too short to do so through the Permanent Representations in Brussels, or when a direct approach by the ambassadors was believed to have a greater impact.

The Permanent Representation was the only centre where the increase in work was very considerable indeed, and where the only way of dealing with it was to work harder and longer. The extra work consisted of: maintaining close contacts with the other Permanent Representations, with the Commission, and with the Council Secretariat; coordinating the meetings of the working groups; chairing the larger part of the group meetings; reporting on group meetings; presiding over all Coreper activities; and informing third countries. It was believed that these tasks could only be promptly and effectively carried out by staff members thoroughly acquainted with the issues at stake. A temporary expansion of the staff was therefore considered of little help; consequently the extra work had to be done by the permanent staff.

In conclusion it can be said that the burden of the Presidency, in terms of an additional workload, is real but not excessive for the ministers and the civil servants working in the ministries concerned. With regard to the Permanent Representation, however, one is left with the impression that it is charged with so much extra work, that only a highly qualified staff is capable of performing its tasks efficiently and for a limited period of time only. It is therefore not surprising that at the Permanent Representation the suggestion of extending the Presidency from six months to one year, was rejected as 'physically unacceptable'.

In discussing the EC Presidency, a number of people expressed the opinion that the future of the Communities does not depend on the management of the Presidency. The key problem in the EC is the rule of unanimity in the decision-making of the Council. As long as this remains unchanged, the Communities will be in trouble, no matter how skilfully the Presidency is handled. This does not mean that the Presidency is not important; on the contrary, most people think that its role has grown, but they do not find this grounds for satisfaction. To some it is a necessary evil, to others it means the wrong choice of two evils.

What is the task of the Presidency? Ideally, the President should see it as his duty to support the European Commission and to promote agreement between the Commission and critical Member States. In more realistic terms, the President must act as a mediator between the Commission and the Member States, in working groups, Coreper and the Council. All illusions aside, the President must try to bring the files closer to a decision by seeking compromises between the Member States.

The latter formulation reflects the Dutch view on the reasons for the strengthening of the Presidency: the European Commission is not performing its duties properly anymore; it is not the institution which pushes the Member States further towards integration, it fails to submit compromise proposals to the Council. This deplorable development created a vacuum in the EC framework, which was to be filled by the Council Presidency. It means that the President now has to play an active role in suggesting compromise solutions, but as one person commented, it also means that a further strengthening of the Presidency implies a further weakening of the Commission, and hence a further erosion of the Community elements in the EC.

Others argued that, in this reasoning, cause and effect have been shifted. The supranational character is not undermined as a result of the strengthening of the Presidency, but the position of the Presidency had to be reinforced because of the gradual disappearance of the supranational elements in the Community. In their economic relations, the Member States have increasingly stressed the overriding importance of their national economic interests. Their discussions and negotiations have become more and more geared to this one aim: the promotion and protection of national interests. European integration was left for what it was: an ideal for better times.

In such a political and economic climate, the European Commission could not hope to be successful as promoter of further integration, nor can the Commission be expected to play such a role effectively for quite some time to come. In the prevailing context of intergovernmental negotiations, the Presidency must try to act as an honest broker. This function has become more difficult to perform successfully as well as more essential in the decision-making process of the EC, as a result of the deteriorating economic condition of the Member States and as a by-product of the increase in the number of participating countries. The economic plight of the Member States makes them very reluctant to accept solutions which have a negative impact on their national economy. To work out compromises acceptable to all Member States is, indeed, a balancing act demanding considerable qualities from the performing artist. An increase in the number of Member States makes compromises even more difficult to attain and consequently an effective performance from the President-in-Office even more essential. The entry of Spain and Portugal must necessarily, in this perspective, lead to a strengthening of the Presidency.

Not all Dutch officials questioned on this aspect agreed with this analysis. A dissenting opinion held was that a decrease in the influence of the Presidency is rather to be expected. In a purely intergovernmental decision-making structure, it is the powers of the participating States that determine the outcome of discussions and negotiations, rather than the good offices of a President pro tem.

Some comments pointed out that a distinction must be made between the Presidency of the Council and its EPC counterpart. The EPC structure puts the responsibility for managing the arrangement exclusively in the hands of the President. An enhanced status for EPC and an increase in its activities do affect the position of the Presidency. Such an increase in influence is deemed acceptable even by Dutch officials, as it does not cause a loss of supranationality. One commentator, however, believed that the strengthening of the EPC Presidency automatically leads to an enhanced position for the Council Presidency. The publicity surrounding the EPC President also makes him a more central figure in EC matters; after all, it is the same person in a dual capacity.

It has already been mentioned that, in the Dutch view, the President's scope for action is limited. He cannot accomplish much unless the Commission submits proposals to the Council and the Member States are willing to co-operate positively in the decision-making. It is not surprising that, when asked for criteria to assess the performance or the success of a Presidency, Dutch officials tend to concentrate on organisational features rather than on substantive accomplishments. A good Presidency:

- maintains smooth co-operation with the Council Secretariat and the Commission;
- is 'technically' well organised;
- is impartial in its organisation;
- provides well-prepared reports;
- maintains a balanced time-schedule;
- coordinates the activities of groups, Coreper, and the various Councils;
- stimulates discussions and decision-making;
- watches over good working relations between the institutions and the national delegations;
- supports the European Commission;
- takes initiatives in the Council if the Commission fails to do so, and in EPC whenever the occasion presents itself.

If these conditions are met, the people involved can be satisfied with their Presidency. They may claim to have been successful according to Dutch standards if their efforts have resulted in:

- bringing various issues nearer to a solution;
- more unified action of the Ten;
- majority decisions in the Council.

Apart from the latter, these targets can hardly be called over-ambitious. But even modest aims, the Dutch argue, can only be attained in the Council with great difficulty. Therefore, the people who have to discharge the tasks of the Presidency, should be selected carefully. The quality of the chairmen is the key to a successful Presidency. The ideal chairman must be good in establishing personal contacts with colleagues, with officials of the Commission and with staff members of the Council Secretariat. He must have a good command of more than one Community language. He must be objective in his conclusions and have the skill to summarise discussions in such a way that conclusions can be drawn and agreements formulated. He must take sufficient time to prepare himself for the meetings he is to chair. He must have experience in international fora and he must know how to handle international discussions. He must be strong enough to dissociate himself from the interests of his own country. Finally, and perhaps most important of all, he must have the ability to sense which compromises might be feasible, and how reluctant delegates may be lured into an agreement.

Although this ideal type was not always available in sufficient numbers, the Dutch certainly tried hard to recruit the best qualified people in the various ministries. Only those who had to preside over the Council meetings could not be selected on the basis of the criteria mentioned; indeed, a weak spot in the organisation!

When asked whether the Presidency is an advantage or a disadvantage for a country in charge of it, most people answer in terms of a plus here and a minus there, with a slight tendency to stress the negative side of the balance sheet. On the positive side, reference is made to the agenda as an instrument in the hands of the President through which he can influence debates and procedures. He can decide how much time is to be spent on which issues, he can avoid clashes and bring discussions to an end. If he does this in an impartial way, if he demonstrates understanding for different opinions, and if he untiringly tries to bring the parties in conflict together, he will gain the respect of his colleagues. The goodwill thus accumulated may at a later date turn out to be a rather useful effect of the Presidency. In EPC, the preparation of discussion papers provides the Presidency with an opportunity to put in some of his country's ideas, a chance he may not have when amending reports drafted by others.

The negative side of the Presidency does not primarily consist of the extra work-load, nor of the direct costs involved in the Presidency, which apparently are not excessively high, although no one seems able to give precise figures! What really mattered was that, in order to make a success of the Presidency, the Netherlands must enable the President to reach agreements. This can be done by being very co-operative, by above-average willingness to compromise and to make sacrifices in order to solve a problem. This cost aspect seems to be considered less important to the Ministry of Foreign Affairs than to other ministries. For representatives of the latter it is apparently sometimes difficult to give up positions that have been successfully defended in the course of negotiations, only in order to enable the chairman to achieve success. The Ministry of Foreign Affairs does not believe that concessions are ever made just to please the chairman. If a serious conflict arose between the Dutch delegate and the chairman, the outcome would more likely be a postponement of the decision rather than any substantial concession on the part of the Dutch.

Despite these costs, few people would want to miss the opportunity of being in charge of the Presidency from time to time. It is considered useful because it involves the country, as a whole, more directly in EC and EPC questions. Those engaged in running the Community become once again aware of the relative weight of national interests. At the same time they may, through their own efforts, make a contribution to the solution of Community problems, thus promoting in very general terms Dutch interests. Yet in the technical ministries, the Presidency is seen mainly as a burden, a task determined so much by circumstances, rules and regulations, that hardly any initiative is required or needed. The Ministry of Foreign Affairs is more optimistic about what it can do: the very task of the Presidency is to take initiatives and not to wait for the inevitable. It is pointed out that many problems shared by the EC Member States are not dealt with in the treaties of Paris and Rome; for the solution of these problems initiatives have to be taken by the Member States and the Presidency provides a natural opportunity for any Member State to develop such new activities. It should however be added that this view is held more firmly at the top rather than by the rank and file of the ministry. Obviously, those in a position to initiate are more inclined to see the Presidency in this light rather than those whose work is largely restricted to less prestigious day-to-day affairs. In fact, it is only among the top officials that we have found people who are really looking forward to the next Presidency, because it would give them another opportunity to be in the centre, to be in touch with all those who are politically important in the Communities, to receive information from all quarters, and to try and effectively use this information in efforts to improve the chances of progress in the EC.

Finally, differences in the assessment of the various activities inside the Ministry of Foreign Affairs should be mentioned. Reference has already been made to the opinion that EPC constitutes by far the largest part of the presidential duties; EC questions being dealt with by the Brussels institutions. Those people in the ministry charged with EC affairs strongly disagreed, pointing out that one or two meetings of the Ministers of Foreign Affairs and a handful of working groups could hardly be compared with the countless meetings and activities the EC Presidency has to take care of. These differences in view seem to be a clear indication that the separation of Community and EPC matters is very effective indeed.

What difference does it make as to whether a presiding country is a major or a minor Member State? Quite a lot, according to some people; not very much, according to others. Obviously, the more powerful states have a greater impact on what is happening in the Communities. They have more men and means at their disposal and are, therefore, in a better position to exert pressure also, or primarily, to promote their own national interests. Although, beyond that, they are faced with the same 'handicaps' as small states: the Commission, other Member States and international circumstances.

The thesis that major Member States prefer to reserve successes to themselves, implying that major decisions can only be taken when one of the major states holds the Presidency, was considered very close to the truth by only a few officials. The majority of those people interviewed disagreed, pointing out that no Member State could obstruct decisions for which deadlines have been set. Moreover, it was argued, there are plenty of 'hot' issues which the major states leave with pleasure to the smaller members. In other words, being small is no excuse for being ineffective.

The Dutch do not think that any of the proposals for change in the Presidency should be implemented. An extension of the Presidency from six months to one year may have the advantage that the prospect of holding the Presidency for a full year induces the Member States to be more audacious in its planning; a six-month period might be considered too short to accomplish anything, which may lead to inactivity with regard to a number of issues. This possibly positive effect of an extension is more than offset by the disadvantage attached to it: the physical burden would be too great; the Member State holding the Presidency would acquire too much influence; a weak Presidency would have serious consequences for the Community; a Member State would only be in charge once every 10 or 12 years. In more plain terms, it was said that the Member States do not trust each other enough to allow one of them to lead the Community for a period of more than six months, a span of time in which too much harm cannot be done.

The idea of a troika, in which the past, present, and future presidents co-operate, was rejected as unnecessary. Its main function would be to guarantee continuity, but this is already provided for by the Council Secretariat. In EPC, no permanent Secretariat exists, but practical problems rule out a troika. A language problem exists, as the ministry charged with the Presidency normally conducts its business in its own language, with which the other troika members may not be familiar. Moreover, their hosts would not want them to interfere in anything but EPC matters. A certain degree of isolation would be required and definitely would not provide a good working climate for EPC.

Apart from these objections, one overriding argument exists against any proposal for changes aimed at strengthening the Presidency: more influence for the President implies a weakening of the position of the Commission and most Dutch officials and politicians equate this with abandoning all hope for a supranational Europe. This, to paraphrase De Gaulle, was not what we had in mind when we established the EEC.

In addition to this argument, the Dutch point out that the problems of the Community are not caused by any deficiencies in the Presidency, but by the failure of the Council to apply the decision-making rules as laid down in the Treaty of Rome. This is where a change is needed!

All this refers to the European Communities. The case is different for EPC, where no supranational Commission is involved, and where the problem of the Presidency consists primarily of the excessive workload. The solution for this problem, a Dutch diplomat suggested, could be found in establishing an administrative secretariat as an instrument at the disposal of the Presidency. Its staff could be recruited from the Permanent Delegations in Brussels, thus guaranteeing the intergovernmental character of the institution. It would have its office in Brussels where, as a rule, all EPC meetings could be held. The establishment of such an administrative centre would alleviate the burden of the Presidency, while preserving the purely intergovernmental character of EPC.

Dutch objections against this proposal once more illuminate the key problem for the Netherlands. A secretariat, it is argued, no matter how much its administrative task is stressed, will be used to prepare reports and other papers of political content. This means that the major states will make sure that they control the key functions; in a short time the secretariat would become a tool for the major Member States, rather than a neutral instrument for the Presidency. The Netherlands' contribution would definitely be smaller than the present system allows and therefore such a secretariat would not be in the Dutch interest.

In this argument we have found the common basis for Dutch attitutes **vis-à-vis** the Presidency of both EC and EPC; it is the concern for being dominated by the large Member States, and fear that Dutch interests will be subordinated to German, French and British interests. In order to protect themselves against these threats, the Dutch want an independent Commission as their ally, a Commission that would not make proposals without taking Dutch interests into account. This ally must be as strong as possible, it must be strengthened at the expense of the Council of Ministers, i.e. of the Member States, or more precisely, of the major Member States. For the same reason, the Dutch do not want an EPC secretariat that might enhance the influence of the major Western European powers.

SUMMARY AND CONCLUSION

It is not difficult to summarise the Dutch position **vis-à-vis** the Presidency, as a large measure of agreement exists on this issue among civil servants and politicians. Facts and opinions may be summed up as follows:

Facts
1. Virtually no extra manpower was employed to carry out the additional work caused by the Presidency.
2. In the Netherlands, existing structures were used to prepare the Presidency; the key to the smooth operation was the interministerial Coordination Commission and the Council for European Affairs.
3. The Permanent Representation played an essential part in the planning and coordination of activities in Brussels; the assistance of the Council Secretariat was considered excellent and

indispensable.
4. In organisational terms, EPC and the European Council were a much heavier task than the EC Presidency.
5. The financial costs attached to the Presidency were not excessively high.
6. The Presidency has had no lasting effect on the Dutch administration.

Opinions
7. The President's task is to stimulate progress in the decision-making process and to search for compromises; to take initiatives is not his prime responsibility.
8. A strong Presidency may be needed when the European Commission is weak, but the remedy for a weak Commission is not a strong Presidency but a better Commission.
9. The effectiveness of the Presidency depends on the quality of the people chairing the meetings. The effectiveness is not to be enhanced by new institutional arrangements, but by a better selection of chairmen by the Member States.
10. Special training for chairmen is not considered useful; people selected for a chairmanship should either know how to deal with it, or not be selected.
11. The effectiveness of a Presidency is enhanced by:
    -   a strong Commission;
    -   close co-operation with the Council Secretariat;
    -   majority voting in the Council;
    -   critical selection of chairmen for groups and other bodies.
12. Freedom of action for those charged with organising and presiding over meetings at all levels is also essential for an effective Presidency; Presidents under strict national control are likely to be ineffective and unsuccessful. This condition for a successful Presidency is more often met by the smaller Member States.
13. An institutionalised reinforcement of the Presidency would be an obstacle to an eventual and necessary strengthening of the European Commission; for this reason it is to be opposed. All proposals aiming at such reinforcement are therefore rejected.
14. The importance of the Presidency should not be overestimated; the margins for new initiatives and action are very narrow, as EC questions are mainly dealt with in Brussels and EPC activities are largely determined by external developments.
15. The Presidency is a liability insofar as the presiding state has to make more concessions to facilitate agreement; in EPC it might be an asset as the presiding country can exert greater influence on the formulation of common standpoints. Increased goodwill is the most one can hope for.

As mentioned earlier, the critical attitude of the Dutch is a defensive posture. It is based on concern about being dominated by the larger countries and on the belief that the European Commission could help them defend their legitimate national interests. There are some people in the Netherlands who, in their work with the Commission, have come to conclusions which deviate considerably from the official Dutch position. One of them completely discarded the notion of a European Commission as the guardian of the interests of small states. As he put it, 'the Commission consists of scoundrels from Germany, France and Britain, who first and foremost try to promote the interests of their own country because, after some years in Brussels, they all want to go home and find a nice position waiting for them. This being so, no Dutch interest is served by doggedly insisting that the future of the Netherlands depends on the position of the Commission. Rather, the Dutch should face the facts and acknowledge the intergovernmental nature of the European Communities, accept that in such organisations states take the decisions and that consequently a more effective Council is a good thing to strive for.'

It is clear that this is a minority view of officials in The Hague; there is no indication that these heresies will soon be adopted by a majority of the Dutch policy-makers. As long as the Dutch stick to the ideal of a supranational Community - and they have been doing so for over 25 years - they will hardly be prepared to consider any proposal to enhance the effectiveness of the Presidency. If they reach the conclusion that their ideal is an illusion, they may turn around and pursue a different course to salvation. In this respect there are no grounds for early optimism; once an idea has been elevated to the status of principle, the Dutch find it very difficult to abandon it. In Dutch politics the supranational character of the European Communities is such a principle.

NOTES:

(1) With the collaboration of Brigitte Buis and Sian-Lie-Thio.
(2) The Council for European Affairs (REZ) consists of:

- the Prime Minister;
- the Ministers of:
     Foreign Affairs
     Finance
     Economic Affairs
     Agriculture and Fisheries
     Transport
     Employment and Social Security
     Development Co-operation
     Housing, Planning and the Environment
- the State Secretaries for European Affairs and
     International Economic Relations;
- The Permanent Representative;
- from the Ministry of Foreign Affairs:
     Director-General European Co-operation
     Director-General International Co-operation
     Director-General Political Affairs;
- from the Ministry of Economic Affairs:
     Secretary-General
     Director-General External Economic Relations;
- from the Ministry of Finance:
     Treasurer
- from the Ministry of Agriculture:
     Director-General for Agriculture;

Each minister is allowed to bring along one senior civil servant; a ranking official from the Prime Minister's Cabinet acts as Secretary of the REZ.

The REZ was established in 1963; its task is 'to prepare the decision-making in the Cabinet on all important internal and external questions concerning the European Communities, as well as on important issues in the framework of EPC, insofar as these are related to the functioning of the European Communities and pertaining to decisions which are to be taken by the European Council'.

(3) The Cabinet consists of ministers only. State Secretaries are present at Cabinet meetings in an advisory capacity only when matters falling within the realm of their responsibility are discussed; the only exception is the State Secretary for European Affairs, who has access to all Cabinet meetings.

(4) The 'Jumbo' Council took place on the initiative of the Minister of Employment and Social Security. Another instance of a decision connected with the EC Presidency, in which personal ministerial views seem to have played a role, is the designation of Maastricht as the meeting place for the European Council; this was a very personal decision by the Prime Minister.

Chapter 11

THE PRESIDENCY OF THE COUNCIL OF MINISTERS OF THE
EUROPEAN COMMUNITIES: THE CASE OF THE UNITED KINGDOM
Dr Geoffrey Edwards, London

THE UNITED KINGDOM AND THE EUROPEAN COMMUNITY

The UK Background

The European Community has been a highly divisive issue in British
politics. The very question of membership has split political parties as
well as public opinion. Rarely has the public been as committed to
membership as in the 1975 referendum. The Community has been the
inspiration of innumerable myths and half-truths which have only too
clearly revealed the fact, bemoaned by Lord Carrington in 1981, that
'the benefits of Community membership are not properly under-stood or
appreciated' (1). As a result the Community has frequently been blamed
for a whole range of ills and problems.

There have, of course, been a number of reasons for this lack of
appreciation. The British have frequently seen themselves as the odd
men out in Europe, whether because of a sense of tradition, of being 'off-
shore islanders' or because they have felt themselves obliged to join -late
and only after two French vetoes - to overcome or ameliorate adverse
economic circumstances. These negative factors have invariably been
complemented by many positive ones, yet issues such as sovereignty, the
CAP and the inequitable distribution of costs and benefits both between
and within Member States have frequently thrown insuperable
difficulties in the way of more positive or maximalist European policies.

These difficulties have been particularly apparent in the attitudes
adopted by the Labour Party. Labour opposed entry in 1972 and, the
referendum and ten years membership notwithstanding, remains formally
committed to withdrawal. But the party has not been united behind the
policy and to a considerable extent the split over Europe has coincided
with left-right divisions. Even after many of the leading pro-marketeers
left Labour to form the Social Democratic Party, there was still little
unanimity on Europe and, since the 1983 general election, attitudes
appear to be undergoing important further changes, which may at last
lead to the full acceptance of Britain's membership.

The actual question of membership has not caused a split in the
Conservative Party to nearly the same degree. The party, together with
many Liberals, formed the backbone of the pro-European committee

237

during the referendum. There have naturally been divisions with, on the one side, some committed federalists and, on the other, perhaps an equally limited number of sceptics, with the majority made up of those taking a pragmatic view of the construction of Europe.

In view of the political importance of the Community, its impact on the political process has not been as singular as might have been expected. It has not, for example, led as in the Danish case to any significant efforts to strengthen or maintain parliamentary control over government. The more effective source of influence over government policy has often been the House of Lords (a chamber the Labour Party is committed to reforming if not abolishing), through the reports of its highly accomplished scrutiny committee. The House of Commons, on the other hand, has been able to exercise only a weak supervisory role (a symptom of, if not a further contribution to, the predominance of the Executive), in part because of the divisiveness of the Community issue itself. The House of Commons scrutiny committee has been primarily interested in determining which Community draft proposals are particularly sensitive and to recommend such items for debate in the House. However, it has then come up against certain problems, including the difficulty of fitting any large number of debates into the timetable and of finding a suitable motion for debate (most are dealt with on a 'take note' basis). It has not always been easy to adapt the normal style of the House of Commons to the consideration of proposals that are not yet government policy.

The importance of the Community has nonetheless imposed significant additional demands on the Executive, particularly in terms of the central coordination of policy. The practice of closely coordinating policy positions is of long standing; it grew naturally out of the need for ministers to have a united position first against the Crown and then against Parliament, i.e. the doctrine of collective ministerial reponsibility (2). The fact that a wider range of ministers with differing views on the question of British membership and/or on the construction of Europe were involved directly with Community decision-making has placed considerable strain on that responsibility, not least in the 'agreement to differ' adopted by the Labour government immediately before the referendum. Even in more normal circumstances the political importance of coordination has been considerably heightened. One consequence of this has been that once positions are agreed, so adherence to them has become more rigorous.

Policy considerations as well as bureaucratic traditions have reinforced the view that the keynote of any Presidency of the Council of Ministers is efficient management. It has been widely held that every Member State is constrained in its attempt to achieve all the objectives it has set itself for its Presidency; after all, six months is a short period and timetables are very largely predetermined. Nevertheless, British ministers and officials have been convinced that the smooth running of the Council and political co-operation machineries can be a major contribution both to the development of the Community and the advancement of favoured policies, and to the limitation of damage and the minimisation of costs. The danger has always been that efficiency becomes an end in itself. The emphasis on efficiency inevitably encourages a low key approach that has limited impact on the public. In many respects it fits the traditional pattern of anonymity on the part of the civil service; at least in the early years British officials were unused to the more open system in Brussels and the higher profile of officialdom. Moreover, even when they may have been inclined towards a more ambitious approach, ministers for their part have been constrained by the existence of major problems for the UK which have limited any public relations advantage that might have accrued from the Presidency.

In 1977, the Labour government was inevitably most affected by its internal divisions over continued membership, although these were compounded by left-right rivalries. Too many in the party remained hostile to the Community, including several key ministers, for the government to exploit what opportunities might have existed for a more positive approach to Europe. The background conditions for the first British Presidency were not particularly propitious.

The Conservative government, elected in 1979, was clearly in favour of continued British membership. Moreover, while there was considerable interest in, for example, the further development of political co-operation it was equally clear that there was a need to confront the problem of Britain's contribution to the Community budget. In the ensuing efforts to persuade its sceptical partners of the inequitable basis of Community funding, disillusionment with the EC increased - within the government as well as the wider public. Agreement on the 30 May Mandate which held out the prospect that, to quote Lord Carrington, 'No Member State is ever again to be faced with an unacceptable budgetary situation' (3) was therefore of particular importance to pro-marketeers; many hoped that it presaged conditions in which there could be a profound change in the United Kingdom's relationship with the rest of Europe. Conversely, further nagging was expected to increase British dissatisfaction, condemning the Community to remain an easy scapegoat for British problems. In such circumstances, the 1981 British Presidency took on an added significance.

The Formulation of British Policy Towards the Community

The Cabinet structure (4)

The Cabinet:
Is chaired by the Prime Minister. It receives weekly reports on Community matters for information purposes. Discussion is usually led by the Foreign Secretary except when specialist councils have recently met.

OD Committee:
The standing committee on foreign affairs and defence is chaired by the Prime Minister. 'The timing and agenda of meetings...are a matter for the Prime Minister, advised by the Secretary of the Cabinet and the Cabinet Secretariat. Meetings are arranged as required.' (5)

OD(E):
Chaired by the Foreign Secretary; it deals with Community business. The Foreign and Commonwealth Office has double representation since the Minister of State also attends. Meetings are open to those ministers whose departmental interests are involved. Meetings are again arranged as required.

EQ(S):
A standing committee chaired by a Deputy Secretary in the Cabinet Office. It meets at under secretary level, usually but not necessarily, weekly in order to discuss more strategic Community issues.

EQ(O):
Chaired by an Under Secretary in the Cabinet Office. It meets at assistant secretary level usually two or three times a week but this depends on the demand. Meetings are open to those who wish to attend. It services OD(E) and deals with issues before Coreper.

In addition, there are a number of ministerial and official standing committees dealing with Community and Community-related issues. There are, for example, official sub-committees on enlargement issues and on British staffing in Brussels. There are also **ad hoc** committees of ministers and of officials. None of these committees are, officially speaking, public knowledge; Cabinet officials neither confirm nor deny their existence and their structure, membership and discussions are shrouded in the mystery conferred by the United Kingdom's Official Secrets Act. This, once again, derives from the collective responsibility of the Cabinet which - at ministerial level, in theory, and at official level, all too often in practice - demands that deliberations are conducted in secret.

It has been suggested that there is little regularity in the meetings of the Cabinet committees; they are arranged as required. They take place, of course, in addition to the myriad of meetings and contacts held informally at all levels. The initiative for a formal committee meeting may come from any department although the Cabinet Office is usually responsible. One meeting that is now held regularly every week is that between the UK Permanent Representative and Whitehall-based officials to discuss forthcoming business. These meetings began on Britain's entry into the Community and had the aim of ensuring that the advice of the Permanent Representative on policy and tactics could be fully taken into account. The usefulness of the meetings was greatly enhanced during Britain's first Presidency and they have remained an important feature of the British system. Even here there is considerable emphasis on flexibility; attendance is open to those who need to attend because of the subjects under discussion and the agenda is often finally fixed only the day before. Some additional flexibility is added to the system since in those areas where a Whitehall department's experience and skill and/or interest are generally recognised, it may be asked to take the lead role. However this is rare. One example is the chairmanship by the Treasury of the Inter-Departmental EC Projects Group, which deals with questions relating to budgetary refunds.

Within the Cabinet Office the main burden of coordination falls on the European Secretariat. This is headed by a Deputy Secretary with an Under Secretary, two Assistant Secretaries and four Principals. Each Principal is inevitably responsible for a wide range of issues (typically divided up as follows: institutional questions; CAP/budget; internal trade and industry; the rest). Officials are seconded from Whitehall departments with the Deputy and Under Secretary usually from economic departments and not the Foreign and Commonwealth Office.

This structure differs slightly from that which existed on Britain's accession to the Community and under the previous Labour governments. During entry negotiations the Secretariat had been headed by a Deputy Secretary but the post was upgraded in 1972 when a Second Permanent Secretary was appointed, in part to emphasise the significance of accession. It remained a Second Permanent Secretary post until 1977 largely because of the continued political sensitivity of Community issues within the Labour government. However it was one of the recommendations of the Central Policy Review Staff (CPRS) Report in 1977 that the Secretariat should be headed by only a Deputy Secretary, as in other sections of the Cabinet Office, on the grounds that the referendum had settled the question of Britain's membership (6).

The line of authority which now exists within the Cabinet Office is not without its ambiguities. Under the Labour Government the Secretariat worked to the Foreign Secretary. This was largely a result of Labour's internal split which was partly resolved when the Prime Minister, Harold Wilson, gave James Callaghan, the Foreign Secretary (and Mr Wilson's successor in the premiership) overall responsibility for renegotiating Britain's terms of membership. Under succeeding governments, while the Foreign Secretary has retained overall responsibility for Community policy, the head of the European Secretariat has had direct access to the Prime Minister. This inevitably reinforces the importance of the Cabinet Office which, in terms of size and support, might otherwise be at a disadvantage in the decision-making process on Community issues. Any disagreements which persist are dealt with at ministerial level.

Cabinet Coordination

The main functions of coordination in the Cabinet at both ministerial and official levels remain those outlined in the CPRS Review. They are:

a) to manage the day-to-day conduct of British policy in the Community;

b) to ensure that the requirements of Parliament are met over European secondary legislation, forecasts of business and so on;

c) to reconcile departmental views when differences occur;

d) to ensure that national policy, especially in the economic and industrial fields, does not break Community rules;

e) to coordinate UK tactics, e.g. to try to make sure that the pursuit of an objective in one part of the Brussels machine will not jeopardise the UK's chances of achieving a more important objective in another part;

f)   to ensure strategic consistency, i.e. to make sure that the UK's immediate objectives at any one time are not only compatible with each other but also with its longer term objectives in the Community;

g)   to ensure that the course the UK pursues in the Community does not put at risk good relations with other friendly countries, in or out of the Community. **(7)**

Moreover there remains validity in several of the reasons put forward by the CPRS for coordination to take place in the Cabinet Office rather than elsewhere. These include:

i)   the need for an overview of Community matters; 'EEC policy will continue to be more than the sum of a number of sectoral policies'. Moreover, the Community was seen as becoming the channel through which the UK operated over a wide range of international economic and political activity so that the government's ability to influence the Community's position would depend increasingly on the line taken on issues under discussion in the Community.

ii)   The need for coordination since 'the potential for intersectoral trade-offs may be exaggerated but it exists'. **(8)**

iii)   The need for a watchdog and a guide in order to help Whitehall spot the opportunities offered by membership.

The relative importance of the different functions described above has inevitably varied during the period of Britain's membership of the Community. However, the reconciliation of differing departmental views has frequently been regarded as vital. While, for example, the Foreign and Commonwealth Office has laid some claims to the necessary overview of Community affairs, suspicion of the foreign service has often run deep in Whitehall and has in some cases been reinforced by hostility to or lack of enthusiasm for Community membership. Given the extent to which Community activity involved public expenditure, the Treasury has also been insistent that its views should be clearly heard. Differences between the Treasury and spending departments such as the Ministry for Agriculture, Fisheries and Food (MAFF) are perhaps endemic in the Community as well as nationally. Among competing claims the Cabinet Office, staffed by officials seconded from all over Whitehall and with direct access to the Prime Minister, provides the necessary impartiality. It is however an impartiality among departments; the neutrality of the Cabinet Office on the question of Britain's participation in the construction of Europe has sometimes been suspect to more reluctant Europeans.

The need for close coordination of Community positions has also contributed to a significant change in the formulation of British policy and the relationship between the Foreign and Commonwealth Office and the rest of Whitehall. No longer are there many easy distinctions to be made between external and domestic issues. Community membership has meant that subjects of hitherto domestic policy have become externalised, requiring negotiation with fellow member governments. Conversely, external issues have many more domestic consequences.

Domestic Whitehall departments have therefore been drawn much more into the international arena and the Foreign and Commonwealth Office has become involved in many more domestic issues. The development of European Political Co-operation (EPC), for which the Foreign and Commonwealth Office retains the predominant responsibility, has in consequence been welcomed with an additional sense of relief within the Foreign and Commonwealth Office.

The structure of decision-making on Community issues in the key departments of the Foreign and Commonwealth Office, the Treasury and the Ministry of Agriculture, Fisheries and Food is as follows:

(i)   the Foreign and Commonwealth Office

- The Secretary of State
- Minister of State
- Parliamentary Under Secretary: (under the Labour government 1976-79)
- Permanent Under Secretary
- Deputy to the Permanent Under Secretary & Political Director (supervising EPC)
- Deputy Under Secretary (responsible for economic affairs and Community business other than EPC)
- Assistant Under Secretary (supervising the European Community Departments)

European Community Dept. (External)	European Community Dept. (Internal)
Head of Dept. (Grade 4)	Head of Dept.
Assistant Head (Grade 5S)	Assistant Head
Political Correspondent and 6 Desk Officers	10 Desk Officers

There has been little alteration to the structure of decision-making on Community affairs since accession. It will be noted that while there is a division of responsibilities for EPC and Community affairs at Deputy Under Secretary level, this is not held to below that level exclusively; the European Community Department (External) deals with both Community external relations and EPC although the Correspondent works directly with the Political Director.

(ii)   the Treasury

- Chancellor of the Exchequer
- Financial Secretary
- Permanent Secretary
- Second Permanent Secretary (Overseas Finance)
- Deputy Secretary
- Under Secretary

Division European Community I   Division European Community II
Assistant Secretary   Assistant Secretary

3 Principals

Division I deals with British budgetary contributions. Division II coordinates the Treasury's position generally on Community budgetary questions and the department's interests in other matters. Other divisions intimately involved in Community work include the Agriculture and Industry divisions, the latter dealing with the public expenditure aspects of the Regional and Social Funds. Coordination takes place largely on an informal **ad hoc** basis; a more formal structure has been eschewed in the interests of maintaining flexibility and efficiency.

Under the last Labour government, the Chief Secretary to the Treasury was the number two on Community business. Apart from this there have been again few changes since accession.

(iii) The Ministry of Agriculture, Fisheries and Food

- Minister of Agriculture, Fisheries and Food.
- Minister of State (Commons)

Permanent Secretary

Deputy Secretary (Agricultural Commodity)	Deputy Secretary (Fisheries and Food)	Deputy Secretary (Land and Resources)

Under Secretaries supervising commodities (e.g. pigs and poultry or milk and potatoes)

Under Secretary (European Community Divisions and chairman of the Departmental Committee on Europe (DCE))

European Community I (Community price fixing, etc.)

Assistant Secretaries

Assistant Secretary

Principals

European Community II (information, briefing, etc. services the DCE)

Assistant Secretary

In view of the frequency of meetings on agricultural issues - monthly councils, weekly meetings of the Special Committee on Agriculture, the occasional meetings of Coreper on agricultural issues, and the Attache Group - MAFF established the Departmental Committee on Europe (DCE). This meets weekly, normally at under secretary level, to report on meetings held and to assess the requirements of forthcoming meetings. An official from the UK Representation usually attends.

(iv) Elsewhere in Whitehall most departments have an overseas, external or international relations division which generally acts as a contact and coordinating point on Community issues. In some cases, such as the Department of Employment, these may have a specific Community management role; in other cases the work of a particular division may in practice be largely or wholly concerned with Community work, on steel, regional policy, etc. Within the newly re-integrated Department of Trade and Industry there is now a single coordinating division for Community affairs, the European Commercial and Industrial Policy Division.

THE UNITED KINGDOM AND THE PRESIDENCY OF THE COUNCIL

Administrative structures

Structural changes for dealing with the additional responsibilities of the Presidency were largely confined to the Foreign and Commonwealth Office both in 1977 and in 1981. Some changes to the European Secretariat of the Cabinet were considered in 1977 but were not pursued. This was because it was considered that the tasks of the Presidency did not directly affect the coordinating role of the Cabinet Office but related more to the number and organisation of meetings and the need for closer liaison with other Community institutions and the Member States - both functions better suited to the traditional role of the Foreign and Commonwealth Office. However, the replacement of a Second Permanent Secretary by a Deputy Secretary as recommended in the CPRS Review was delayed until after the British Presidency had taken place. During preparations for the 1981 Presidency changes to the Secretariat were again briefly considered and discarded. One of the principals was simply given the responsibility of ensuring that the Presidency dimension was taken into account. Otherwise, the Cabinet Committee structure was merely stretched to absorb the greater frequency of meetings and the larger number of papers, briefings, etc.

Similarly, elsewhere in Whitehall the needs of the Presidency were fitted into the normal structure of decision-making. In the Ministry of Agriculture, Fisheries and Food for example, one of the Assistant Secretaries for coordination was given additional responsibilities for ensuring that arrangements worked smoothly, particularly those made for the informal meeting of Agricultural ministers. An innovation made in 1977 and considered valuable enough to repeat in 1981 was a freeze on posts relevant to Community work some six months before the Presidency began in order to ensure expertise and familiarity with the subjects in hand. This was more or less possible in the Foreign and Commonwealth Office, the UK Representation and the Cabinet Office. It proved rather more difficult in other Whitehall departments although efforts were made to ensure that at least some key officials remained in their posts; as one (anonymous) official put it, it was impossible 'to interrupt normal haphazard career arrangements.'

In the Foreign and Commonwealth Office a number of measures were taken, most notably the establishment of a Presidency Secretariat. At ministerial level, one of the last appointments made by Harold Wilson as Prime Minister was John Tomlinson MP as Parliamentary Under Secretary with specific responsibilities for helping with the preparations for the Presidency. The total complement of the Presidency Secretariat in 1977 was 49, including clerical and registry support. Its head was a Grade 4 official (John Weston) who had served in the UK Representation (and who had also been Assistant Private Secretary to James Callaghan when Foreign Secretary). The Secretariat was divided into three teams: six officials dealing with European Political Co-operation; three (one of whom doubled with responsibilities in the news department of the Foreign and Commonwealth Office) responsible for liaison with Community institutions; and eight officials dealing with actual meetings and their arrangement. These latter officials had close links with a special conference unit that was established since the UK Presidency coincided not only with the Queen's jubilee and all that that entailed, but also with a Commonwealth Conference, a Western Economic Summit and a NATO council.

The functions of the Secretariat clearly reflected the priorities of the government: the efficient working of the Council machinery and the smooth running of meetings; the importance of EPC, which was considered likely to impose a particularly heavy burden; the coordination of UK policy and the demands of the Presidency; and the effective presentation of the UK Presidency.

The size of the Secretariat was considered something of an over-insurance even in 1977. Certainly the Secretariat itself in its recommendations suggested that fewer people would be necessary in future Presidencies. In fact the Secretariat established in 1981 had a total complement of 33.

The 1981 Presidency Secretariat was again headed by a grade 4 official (Adrian Fortescue). However, unlike its predecessor, the 1981 Presidency was made a part of the European Community Department (External). The change was designed to emphasise the administrative role of the Secretariat although it also reflected the view that, in London, the major business of the Presidency was concerned with political co-operation. The change was considered appropriate for several other reasons, including a belief that there had been an over-reaction in 1977, and that Britain had had five extra years of membership in which to become familiar with Community procedures and practices. No special unit to liaise with other Community institutions was set up. Very much more was left to the Permanent Representative or, in London, to the European Community Departments themselves. In addition, it was considered possible to reduce the EPC unit from six to three because of the greater familiarity among Foreign and Commonwealth Office departments with the various EPC working groups. However the overall size of the Secretariat was also reduced through the introduction of some of the products of modern technology, including a word processor.

Preparations for the Presidency 1977

It was perhaps inevitable that the first British Presidency should attract considerable attention and comment. It was clear that preparations had begun well in advance and that by the spring of 1976 'Whitehall was beginning to gear itself up to assume the responsibilities of the Presidency. Officials were examining its duties and looking at the experience of other governments in the chair, and in Brussels the UK Representation was assessing the resources that it would be able to draw on.... The European Secretariat in the Cabinet had started to define the special requirements of the Presidency in terms of both formal organisation and policy formulation' (9). The Foreign and Commonwealth Office's Presidency Secretariat also took a leading role both in coordinating likely requirements and in preparing to take over responsibilities for EPC from the Dutch. One innovation already referred to was the freeze on postings some six months before the Presidency began. There was, too, an added emphasis on the weekly discussions held in the Cabinet Office with the Permanent Representative.

Ministers, it was noted, took somewhat longer than officials to focus on the Presidency. 'Partly this reflected the general tendency of ministers to think in shorter time-scales than officials, and to be preoccupied with their immediate political problems' (10). These problems were of no small magnitude even if self-created. The change in government in March 1976 had brought several ministers to key posts who were fresh to Community business, including the Foreign Secretary, Anthony Crosland, and the Minister for Agriculture, John Silkin. Moreover, despite the 1975 referendum, there remained many ambiguities in the Labour government's policy towards the Community. There was an attempt to draw out the main objectives of British policy during the summer of 1976, but the framework in which officials had to prepare for the Presidency was neither wholly clear nor wholly consistent. Once the imminence of the Presidency had begun to concentrate ministerial minds, for example, officials then had to point out that little political mileage was likely to be gained from it. It was emphasised repeatedly that the primary role of the Presidency was that of impartial, competent management and that grand initiatives were doomed to failure, at least within the brief span of six months. Nonetheless there were pressures on the government to take a high profile. There were many in the rest of the Community who looked on the first British Presidency as the ideal opportunity for Labour to show that it had overcome its divisions and had achieved a new sense of purpose which could enable it to play a full part in the construction of Europe. However, it was soon clear that the lack of consensus within the party meant that it was impossible seriously to consider a politically advantageous term of office.

The 1977 Presidency

There were mixed reactions to the UK's conduct of its first Presidency. It was quickly apparent that the Presidency was only one of several pressing issues with which the government had to deal. The sudden death of Anthony Crosland inevitably cast a long shadow over the Presidency. His successor, David Owen, while personally a strong pro-European, was often more preoccupied with the problems of Rhodesia. Nor could he have been expected to exercise the same political weight as Crosland, especially against such intimately involved ministers as John Silkin at Agriculture and Anthony Wedgewood Benn at Energy. Issues such as direct elections to the European Parliament created tensions and further divisiveness. Moreover, the government after March 1977 survived only with the support of the Liberal Party. This did not result in any significant Liberal influence on policy. Its effect was largely to focus people's attention on elections, less because they were regarded as imminent than because Mr Callaghan was not expected to lead the Labour Party for long after them and the question of the leadership of the Labour Party is invariably extremely newsworthy. It was suggested in 1977 that 'ministers were tempted to try to improve their chances of the succession by stressing their scepticism about Community co-operation and their vigorous defence of national interests. Not surprisingly, therefore, ministers in the chair found themselves looking over their shoulders at party reactions and press comments' (11). Mr Benn went so far as to provide a fairly sumptuous public record of his chairmanship (12).

At the less political level, conclusions on the British Presidency also varied. Some procedural and managerial innovations were generally welcomed. These included the division of the European Council's agenda into two parts; topics for discussion and those requiring a decision or some form of joint statement. Other innovations were the cross-reporting between the Political Committee and Coreper and the initiation of the Troika procedure. However, not everyone was entirely convinced that the British approach to efficient management was quite the right one for the Community. This was particularly so in the Council Secretariat where there was a common feeling that the British were attempting to do too much of the Secretariat's work. A similar criticism was voiced in the Commission, although the government's relationship with it was in general somewhat complicated by the position of Roy Jenkins as the new Commission President. Some national representatives, at both official and ministerial levels found the attempt to begin and to end meetings on time exceedingly welcome; others did not, particularly when sensitive issues were on the agenda and when a thorough and lengthy explanation would have seemed in order. However, the positive achievements in terms of efficiency were rarely enough to compensate for an approach which was almost entirely negative; 'the arguments of those in the Community who resented the preoccupation of the British with their own narrow concerns had been fuelled by that approach' (13).

Preparations for the 1981 Presidency

In 1981 there were inevitably those who feared that the 30 May Mandate would preoccupy the British Presidency. But, budgetary differences notwithstanding, the circumstances were in general very different from those of 1977; the Conservative government's support for British membership, for example, was clear. There was also, of course, a far greater familiarity with the Community and the needs of the Presidency among officials. Nonetheless, efficient management remained the key to the overall British approach. Thorough preparation and sound organisation, while not necessarily guaranteeing progress, were regarded as likely to provide the best conditions in which it might be achieved - and it was obvious that the government was determined to make as much progress as possible on the mandate. It was also recognised that EPC had grown in importance, a development which was widely welcomed in the UK. Its further development was therefore to be encouraged and this too was likely to demand both extensive preparation before and hard work during the Presidency.

A belief in the necessity of investing time and resources in the Presidency was reinforced to some extent by the conclusions of the Three Wise Men, whose report was published at the same time as officials in Brussels were beginning to think about the needs of the 1981 Presidency. The Three Wise Men pointed clearly to the need for greater authority on the part of the Presidency in terms of both management and political impetus, and that 'the virtual breakdown in the Council's work under some particularly 'bad' presidencies' indicated that if the Presidency did not do the job 'there is no longer anyone else who can fill the breach' (14). Significantly, perhaps, the particularly 'bad' presidencies were those whose faults lay either 'in weakness or an over-autocratic approach or both' (15).

A more relaxed British approach to the Presidency in 1981 was very clearly discernible. There was of course the wider pool of officials experienced in the ways of the Community in all the key departments of Whitehall. In addition the official reports of the 1977 Presidency were available which suggested useful models and guidelines. However, it was still considered desirable both to establish a special Presidency Secretariat and to undertake lengthy preparations. The head of the Secretariat took up his responsibilities in January 1981 and a freeze was imposed on posts in the European Community Departments of the Foreign and Commonwealth Office and in the UK Representation. The task of alerting the rest of Whitehall through the Cabinet Office was also begun early, not least because of the formal requirement for the dates of the Foreign Affairs, Agriculture and EcoFin Councils to be known seven months ahead of a Presidency.

One of the earliest undertakings was a comprehensive review of all the dossiers before the Council which was carried out by the UK Representation in consultation with the Council Secretariat and UK ministries. The purpose of the exercise was two-fold: to assess the number of meetings within the Council structure that were likely to take place; and to elicit from the dossiers that were not wholly dead items for possible inclusion in the British Presidency programme. There were few surprises but the review was considered useful; not only did it suggest those areas where some added political impetus might have greatest impact but it also helped officials to sketch in a timetable of working groups and Coreper meetings which would allow for improved coordination. The draft agendas were revised as the Dutch Presidency progressed. They contributed to a smooth take-over on 1 July 1981.

The assessment of the number of working groups likely to meet, the nomination of chairmen and national representatives, travel and other arrangements are inevitably among the most tedious and time-consuming of preparations for any Presidency. Most British chairmen had been provisionally assigned their posts by mid-1980. To a considerable extent the task was made easier by designating officials from the Permanent Representation whenever possible. The rationale behind this was a strong belief that good chairmanship was something that could not be taught except by being in the chair and that those most familiar with and experienced in decision-making in Brussels would be in a better position than officials sent out from Whitehall to carry out the duties of the chair.

A similar attitude to acquiring the skills of chairmanship was held by those in the agricultural sector which proved to be the major exception to the rule of Brussels-based chairmen. It has been variously estimated that between 30 and 40 working groups on agricultural issues could meet in any six months in addition to Councils, the Special

Committee on Agriculture (SCA), meetings of Coreper on agricultural topics and so on. At Council level, the minister was designated chairman, with the responsibility of representing the UK devolving on the Minister of State (Commons). Since both ministers normally attended agricultural councils no problems were foreseen (it was after all the less hectic part of the agricultural year with no price-fixing councils). The SCA was to be chaired by an official from the Permanent Representation. Below that level, the Ministry of Agriculture, Fisheries and Food was obliged to adopt a different practice from other departments; the resources of the Representation were obviously not enough to deal with all the working groups likely to meet. Moreover, although the number of the ministry's staff seconded to the Representation was increased by one, it was for the purpose of improving coordination rather than providing an extra chairman. But since many home-based officials from the Ministry of Agriculture, Fisheries and Food were constantly travelling between London and Brussels, the argument about the Representation's greater familiarity with Community decision-making did not arise. The ministry was well able to choose the home officials it believed had both expertise and an aptitude for chairing meetings. Indeed the choice was made even wider by the need to take into account the interests and/or claims of the Agricultural Departments of the Scottish, Welsh and Northern Ireland Offices.

In view of the decisions taken on the chairing of working groups it was not considered necessary to devote many resources to the preparation of chairmen. Few courses were given at the Civil Service College, for example, although those that were held were warmly welcomed, particularly by officials in more peripheral departments. Some departments of course held their own meetings to discuss the demands of the Presidency and the overall British approach. The Ministry of Agriculture, Fisheries and Food, for example, held an afternoon meeting attended by the minister in the Permanent Representation and the officials who had been nominated as chairmen of working groups. Elsewhere in Whitehall, especially in departments less intimately involved in Community business, the extent of any preparations varied considerably; much inevitably depended on the degree of interest shown by the minister or by individual officials. Otherwise, general guidelines were issued for chairmen of working groups in the form of a small booklet. These reminded chairmen that their primary purpose was to lead the working group to a decision and that the task of promoting the UK's point of view belonged to a different person. The guidelines also suggested procedural techniques which might be called in aid in bringing about a consensus or defusing a conflict, such as the use of short adjournments, or calling on the Commission either for additional information or for a compromise proposal. They urged chairmen to resist the temptation to hand over a dossier to Coreper until as much work as possible had been done on it. They also laid down some ground rules for contacts between chairmen and Members of the European Parliament (MEPs), especially British MEPs, and rapporteurs of EP Committees, which emphasised the need for discretion and care. These contacts had in fact been an issue raised at the Civil Service College courses.

The actual timetable of meetings is, to a considerable extent, beyond the control of any one Member State. However, the actual arrangements for meetings can fall heavily onto officials. In Brussels, the Council Secretariat is closely involved in these preparations, although in juggling the requirements of rooms and interpreters the British found the appointment of a Grade 9 Assistant Coordinator in the Representation very useful. It also left the Presidency Coordinator (a Grade 5 official) better able to carry out other tasks, including representing the UK on the Antici group and dealing with other Presidency arrangements. Even so, there were inevitably problems, not least those caused by departments either overlooking the likely need for a Council or working group or suddenly seizing the initiative to hold one. The combined weight of the Cabinet, the Foreign and Commonwealth Office and the Permanent Representation of the UK was not always enough to discourage some private enterprise by other departments, invariably towards the end of a Presidency. Some 33 Councils were in fact held under the British Presidency in either Brussels or Luxembourg.

Informal Council meetings and meetings held within the framework of political co-operation in the UK were very largely the responsibility of the department concerned and the Foreign and Commonwealth Office. The number of informal Councils (six during the 1981 Presidency) was in marked contrast to the practice in 1977 when Messrs Rogers and Benn were refused such meetings on transport and energy. In addition, four other meetings were arranged at Council level, six meetings of Political Directors and over 20 meetings of EPC working groups. The European Council meeting in London inevitably added to the burdens of preparation. Great pains were taken to keep to agreed schedules and to ensure the success of meetings. Considerable care was taken over venues, catering and, of course, protocol. Some delicacy was required, and expertise gained, at informal ministerial dinners in drawing up seating arrangements for ministers and their spouses which balanced the demands of protocol, linguistic abilities and ministerial preferences.

By the end of 1980 the more intense period of preparation was underway, including the more direct involvement of ministers. Within the Foreign and Commonwealth Office the Minister of State, Mr Hurd, was given particular responsibility for the Presidency. As far as other ministers were concerned, although the Conservative government had been in office since May 1979 it was, as in 1977, a case of once having alerted ministers, officials then had to persuade them that the primary tasks were managerial. However, a number of strategy papers were also drawn up early and circulated among departments with the aim of achieving ministerial clearance three or four months before the Presidency began.

The 1981 Presidency
Its budgetary contributions had inevitably been a predominant concern in Britain's preparations and, as Lord Carrington made clear in his speech to the European Parliament on 8 July 1981, the government attached the highest importance to making progress on the 30 May Mandate. With a triptych of 'renewal, enlargement and identity' which Lord Carrington described as forming the basis of further Community development, the

Mandate was seen as the very foundation of the Community's renewal. It was recognised that progress was likely to be complicated by the fact of holding the chair but, equally, it was clear that every effort had to be made to achieve as much progress as possible. However, efforts were made to persuade the rest of the Community that the Mandate would not overwhelm the rest of the work of the Community entirely and that an impetus would be given in other sectors to achieve further agreements. Among these other sectors priority was given to the further development of the internal market including services, especially insurance, (the Chancellor of the Exchequer in fact placed it on the agendas of four out of the five finance council meetings).

Lord Carrington also expressed his hopes for the further development of political co-operation. Principal concerns were the Middle East and what came to be known as the London Report. Lord Carrington argued that in the Middle East the Community was being more than simply reactive and declaratory and indeed the Multinational Force and Observers (MFO) in the Sinai became a major preoccupation. The need to strengthen the framework of political co-operation also featured prominently in Lord Carrington's programme. Ever since the failure of the Nine to act coherently and expeditiously after the Soviet invasion of Afghanistan, Lord Carrington had felt strongly that EPC needed to be developed further. Work had begun under the Luxembourg Presidency and continued under the Dutch. The British contribution during the Presidency was to be important and they were able to take advantage of the change of government in France. The British approach was however wholly in keeping with the general emphasis on a practical, step-by-step approach. The ambitiousness of a Genscher-Colombo type initiative was carefully avoided.

The key to a 'successful' Presidency for Lord Carrington remained the smooth running of the Community and political co-operation machines. Responsibility for political co-operation lay primarily if not exclusively, with the Foreign and Commonwealth Office. The Presidency Secretariat found itself, in practice, able to concentrate on political co-operation affairs, notably the drafting of the London Report. The European Community Department (ECD) (Internal) and the rest of ECD (External) not dealing with EPC, the Cabinet Office and, of course, the UK Representation concentrated on Community business. But in Whitehall, the Presidency as such tended to add only marginally to the length and frequency of meetings.

For the Permanent Representation, the Presidency became an overwhelming preoccupation, although once it had begun and the adrenalin was flowing, many officials reportedly enjoyed the six months. As the Representation had undergone some reductions in staffing after 1977 (though it remained one of the largest in Brussels), seven additional desk officers were appointed to, inter alia, the agricultural, industry and development sections. Close internal coordination was maintained by almost daily meetings of all officials. In addition, as was noted earlier, the Grade 5 official on the Antici Group was appointed the Presidency Coordinator and was responsible, subject to the Head of Chancellery, for most of the Presidency arrangements. In many respects he acted as the Ambassador's assistant. The burden on the Ambassador and his Deputy was particularly great. The 'normal' heavy workload of any Presidency was intensified for the Ambassador by the need to press on with the 30 May Mandate - his weekly meetings in Whitehall were frequently dominated by the issue. For the Deputy Permanent Representative, the major problem was in reaching the necessary consensus on the Community's 1982 Budget. It had been anticipated that he would represent the UK in Coreper II in addition to chairing Coreper I. For the most part this proved impossible; it was estimated that Coreper I had itself met on 100 occasions during the six months.

During the preparatory period the Permanent Representative was in close contact with the Council Secretariat. Extensive collaboration took place with its officials for example, in the comprehensive review of dossiers before the Council. During the Presidency, relations were often described as 'proper', which suggests, perhaps, a certain lack of warmth in the relationship although it was certainly better than during the 1977 Presidency. In some policy areas contacts were close; in others the British tended to look to their own resources. The situation, in other words, was not atypical of the relationship of most of the bigger Member States with the Secretariat.

Relations with the Commission generally intensified before and during the Presidency. A preparatory meeting was held, for example, between Lord Carrington and Mr Thorn, and the Ambassador also had regular meetings with the Commission President. However, in general, relations with the Commission tended to be influenced, as was the Report of the Three Wise Men, by a belief that the Commission could no longer fulfil completely the role originally designated to it under the Treaties that in several vital areas the Presidency had had to step in. A result of this was, for example, a reminder to chairmen that, formally, the Commission had to make proposals, and that any mediation or package-broking by the chair had to be done with an additional element of tact. Moreover, while it was recognised that the Dutch acted with perfect propriety in establishing little or no contact with the British as the in-coming President on Community matters since the maintenance of continuity was regarded as a Commission and Council Secretariat responsibility, it was nonetheless held that the minimum of disruption should be allowed. To this end, the British had worked out draft agendas which enabled them to take up matters without further pause for reflection. Towards the end of its Presidency the British also invited the Belgian Coordinator to its agenda-setting meetings with the Council Secretariat so that the Belgians would be in a better position to take up those items which particularly interested them and, at official level at least, would know exactly what was going on.

While contacts with the Council Secretariat and the Commission conformed largely to expectations, the additional workload falling on the Presidency from the European Parliament proved a surprise - indeed, an extra official had to be appointed to the Representation during the Presidency. The demand of Parliament for attention and information was clearly indicated by the fact that some 63 oral parliamentary questions were put down. Although not all these were actually reached, officials had had to prepare for possible supplementaries. In addition ministerial visits had to be prepared for in other ways and some 13 ministers from

10 different departments attended either plenary sessions or meetings of parliamentary committees. Mr Hurd, the Minister of State at the Foreign and Commonwealth Office, attended monthly; in total there were over 40 ministerial visits during the six months. This highly creditable performance was achieved despite agnosticism on the part of some individual ministers on the question of the further development of Europe, their preoccupation with other issues or simple apathy In addition, of course, Mrs Thatcher agreed to address the Parliament to give an account of the European Council, thus establishing an important precedent. A second innovation during the British Presidency was a meeting of foreign ministers with the enlarged bureau of the Parliament and the President of the Commission to discuss the future of the Community's institutions.

AN ASSESSMENT

Lord Carrington, in his concluding speech as President of the Council, told the European Parliament that the 'keynote' of any Presidency 'should be to contribute in a business-like and effective manner to the continuation of the Community's affairs' (16). An element of satisfaction that this had indeed been achieved was however offset by disappointment that more progress had not been achieved in areas of particular importance - to both the Community and to the UK. As Lord Carrington declared in the same speech, 'We have tried to demonstrate the tenacity and endurance which are needed in every Presidency, but even they are not enough if there is no common will to reach conclusions and that, I fear, is what is too often lacking in our deliberations' (17).

The qualities referred to by Lord Carrington were perhaps best shown in the efforts made to win a consensus on the 30 May Mandate. There is a widespread belief in the UK that more progress had been achieved than had been expected even if, ultimately, hopes of a breakthrough had been dashed. The Presidency's ability to maintain a momentum by, for example, increasing the frequency of meetings, carried the exercise a long way forward. But as Lord Carrington was to say:

> I think in my heart of hearts I never imagined that we would get a full agreement. I think in European terms, the pie wasn't cooked. The Community is rather inclined not to make disagreeable decisions or sensible compromises until the twelfth or sometimes the thirteenth hour... (18).

But the view that the Presidency is costly in terms of national interests had been only partially reinforced.

The efforts made on the Mandate inevitably highlighted a problem that is faced by all Member States: the division between the demands of an impartial chair and the interests of the Member State. Doubtless all Member States hope that during their Presidency, they will get the overall balance about right; it is of course a matter of interpretation. Certainly in the UK case, pains were taken in the guidelines issued and in departmental meetings to emphasise the separation of roles between the chair and the national representative. There were occasions when some Brussels-based officials considered that departmental briefs failed to maintain the separation very clearly but they were not frequent. It was sometimes apparent that the more peripheral departments found greater difficulty in making the distinction clear although they were also some of the most enthusiastic about making an impact and a contribution. It was on occasions equally clear that the determination of British interests did not allow the chair any particular flexibility - British hostility to proposals on statutory employee participation is such an example during the 1981 Presidency.

It is perhaps a truism that the 'success' or 'failure' of a Presidency rests heavily on the individuals who take the chair. As Lord Carrington remarked:

> It is very hard work. I didn't fully understand, I think, two-and-a-half years ago when I became Foreign Secretary, that I was going to be expected to understand such abstruse subjects as multi-fibre agreements and cocoa agreements and things of that kind...But it has proved, of course, that because, as President, I have to take the chair, I really do have to know about these things and they are inevitably complicated and one does realise the problems the differences of interest that there are between the various countries... (19).

Negotiating and drafting skills are at a premium. However, at the official level, the British system does not always encourage the wider use of an individual's initiative. The UK has a reputation in the Community for imposing particularly tight instructions on its negotiators with innumerable contingencies allowed for, fall back positions indicated, and so on. At its worst, critics aver, this means that in circumstances not accounted for, officials cannot move until they have referred back to Whitehall. Certainly in areas where the UK is in an awkward minority position or when officials are tackling new or unfamiliar issues, instructions are often closely drawn. Holding the Presidency may reinforce these pressures so that a chairman may well be inhibited by the knowledge of what the British government will consider unacceptable. On the other hand, of course, it could be argued that it can be a help to know what at least Her Majesty's government will accept. But it is also sometimes the case that where the UK occupies the middle ground (on many trade issues for example) or where officials are more experienced, greater flexibility can be allowed. This may be the result of an experienced official successfully arguing against his instructions or placing the government in an untenable position. While difficult to substantiate, there have been suggestions that during the Presidency, Brussels-based officials were able to supplement their own authority by the skilful use of the demands of the Presidency to modify Her Majesty's government's position.

It needs to be remembered, however, that the brief given to officials is already the result of prenegotiation among Whitehall departments. It is not surprising therefore that a shift away from an agreed position in Brussels requires further inter-epartmental clearance, including the agreement of ministers. Whatever the inter-departmental differences over the intrinsic merits of a particular proposal, swift decision-making has not always been helped, in the past at least, by a lack of enthusiasm for Community matters on the part of many ministers. Outside the Foreign and Commonwealth Office, where even under Labour governments ministers were in general more favourable than not towards the Community, and the Treasury and the Ministry of Agriculture, Fisheries and Food, where an interest in Community affairs is unavoidable, attitudes towards Europe have varied enormously, from the enthusiastic pro-European to the implacably hostile. Such differences have inevitably heightened the importance of coordination while simultaneously placing difficulties in its way.

The experience of two presidencies has, in general, confirmed the British in their belief in the value of thorough preparation. Among the measures taken that were considered particularly useful were: the weekly meetings between the Permanent Representative and Whitehall-based officials to discuss forthcoming meetings; the establishment of a Presidency Secretariat within the European Community Department of the Foreign and Commonwealth Office; the role of a Presidency Coordinator in Brussels; the use of the Permanent Representation for most chairmen (although this of course is possible only so long as the UK Representation remains at its present large size); and the comprehensive review of all dossiers before the Council. An area where greater resources are likely to be devoted in 1986 or 1987, depending on whether Spain and Portugal have become members, is in preparing for and dealing with the European Parliament. The pressures exercised by MEPs for greater participation in the Community's decision-making process, by means of, for example, greater influence over, or at least more information on, the progress of topics through the Council machinery, are likely to increase. Since parliamentarians are often sensitive to the dignity of their office, there are likely to be heavier demands on Ministers to provide that information and to participate more extensively in the Parliament's deliberation.

The second British Presidency also confirmed many in their belief that any reforms involving the Presidency should not include the extension of the six-month period of office. A number of arguments were recognised in favour of, say, a year-long Presidency, not least a lessening in the disruption sometimes caused to Community business when Member States take over with a different set of priorities. A longer period might create greater opportunities for a real impetus to be given to the further construction of Europe. However, such an argument presupposes that Member States will forego (and for longer) the tendency to adopt a low profile and a damage-limitation policy during their Presidencies, a tendency which is particularly marked among the Big Four. The Presidency is seen, that is, to have costs in financial terms but more importantly in terms of constraints on the promotion and protection of national interests. Moreover, the strain especially on the Permanent Representative and his Deputy could be unacceptably great if presidencies were extended beyond six months. At ministerial level too, few Member States are likely to afford the time and resources necessary, particularly on the part of the foreign minister with his (or her) dual responsibilities for political co-operation as well as Community issues. But even if individuals are dispensable, a more profound argument is put forward for retaining the present term of office: anything which weakens a government's full responsibility for advancing the Community's business would gravely weaken the Community. If each Member State were to hold the Presidency for longer than six months, the infrequency with which it took its turn would mean a considerable loss of awareness and experience of the responsibilities that are imposed by the Presidency. Being obliged to prepare a programme and to advance it in the Community's interests is regarded as a salutary lesson for all goverments. Moreover, in political terms - and not solely those of the UK - the Presidency creates opportunities for governments and the Community to have a more positive impact on national electorates.

However, while holding to the importance of a six-month period of office, many officials are increasingly concerned about the problem of continuity. The provision of continuity was one of the first tasks of the Presidency outlined by Lord Carrington in his programme speech in July 1981 **(20)**. It is accepted that issues, and working groups, have a momentum of their own and that all Member States are similarly bound by timetables that have already been agreed. The Council Secretariat also exists to contribute to a smooth hand-over between Presidencies. The Commission, too, has a general responsibility to ensure progress. However, at the same time, most Member States seek to make some sort of impact during their Presidency; programmes, however modest, are announced and sometimes even followed through. Usually there is an element of individuality in these programmes even if the problems addressed vary little from one Presidency to the next. Each Member State, that is to say, seeks to create a certain impetus and use its good offices to further dossiers of particular interest to itself as well as to the Community. There is therefore an inevitable stop-go effect in areas where the emphasis is shifted.

There is no unified British approach to overcoming the problem of discontinuity although a greater recognition by others in the Community that the problem is real would generally be welcomed. There have been some efforts to raise the question in discussions on institutional reform. It has in some respects been taken up before, by the Three Wise Men in their report, for example. Consideration was given by them to ways of sharing the burdens of the Presidency, of establishing ministers for Europe, of borrowing the Troika principle from political co-operation and so on. It is perhaps time to look again at many of the issues raised in that report. Certainly the Presidency is widely considered in the UK to be a vital element in any further discussions on the Community's institutional development.

REFERENCES

(1)   Verbatim Service 83/81 18 June 1981.
(2)   For a discussion of the doctrine of collective responsibility and the strains imposed upon it even before Community membership, see J.P. Mackintosh, The British Cabinet 2nd edition 1968.
(3)   Debates of the European Parliament, 8 July 1981, p.118.
(4)   See The Economist, 6 February 1982.
(5)   Falkland Islands Review. Report of a Committee of Privy Councillors-Cmnd. 8787. January 1983, Annex B, p.93.
(6)   Central Policy Review Staff, Review of Overseas Representation, HMSO 1977, p.44.
(7)   CPRS Review, op.cit., p.42.
(8)   Ibid, p.43.
(9)   G. Edwards and H. Wallace, The Council of Ministers of the European Community and its President in Office Federal Trust, London, 1977, p.77.
(10)   ibid p. 78.
(11)   Edwards & Wallace, op. cit. p. 92.
(12)   The United Kingdom and Community Energy Policy: A Record of the UK Presidency of the Energy Council, January-June 1977, Department of Energy 1977.
(13)   Edwards & Wallace op. cit. p.92.
(14)   Report on the European Institutions presented by the Committee of Three, (The Three Wise Men Report) 1979 p.35.
(15)   ibid.
(16)   Debates of the European Parliament, December 1981, p. 201.
(17)   ibid, p.204.
(18)   Verbatim Service, 193/81. 7 December 1981.
(19)   Verbatim Service, 194/81. 8 December 1981.
(20)   Debates of the European Parliament, 8 July 1981, p. 118.

Chapter 12

THE PRESIDENCY OF THE COUNCIL OF MINISTERS OF THE
EUROPEAN COMMUNITIES: A COMPARATIVE PERSPECTIVE
Dr Helen Wallace, London

The European Community is above all, in its contemporary manifest-
ation, a negotiating forum, negotiating constantly both over internal
rules and policies and with other countries. By international standards
and given the adverse environment it is remarkably productive. The
volumes of legislation steadily take up more and more space on the
bookshelf. More and more national officials find themselves sucked into
the Brussels whirlpool, whether negotiating themselves, or briefing their
colleagues or implementing the consequent decisions. To those directly
involved it is obvious that the EC actually generates several different
and simultaneous levels of negotiation. What happens in the Council of
Ministers, its committees and working groups constitutes the most
visible expression of Community negotiation. Equally important and
often determinant are the negotiations in national capitals through which
individual governments adopt their own positions, often if not generally
against a back-cloth of contending priorities and pressures from those
who represent the relevant economic interests. In many instances where
EC proposals and actions affect third countries directly or indirectly
lobbying also takes place in EC capitals, quite apart from the formal
negotiations conducted by the EC with other countries or groups of
countries.

Thus, from the perspective of the national official dealing with EC
business, the Community is the cause of one long round of meetings and
briefing. In some areas of work the rhythm is reasonably relaxed:
meetings take place at manageable intervals, the subject matter is fairly
well specified, and the debate ranges (often repeatedly) over familiar
ground. But in many other areas the pace is phrenetic, with meetings
both frequent and at short notice, with papers often arriving late and not
in the correct official language, and with awkward and sometimes
unpredictable linkages to dossiers simultaneously under discussion in
parallel groups and committees. The sheer problem of keeping up
imposes a heavy burden of preparation and consultation and leaves little
time for either perfectionism or measured thought. In most areas of
policy officials are subject to political, administrative and resource
constraints which limit their margin of manoeuvre, quite apart from the
need to examine the merits of the particular case in its own right. Even
under 'normal' conditions this adds up to a fairly taxing workload. During

261

the Presidency the load increases both quantitatively and qualitatively to the extent that those in the chair have also to assume managerial, mediatory and representational duties and to acquaint themselves in greater depth with the positions of other governments.

The Requirements of Community Negotiation
Unless this 'real world' of the Community as seen from national administrations is understood, it is difficult to comment sensibly on either the impact of EC membership, or more specifically, the Council Presidency. Increasingly the literature on international negotiation has come to acknowledge that, as one scholar has put it, negotiation is 'a management process' (1). The implication of the argument is that optimising strategies rarely work and that maximising or, to quote Herbert Simon, 'satisficing' (2) strategies are more realistic - often the desirable has to be sacrificed for the possible. The outcome may be neither to achieve an appropriate solution at the EC level nor an adequate squaring of domestic interests. These features obtain in many international fora, but they are evident in the EC in a particularly distinct form for (at least) three reasons. First, in most areas EC decisions have to be reached by <u>consensus</u> both in Brussels and amongst relevant policy-makers at home. Secondly, consensus is dependent on the formation of <u>coalitions</u> amongst those with common or compatible interests. Thirdly, EC decisions really matter and have, by and large, to be <u>implemented</u> and executed.

Achieving <u>consensus</u> requires packages of interests and/or arbitration amongst competing interests in capitals and within the Council of Ministers. One government or a minority coalition in Brussels may often constitute an effective veto group. Within each government a reluctant minister or ministry (or part of a ministry) may have enough leverage to put a brake on movement. To move forward requires skilled negotiation, a high level of information and understanding of the objectives and requirements of partners and a capacity to formulate what Roger Fisher calls 'yesable' propositions (3). To say yes to partners presupposes the ability of the national negotiator to deliver the effective, as well as the nominal compliance of his own government.

Constructing <u>coalitions</u> is crucial to the stitching together of a broader consensus. To reconcile eleven points of view (the Member States and the Commission) involves alliances amongst like-minded governments and often a readiness to include in the package some 'side-payments' to carry along those who are reluctant to agree - less for reasons of principle than because of an important but subsidiary material interest. In practice, member governments rarely have identical interests and objectives and a coalition thus requires a willingness to modify positions enough for similar but different interests to be made compatible. Side-payments often mean acceptance of a rather untidy package with some inconvenience to, or additional burden on others.

Community legislation is <u>implemented</u>, executed and enforced in the Member States, albeit with different degrees of rigour, precision and speed. Implementation is the subject of another research project, sponsored by the European Institute of Public Administration (4), but is also relevant to our analysis of the way in which the Council works and the impact on national administrations. A major consideration in the formulation of national negotiating positions is an assessment of whether a proposal, if adopted, is capable of implementation practically and technically as well as politically. It is now well substantiated that governments often delay or withhold assent because implementation will take time or require substantial modification of established national practice (5). Sometimes assent is given only subject to special derogations or complex additions or amendments to the negotiating text. All in all, Community negotiations require of national officials special skills and a high degree of ingenuity, quite apart from the broader framework of political preferences and priorities chosen by ministers.

Experienced negotiators argue that effectiveness depends on **inter alia**:

1) clear identification of objectives in terms of the ideal, the realistic and the minimum which is tolerable;
2) a thought-out strategy about how to achieve policy objectives;
3) careful tactical judgments about how and when to deploy the strong cards;
4) measured evaluation of the likely positions of other participants and where they are supple, and also of their bargaining power;
5) availability of adequate information, not just about one's own position but about the issues as they affect other participants; and
6) an ability to look at different ways of achieving objectives so that more than one solution can be envisaged in order to achieve agreement.

The implications in the EC context are that national officials dealing with EC proposals need to perform at least four different tasks in preparing for EC negotiations, namely:

a. evaluate the technical merits and consequences of each proposal;
b. assess the individual proposal within the framework of the government's political priorities;
c. gather intelligence about other member governments; and
d. determine negotiating strategy and tactics.

Moreover, since the Brussels negotiating process is iterative, in practice national officials have continually to reassess and to adjust to changes in the debate. Agreement almost invariably depends on movement in national positions as the dynamic without which progress is impossible.

National Policy Formulation

The various processes and procedures adopted within each national capital have thus evolved in order to provide each government with the resources, as far as possible, to perform these tasks. Each government, irrespective of its broad stance on the EC, is quite rightly keen to get the best possible outcome, issue by issue, in terms of the interests and objectives generated in domestic discussion. But precisely because the political and administrative habits and traditions of each Member State are idiosyncratic, the particular methods chosen for handling EC business differ markedly from one to another. This idiosyncracy comes clearly through the individual country studies which form the body of this volume. In each we can trace the influence of constitutional conventions, political constellations and administrative practice, quite apart from the fact that in substantive and material terms governments have particularist needs and objectives, often embraced against the back-cloth of both party and national doctrines.

Foreign Ministers and Home Civil Servants

Yet there are some common threads which run, explicitly or implicitly, through each example. There is a recognition in each capital that EC business is **sui generis.** The particular context, agenda and constraints of the Community mean that the 'normal' processes of domestic government cannot automatically be extended to incorporate the management of EC work. The most obvious illustration of this is that the Community involves a special dialectic between diplomats and home civil servants and their ministerial overseers of an intensity and character that is not recurrently found in other areas of domestic work and which obtains to only a more limited extent in most other areas of international work. In all Member States, Foreign Ministers continue to play an extremely important part in helping to prepare and articulate national negotiating positions. This is quite understandable in so far as EC business involves negotiations with other governments (both EC partners and third countries), and after all the stock-in-trade of the good diplomat is negotiation. In some Member States, the logic has been extended to make the Foreign Ministry the central coordinator of EC policy - notably Belgium, Denmark, Greece, Ireland, Italy, Luxembourg and the Netherlands. Yet equally striking is the extent to which diplomats are more often the coordinators than the direct negotiators, even though once a dossier moves up to ministers, Foreign Ministers in the General Affairs Council may take up the final responsibility for negotiating the agreement. Domestic ministries are actually numerically the main providers of negotiators for Council meetings at ministerial and official level. Thus responsibility for negotiation on the spot in Brussels tends to confer an expertise and influence on the sponsoring ministries which diminishes the influence of diplomats and Foreign Ministers (outside their prime fields of political co-operation and external relations). To achieve a constructive balance between these two wings of the national administration has proved as difficult in capitals as within the Council machinery in Brussels. While the respective roles of diplomat and home officials should ideally be complementary they are frequentiy competitive, and only with mutual tolerance and trust can this be satisfactorily resolved.

One of the reasons for European Political Co-operation (EPC) continuing to be so different in character from Community business is precisely that it avoids the need for a dialectic with the rest of government. It has remained largely the preserve of diplomats and

Foreign Ministers and thus escapes the heavy procedures and constraints of interministerial coordination, as the case studies bear out. Instead the preparation of policy positions rests with the diplomatic experts and with their posts abroad. But there is another crucial difference in that much of EPC activity lies, as the home civil servant would see it, in the stratosphere of abstract debate. In this sense EPC is not, at least yet, rooted in a negotiating process designed to produce tangible output or concrete substance, but rather focused on gradually shifting broad attitudes and promoting common analyses of major international issues. Negotiation, as distinct from discussion, is confined to the wording of declarations and exhortations rather than detailed legislation. Meetings are an end in themselves in a way that few would argue is true of Community business. However, once the participants in EPC want to engage in common action, they are generally obliged to resort to the Community framework, at which point substantive interests have to be incorporated through the coordinating processes in capitals and the machinery of the EC. It is hardly surprising that diplomats should find EPC so welcome a relief from the (for a diplomat) often tedious and technical dossiers emanating from the EC framework, nor that they should find it irksome when their agreed consensus cannot readily be translated into instant Community action.

Central Coordination

A second illustration or element is the role and powers of the centre of government. It is self-evident that no government is likely to achieve a consistent and overarching political or negotiating strategy unless either there is a high degree of domestic consensus on EC issues or there is an effective capability at the centre for reconciling different viewpoints and imposing a sense of direction. It may even be that elements of both are needed for a high success rate to be achieved in Brussels negotiations without too many costs being attached. Obviously there are several ways of achieving central direction of policy - a strong President or Prime Minister may provide the steer; a particular ministry may be the instrument, usually the coordinating Foreign Ministry, though it does not follow in all cases; or a particular and more novel central agency may perform this function, as has broadly been the case in France and Britain. But what is crystal clear is that idiosyncratic national practice is the determinant of what is possible, since the way in which governmental systems work differs so much in this respect. Lessons cannot be easily transplanted from one national context to another. It is not for example possible for the German Chancellor's Office to perform the same functions as the British Cabinet Office without changing fundamental conventions, practices and political hierarchies.

Changing Ministerial Hierarchies

A third element is the prevailing ministerial hierarchy in each capital, in turn a function of deeply entrenched practice, particular economic interests and the influence of individual office holders. Again here the experience of each Member State tends to be somewhat idiosyncratic, as the case studies demonstrate, but some common themes emerge. One recurrent feature, not brought out in the national profiles in this volume, is the considerable involvement and influence of ministers and officials responsible for trade policy (the specific titles and ministerial structures vary). The importance of the internal market as an issue area and the extent of EC negotiations with third countries make these primary and intensive areas of work for the relevant national policy-makers. Interestingly, however, these activities are managed somewhat separately from other areas of work and are often coordinated at the national level outside the 'core' agenda of policies which involve expenditure. Particular problems of coordination arise especially between the trade and industry components of the subject matter; depending on ministerial structures this may involve one or several different ministries.

But often as relevant, if not more so, are the contacts between the responsible ministers and officials and the various commercial and industrial interests. Complex though the issues are, in the past the trade field has had its own momentum often induced by an externally imposed agenda, which has driven EC-wide agreements forward, even in periods in which much less progress was being made on other issues. The result has been somewhat to insulate the trade field within a separate compartment and to leave its management both in the Commission and in capitals to a small circle of specialists. It is striking that the national case-studies by and large have not dealt with the area in any great detail. Yet current trends should lead us to question whether we can expect this pattern to continue. Trade issues have become more controversial and the preservation of the Community's internal market is now under considerable pressure, most visibly from the French and Greeks, but more surreptitiously and perhaps more subtly from other quarters. This suggests that we should expect to find national policy coordination and the preparation of national negotiating strategies becoming more problematic and more time consuming, and perhaps becoming more closely linked to other subjects on the agenda for both substantive and tactical reasons.

So far consistently rather more visible has been the involvement of Ministers and Ministries of Agriculture as a result of the historical and contextual 'accidents' which gave agriculture pride of place on the EC agenda and in the EC budget. It has followed that agricultural issues have been inescapably a dominant preoccupation, not just for the specialists, but for Foreign and Finance Ministers and for those responsible for the central coordination of policy and negotiating strategy. Here there is a manifest discontinuity between national and EC theatres; however important agriculture is within national economies (with perhaps the exception of those very few Member States where agriculture counts for a very large proportion of national economic output), in practice other parts of economic, welfare and industrial policies are far more consuming of national political and administrative energies. Perversely, the prominence of the Common Agricultural Policy (CAP) has served to reinforce the standing of Agriculture Ministers and Ministries on the EC stage, even against the downward trend of agriculture in the labour force. Even in the UK, the ministry is a major policy actor to an extent which would hardly have been expected without the goad of the CAP. The precise mechanisms through which the CAP is both negotiated and implemented make Agriculture Ministries both inextricably engaged in bargaining with other ministries in capitals and extremely influential on the detail which falls to their specific charge. At a minimum, they can constitute a fairly unassailable veto group; at a maximum they have, at least in the past, been able to bargain up their share of the EC budgetary cake with the pork-barrel politics reminiscent of American federal policy-making. So far, neither at the EC level nor within national capitals have countervailing forces been effectively marshalled, though the exhaustion of own resources and the Stuttgart Mandate may turn this trend around.

Yet the most likely countervailing force has always been the combined weight of national Finance Ministries. It is a commonplace commentary on public administration that within national governmental processes Finance Ministries enjoy high prestige, an impressive quality of personnel, leadership by senior members of the incumbent government and considerable political leverage. One of the surprising features of the EC policy process and institutional landscape is that they have not reflected their national counterparts. On the contrary, Finance Ministers and their officials have had to compete for primacy, often unsuccessfully, with 'spending' ministers, notably agriculture but others too. The nature of the EC budget arrangements, at least in the past, has been to make the financial costs of policies a secondary consideration or rather to leave the battle to be fought in capitals. After all, if the logic of national processes were to be extended to Brussels, we would expect Finance Ministers either to be the central coordinators or to have to give formal and active assent to expenditure proposals. So far neither role has been assumed collectively, though again current developments may be altering the correlation of forces. Nonetheless at the national level Finance Ministers continue to exercise a more pervasive influence on their governments' policies and negotiating positions. In all Member States, relevant Finance Ministers and officials form part of the inner circle of influential policy-makers on EC subjects. In France, for example, the head of the coordinating agency (SGCI) had until recently to be an Inspecteur des Finances. In the UK, Her Majesty's Treasury has certainly had a very large influence on policy towards the EC, not least because of the primacy for the government as a whole of the budget issue. The increasing salience of the budget issue for all member governments is beginning to be reflected in a more prominent role for Finance Ministries. There will, however, continue to be limits on how far this can be translated into collective agreements without some structural adjustments in the EC process.

Managing Technical Dossiers

Once one moves away from the glamorous, if frustrating, 'core' agenda of the EC the picture of Community business from national capitals changes strikingly. A very large proportion of the working groups of the Council of Ministers deal with more mundane and more technical issues to do with the four freedoms, the internal market, harmonisation of laws, the customs union and so on. These highly diverse areas of work engage in EC negotiation officials from ministries which are much more marginally involved in EC and international work. From a worm's eye viewpoint this creates problems more than opportunities. National officials may well be reluctant to change established and tested national practice in favour of some alien approach which often looks like change for the sake of change to no obvious good effect. The aura of xenophobia which easily pervades such negotiations is impressive and indeed understandable. A Brussels regulation or directive may well be acceptable if it puts the onus on others to conform to one's own practice, but for those required to adapt the irritations are clear and may be costly in terms of technical, administrative and legal adjustment and resources of time, energy and sometimes money.

Negative though this may appear as a reaction, it helps to explain why progress has been so inordinately slow in many such areas of work, except in those cases where some particular technological, commercial or other external impetus serves to inject some momentum towards agreement. The room for misperception is great: 39 000 norms may be a perfectly sensible protection of industrial and other standards to the German, but appear as devious protectionism to the French critic. These problems are compounded by the experience of actual Community legislation which often emerges as an untidy hotch-potch, difficult to administer and not quite serving anyone's precise and substantive needs.

For those concerned with formulating overall national policy such areas of work create real problems. It may well be both difficult and unrewarding to invest the effort and resources into mastering the technical dossiers. But, if not watched, a particular dossier may suddenly escalate in terms of political saliency and controversy - lead in petrol is a good case in point. The technical experts may get into trouble because they are insufficiently familiar with the detailed processes of the EC or with the legal implications of particular formulae. From the perspective of the experts the intrusion of Foreign Ministries and central coordinating agencies makes still more awkward the consideration of EC proposals by expanding into territory which goes far beyond the substantive and technical issues. In all Member States there is a tension between the desire to steer such dossiers on a course that takes linkage and broader dimensions into account and, on the other hand, an inclination to let those who understand the substance get on with it. There is no single or perfect answer to this dilemma. Practice has varied across Member States and from one dossier to another. In part the dilemma is offset if the responsible experts are adequately educated about and sensitised to the special characteristics of the EC and if the guiding reins can be pulled with a light and supple hand by the central coordinators.

Amongst the more technical areas one stands out as an exemplar of a more co-operative approach. In the development of the customs union the customs services of the Member States have worked together remarkably closely, helped by the early achievement of agreement on commitments in the Treaty of Rome and by the automatic acceptance by relevant national officials that they have to co-operate across national boundaries. None of this necessarily implies that agreement can readily be reached EC-wide on all dossiers, but it suggests that the nature of bargaining and negotiation is more consensual than conflictual. Also the accumulated experience of working within an EC framework of rules for many years and of having to master in some detail the knock-on effects of the Common Agricultural Policy and the 'own resources' system help to equip national officials for their EC role. Here too is an area of work, like the trade field, in which, at a rather more technical level, business is conducted without the regular intrusion of central coordinators. But again, as on broader trade issues, the politicisation of dossiers because of commercial competition and incipient or occasionally strident protectionist reflexes may bring a hitherto rather more self-contained area of work into the centre of the stage. This would then require a greater attention from the central managers of policy.

Career Planning and Special Skills

Running through all of the examples quoted is the recurrent theme that Community work requires some special skills and knowledge on the part of national officials. In all of the Member States the central direction of policy rests in practice with a fairly small group of specialists located in key ministries and, where they exist, special coordinating agencies. This is true however diverse the procedural arrangements for formal coordination. In some cases many of the same people have been in relevant posts for a very long time and indeed the personnel systems, either generically or for explicit EC reasons, serve to promote stability of experienced staff. The British and French have diverged most because of their habits of greater mobility, though they too in practice draw on a core of EC specialists (even if not necessarily always a result of positive career planning). The existence of such a pool of officials is almost certainly a significant factor in enabling governments to cope with Community work, whether by oiling the wheels of the formal machinery or sometimes by substituting for inadequate machinery. It is probably also the case that the more mobility there is, the greater the likelihood that national blinkers and inexperience will combine to inhibit effectiveness. Of course there is a risk that old European hands may become so committed to the common EC enterprise that their judgement is 'warped', but the actual substantive interests and domestic political constraints to which national officials must generally respond are a powerful counterweight.

As one moves away from the centre to the myriad parts of government on which the Community impinges, so special knowledge and experience is more scattered. Here two factors intervene. First, in those countries, notably the Benelux countries, in which substantive interests are intimately bound up with interdependent relations with EC partners, the Community dimension is an automatic element in policy formulation - a given of normal day-to-day work. This is much less the case in those countries where either a more unilateral approach can be sustained or, as in the Danish case, other poles of transnational co-operation exist. Second, to some extent the EC provides an area of work with high prestige and opportunities for an impact that are sufficiently attractive to draw able officials into the fold. Community work after all requires an official to be linguistically and legally adroit, resourceful in negotiation and brokerage, geographically mobile and open to different ideas. Such skills and aptitudes can to an extent be taught and training programmes are in some cases provided, though there are still many officials, even in 'old' Member States, who are thrown into EC negotiations with little prior preparation. However, most Community hands would argue that an accumulation of first-hand experience is invaluable.

Is There an 'Ideal' Model?

It is tempting to infer from what has gone before that there ought to be an ideal model for member governments to guide their management of Community business. The most obvious prescription would be for carefully constructed and tightly structured central coordination with posts staffed by superbly trained officials with deep knowledge of the EC and with systematic channels of communication within the national administration and to and from external posts, notably the Permanent Representation. The model would equip a government to devise and pursue a political strategy on the basis of which negotiating strategies and tactics could be rigorously determined. It would ensure that left and right hands were operating in tandem and enable governments to achieve the maximum effectiveness in Community negotiations and to respond quickly and coherently to change. We should, however, be wary of proceeding down this path. In the first place, as the case studies and this chapter have pointed out, each governmental system is in some key respects **sui generis.** What works in one context cannot necessarily be transplanted and an artificially imposed approach could squeeze out or distort policy management and separate negotiating effectiveness from either bargaining power or substantive issues. Some governments carry more weight than others either across the board (as for example the German with its considerable economic achievements) or in a particular sector (the Dutch on transport). Moreover, those governments defending positions that lie close to the Commission's proposals and/or to where the core of a consensus lies amongst all partners start with a great advantage, while those who are in a minority or unconventional position start with the odds stacked against them. Smooth policy management and adroit negotiation cannot at the end of the day override the deep structures, though they may produce a better outcome than a more detached observer would expect.

However, a rather more fundamental criticism is that the evidence is at best unclear on whether such an ideal type (supposing it were capable of application) is actually appropriate to the realities of Community negotiation. Examples from outside the EC may serve to clarify the point. Many Europeans complain at the profound difficulty of negotiating with the Americans. American policy is confused; different parts of the administration speak with different voices; the extent and thrust of presidential involvement varies; and getting past the Congress can be both unpredictable and require further modifications. As counterbalance the American government can deploy political and economic leverage by force of power, resources, size and so on, yet these latter factors do not on their own explain adequately the extent of American influence. Other partners are compelled to look in some fine detail at what might be an acceptable deal to square differing US interests; uncertainty breeds a willingness to go for 'satisficing' rather than optimising strategies; and deals have to be struck with particular parts of the American administration in the absence of an overall package. Conversely the Japanese, with their more impenetrable political system and often more rigorously defined objectives, tend to aim for watertight bargains in which their benefit is clear. But they leave themselves little room for flexibility, movement and compromise and deny their negotiating partners the opportunity to build packages and introduce side deals. Extreme though these examples may be, they suggest that a government may derive some advantage from being able to pursue particularist interests outside the framework of an overarching and thereby constraining approach, making it more difficult for others to subordinate the particular to questions of general principle. It is not necessarily to the disadvantage of the Germans that they lack an explicitly strategic view, nor always to the advantage of the French who prise their overarching approach so dearly.

In the Community arena the institutional and negotiating processes are actually in major respects quite close to the US pattern. Apart from the European Council, the fora do not exist for pursuing overarching strategies and, however important, the exhortations of the European Council are quite often not picked up at the working and more segmented levels of negotiation. Consistency of national purpose may be desirable, but is far more likely to be achievable within than across sectors. The pursuit of a grand strategy may leave little room for flexibility or modulated response to unexpected shifts in the dynamics of an individual negotiation. It may leave a government hooked on a conventional argument of principle which has already been overtaken by practice. Such an approach may make it obvious what proposals have to be resisted but close minds to other options which might reach similar objectives by a different route. In other words, elements of constructive 'anarchy' may yield negotiating success. Obviously this line of argument should not be exaggerated. Skills, experience, expertise, careful preparation and forethought are all necessary attributes, without which Member Governments are likely to be comprehensively out-manoeuvred. But a balance needs to be struck between rigour for its own sake and the pull of individual special interests. An ideal model would have to combine coordinated strategy with tolerant flexibility. No mechanism or process is likely to be so finely tuned as to rule out the possibility of errors of human judgment. A centralised approach makes it more feasible for the judgments of those at the centre to pervade the wide spectrum of EC issues. A more loosely coupled system while lacking coherence relies on a series of smaller and theoretically more corrigible judgments.

Over the years a shift is observable from the two extremes towards a median point, as the respective records of the French and German approaches demonstrate. The initial highly centralised approach of the French has been moderated and become more open-ended, and diversified, even in some respects contradictory. In part this reflects what may be temporary political differences of approach at a ministerial level but it also bears the mark of adaptation to a Community system and of the close bilateral relationship with the Federal Republic of Germany. Conversely, in the Federal Republic of Germany and Italy, successive efforts have been made, with varying success, to achieve a more aggregated approach. Effectiveness in negotiation differs from case to case as well as from country to country and, in any event, the current problems of the EC agenda make it easier for participants to put on the brakes rather than to press the accelerator. In the absence of clear political strategies the prizes fall perhaps most easily to national negotiators who are skilful on particular dossiers. This gives considerable importance to individual capabilities and to the viability of particular proposals. But in addition we must not let go of the coalition point: EC negotiations require an acceptance that bargaining has to be seen in terms of variable sum games and of partnership. The political cultures of some Member States are more attuned to this than others - the Dutch having historically been perhaps the most noted practitioners of this art.

Equally striking in the country studies is the emphasis of policy-making machinery in capitals on current business. There is little recent evidence of a 'think tank' approach or of longer-term planning. The French government has periodically sponsored studies of the EC and French interests over the longer term, which have fed, to some extent, into official thinking (6). The Genscher-Colombo proposals sprang in part from a German concern to take a longer view. There has been some exploration of longer-term scenarios and options in the Netherlands. But these are rare examples and there has been little impetus to push for the wide-ranging approach which produced, for example, the Tindemans Report in the mid-seventies. Some governments, notably the Italian and Benelux, take as given a commitment to strengthening the Community fabric as a long-term aim, but this has not really been reflected in substantive proposals to cover the medium-term options.

The implications for the Presidency
The first and most obvious point is that it is unrealistic to expect governments to act out of character for the six months duration of the Presidency. Rather the strong and weak points of their 'normal' approach are likely to be thrown into relief. The framework of their general attitude to the EC and the particular interests which concern them will influence their behaviour and margin of manoeuvre. Those governments, notably the Danish, British and French, which have been prepared on key issues to sit it out in a minority or blocking position, are unlikely suddenly to become arch-conciliators, while the Italians or Luxembourgers will slip more readily into the role of mediator. The Dutch, imbued with a long-standing, even ideological, commitment to reinforcing the Commission find it difficult to promote the office of the Council Presidency, whereas the French are always tempted by the prospect of political initiatives. A government hampered by structural administrative weaknesses, such as are found in Italy and Greece, can hardly be expected to discover the key to administrative reform while in the Council chair and is thus likely to have to rely on the abilities, albeit

often considerable, of individual ministers and officials. Governments such as the British or French which pride themselves on their smooth coordination of national negotiating positions will endeavour to deploy this as a real asset in managing Council business. Those which have pursued a more disaggregated national approach, including for example the Germans, may not shake off entrenched habits but may well seek a reinforcement of key points in their administrative and policy processes in order to make the best possible job of the Presidency. All governments find themselves under pressure to show themselves to advantage under the Presidency spotlight both in terms of actual Council and EPC output and in terms of peer group evaluation. They wish to show themselves to be impartial, though they may not always convince their partners of this. In some governments explicit and careful attention is paid to separating instructions to Presidents from those to national spokesmen, with the extreme case in the last Danish Presidency of chairmen being forbidden to read the national negotiating brief.

Thus, by and large, national conduct of the Presidency is an extrapolation from 'normal' business rather than a sea-change. Most would argue that good and careful preparation helps, but only up to the point where the extent of controversy and consensus or unexpected events impose their own logic. In all cases able chairmen, both Ministers and officials, can substitute for formal resources by the individual skills which they can deploy, but again subject to the limits of the real agenda and the constraints on consensus. In all cases the Permanent Representations play a key role, and it is on these - their staffing, political profile and communications networks with capitals - that much of the mobilising effort is concentrated. Some would argue, although here experience and views differ, that the extent to which a government and especially its Permanent Representation is able to work closely and constructively with the Council Secretariat is an important factor affecting performance. It is interesting here to note that the German study suggests that German views have actually evolved into a more positive attitude towards the Council Secretariat than hitherto, while governments from the smaller Member States, Luxembourg being the extreme example, rely especially heavily on it.

In capitals the extra increment of time, resources and staff is sought largely amongst those who deal with EPC. The role of the Presidency as both chair and secretariat makes this virtually inevitable. It is noteworthy that the establishment of the 'flying secretariat' based on the 'troika' principle has been identified in all of the country studies as a positive and useful contribution to improving the infrastructure and facilitating continuity. Only the Luxembourg study suggests explicitly that the point is fast arriving at which the workload for national Foreign Ministries and posts abroad may become overwhelming. Again this is an extreme example given the tiny size comparatively of the Luxembourg diplomatic service. For the larger Member States finding suitably experienced diplomats is not in itself a major problem. However, the consequence may be to suck into the EPC network particularly able individuals, but with the opportunity cost that units dealing with other parts of the world or issue-areas may be either under-staffed or less competently staffed. The particular demands of EPC both in 'normal' times and during the Presidency may also have served to reinforce the dichotomy between the political and economic directorates of Foreign Ministries. So far this has produced some awkwardness of communications and some divergence of priorities or perception. It would become a more serious problem if an attempt were made qualitatively to reinforce EPC activities, for which the current, essentially rather **ad hoc** Presidency arrangements do not suggest any obvious solution.

For the rest of the national administration, the main burden of the Presidency comprises more travel, longer meetings in capitals, heavier workloads and keeping people in key posts for the relevant preparatory and operational periods. Governments of recent adherents and/or any who have a distinctive political objective tend to view the Presidency strategically. This may be primarily directed at demonstrating to others that the relevant government can and will perform competently, a particular hallmark of the approaches of the first Irish and Greek presidencies. The strategy may be designed to achieve very specific policy outcomes. In either case good advance preparation is required together with a medium-term perspective over a period of a year or so and attention with some fineness of detail and nuance to other Member States and the Commission. The country studies both support and undermine these propositions. Efficient management of business and competent handling of the liaison and representational functions of the Presidency are unlikely to be achieved unless a substantial investment of effort is made. But to move from good groundwork to effectiveness on identified dossiers is much harder, partly because of extraneous events and partly because consensus building in the Council at all levels has become harder, not easier with the passage of time.

Consequently, two rather contradictory trends can be observed in the country studies. It seems by and large to be the practice of governments to judge that a serious effort and application of resources and energy is desirable. Yet, there are perhaps fewer illusions than in the mid-late seventies that this will yield many tangible gains. A further complication is that, unless a government has remarkable stability of both ministers and officials, it is hard for experience to be accumulated from one Presidency to another. Successive enlargements of EC membership have elongated the cycle of rotation amongst member governments, and it will be increasingly the case that a new 'learning process' within individual governments will be required from one Presidency to the next. Practices such as those of the British to produce for internal consumption a **post hoc** report on the experience of a particular Presidency are one means of facilitating that learning process.

For electoral and parliamentary reasons, high gearing cannot always be achieved at ministerial level. Several of the country studies point up the dislocating consequences of changes of government. These are less problematic for those countries in which a broad consensus on EC issues persists across political parties, than for those in which distinctive party views obtain, or where attitudes towards the EC are evolving. While this study is not primarily concerned with the politics of EC negotiation, it stands to reason that the performance of officials is actually and correctly circumscribed by the political views, preferences and priorities of ministers. Here there is a distinction to be drawn between EPC and Community business. The nebulous character of EPC and its lack of firm underpinning (either institutionally or substantively) make ministerial interventions both more influential and less predictable than in Community business. A persuasive and widely respected Foreign Minister may from the chair persuade what are after all the other members of a highly exclusive club to move forward, as did Lord Carrington in pressing for what became the London Report of October 1981, though he was helped by the fact that some of the ideas had been in circulation previously. Conversely there are few carrots or sticks available to counteract a Foreign Minister prepared to hold out on his nine other colleagues, as became clear in the debate over the Korean airliner in Athens in September 1983. Yet there is too a learning process as the subsequent Greek conduct of EPC demonstrated.

Community business is quite different. The options are more circumscribed, the room for manoeuvre is generally limited and the weight of precedent and existing commitments is often overwhelming. Some scope may sometimes be available for an individual minister in the chair to make a remark or indeed for a government as a whole to unblock one or several dossiers. Even in a case where the presiding government has major and substantive interests, it may be possible from the chair to achieve a constructive compromise, as under the German Presidency on the EMS realignment of spring 1983, but such examples are striking for their rarity in the country studies. More prevalent are examples of governments at both political and official levels being locked into the defence of established lines of argument whether to promote or to resist particular outcomes. In these instances the Presidency may permit or even encourage a marginal shift of position by pressuring the reluctant in national capitals to accept a less than ideal decision from their perspective. The combined force of habit and substantive interests, however, militates against more radical reorientation.

The new or perhaps rather the increasingly prevalent dimension for ministers is the growth of bilateral consultations as an adjunct to developing coalitions and seeking compromise in Brussels. The forging of a Presidency compromise on critical dossiers has required in the case of the Stuttgart Mandate an extraordinarily intensive round of meetings of Councils and Jumbo Councils with an enormous consequential burden on the Presidency and the Council Secretariat. Here it is questionable how far the Presidency as such, however well prepared, can be a catalyst of agreement, though there are some indications that those responsible for EC policy in Paris would like to avail themselves of the chair to steer debate forward. But in this area, as now in many others, steering in Brussels depends on careful charting of the waters through bilateral discussions by the Presidency (as well as among other combinations of member governments). The consequence in crude terms is significantly to increase the workload of ministers and key officials, since on critical issues extra staffing cannot provide people with the appropriate experience and status. Perhaps more importantly it requires an intellectual and conceptual willingness to look at the EC negotiating process in the round without the understandable but confining blinkers of the national spokesman.

Thus far we have concentrated on those elements of the Presidency which impinge on the **cognoscenti,** which is where its impact is most discernible. But beyond in each Member State there is a broader and at least partially attentive public and at the European level a very attentive public in the form of the European Parliament (EP). In the latter case it is clear that presidencies in turn now devote much more effort than used to be common to maintaining a dialogue with the EP and practising concertation. Of course this partly results from the formal powers and procedures of the EP, but it is perhaps also indicative of a concern both for public presentation and to minimise obstructions to the Community's legislative and budgetary processes. This now has significant repercussions for the time and workload of ministers and officials from the Presidency. At the national level the picture looks very different. Here the country studies yield little hard information on parliamentary activism. Instead we see the often rather sketchy parliamentary controls in a formal sense impinging on the Presidency at the margins, though of course where substantive issues are controversial or where the formal controls, as in Denmark, are significant the parliamentary dimension can be important. As for broader public opinion only two major points emerge. First, there is some evidence that the Presidency of the European Council does lead Heads of State and government sometimes to play to their domestic audiences. We could for example expect the French Presidency of 1984 which coincided with the second direct elections to the EP to reflect this. Second, in earlier studies there were indications of national presidencies using the period in office to educate and inform domestic opinion on EC issues and the Community record. This does not seem to have become a more general phenomenon. Rather presidencies, with rare exceptions, are geared primarily towards coping with EPC consultations and EC negotiation and towards having an impact on partner governments and even on domestic opinion in other Member States. In other words the image of a country as transmitted by the Presidency to other parts of the EC or to third countries (in external relations and EPC) does consume attention, but much less the image of the Community within the Member State.

From Glamour to Grind and Beyond

It is difficult to draw satisfactory or satisfying conclusions from the disparate experience of the Ten. In the mid-seventies it looked as if the Council Presidency might develop into a more active, dynamic and glamorous vehicle for EC consensus-building, though there were always those who cautioned against the plausibility of this prognosis. In the early eighties the sceptics have been vindicated in that the grind is a more impressive feature of what the Presidency entails and what it might achieve. Equally there were those who argued that some more permanent secretariat for EPC would be recognised as essential precisely because of the limitations of the Presidency. In this area, since the Soviet invasion of Afghanistan, we have perhaps begun to approach a half-way house, the construction of which has begun with the 'flying secretariat' and the other reforms of the London Report. But as long as EPC is primarily exhortatory we are unlikely to move beyond this.

Yet, it would be quite wrong to infer that the Presidency does not require careful national preparation. All the evidence both of the country studies and of the observable experience of Council negotiations and EPC consultations suggests that inadequate preparation of and/or incompetent performance in the Presidency can contribute negatively to policy outcomes. There may be few tangible prizes (beyond the respect of one's peers) for making the required effort, but there are manifold recriminations to suffer if the Presidency is ineffectual or, worse, partisan.

In searching for explanations of this rather downbeat assessment we need to look at both Community and national levels. At the Community level and within EPC, as has repeatedly been shown, part of the problem lies in the real world agenda and the genuine difficulties of substance and interest. In the EC specifically the Council structures do not encourage effective presidential management, however ably attempted. EPC is different because of the greater homogeneity of subject matter and participants, and because the framework is a good deal more supple. But even here the churlishness of the Soviet government in invading Afghanistan over the Christmas holiday period (1979-80) did suggest that suppleness could be overdone. But another factor impinges - namely the interrelationship between the forum of the member governments and the collective expression of the whole. In the strict EC context most participants would accept that progress in negotiation requires a constructive relationship between the Council and the Commission, irrespective of any wider argument about constitutional roles and powers. This partnership to be effective depends on an active dialogue between the Council Presidency at all levels and the Commission (both college and services) to which each must contribute sensibly and sensitively. The period leading up to the May 1980 Mandate under the Italian Council Presidency is a positive illustration. It is, however, difficult to resist the conclusion that the Commission is now less capable than often hitherto (at least in some crucial areas) of making a forceful contribution to the negotiating process both formal and informal or perhaps that it has become so preoccupied with defending its own corner that it focusses less clearly on the overall community interest. Explanations for this lie beyond the remit of this study. In such circumstances it is somewhat unrealistic for the Presidency to perform both its own functions and to fill a lacuna left by a more cautious and less coherent Commission. Governments are not equipped to perform the 'think tank' and motor functions of the Commission. Conversely apparent 'success' by a particular presidency in a specific policy sector may be a reflection not just of the incumbent government's approach but also of a Commission contribution which is purposive and well-judged. The processes of EPC which lacks a collective expression obviously cannot be subjected to this kind of analysis.

At the national level there are three major obstacles to a more extensive role for the Presidency. First, the substantive interests of the incumbent government may and often do simply get in the way, still a greater problem for the larger than for the smaller Member States which stand to gain greater international visibility. Second, the volume of work deriving from the Presidency does appear to produce a heavy and somewhat excessive load for in practice a relatively small number of national ministers and officials, at least outside the more technical subject areas. Overload is unlikely to yield high levels of performance across the board. In practice persistent attention and political energy are likely to be restricted to a handful of priority areas. Thus most governments approaching the Presidency tend willy-nilly to find themselves focusing on a dossier approach with some attempts at linkage amongst those dossiers which are currently of critical importance. Their time frame is unlikely to spread much beyond the period immediately following their own tenure of the chair. Such an approach cannot be expected to generate a detached and strategic view of the collective Community interest.

For all of these reasons, the Presidency of the Council and of EPC should be seen as an essential element of steering through current proposals and of expressing the state of agreement amongst member governments to date, whether within the Community or to third countries. But it does not provide a basis for a new institutional and negotiating dynamic. Significantly the country studies did not reveal much enthusiasm for building up the role of the Presidency further. Nor is institutional reform, at least in the sense of reallocating functions amongst the institutions, high on the Community agenda. The burst of ideas about the Presidency which circulated during the 1970s find little resonance in the recent experience of member governments in attempting to make the best possible job of a necessary but unglamorous task.

Other options of course theoretically exist. On the NATO analogy, chairmanship could be provided by the senior officials of the Council Secretariat, thus firmly dissociating the chair from any substantive special interest. Alternatively, the Commision might assume the chair, though it is difficult to marry this with an exclusive right for it to propose new legislation and such a change could not plausibly extend to EPC. At ministerial level the main burden could fall on a single and full time minister for the six months' duration or possibly longer. But the climate does not seem to favour a radical reappraisal, nor is there any one suggestion which would command widespread assent. In the EPC context the whole drift of developments has been to follow modest incrementalism. In the EC context governments seem inclined to favour the system of which they are periodically the embodiment. Indeed current debates over a more variegated or differentiated Community, on whatever formula might emerge, suggest that efforts to establish a clearer focal point and a more specific role of leadership or agenda and strategy definition are misdirected. Such patterns as we can observe rather point to a reinforcement of the notion of collective leadership: in the EC case gradually bringing together the Presidents of the Council, Commission and Parliament; and in EPC perhaps some gradual extension of the troika principle.

REFERENCES:

(1)   Gilbert Winham, 'Negotiation as a Management Process', World Politics, 30,1, October 1977.
(2)   H. Simon, 'A Behavioural Model of Rational Choice', Quarterly Journal of Economics, 69, February 1955.
(3)   R. Fisher and W. Ury, Getting to Yes: negotiating agreement without giving in, Hutchinson 1982.
(4)   EIPA research project on 'The implementation of Community legislation by Member States', under the direction of Prof. F. Capotorti, Prof. G. Ionescu and Prof. H. Siedentopf.
(5)   See D.R. Lewis and H. Wallace (eds.), Policies into Practice, Heinemann Educational Books, London, 1984, chaps. 8-10.
(6)   Eg. L'Europe: les vingt prochaines années, Commissariat du Plan, Paris, 1980; Quelle strategie européenne pour la France? ibid. 1983.